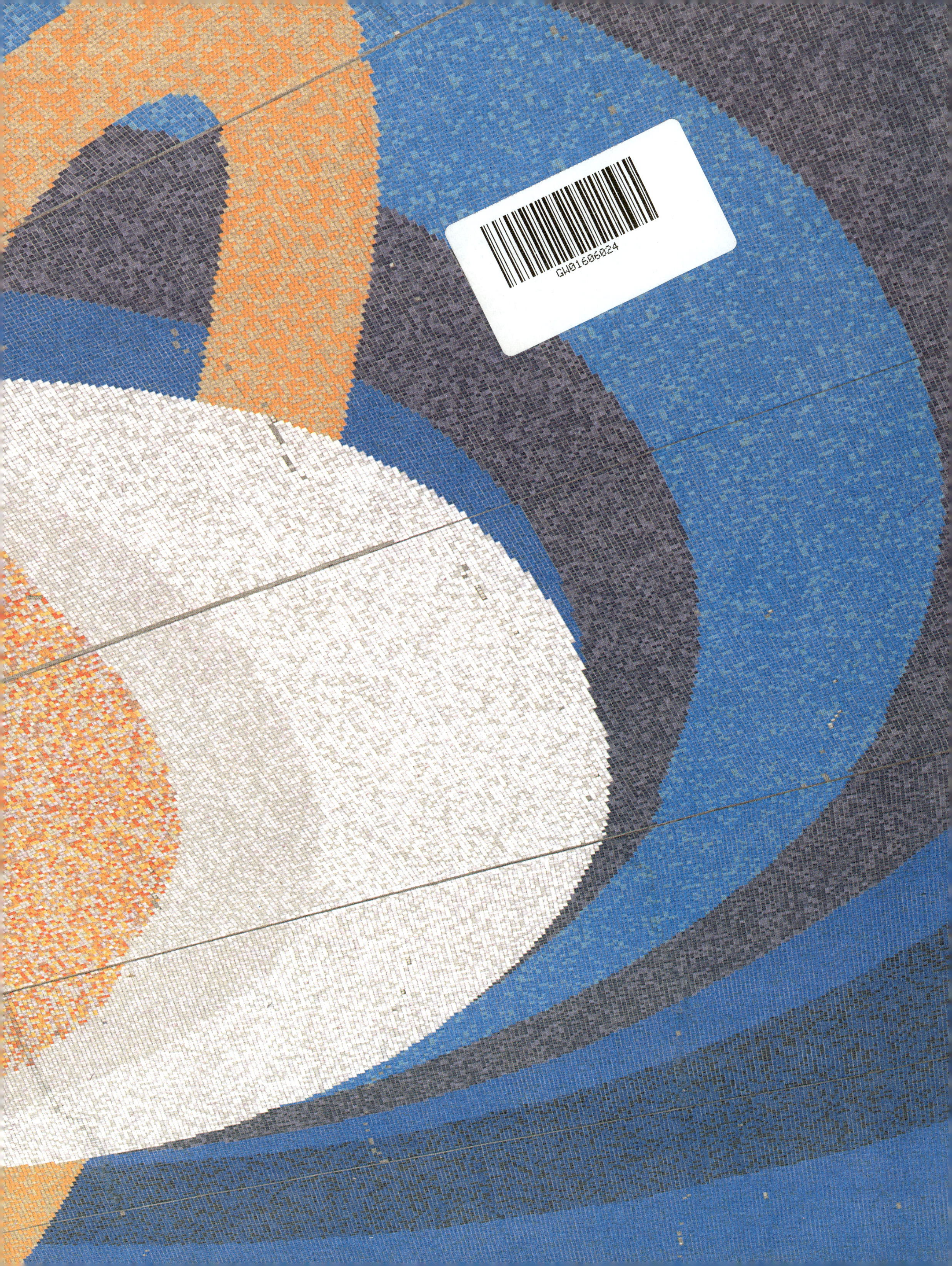

بسم الله الرحمن الرحيم

الأخت العزيزة ... جمرتا

مع تحياتي واحترامي لك

اهدي كتاب اللغة في جدة

واعرف انك تحبينه زيي

وابنتي هاني تدرساهم فيه

محمد ومحمد سعيد ناصر

٢٧/٥/٩٢

JEDDAH
CITY of ART

THE SCULPTURES AND MONUMENTS

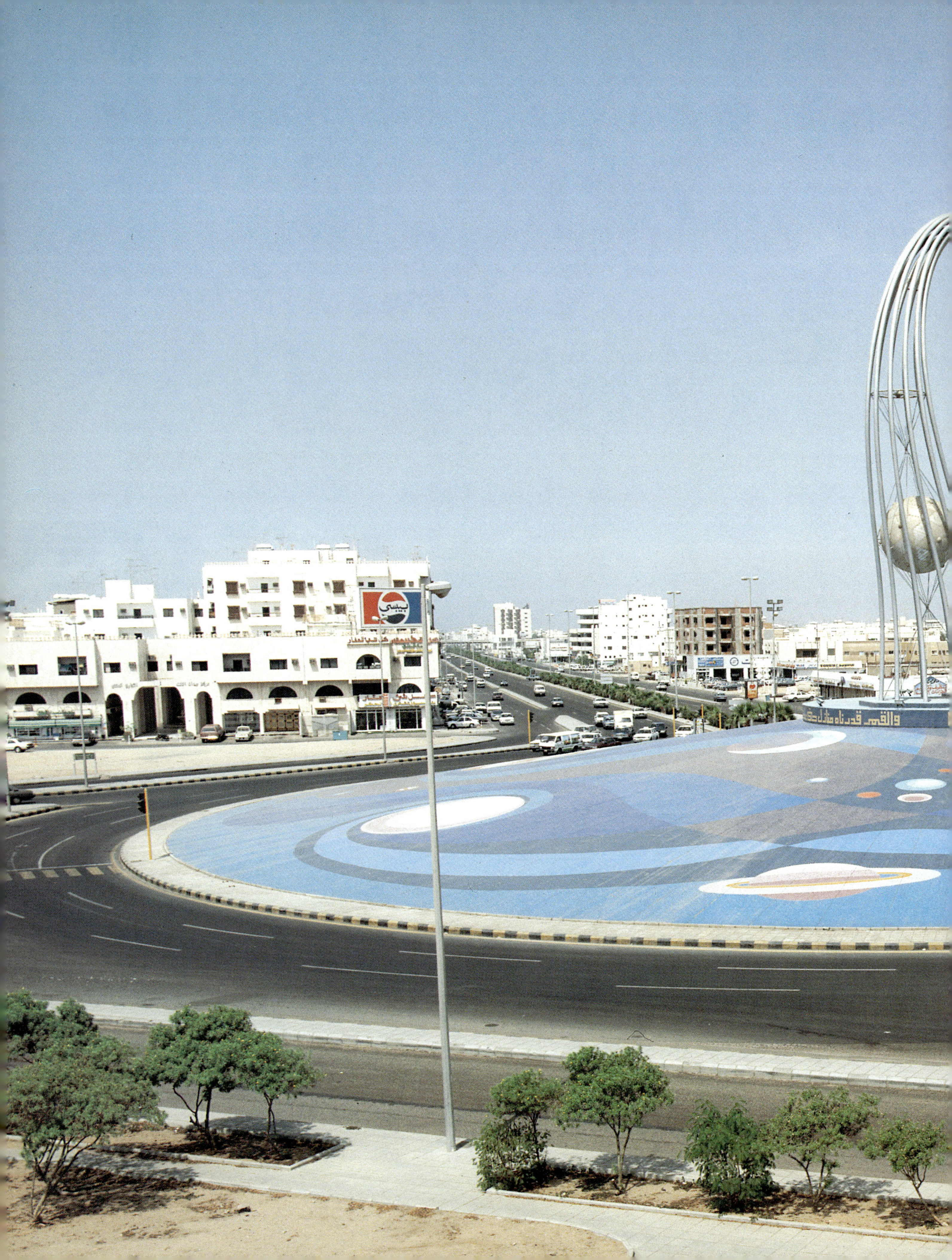

بيبسي
والقمر قدرناه منازل

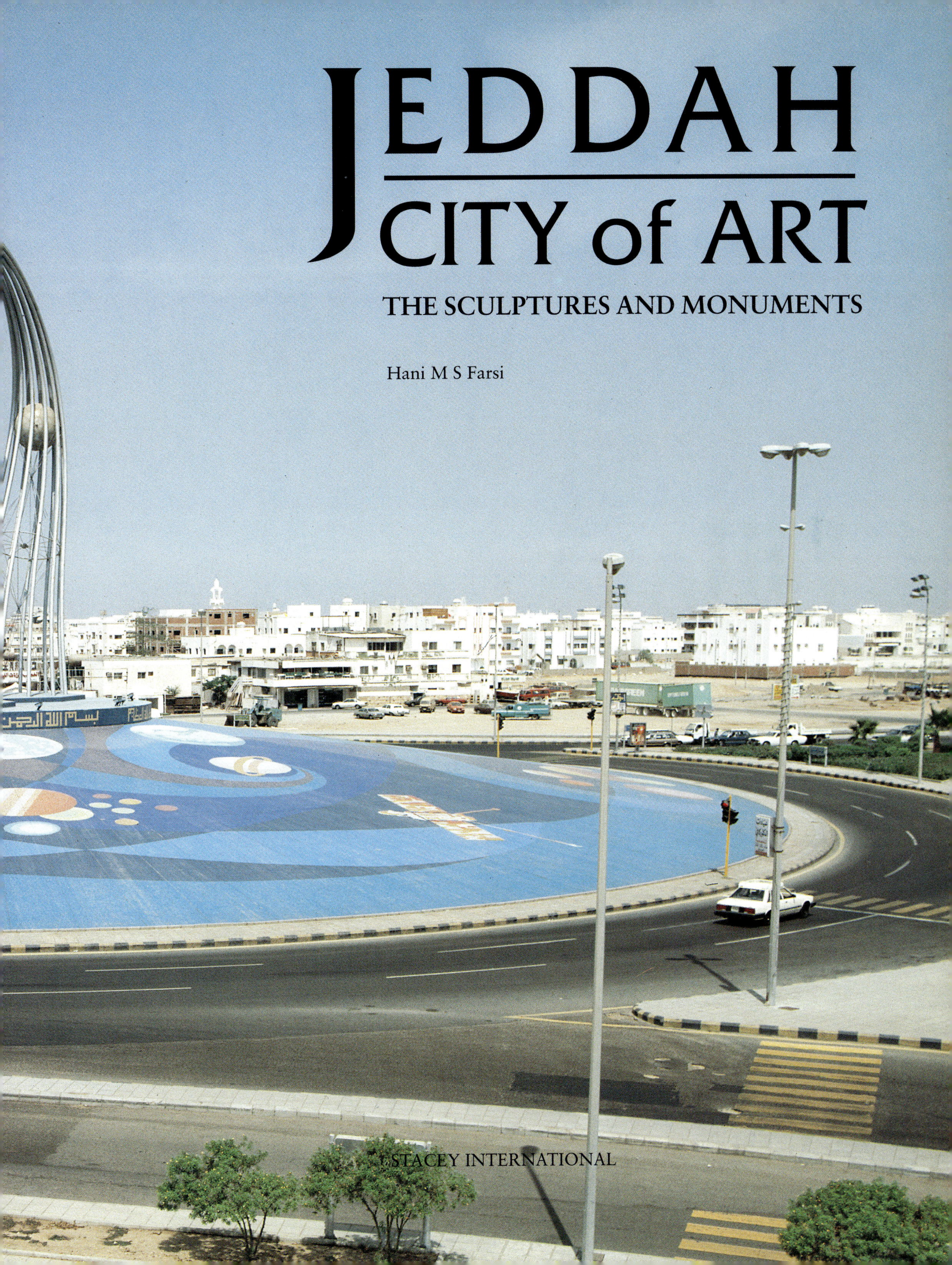

JEDDAH
CITY of ART

THE SCULPTURES AND MONUMENTS

Hani M S Farsi

STACEY INTERNATIONAL

SUPERVISORY EDITOR
Hani Mohamed Said Farsi

ART DIRECTOR
Josephine Cotter

PRINCIPAL PHOTOGRAPHER
John French

EDITORS
Peter Fagan
Jill Waters
Kitty Carruthers

CARTOGRAPHER
Andras Bereznay

RESEARCH ADVISERS
George Duncan
Hassan Dajani
Desmond Day
Faris Azzee
E. F. Haddad
William Facey

◀◀◀ Detail of the base of Ottmar Hollmann's *Cosmos* (*Al-Falak*). This mosaic base, which was conceived by Salah Abdulkarim and implemented by Julio Lafuente, comprises roughly two million pieces of mosaic; orginally laid out in Italy and then shipped to Jeddah it took two months to reassemble.

◀◀ **KING FAHD FOUNTAIN** (1)
The world's highest waterspout dominates the city's shoreline. At night, floodlights turn the falling spray into a delicate coloured veil.

◀ Ottmar Hollmann's **COSMOS** (*Al-Falak*) (2) is a dynamic, soaring representation of the Solar System.

▶ **SUNFLOWER FOUNTAIN** (3)
Eila Hiltunen
Stainless Steel

Much care went into selecting the correct grade of corrosion-resistant stainless steel for this sculpture since it stands in one of the Corniche lagoons.

The numbers appearing on the captions refer to the location map on pp.50-51.

All photographs are by John French except those illustrations listed below which are reproduced by kind permission of:

Aga Khan Award for Architecture 75; Baz East 84; Mohamed Said Farsi 11, 13 (bottom left), 19, 22, 23 (right), 25, 26, 27, 28, 33 (bottom), 35 (top), 36 (bottom right), 41, 62, 65 (bottom), 67 (centre and bottom), 70 (bottom), 90 (top and bottom), 146 (top), 155 (bottom right), 176; Henry Moore Foundation 37 (top left); Lafuente, Julio private archive 23 (left), 24, 26 (left), 28 (bottom), 68/69, 143, 164; T. E. Lawrence archive at the Conway Library, Courtauld Institute of Art 12, 13 (top), 18 (top), 38; The National Commercial Bank, Jeddah 16 (bottom left), 54 (bottom left); Saudia 15; W. Spencer Tart 17; Trustees of the Science Museum, London 30.

Set in 11/13 Sabon Roman by
SX Composing Limited
Rayleigh, Essex, England.
Colour origination, printing and binding
by Tien Wah Press, Singapore

Published by Stacey International
128 Kensington Church Street
London W8 4BH

British Library Cataloguing in Publication Data
Farsi, Hani Mohamed Said
Jeddah, City of Art – (Arabian library).
I. Title
953.8
ISBN 0 905 74366 0

CONTENTS

	PREFACE	7
Section One	The CITY as ART	9
Maps	The Growth of Jeddah	10
	Jeddah on the Arabian Peninsula	10
Chapter 1	JEDDAH: The OPPORTUNITY	11
Chapter 2	The SOURCES of MOHAMED SAID FARSI'S VISION	17
Chapter 3	FULFILLING the TASK	25
Chapter 4	SOME MAJOR ARTISTS and THEIR WORKS	30
Section Two	The SCULPTURES and MONUMENTS	49
Map	The Location of the Principal Sculptures and Monuments	50
	The CORNICHE	53
	The AL HAMRA OPEN AIR MUSEUM	99
	The INTERSECTIONS and PARKS	133
	INDEX	174

This book is dedicated to my father
who has taught me to remove what is superficial
and preserve what is essential.

HANI M S FARSI
August 1991

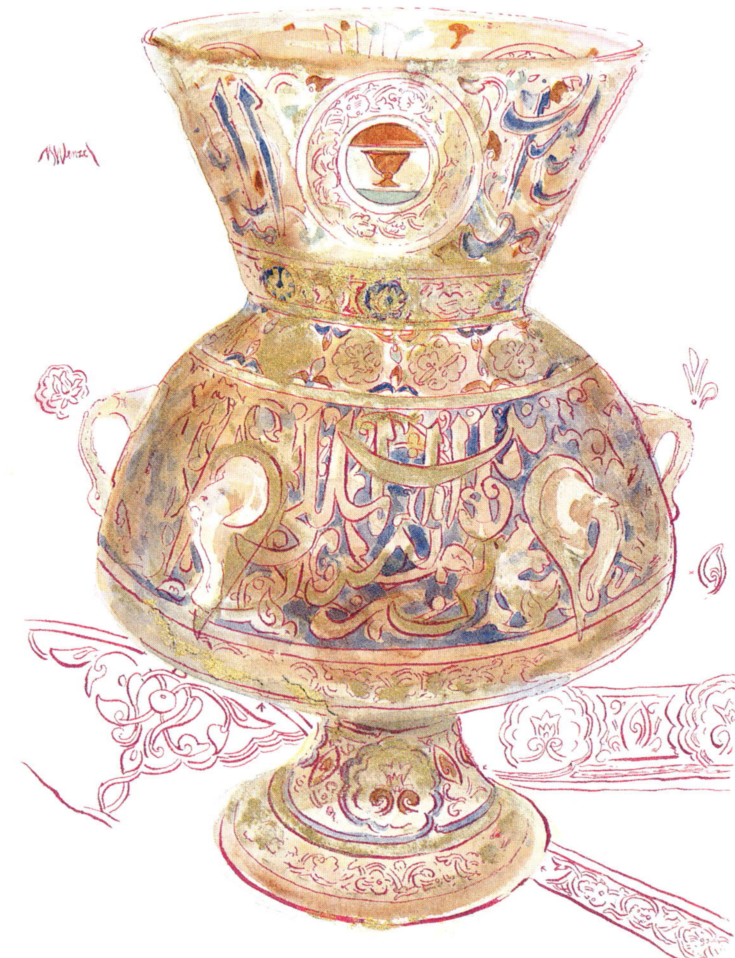

□ An enamelled Mameluke mosque lamp dating from about 1330 CE. For centuries such mosque lamps have embodied the supreme artistry of Islamic craftsmen. This traditional art retains a crucial importance for many contemporary Arab artists and several of the sculptures featured here show this influence.

PREFACE

What is it that makes a city? Two decades ago Mohamed Said Farsi set out to find the answer to this question. Twenty years before that, as a young man, he knew Jeddah as a small, intimate walled city, hardly touched by the twentieth century.

This upbringing and his ambition, from an early age, to be an architect, were the corner-stones of an instinctive awareness of and sensitivity to history and tradition. It would be impossible for him, in looking forward, to lose sight of the past.

After studying architecture and town planning in Alexandria, he entered government service in 1963. In 1965 he became the Planning Officer for the Western Region of Saudi Arabia, an area larger than the United Kingdom and containing not only the port city of Jeddah but also the Holy Cities of Makkah and Medinah.

During this period as Planning Officer, and prior to his appointment as Mayor of Jeddah, Master Plans for these cities were prepared under his responsibility. This process started in 1970, at a time when the future structure, form, concepts and aspirations of Jeddah and the Holy Cities of Islam were defined. Such was the importance attached to this work that these cities were the first in the Kingdom to have their Master Plans approved by the supreme governing body – the Council of Ministers. Indeed, King Fahd, who at that time was Crown Prince, personally reviewed these projects.

When in 1972, Mohamed Said Farsi became Mayor, Jeddah had grown from the almost medieval city of his childhood to a large city of more than 300,000 people. However, as a direct consequence of the vast increase in oil revenues and the ambitions of the National Five Year Plans to invest this revenue in the growth and well-being of the Kingdom's future, the population of Jeddah was to grow fivefold over the next decade – to well over one and a half million.

It is most probable that, even with the fortuitous circumstance of an approved plan (and one, it should be added, which was sufficiently far-sighted to plan for two million people), this growth rate would have resulted in chaos and deficiencies in every aspect of civic, social and essential urban services without the colossal and totally dedicated effort sustained by the Municipality of Jeddah.

Of course, such an enormous task was not accomplished without many short term discomforts and inconvenience to the people of the city. Nor, it must be said, was it the achievement of any one person or agency. But Mayor Farsi was the driving force and overall co-ordinator who not only ensured the provision of the basic requirements (and let us not minimise the importance of providing sufficient water, electricity, sewage disposal, telephones and – fundamental to an affluent and mobile society – roads with the capacity to take the demand for travel placed on them) but also attended to the much more subjective aspects of city building such as the quality of architectural design and layout, landscaping and beautification.

A city should fulfil the needs of its inhabitants and give them a sense of identity and belonging. If, in achieving these worthy objectives, a city does not give joy and delight, then it is not truly a city for people.

It is the supreme measure of Mohamed Said Farsi's stewardship as mayor that he succeeded in achieving all of these objectives. Jeddah, with its green boulevards, gardens and open spaces, its carefully preserved core, its majestic interplay with its raison d'etre – the sea – and its many sculptures and monuments, fulfils the needs of its people and brings delight to residents and visitors alike.

Jeddah stands out as an example of how an ancient Arab city can grow and adapt as it enters the twenty-first century.

George Orr Duncan MBE
B. Arch Dip TP PhD ARIBA ARIAS MRTPI FRSA

August 1991

Section One
The CITY as ART

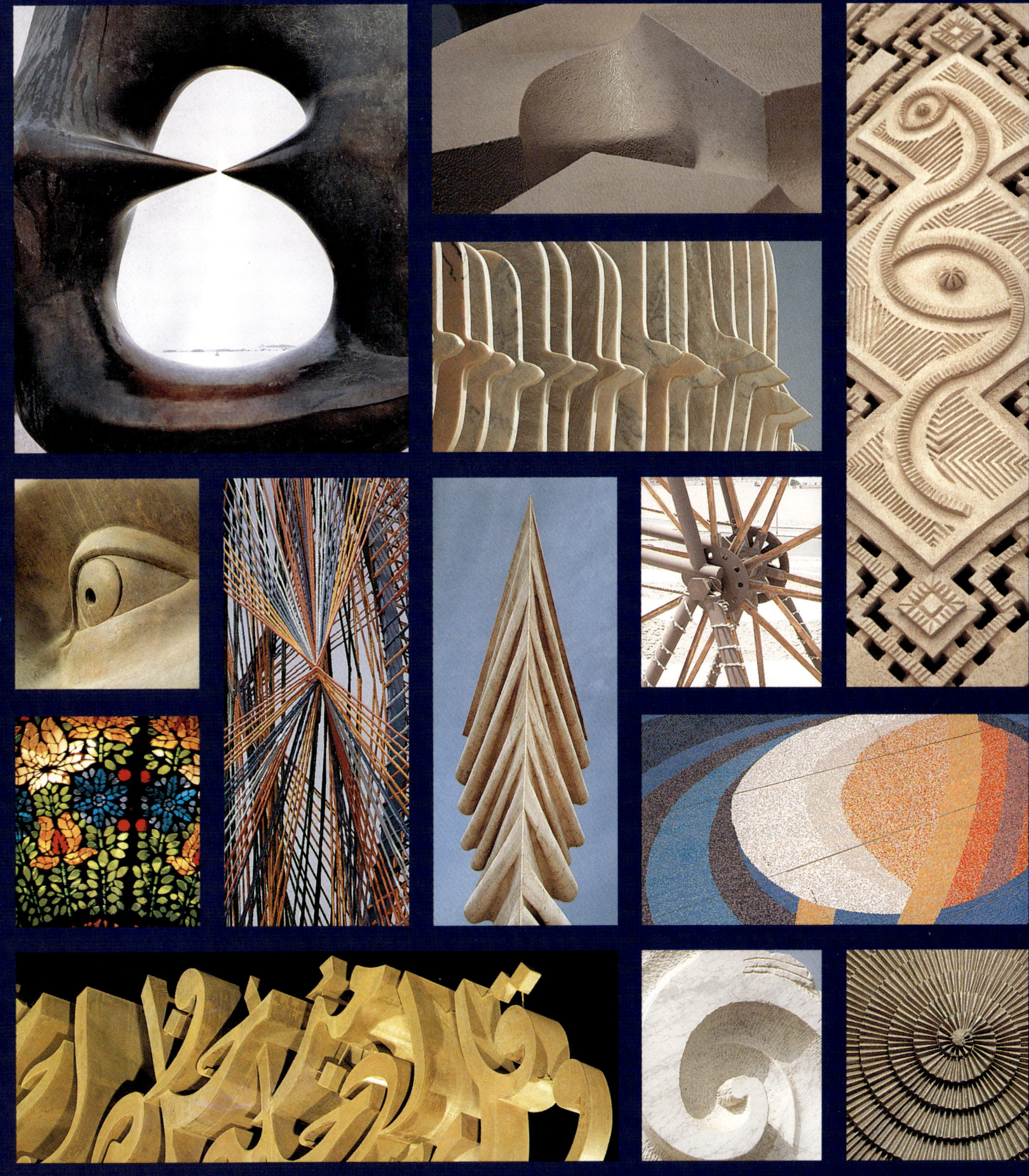

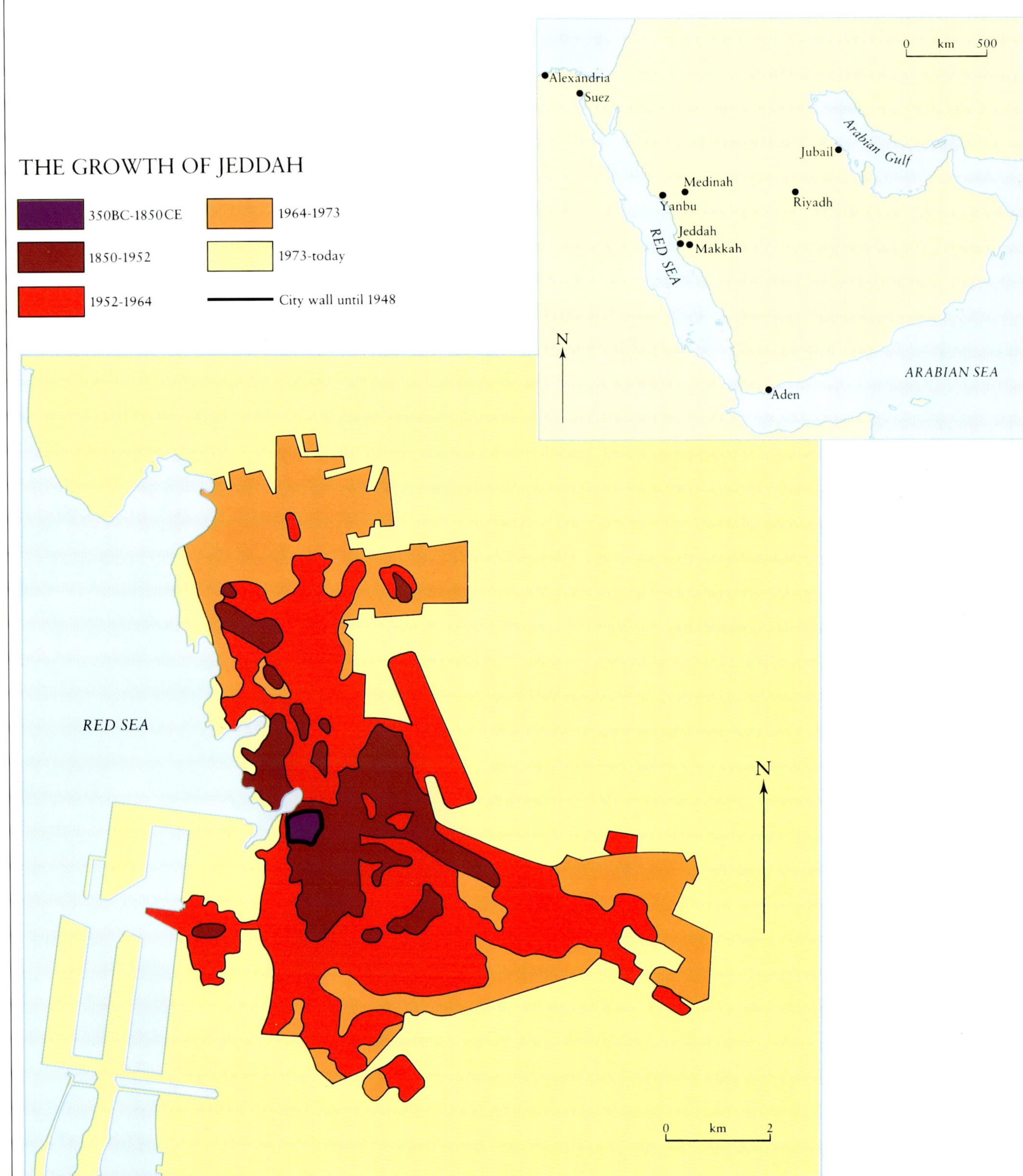
THE GROWTH OF JEDDAH
350BC-1850CE
1850-1952
1952-1964
1964-1973
1973-today
City wall until 1948
RED SEA
N
0 km 2
0 km 500
Alexandria
Suez
Arabian Gulf
Jubail
Medinah
Yanbu
Riyadh
Jeddah
Makkah
RED SEA
N
ARABIAN SEA
Aden

CHAPTER ONE

JEDDAH: The OPPORTUNITY

When Mohamed Said Farsi first saw Jeddah at the age of five it was the compact walled town it had been for the previous nine centuries. Although few of its fine merchant houses were much older than a century, to the young Farsi's eye it might have appeared a city sealed from time and change. The phenomenal transformation that was to overtake Jeddah in the coming decade was utterly unpredictable.

In those previous nine centuries Jeddah variously fulfilled its role as the port for Makkah's pilgrims, the entrepôt for such trade as that region of the Hejaz hinterland offered, as the local market, and until the coming of steam, as a victualling point for ocean traders using the Red Sea route to Europe. Like any Arabian port of the era, its population and physical size had been curtailed by its limited wells of fresh water and by the requirements of defence and workable administration.

The beginnings of a port were already there by the fourth century CE. For the site of Jeddah, incorporating a natural lagoon, was found to lie at that point

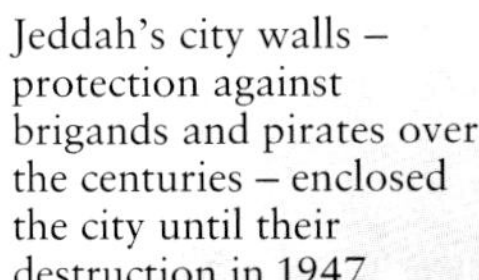

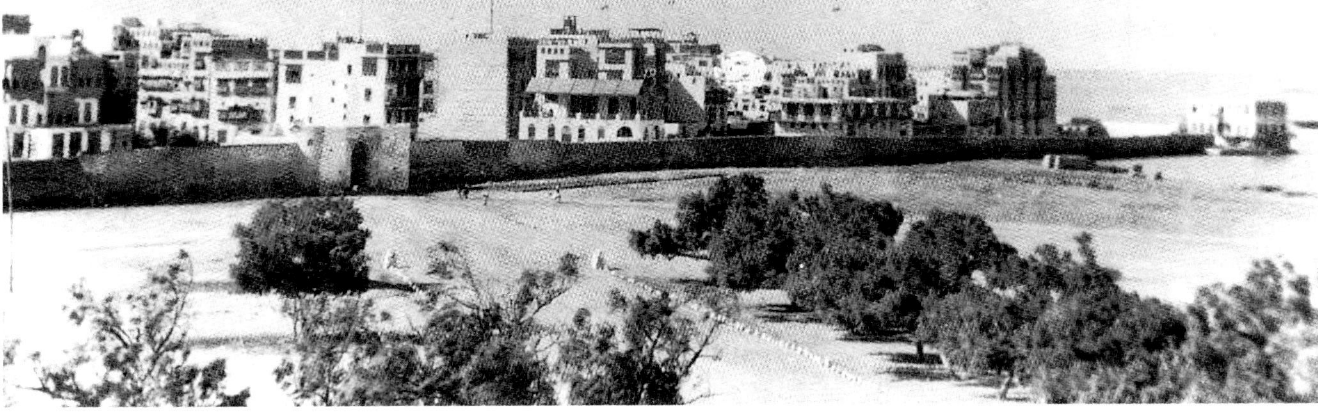

Jeddah's city walls – protection against brigands and pirates over the centuries – enclosed the city until their destruction in 1947.

where the vicious coral reefs that rim that whole stretch of the Red Sea coastline give way to allow a natural passage to and from the shore. Mediterranean appetite for frankincense from Arabia had always existed. Now a safe port between Aden at the mouth of the Red Sea to the south and the offloading point of Suez to the north was to give Jeddah a natural role as a provider of water and food for frankincense-laden vessels. In parallel to this role, Jeddah became a mart in its own right; and when, later, Europe's appetite for spices from further east began to grow, Jeddah became a trading post for ships and goods from the Orient.

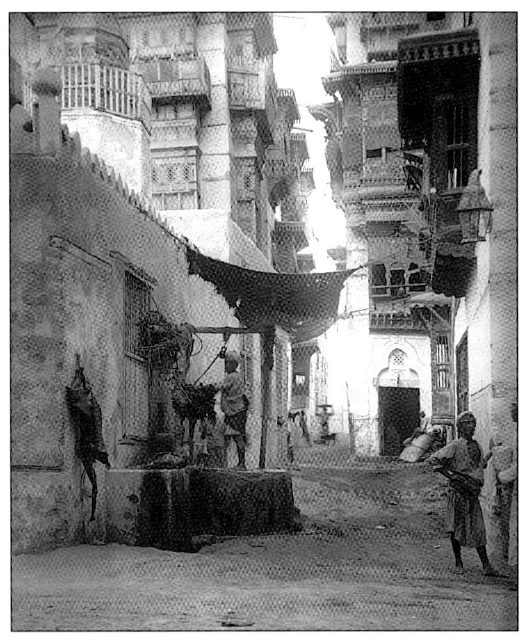

► Jeddah as photographed by TE Lawrence in 1916: Mohamed Said Farsi's conservation policy has ensured that many of these traditionally-designed buildings still survive.

Meanwhile, with the arrival of Islam in the seventh century CE, Jeddah was soon to establish itself as a thoroughfare in another direction. Jeddah was linked by a second natural passage to the world beyond – this time by the course of the Wadi Fatimah through the mountains behind the town to the Holy City of Makkah, a mere two days march – 75 km – inland. In the 24th year of the Islamic era (646 CE), the Caliph Uthman designated Jeddah as the appropriate landing for Makkah. Jeddah, the Caliph decided, was more secure from pirates than the earlier choice of Shuwaiba to the south.

Thus the city-port which was to become known as the 'Bride of the Red Sea' had entered upon the role which was to make it a byword throughout the growing world of Islam – and indeed the world beyond Islam. As early as the tenth century CE the traveller and geographer Al-Makdisi described the town as "fortified and well populated. The people are traders and are wealthy. The town is Makkah's treasury and Yemen's and Egypt's emporium."

Jeddah's very success, however, made it an object of the cupidity and rivalry of outside powers jockeying for influence in the region. It endured its crises and phases of turbulence as from time to time it passed out of Arab hands into those of the Persians, Egyptians or Turks or felt the long reach of the Portuguese, Dutch and English.

A millennium after Al-Makdisi – and a mere generation before Mohamed Said Farsi's first visit – T E Lawrence described his arrival in Jeddah:

"It was indeed a remarkable town. The streets were alleys, wood- roofed in the main bazaar, but elsewhere open to the sky in the little gap between the tops of the lofty white-walled houses ... House-fronts were fretted, pierced and pargetted till they looked as though cut out of cardboard for a romantic stage-setting ... The atmosphere was oppressive, deadly. It was not burning hot, but held a moisture and sense of great age and exhaustion such as seemed to belong to no other place."

It would appear that little had changed in terms of scale and atmosphere between the two travellers' visits. But one notes that accounts of both chroniclers, and those of numerous other visitors in the intervening centuries, underlined Jeddah's role as a gateway to the outside world and the entry point into the Hejaz of new ideas.

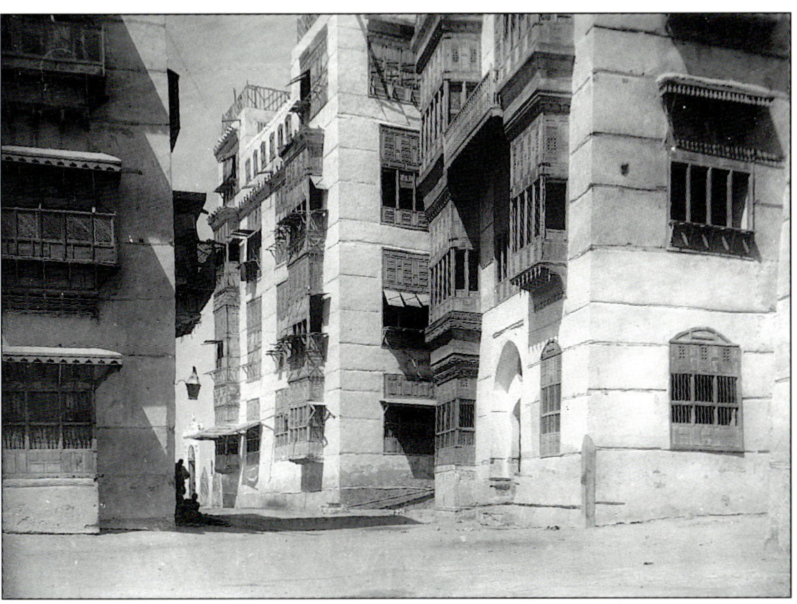

▲ The *rawashin* – fretwork-screened balconies – and narrow streets of old Jeddah made a deep impression upon T E Lawrence when he first visited Jeddah during the First World War.

Change, in historic terms, rarely seems dramatic at the time, but the explosive development of Jeddah that followed the discovery of oil in 1938 is an outstanding exception. A population which had remained stable for at least a century – and probably centuries – at around 25,000 was to increase sixtyfold by the early 1990s. Some residential spread occurred in the thirties and forties as building work spilled over into the land to the north and south-east of the old walled town along the Makkah road beyond the walls. Then, in 1947, down came the walls. Victims of the same demolition were the old gates – later to be reconstructed as a reminder of Jeddah's past.

The first oil 'boom' of post-1947 Jeddah induced a headlong building of roads, public services, royal palaces and luxurious villas. The quarantine hospital, the Petromin refinery, the new harbour and the Khozzam Palace (later used as the Foreign Ministry) were all either completed or started between 1947 and 1956. Then the closure of the Suez Canal in the war of 1956 suddenly dampened development, and investment confined itself mainly to public works such as a new harbour and the first airport.

With the accession of King Faisal ibn Abdul Aziz in 1964, the growth of Jeddah was resumed, but at a slower pace. The previous year, Mohamed Said Farsi had returned to Jeddah after qualifying as an architect at university in Alexandria and was appointed Town Planning Officer.

The challenges that lay ahead were awesome. How was Jeddah to expand? How swiftly? What role was Jeddah to play in the commerce and industry of the new country? How, throughout all this, were the needs of residents – both Jeddah's existing inhabitants and the newcomers – to be catered for?

The achievements of the Jeddah municipality over the next twenty years were based on the bold and progressive ideas of the team which co-ordinated the city's growth. In 1968 the Saudi government invited a United Nations-appointed international committee to

▼ Countless numbers of pilgrims passed through the Makkah Gate before it was swept away in the expansion of the late forties. Today a replica stands as a reminder of that past.

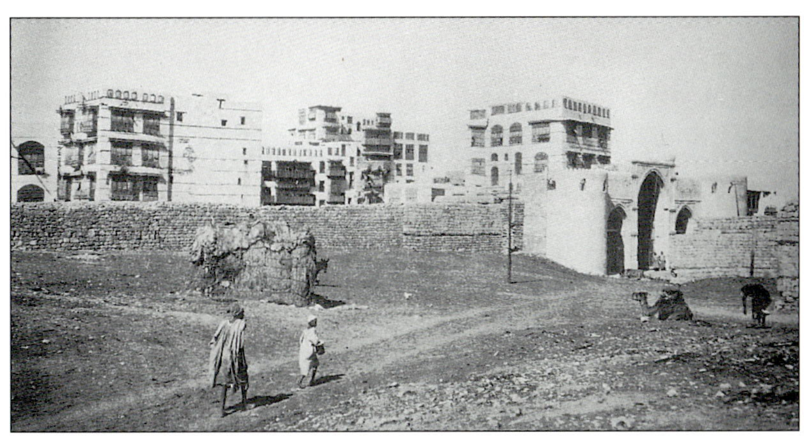

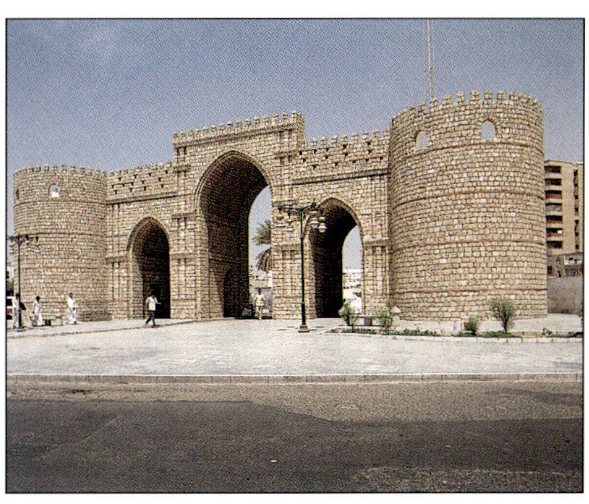

advise on a programme of regional and city planning for the whole Kingdom. A year later, a British firm of consultants was asked to develop a plan for the cities of the Western region; this included Jeddah. The key role of liaison officer was given to the same Mohamed Said Farsi, then Director of the Western Region Planning Department. It was he who supervised the work of the Saudi team and supported the consultant's project director. He became Mayor of Jeddah in 1972 and remained centrally involved with the conception and implementation of the entire Jeddah master plan.

The port of Jeddah was a development priority: work on its further expansion began in 1966, and the first phase was completed on target in 1973. Nine deep-water berths were constructed, increasing the port's capacity from its 1950s level of 600,000 tonnes to 1,500,000 tonnes in 1974. By this date, however, the vastly increased revenues from raised petroleum prices were available for investment. Thus, a mere two years later, some two hundred ships could be seen riding at anchor off the port of Jeddah, facing a four to six months wait to discharge their cargo.

▼ Jeddah's quayside in the late forties: port expansion was a major priority during the sixties and seventies.

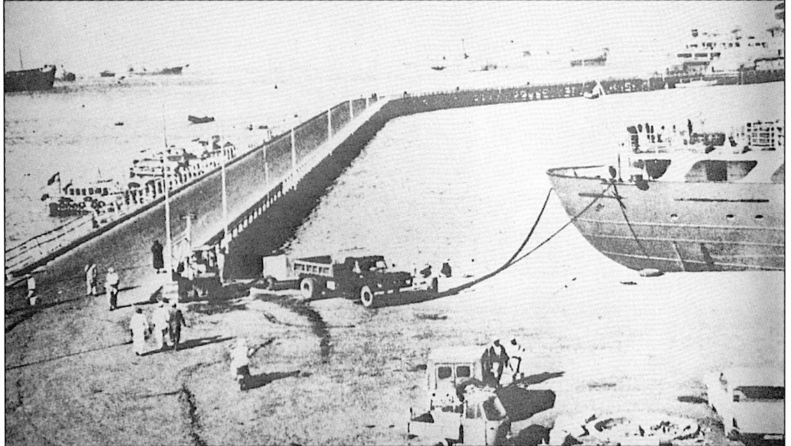

The frustration of those pioneering construction was acute, forcing them to the desperate expedient of unloading everything by helicopter – even cement! Drastic action had to be taken, and by 1977 Jeddah had 14 berths in operation, handling approximately 8 million tonnes of offloaded cargo a year. By 1980 another six deep-water berths had been added, putting an end to congestion.

Alongside rapidly escalating freight imports was another soaring influx: that of people. Into the city poured the migrant labour – from neighbouring Islamic states like Yemen and regions such as Eritrea, from further afield in the Islamic world, and some indeed from the Saudi hinterland itself. There was a wondrous clutter of folk, in every sort of temporary accommodation, often with their wives and children.

Simultaneously, there was a vast increase in the numbers of pilgrims bound for or returning from the Holy City of Makkah. In 1954, the number of pilgrims entering Saudi Arabia for the Haj and the Umra pilgrimages was 37,630. Most of them came by sea. By 1965, this figure had increased to 283,319 and had doubled again by the early 1970s to nearly half a million, mostly now by air. The logistical problems involved in coping with this human tide were enormous, and the Saudi government had always attached great importance to the efficient and safe administration of the pilgrimages. Hundreds of millions of riyals had to be spent to ensure adequate water and sanitation as well as accommodation and health care for the pilgrims.

The numbers of pilgrims arriving in Jeddah continued to rise. Up to the 1960s, the city had little expectation of a role as a focus of international air travel. After all, Saudia's original fleet had been three battered Dakotas (one of which is now preserved as a monument in front of the old terminal building). Thousands were wanting to enter – and by air. Annual passenger figures were approaching 8 million when, in 1974, work started on what still seems to have been a visionary project: King Abdul Aziz International Airport (KAIA), far to the north of Jeddah as it then was.

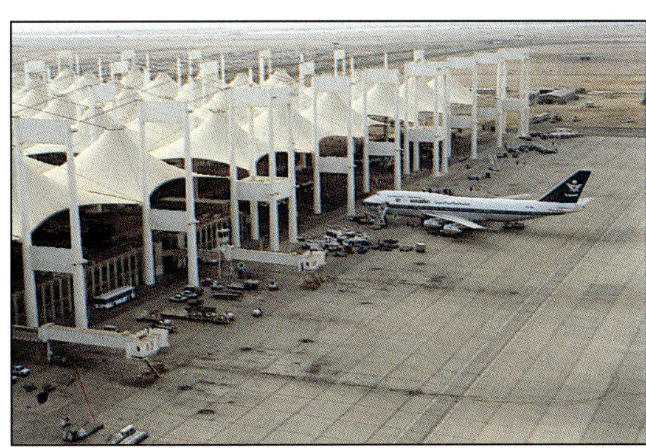

► The tent-like structure of the Haj Terminal at King Abdul Aziz International Airport was a winner of the Aga Khan Award for Islamic Architecture in 1983.

KAIA was to take eight years to complete. It is still acclaimed as a landmark in the history of both aviation and of architecture. Spanning over a hundred square kilometres, with the magnificent tent-shaped Haj terminal and the gleaming marble of its reception and administrative buildings, the airport is a fitting point of entry to Jeddah and the Holy City it also serves. It was awarded the Aga Khan Award for Islamic Architecture in 1983.

Such triumphs of the marriage of function with aesthetics were to become recognised as a keynote in the development of Jeddah. The new mayor and the town planners were never for a moment to lose sight of the requirement of the new Jeddah to emerge as a place beautiful and original in its own right.

In the early days, expansion was haphazard and unsightly. Poor quality housing sprang up along the Makkah road. Quick-built factories. Temporary tenements for hundreds of migrant workers. The congestion was often grievous, and the scramble for accommodation hectic. Where greenery was introduced, the goats ate it. During these 'frontier' years as that part of the old town nearest the sea was redeveloped, some of the finer old buildings of Jeddah disappeared. The dangers of over-enthusiastic speculative building were swiftly perceived. From the early 1970s on, efforts to preserve the precious heritage of 'The Bride of the Red Sea' were to play a key role in the planning of new development.

Jeddah was also the diplomatic capital of the country and as such host to a substantial and fast-growing international community. The swelling congestion of embassies and their staff were based in Jeddah until the mid-1980s when transferral to Riyadh at last began. This international community, coupled with Jeddah's population of expatriate business executives and their families, brought about a great appetite for recreation on the beaches and particularly at Obhor Creek to the north. Week-ending Saudi residents likewise took to heading for the sea-shore, north and south. Thus the line of the shore was to become a central part of the beautification of expanding Jeddah; and it was to reflect a relaxed and cosmopolitan atmosphere. Meanwhile, back from the shore, formal sports facilities and stadia were being built from the mid-1970s for the city's youth.

Function and beauty. The perennial problem of water manifested itself both in shortages and the occasional devastating surplus. A storm water channel was dug to protect the city from violent floods that once or twice a decade would sweep down the wadis from the basalt hills of the Hejaz.

Water resources remained prominent on the agenda as the population continued to swell inexorably. The old thundering, desalinating *Kindasah* (condenser), as it was affectionately known, had already been rendered obsolete by the pipelines constructed from the wells in the wadis Fatimaḥ and Khulays in the late 1940s. By 1974 a population of 600,000 needing 250 litres per person per day made for a total daily requirement of 150 million litres. By 1977, rain-water and well-water began to be supplemented by two of the eventual four huge desalination plants, built along the coast to the north of the city centre. By 1980, the population was already a million.

The dedication of the team which had overseen the planning and development was rewarded by the establishment of a city as well served by its amenities as its role as commercial capital and gateway to a 'new' and prosperous country could call for.

What was true of water was no less true of drainage and sewerage, of electricity and telephones, and indeed of roads and bridges.

In the matter of roads and bridges, flyovers and roundabouts, the marriage of function and beauty was again the keynote. From the mid-1970s onwards, the population of Jeddah became accustomed to awaking of a morning to find yet another new inspired addition to the inventory of the city's public art. They seldom knew what to expect or where to expect it. Beside a flyover. Filling a shop or factory forecourt. Dominating a traffic circle – and the avenues approaching from the four points of the compass.

For many, the mere emergence out of a virtual sea side wilderness of the clear bold lines of a gleaming modern city would have been achievement enough. But what was distinguishing Jeddah from other cities – and not only in the Middle East but in the world – was the persistent aesthetic vision of its planners. Woven into the fabric of the city was the fulfilment of the requirement for this new Jeddah to provide something fresh and relevant to the modern Islamic world.

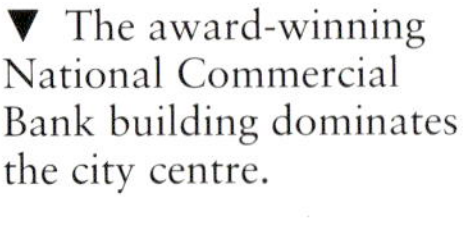

▼ The award-winning National Commercial Bank building dominates the city centre.

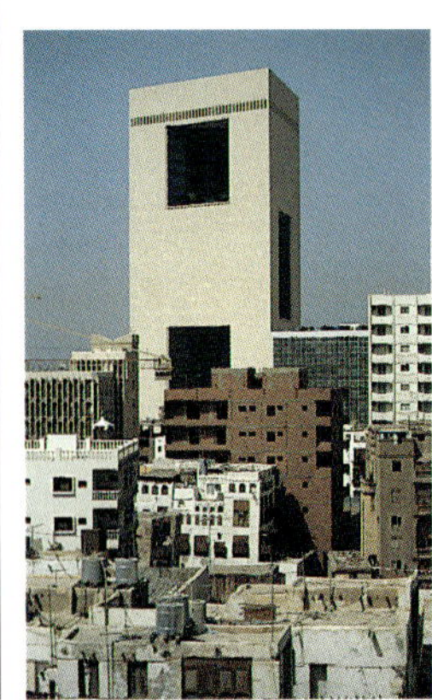

Thus came its dazzling innovative architecture and thus came its array of monuments and public sculptures. Of the great buildings, let us consider the National Commercial Bank – a monolith which dominates the downtown area, on the very edge of the old quarter. It would have been easy to opt for a safe design which would neither offend nor astonish: instead, the bank's architects were encouraged to design with audacious originality. The result was a dramatic addition to Jeddah's skyline and a stimulus to buildings to come.

Nor was the small scale neglected in favour of the grand: ornamentation and attention to detail were constantly included in the master plan, so that almost every bridge or street corner was perceived as an opportunity to please the eye. A simple parapet wall became more than just a safety barrier; an open air leisure or picnic area was a chance to create not only shade but also a work of art.

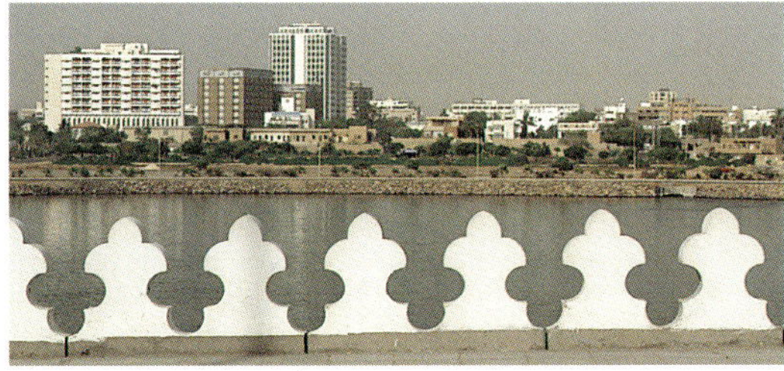

► Even safety barriers provide an opportunity for decoration in Jeddah.

The soul of old Jeddah lingered on in the streets and alleys of the preserved ancient city. The remarkable feature of Jeddah's new development was that countless construction projects succeeded by alertness and imagination in bringing Greater Jeddah its new 'soul'.

No Jeddah entrepreneur or commercial or industrial magnate was overlooked by the mayor and his team in their efforts to exploit the once-and-for-all opportunity that the city's amazing expansion had presented them with. The public sculptures of Jeddah were soon to come into their own and win the city a new international fame. How did they come about? What was the vision that inspired them?

TS/JW

CHAPTER TWO

The SOURCES of MOHAMED SAID FARSI'S VISION

For Mohamed Said Farsi the beauty of Jeddah has always carried a profound and personal meaning. His work for Jeddah has been a labour of love and words alone can do little to convey what is in his heart.

Jeddah was something he dreamed of from his earliest years. Those first years were spent in Makkah, where he grew up close to the Holy Mosque, learning to recite from the Koran and every now and then drinking from the water of the Well of Zamzam. It was shortly after his fifth birthday when his father first took him to Jeddah. That visit changed dreams into a reality. When young Mohamed arrived at the old Jeddah quayside for the first time, he was awe-struck by so vast an expanse of blue – sea blue and sky blue meeting and merging at the horizon. Ever since, he recalls, his heart has responded to the sea's horizons, the smell of the sea and its unknown depths.

After that first visit, he often returned to Jeddah's souks – Al-Nada, Al-Khasikiyah and Gabel – where trade continues to this day.

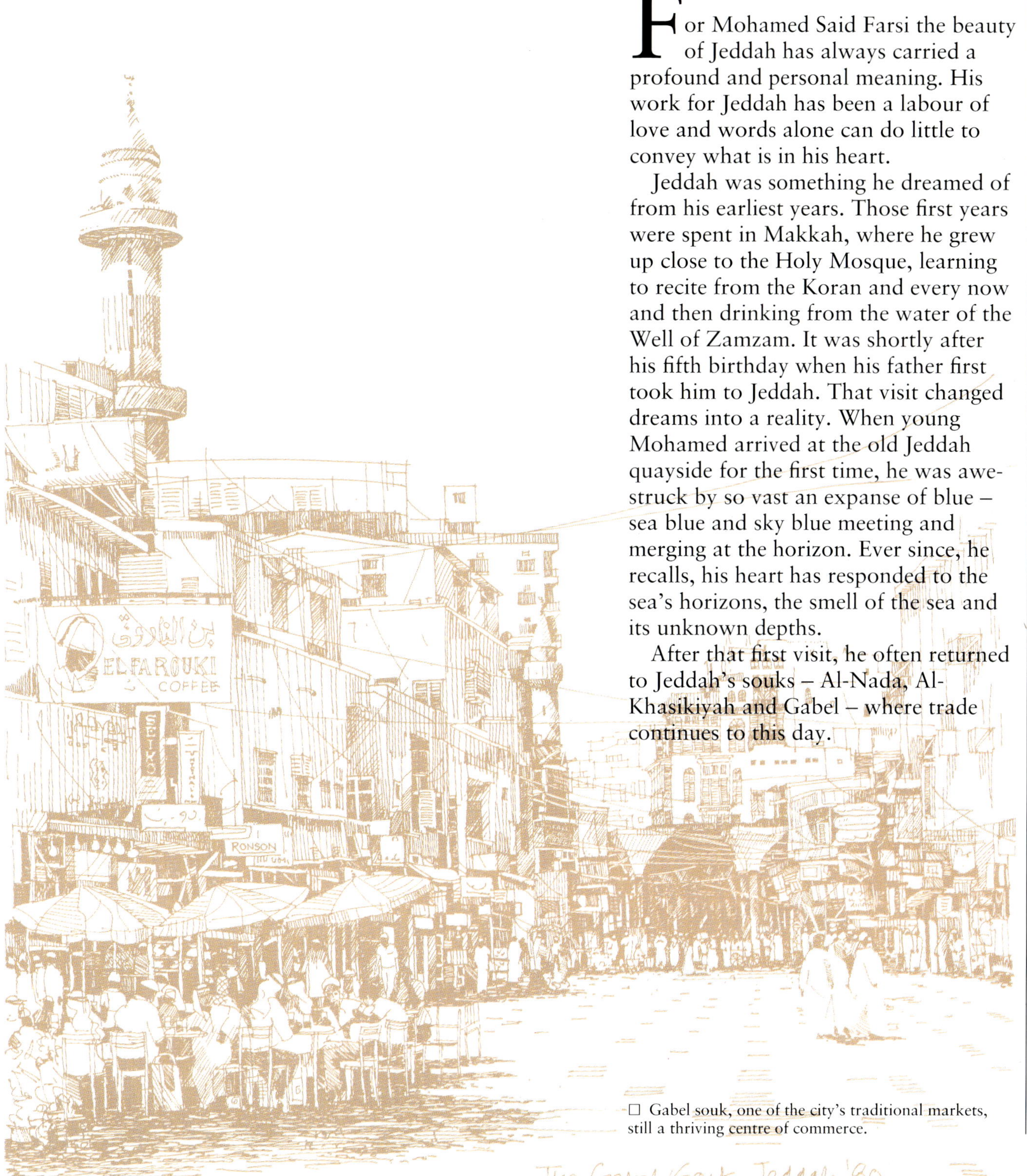

□ Gabel souk, one of the city's traditional markets, still a thriving centre of commerce.

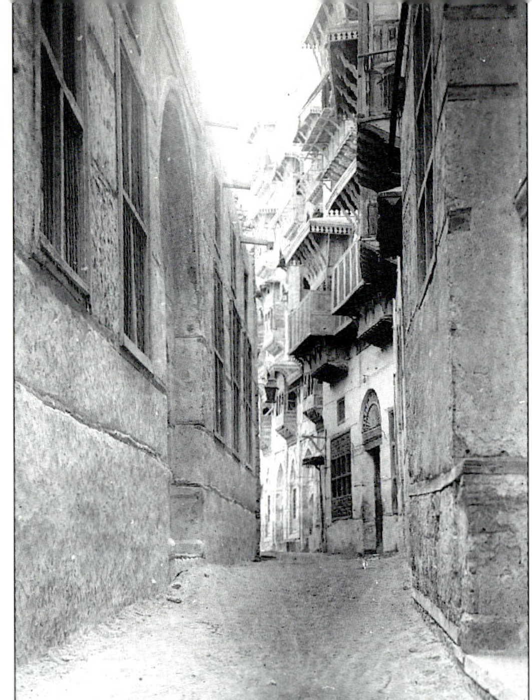

► The old merchant houses of Jeddah, photographed by T E Lawrence in 1916, were characterised not merely by their "pierced and pargetted" *rawashin*, but also by their use of blocks of coral as a building material.

He roamed Jeddah's alleys and streets, which weave like the calcite veins in a block of marble. He threaded their narrow irregular routes between the tall buildings of the ancient city. He remembers how the sea breezes used to provide some relief from the heat of the fierce summer. Those same breezes were sought and caught by the *rawashin* – the projecting bay windows – of the merchants' houses. From those earliest days he was intuitively alive to the rightness of the alliance of function and beauty.

By his late teens he was ready for experience of the wider world. From the old airport of Jeddah – airport is too grand a word to describe Jeddah's old landing strip in those days, with its cluster of buildings – he made his first trip to Egypt, and became a university student in another coastal city. As Jeddah was, and is, the 'Bride of the Red Sea', Alexandria is 'Bride of the Mediterranean'.

Living in Alexandria and studying there, he could not but reflect on the bond that exists between man and the natural creation of God with which man is surrounded. There was the beauty of the Nile in its kinship with Cairo, and of the sea with Alexandria. His awareness grew of the beauty and majesty granted by God. The shores of the sea, so it seemed to him, were for man's guileless delight in the beauty of God's creation. The experience enriched him, sharpening his devotion to Jeddah and to his first love, the Holy City of Makkah Al-Mukurramah.

He could never have guessed how passionate would become his bond with the city of Jeddah. Jeddah is, surely, loved by all its inhabitants. And visitors too, one has discovered, were – and are - constantly astonished by the charm of Jeddah, the cool sea breezes of its night-time and the rhythm of its waves, always so close to the ear of the old city. Yet it could scarcely have occurred to Mohamed Said Farsi that he was to enter into so long and emotional a commitment to Jeddah. The work that lay ahead of him was to become his life and the realisation of hopes he would not have dared to dream of.

In 1963, as a young man of 29, Mohamed Said Farsi was appointed Town Planning Officer to Jeddah. That date, he now recognises, was the beginning of his obligation to the beauty of the place. Already at that time, he remembers, the big questions were crowding his mind. Upon what

▼ Mameluke architecture, as typified by these drawings of mosque minarets in Cairo, provided the inspiration for many of Jeddah's sculptures.

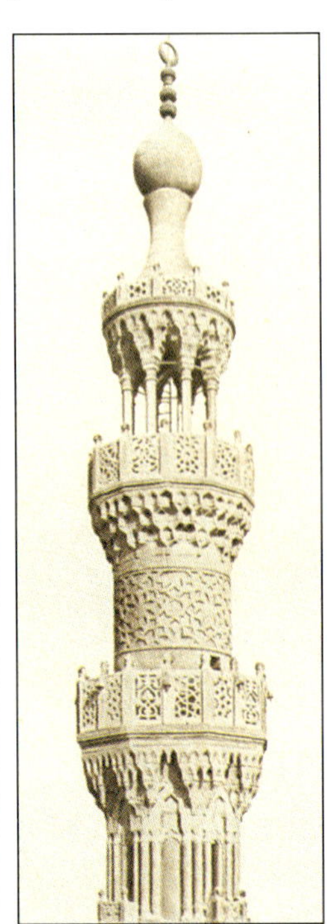

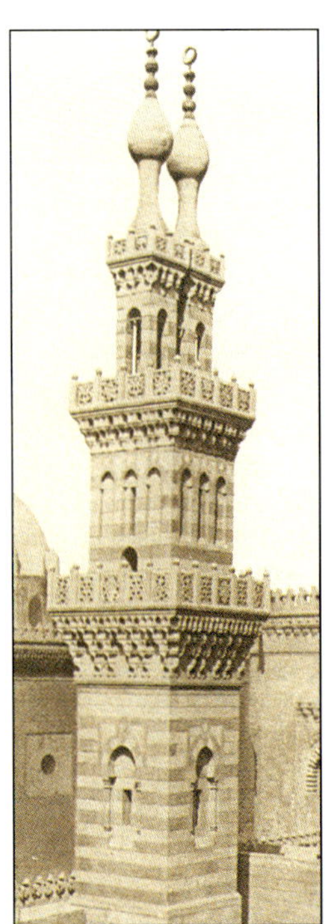

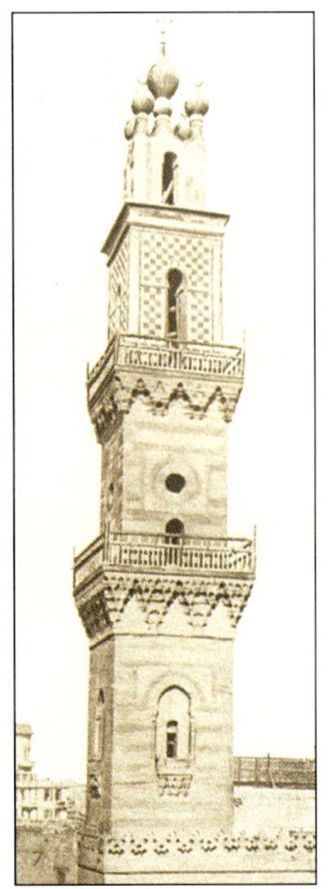

frame should he start to tackle so vast a task? How could his ideas and emotions be given structure and direction? What manner of artistic expression would meet the requirement of such a place at such a time?

Art in Islamic Culture

In the Islamic world, art has followed and is guided by the teachings of Islam. It is a form of art practised from the very first century of the Islamic period. To comply with the spirit and teachings of Islam, each Moslem country reassessed and modified its previous modes and styles of artistic creativity, whether in the field of architecture or ornamentation or artefacts.

In Syria, for example, there evolved the Umayyad style of architecture. There and elsewhere, Moslem craftsmen developed and refined their own styles and techniques not only in architecture but in all branches of applied art – earthenware, ceramics, glass, metals: in the working and carving of wood, plaster and stone; and in textiles and all uses of weaving. The human figure was avoided; abstract forms grew from geometry and rhythm and symmetry and, of course, from the written word. The evolutionary period was enriched by the exquisiteness of the craftsmanship of the pre-Islamic Sassanian and Byzantine periods. Islamic art achieved its zenith, perhaps, during the first Abbasid period.

Alongside the plastic arts, Moslems perfected the 'art of the word' in their early literature and poetry. The tonal values of words and verses assume a sound as of music. The reciting of poetry and performance of musical ballads at the ancient fairs of Ukaz and Mina in the Hejaz played a significant role in the cultural life of the region. The poets and the bards and the musicians drew pictures without a brush.

Islamic thinkers were invariably also artists in music as they were masters of mathematics and physics. Such was Al-Farabi, the inventor of the zither and Ibn Al-Haitham, founder of the science of optics and – incidentally – originator of the idea of a high dam in Egypt. Such too was Al-Kindi, the thinker and translator.

Islamic culture brought about the embellishment of surfaces with inscriptions and the abstract ornamentation of flower or branch or tree. Mohamed Said Farsi compares the artistic structure of Arabic calligraphy to the flow of black shapes over a snow-white landscape, or to a returning rhythmic phrase in music whose tonal values are represented by the shapes of rounded or squared calligraphy. The eye is rewarded in the same way that the ear may be assailed by thoughts that make the music of mind and soul. Arabic calligraphy, he believes, is the truest visual expression of Islamic culture. Its outstanding masters are Ibn Al-Mukla (died tenth century) and Ibn Al-Bawwab (died eleventh century), both of whom anticipated the abstract art of today by a millennium.

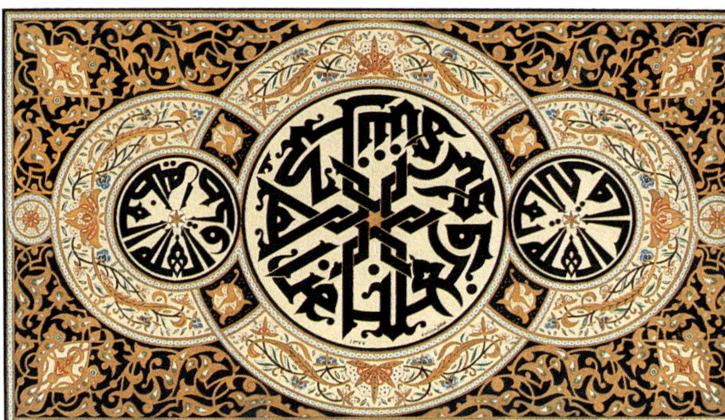

► This example of calligraphy from the Abbasid era – part of Mohamed Said Farsi's collection – was used by Lafuente as a basis for his *Calligraphic Discs*. The quotation is taken from the Holy Koran 21:30.

Eight centuries ago Al-Waseti of Baghdad won fame for his decorative works and calligraphic illumination which were said to reflect the essence of Arabic and Islamic culture as if in a mirror. The Egyptian historian, Dr Tharwat Ukasha, has written of him that he brought his drawings to life and made them the touchstone of the artistic experience of his day.

In times past, what did Arab philosophers have to say concerning beauty? Abu Hayyan Al-Tawhidi, for one, considered art to be of greater value than science. He asked: Why is a good picture liked? Is it through the influence of nature? Is it a personal thing? Is it through the exercise of the intellect or by firing the spirit? Ibn Meskawaih (died eleventh century) responded to Abu Hayyan's questions by defining the effect of beauty as "a condition of influence on someone viewing an object to a point of complete unification between object and viewer." He cites two principal premises of artistic appeal: the temperament of the observer, and 'harmony' in shape, colour and form.

Modern Moslem thinkers subscribe widely to the definition attributed to Shaikh Mohamed Abduh in the nineteenth century: "Drawing is a kind of poetry seen but not heard, and poetry is a kind of drawing heard but not seen." He goes on: "Such drawings record life in its inventory of forms and human experience. They depict man or animals in a state of pleasure, satisfaction and peacefulness."

During that golden age, Arab and Islamic culture bore artistic witness to man's sense of security, continuity and peace. Let there be no doubt that the flowering of culture begins with the elimination of fear and anxiety and turbulence. Mohamed Said Farsi likens this shining period of Islamic culture to the opening of the shutters of a window that cast its shaft of light across a primitive Europe and other regions of a darkened world. At Toledo, Spain, the Islamic academy was a magnet for princes and clergy from all of Europe. Islamic knowledge and learning in the arts and sciences and literature became a source of enlightenment far and wide.

Institutes for learning which subsequently sprang up in Europe reflected this Arab-Islamic influence not only in their scholarship but in the domes and arcading of their buildings and churches and courtyards and their ornamentation. With the passage of time, this Islamic influence began to wane; but it had played its part in the inspiration and development of thought in an awakening Europe.

Such cross-fertilisation of ideas and styles applies no less today. Travel opens up the mind and extends the frontiers of art. In the commissioning of a number of unique works of public art specially conceived and designed for the city of Jeddah, Mohamed Said Farsi toured the cities of the world, travelling from the Arctic Circle in Finland to the Philippines and Indonesia in the tropics. A constant requirement was compliance with Saudi cultural heritage and an acceptance of what the people of Arabia and Islam perceive as being artistic and beautiful. Given that, he reflected upon the question: "How can man translate the feelings and perceptions of his inner creative energy into effective and original art?"

The Elements of Beauty

The recurring theme of the protracted discussions Mohamed Said Farsi had with artists met on his journeys – be it in Brussels or Paris or Rome or Cairo or Jakarta or Helsinki or Madrid – was how one can best find ways to embody beauty and bring delight and meaning to the beholder. Mayor Farsi and the artists discussed the perennial conundrums: "Does one respond to works of art because they are beautiful, or are they beautiful because one responds to them?" and thence: "Is beauty an objective fact or a subjective experience?" Maybe, he acknowledges, the distinction is a false one, since in its 'objective beauty' a work of art cannot

▼Mahmoud Banat's marble book, bearing the inscription *"Science is Light"*, stands outside Dar Al-Hanan school where, doubtless, it serves as a source of inspiration for the students.

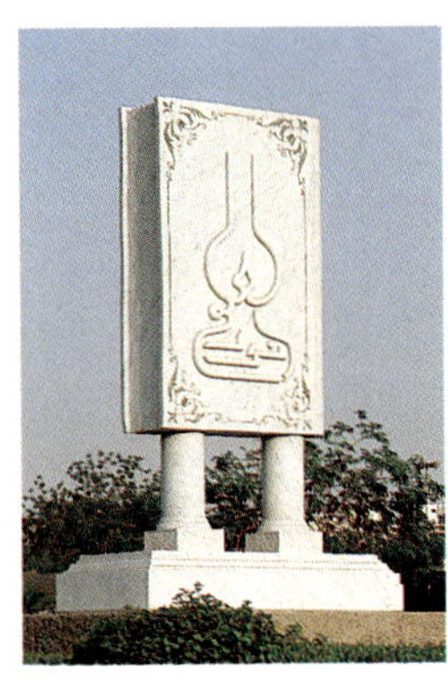

fail to be delved by the eye for the elements which accord it its beauty. Not everyone will be of the same mind. Some will insist that objective 'beauty' can and should be submitted to measurable assessment rather than personal judgement, on the grounds that what pleases one person 'subjectively' may not please another.

Beauty, he believes, does have fundamental and immutable constituents, the mastery of which forms the language of the plastic arts.

The first element, which he thinks is more important than the material from which the work is created, is line in all its guises – straight, curved or broken. Line constitutes the main attribute of the work as a whole. It will spark the first response to the work. It may evoke pleasure and wonder, as do skyscrapers; awe and submissiveness, as do the pyramids, sphinx and temples of ancient Egypt; or a sense of movement and energy, as do drawings which mingle the straight and the curved. Line transmits the first impression of the artist's hand at work.

Next, he says, come light and shade and colour, the thousand tones which tell of the mood of the artist during the implementation of his work. In the plastic arts, colours affect the spirit as do the sounds of the words in literature or recitation. Some colours – such as green and blue – emanate cold emotions; yellow and orange radiate feelings of warmth. Mohamed Said Farsi reasons that it is surely for his mastery of colour – the precision and honesty of his use of colour – that Van Gogh is universally honoured.

Next, the tactile characteristics of works of art: that is, the texture that its surfaces impart to eye or hand. The element of touch, the caress of hand or eye, is of course suggested by the material itself – as by the smoothness of polished marble, the translucency of glass, the sharp edges that iron can give, or the complex darkness of bronze.

Form, he concludes, is the combination of all the elements referred to above – line, colour and texture – within a defined space. In his opinion, fine art emerges from the spiritual beauty or spiritual essence that form illuminates.

The realisation of an object as art is a spontaneous act of giving. Mohamed Said Farsi compares it to a silken song from the lips of a passionate lover and describes it as the subjugation and refinement of the 'thing' in the service of man the beholder. As the academic, Dr Shukri Ayyad has put it: "Beauty is part of life, and life has no value without it." Kamil Zuhairi, the journalist, has written: "In drawing, light whispers to shade. Drawing makes a secret relationship between distance and space. The eye sees as the ear hears, since drawing too has its echo and resonance. There are tones of colour and light in art, in music and in the sound of words."

Mohamed Said Farsi likes to use music as an analogy: in music, he notes, beauty depends upon the melodic and harmonic ordering of sounds on a given range of musical intervals. The composition of the music derives from the composer's (and performer's) mood; how the music is received by the audience response will reflect that mood. Al-Farabi is famous for his claim that he could move his audience to laughter or tears, or lull them to sleep before he left them and went away.

For an architect, inherent understanding of beauty lies in the ratios and harmonies of the three dimensions of solid materials. Unquarried stone is an inert mass: stone as the material of a building however, is something else. The stone tells of the spirit of the artist who designed the building.

For Mohamed Said Farsi the architect, beauty lies in the exquisite proportions by which man was made by the hand of God. Hence, he notes, our common units of measurement – the hand span, the foot, the step (yard or metre) and the span of the outstretched arms of a man which approximates to his height. The golden symmetries and ratios of the human frame are surely there in the successful design of architecture and cityscapes.

Jeddah: the Aesthetic Plan

In the beautification of a city – assuming such a thing takes place at all – the contribution to beauty usually happens after the completion of the building work. In the creation of modern Jeddah, by contrast, everything proceeded in one great harmonious sweep of growth and development. The elements of beauty and function came together in one cohesive surge of realisation.

Mayor Farsi and his team were determined to make Jeddah the first city in the world to turn its face against the convention of the museum and the gallery being the chief repositories of public art. They would commit themselves to taking art out into the streets where it was accessible to everybody, whether at leisure or going about his or her business. Today, perhaps no other major city in the world contains so much in the way of open air sculpture and works of art as Jeddah does. This is most dramatically evident along the Red Sea Corniche.

Jeddah's sculptures and monuments serve as recognisable landmarks and focal points as well as giving delight to those approaching them from all directions. Lewis Mumford, in his *Cities Throughout the Ages*, speaks of the main function of any city being to change power to system, energy to culture and solid matter to vivid symbols of art. Elsewhere in the same work, he tells us that we should not think of the city first as the centre of business and administration but as a basic system or matrix which represents and acknowledges the personality of the 'New Man'.

In Jeddah, the prerequisite governing the selection of the works of art was that they should satisfy the requirements of Saudi culture and environment while at the same time reflecting the situation of the city in the context of world art, both contemporary and ancient. Mohamed Said Farsi and his colleagues had to face the question: What are we seeking for the city in terms of its beautification by art? The answer, they decided, was: To bring delight to the citizen while stimulating him to probe for the work's meaning, to give him a sense of wonder or admiration in its mode of creation and often, also, to stir his sense of history. The rewards of any piece should be no less than those brought by the reading of good literature, or by drama or music. From the delving of a work's meaning and the dawning of appreciation will the eye and the mind derive their satisfaction.

Cities throughout the world have

▼ Mohamed Said Farsi (second from left) inspects the proposed site for one of the sculptures.

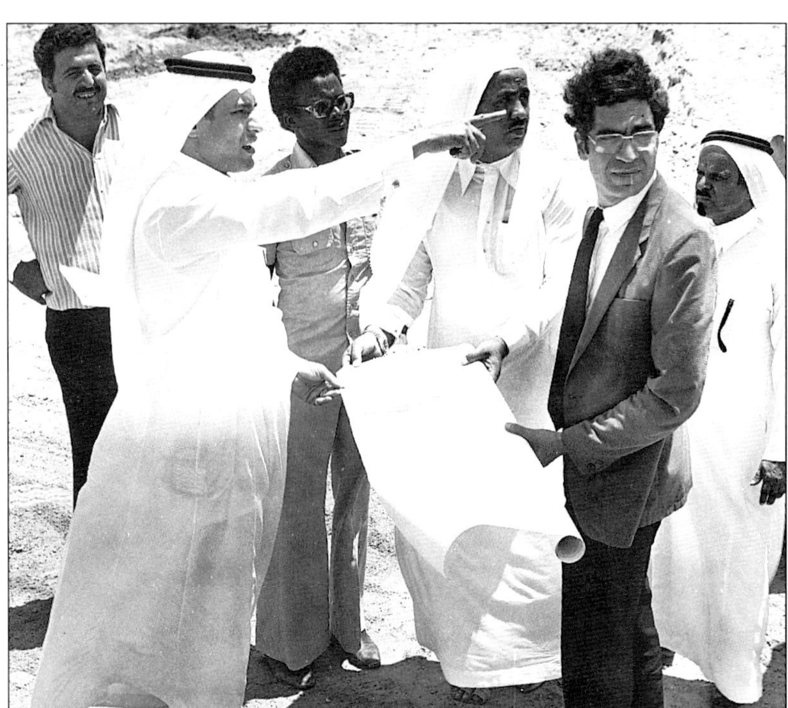

been guided by differing rules and principles, sometimes including the unrestrained representation of the human form in streets and squares. The Jeddah Municipality team, wishing to avoid elements of human representation, selected subjects associated more with beauty in the abstract and with noble emotion and sometimes sheer wit. At the start, they sought beauty in traditional shapes – fountains from water pots and coffee pots and censers. They made sculptures from historic artefacts – like the remains of the archaic 'condenser' – Jeddah's first water purifier. They were soon to turn to the beauty of Arabic calligraphy as inspiration. Ready, too, to look outwards towards international art, the team sought examples of work which were close to Saudi values and taste. Thus they found themselves responding to the works of such great artists as Henry Moore from Britain, or Lafuente from Spain, the Frenchman Vasarely, and César, Miró, Arp, Pomodoro and several others.

For the mayor and his aides, the abstraction of much of modern art was peculiarly apt. He asks: Where lies the appeal of this abstraction? Some have claimed the essence of beauty to lie in what is hidden – in that the hidden element evokes enquiry and stimulates the mind. Baudelaire, questioned on the meaning of contemporary art, replied that it was everything that provoked astonishment and stimulated curiosity. The Mayor tells the story of Salvador Dali climbing the podium to give a lecture on modern art, dressed from head to foot in deep-sea diving clothes. He spent much of the lecture simultaneously freeing himself from the cumbersome clothes and equipment, in which the audience found itself obliged to assist him. Characteristically he explained: "What you have been experiencing is modern art – that which attracts attention and provokes association of ideas."

Here is another factor at work in the choice and placing of the art of Jeddah. On a long journey, a traveller needs to pause and rest, to gather strength for the next stage of his journey. Such is true also of life – a perpetual search for one's own identity and purpose and goals. Thus the Municipality offered them – the citizen and the visitor – examples of beauty to have him pause and ponder.

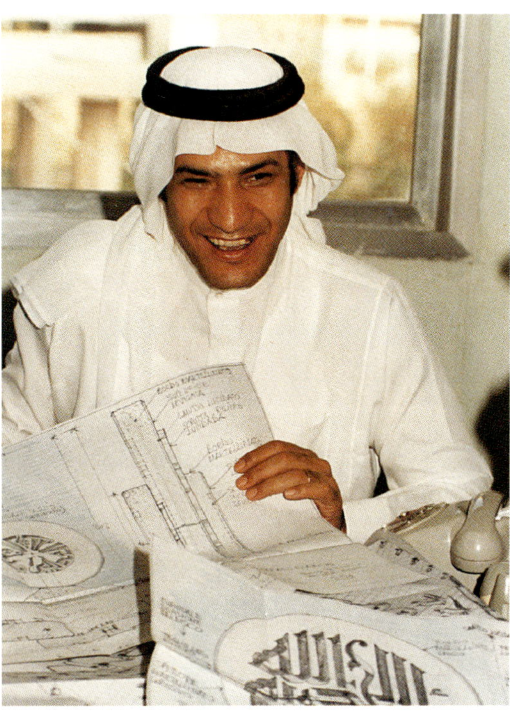

► Mohamed Said Farsi examines the working drawings for one of Lafuente's *Calligraphic Disc* sculptures.

Mayor Farsi was intent on using a variety of materials. Ancient artists used clay long before they turned to bronze. As their tools and skills developed, they would work in stone and marble, granite, basalt and diorite. In Jeddah, artists had the opportunity of an unprecedented range of materials to work with in a single place, and a great variety of surfaces and patina. Mohamed Said Farsi and his advisers extended the idea of 'recycling', to create many sculptures from scrap iron and other 'artefacts' such as aircraft, ships and abandoned factory machinery.

► This decorative screen, hiding a water tank, is evidence of the attention to detail that went into the planning of Jeddah.

Blessed with such a choice of open spaces, and the opportunity for the viewer to move round the work of art and regard it from a variety of angles, artists were able to exercise their ingenuity in playing with the relationships of their works to what lies behind and beside them – be they minarets, or domes, or sea, or open space, or housing or roads and avenues.

It was not an easy task to combine the Mayor's dreams with reality. Yet in the course of time dreams did become real. He watched over and guided the city as it surged north and east into the surrounding plains. He laid down its guidelines and its master plans. He attended to the design of bridges and overpasses, the landscaping of the roads, the provision of rich soil from which gardens have sprung, the extending of street lighting, the planting of millions of trees beside the roads. He watched over the elevations in each new building, and the play of arches and bay windows; he spurred the reintroduction of domes and roof crenellations on new mosques as well as in private houses and boundary walls.

For Mohamed Said Farsi, there was, and is, a simple ending to this tale.

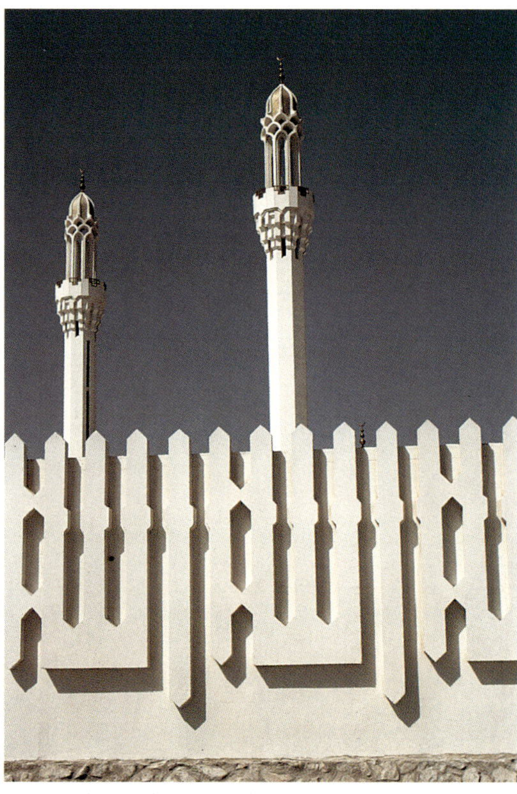

Everything he has done, throughout his professional life, has been for the city. And in all these works of art, there has been one aim: to give Jeddah the aspect of beauty as was in his power in the devoted bearing of the burdens of responsibility as Mayor for the period covered in this book from 1972 to 1986.

HMSF

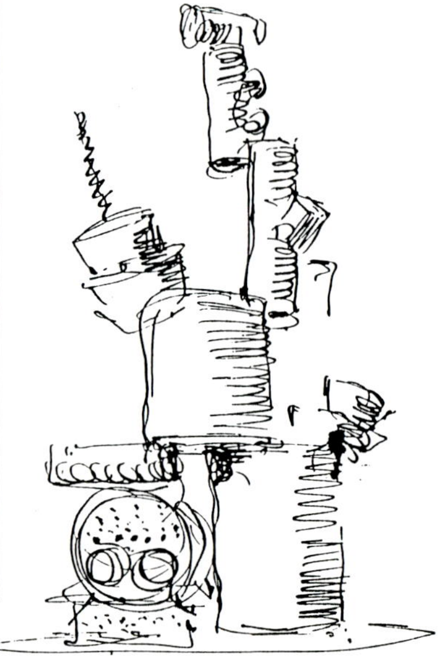

CHAPTER THREE

FULFILLING the TASK

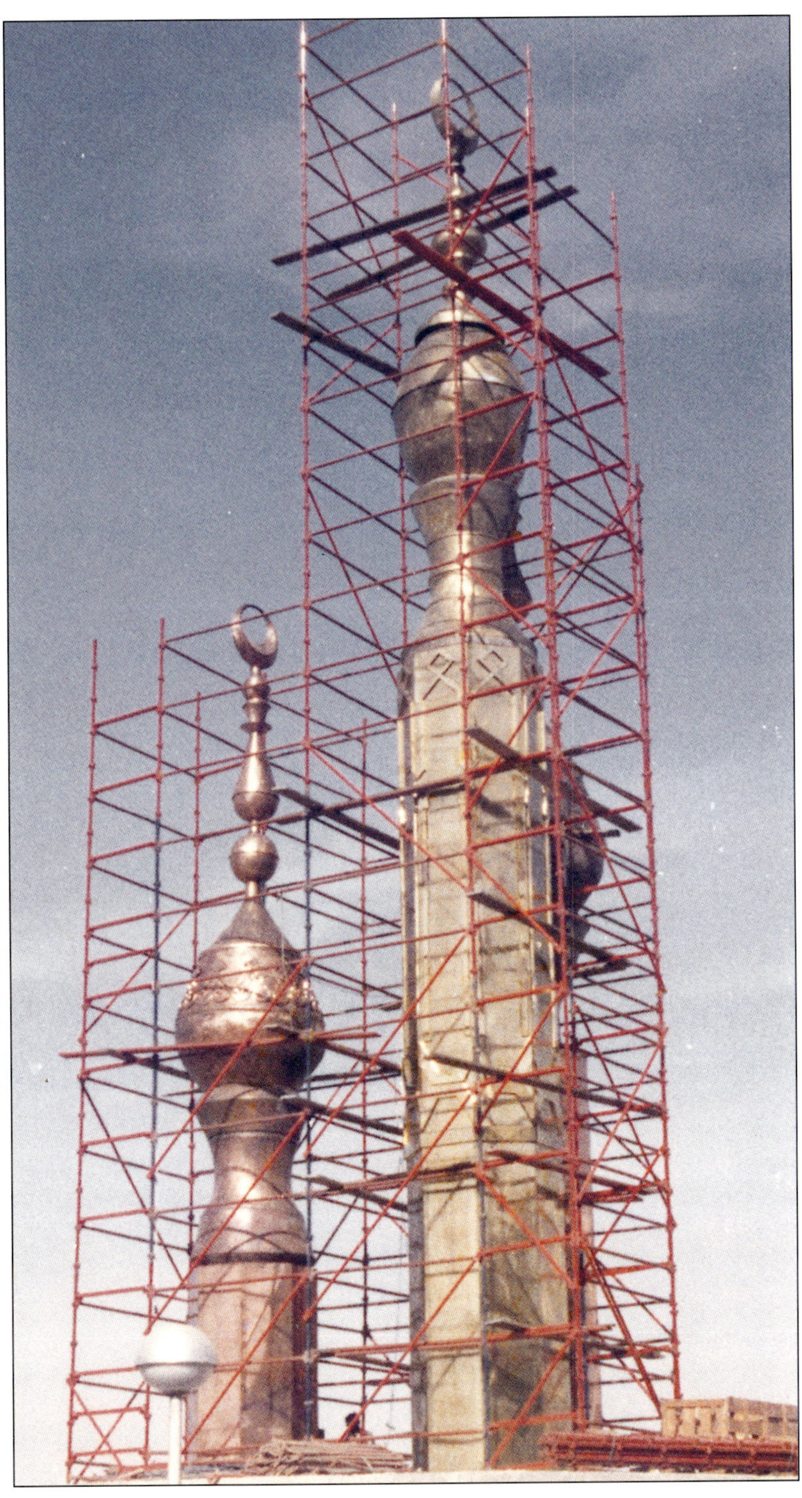

Mohamed Said Farsi's vision of turning Jeddah into an open air art museum – bringing art to the people – was, by any standards, ambitious. In the space of just a few years, he was to enhance the urban landscape of his beloved city, to introduce Jeddah's inhabitants to modern art and to stimulate Arab artists to develop distinctive new forms of Arab Islamic art.

In any context, these achievements would have been outstanding, but to have built up the Arab world's premier collection of sculpture in the midst of the chaos that was Jeddah during the 1970s and early 1980s showed an extraordinary tenacity and single-mindedness on the part of the former mayor.

In common with the other major cities of the Arabian Peninsula, Jeddah endured all the problems of rapid growth and industrialisation – port congestion, power and water shortages, lack of residential and commercial accommodation (visiting businessmen would plead for a couch in an hotel lobby), congested road networks and an embryonic bureaucracy.

In the circumstances, Mohamed Said Farsi's determination that the beautification of his city should proceed step for step with the more prosaic infrastructure projects must have occasioned more than a few raised eyebrows, but the city he left behind him when he finally relinquished the office of mayor vindicated his belief that infrastructure and aesthetics were not mutually exclusive.

◄ *The Mameluke Minarets* under construction.

As mayor, his workload was daunting – colleagues recall that a good time for getting the mayor's undivided attention was around 5.30 in the morning, before the day's work began in earnest. Despite all of the responsibilities of overseeing one of the world's biggest urban development programmes, Mohamed Said Farsi throughout his tenure of office was able to add, on average, one major new sculpture to the city's collection every month. Nor was the acquisition of a collection of around five hundred works simply a matter of selecting sculptures from a catalogue and then reaching for the city's cheque book: Mohamed Said Farsi was active in commissioning new works, meeting the artist and watching over a work as it progressed from conception to installation. He proved to be remarkably adept at finding sponsors to pay for the work.

Something in the region of $150 million was spent on the sculptures and associated landscaping. But rather than looking to the public purse to fund the implementation of his dream, Mohamed Said Farsi turned to private citizens and corporate sponsors who included many of the contractors who were carrying out Jeddah's infrastructure projects. The sculptures are now the property of the Jeddah Municipality and it is a measure of the scale of the collection that some thirty men are employed in the task of cleaning and maintaining the works.

Take the case of one of the city's most imposing monuments – Ottmar Hollmann's *Cosmos*. The artistic achievement of the German sculptor was paralleled by the engineering and logistical achievements of all those who were involved in its fabrication, transport and erection. From conception to realisation the creation of this monument took seven years, involving people in many countries.

Apart from the time and effort required to fabricate this 36 metre high assembly of steel and aluminium and then ship it from Germany to Jeddah, the task of moving the huge components from Jeddah's port to the designated site required the logistical expertise and forethought of a military operation. First, there was the equipment requirement – three huge low-loaders (more commonly used in moving the massive components of

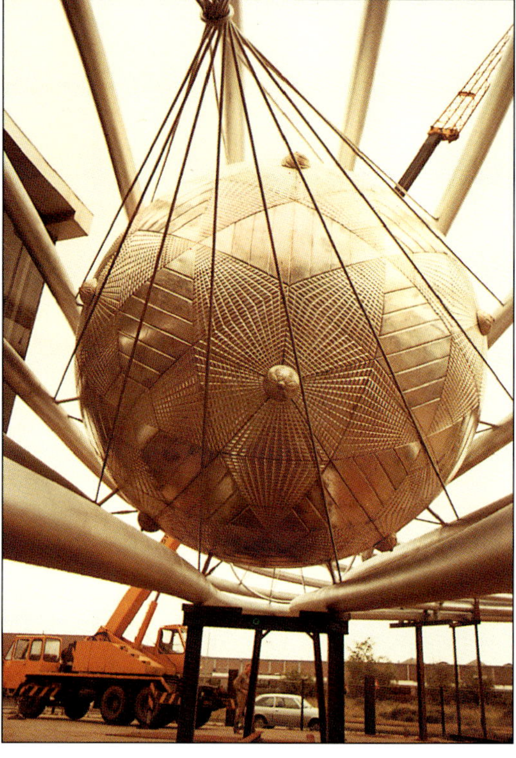

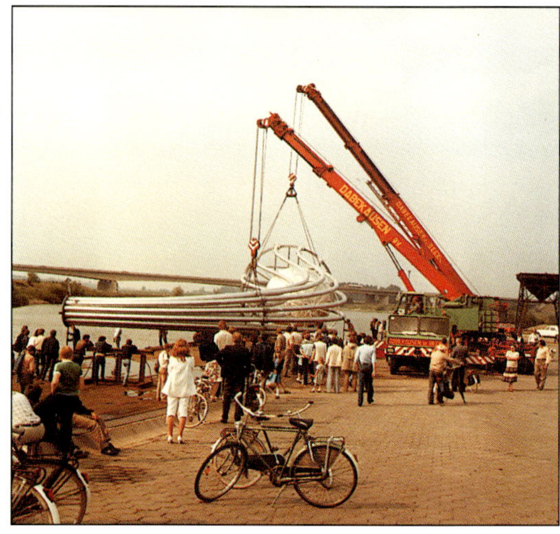

► Moving Ottmar Hollmann's massive *Cosmos* to Jeddah from Germany, where it was fabricated, was a major exercise in logistics.

heavy industrial projects) and two soaring cranes capable of 100 metre lifts. One of these cranes was available in Yanbu – the new industrial city on the Red Sea to the north of Jeddah – but for the second crane the installation project managers had to look all the way across the kingdom – to Yanbu's sister city, Jubail, on the Gulf.

The low-loaders and cranes gave the installation team the mechanical wherewithal to move the monument to site and hoist it into position, but they still had to work out how to get the components from the port to their final destination. By carefully studying maps of the city – and by then driving along the proposed route to ensure that the maps matched the reality in a city changing by the day – the team was able to establish a feasible route from the port. This route was not without its obstacles, however, and on some narrower stretches of road it was necessary to temporarily remove street lights and traffic lights for the passage of the strange convoy.

So as not to bring the city's traffic to a grinding halt, the movement of the components took place in the dead hours of the night, between 1 am and 5.30 am. At the snail's pace of the transporters and allowing for contingencies, the team calculated that the 15 km move would take several nights and, consequently, had to ensure that their chosen route offered suitable empty spaces where the transporters could park during the day, away from the traffic. (In a similar operation to move obsolete coastguard vessels to Warships Square, transporters carrying vessels of up to 300 tonnes took two weeks to progress through the city's streets.) Four nights after leaving the port the convoy finally reached the junction of King Fahd Street and Sari Street where the components were lifted off the low-loaders and slowly hoisted into position.

This commanding monument stands on an 8.5 metre mound which is decorated with a representation of the solar system in mosaic. This base was a major undertaking in itself: the design – by Salah Abdulkarim and Julio Lafuente – incorporates two million pieces of mosaic. The mosaic was first laid out in Italy and the pieces then shipped to Jeddah where Italian craftsmen spent two months recreating it on site.

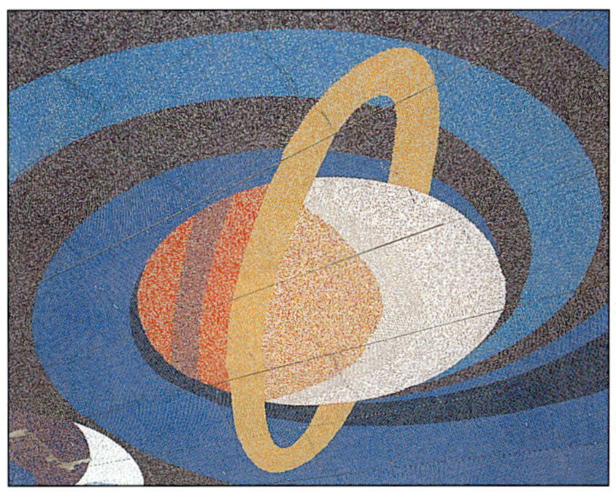

► Two million pieces of Italian mosaic were used to create the colourful base of Hollmann's *Cosmos*. The overall design of the base was by Salah Abdulkarim, while Julio Lafuente was responsible for the detailed work and supervision of the project.

Foreign craftsmen were frequently brought into the Kingdom to help with the installation of major pieces: in one instance workers came from as far afield as Indonesia to spend six months erecting sculptures by Maurice Malsia.

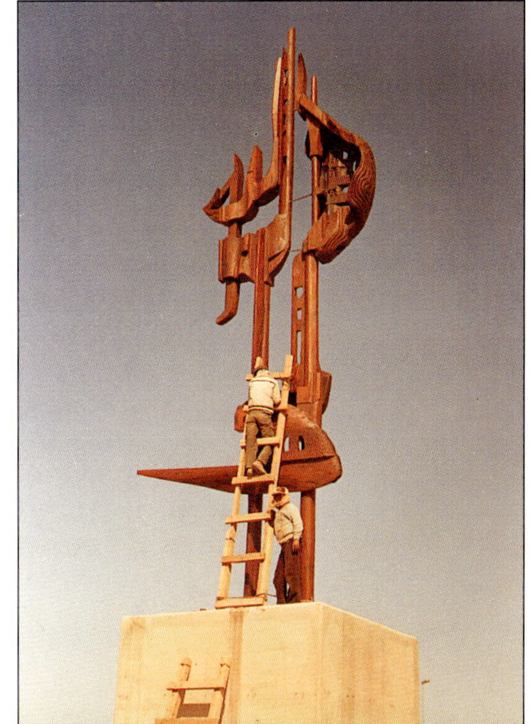

► Maurice Malsia brought assistants with him from Indonesia for the six-month-long task of erecting his petrified wood sculptures.

Hollmann's *Cosmos* was by no means alone in requiring considerable input from structural and civil engineers. Mustafa Senbel's *The Seagull* is – at 50 metres high – the world's largest piece of abstract art and took three years to build, using as much reinforced concrete as a medium-sized block of flats.

► Mustafa Senbel's *Seagull* was as much a construction project as a work of art, requiring tonnes of concrete and steel and an extensive labour force.

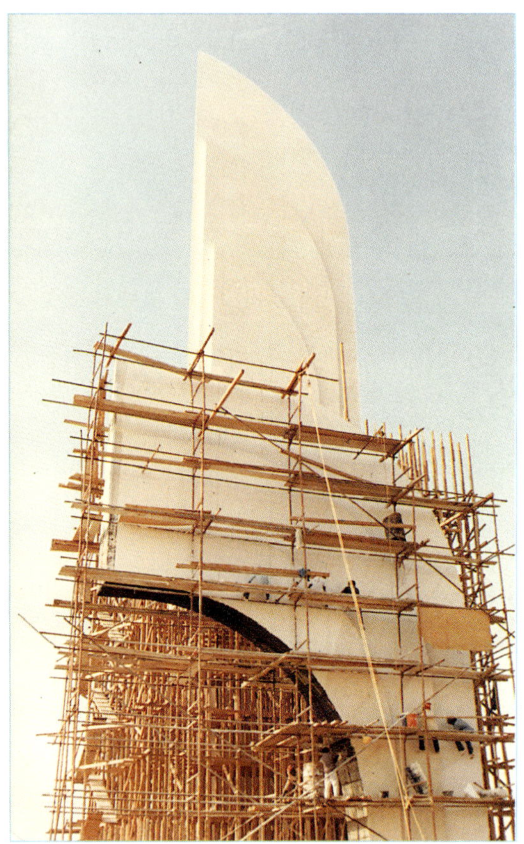

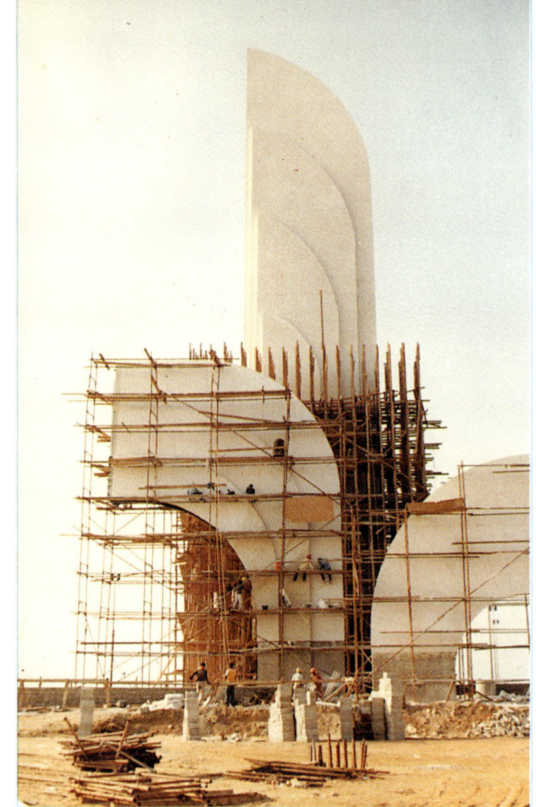

Jeddah also boasts the world's largest bicycle: jokingly referred to as the *Monument to the Unknown Cyclist*, this massive boneshaker is 15 metres high and 25 metres from end to end and was created by Lafuente using scrap materials from the old Mohamed Bin Laden Marble Factory. The 'spare wheel' which makes up part of *The Bicycle* group stands some 90 metres from the bicycle itself, with the whole of the surrounding and intervening space paved and contoured. In this and other major works such as *Cosmos*, *The Direction of Prayer* (*Al-Kibla*) and the four *Mameluke Mosque Lanterns*, much of the impact of the monument (and much of the expense of implementation) derives from the thought and effort which have gone into landscaping the immediate surrounds.

Mohamed Said Farsi gave considerable thought to the siting of each work (in some cases taking months over a decision), believing that the impact of each monument could be greatly enhanced by placing it in an appropriate setting. Thus, the road to the city's current desalination plant is marked by sculptures wrought from the scrap iron of a former plant; the environs of the university are dotted with sculptures representing science and learning, and the end of the runway at the old airport is marked by an old aircraft, mounted on a plinth in simulated take-off (as a matter of interest, the aircraft had been given to King Abdul Aziz by President Roosevelt when they met during the Second World War).

The wishes of the artists were also taken into consideration in placing the works: Henry Moore was reported to be pleased to have his work alongside that of Miró, while Hollmann was able to persuade the Mayor to relocate one of his works from a site on the Medinah Road to a spot near Moore's works in the Open Air Museum.

While the Jeddah collection boasts many works by artists of international renown, Mohamed Said Farsi was equally prepared to acknowledge beauty in anonymous, mass-produced forms and used small shop-bought knick-knacks as models for larger scale works.

He also allowed chance events to inspire new works: the *Cannons* monument stands close to the spot where the old Turkish cannons were unearthed during the excavation of the foundations for a new building.

On a wider level, the whole collection stands as a monument to a remarkable man of extraordinary vision. *Si monumentum requiris, circumspice* – the epitaph of England's great architect Sir Christopher Wren – springs to mind as an appropriate assessment of the contribution which Mohamed Said Farsi has already made towards the beautification of the city which he has loved since his boyhood. If you seek his memorial, look around.

PF

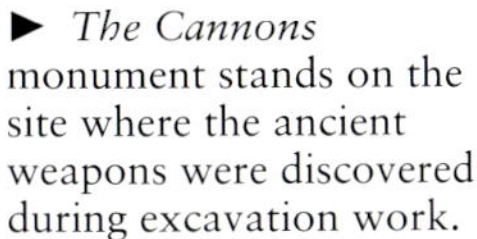

► *The Cannons* monument stands on the site where the ancient weapons were discovered during excavation work.

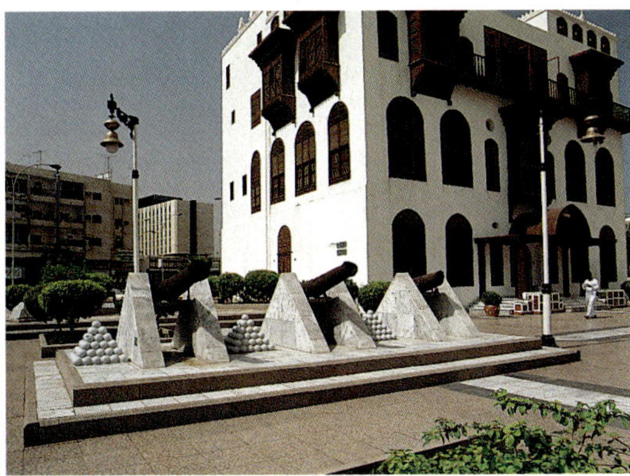

On a more personal note, the various *Heart* sculptures were commissioned by Mohamed Said Farsi after he underwent open heart surgery; that he needed such an operation was evidence of the punishing schedule he had set himself as the guiding force behind the creation of new Jeddah.

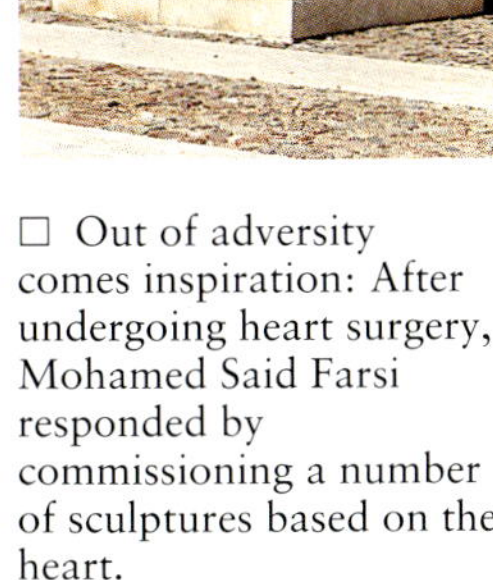

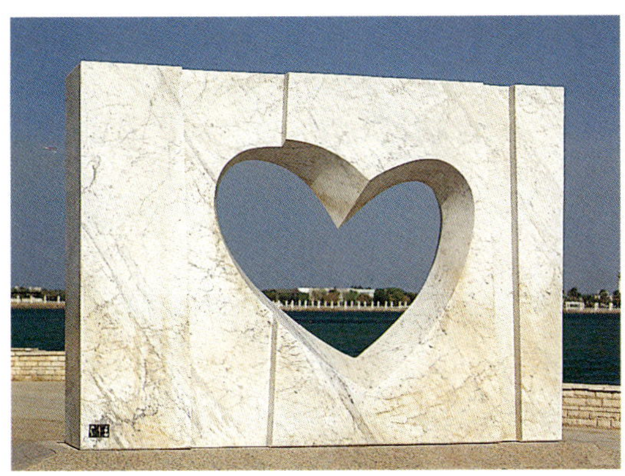

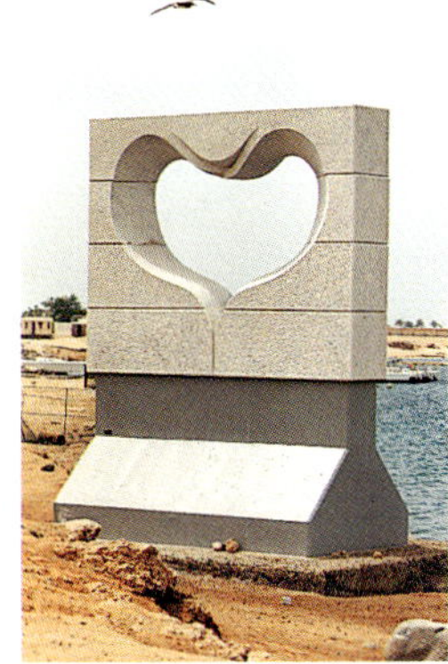

□ Out of adversity comes inspiration: After undergoing heart surgery, Mohamed Said Farsi responded by commissioning a number of sculptures based on the heart.

Artists:
▲ Aref el Rayess
► Salah Abdulkarim
►► Unknown

SOME MAJOR ARTISTS and THEIR WORKS

Introduction by Mohamed Said Farsi

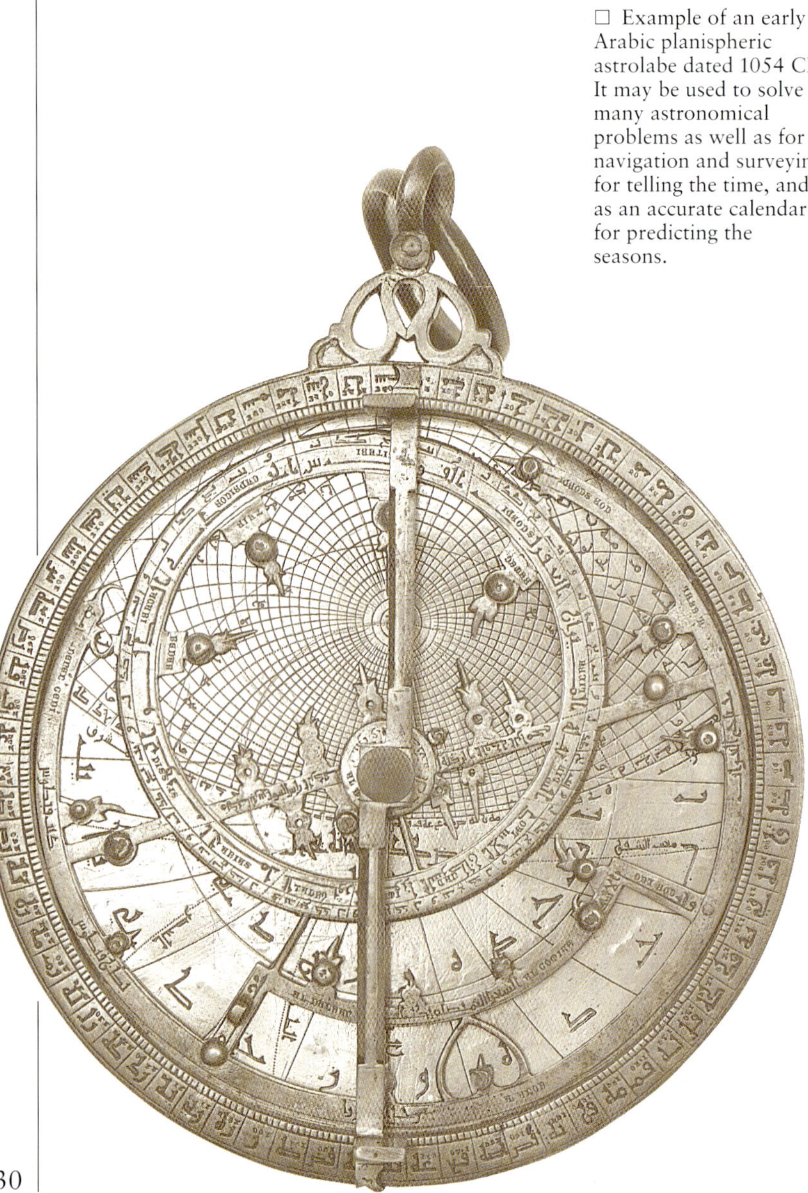

☐ Example of an early Arabic planispheric astrolabe dated 1054 CE. It may be used to solve many astronomical problems as well as for navigation and surveying, for telling the time, and as an accurate calendar for predicting the seasons.

In acquiring sculptures for Jeddah's collection I found myself faced with a quandary: I would have liked to have gathered up every beautiful thing that I could find during my travels, as well as preserving as much as possible of the beauty which we already had in the city, but choices had to be made. Having made my selections, I have had to live with those decisions.

Several major themes ran through my programme of acquiring art for Jeddah's parks and avenues. One of the most important of these themes concerns the achievements of Islamic science. Islamic culture provided fertile soil for the germination of modern sciences such as astronomy, chemistry, medicine and mathematics, and this is documented in the work of Avicenna (Ibn Sina), Al-Razi, Ibn Al-Nafia, Al-Khawarizmi, Abu Hayyan, Al-Basri and Al-Khayyam.

Among the inventions of early Moslem scientists was the sundial, and, fittingly, it provided the subject for one of the first works of art erected in Jeddah. This monument testifies to our heritage and reminds us of the achievements of our forebears. *The Moon and Bow* (otherwise known as *The Sundial*), which is on the North Corniche, takes the form of a spear topped with the crescent and surrounded by arches upon which the hours of the day are marked. As the sun moves the shadow of the spear is thrown across the arches, thereby indicating the precise time of day. This huge sculpture was made in Germany by the artist Ottmar Hollmann.

Another Arab invention – the astrolabe – is represented in a bronze piece on the same intersection as *The Seagull* and also in Hollmann's *Twenty-eight Winding Steps*. The latter is adorned with engravings taken from the book of Avicenna and has a distinctive base in which the significance of the number Seven (the Seven ages of Man, the Seven Heavens mentioned in the Holy Koran *etc.*) is expressed symbolically.

The astrolabe is a simple, yet ingenious instrument which was – and indeed still is – used by sailors as an aid to navigation. The invention of the astrolabe enabled Moslem Arab seafarers to sail around Africa long before the Portuguese sailor Vasco da Gama, and to navigate the Atlantic route to Western Europe . . . and possibly even to America.

By his mastery of the astrolabe Ibn Majid was able to guide Portuguese ships to India and the Eastern seas beyond, although when he subsequently witnessed their cruelty, greed and oppressive treatment of the natives in Bombay and elsewhere, he regretted having aided them. Moreover the opening up of the sea route around Africa cost the Moslem nations dear, since it eventually led to the decline of the overland trade in spices and gold (from Aden via Jeddah to Suez). Europe benefited greatly from this shift, and the resources which it gained stood it in good stead during the Crusades.

Astronomy has been a recurrent theme in the beautification of Jeddah, inspiring such notable monuments as Hollmann's *Cosmos*, which is decorated with a verse from the Holy Koran about the phases of the Moon. The phases of the Moon are also the subject of a sculpture on the Makkah-Medinah motorway. Another astronomical sculpture – Lafuente's *Rotation of the Crescent and Moon* – uses rose-coloured granite octagons to represent the movement of the Moon.

Cartography is yet another science pioneered by Arab Moslems, who were particularly adept at map-making. Al-Idrisi was the first geographer to prepare a world map on a sphere, in the event in graven silver, as a present for Roger II, King of Sicily, in 1138. His use of a sphere, which was derived from a Koranic verse, predated Galileo by hundreds of years. Inspired by this rich heritage, the planning consultant Dr Raouf Helmi, designed a monument which depicts the Master Plan of Jeddah.

At another square on the North Corniche is a sculpture which consists of three curved posts from which plumb lines are suspended in representation of the plumb line which enabled builders to make practical use of the force of gravity long before the formulation of Newton's famous theorem about universal gravitation.

Modern science is also represented by a number of works, including the *Structure of the Atom* – a sculpture which has the nucleus at its core and moving rings to denote the orbits of other particles. This was the first work of art with moving parts in Jeddah.

In this way we made Jeddah the first city to celebrate Islamic art and sciences on every thoroughfare.

▼ A 'map' of Jeddah's master plan created from scrap metal left over from the construction of Al-Anani Mosque.

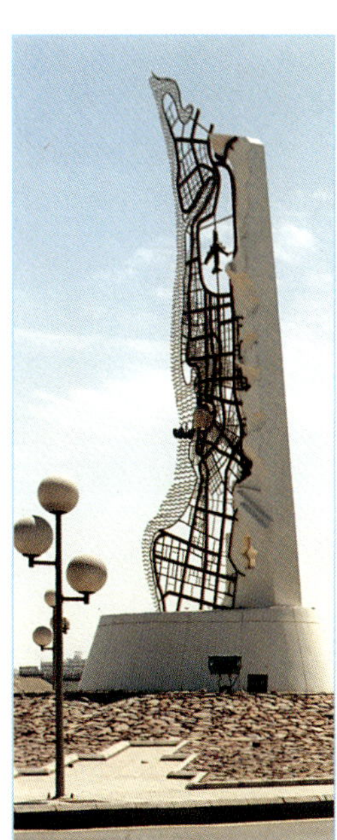

The use of obsolete or scrap material in creating works for Jeddah's sculpture collection became one of my great passions. Various artists and I sought to use materials which, though they had become intrinsically worthless, had in their day performed some useful role.

A good example can be found in a sculpture at the city's old airport which consists of an aircraft formerly used by King Abdul Aziz and now poised on a plinth in simulated take-off. Other obsolete aircraft have been used as distinctive landmarks at squares on the route to King Abdul Aziz International Airport. Many different arrangements and forms of base were used: in the last of these aircraft monuments – *Clouds* by Lafuente – the base combines clouds and waves, signifying the relationship between the earth, sea and sky.

Obsolete ships and launches were also used on a large scale: in one monument a wooden-hulled steamship formerly used by the Coast Guard lies alongside that force's first iron-hulled steam gun-boat. Twenty-nine obsolete boats, including one of 294 tonnes, were offered to the city by H.R.H. Prince Naif ibn Abdul Aziz and these now form the centre-piece of Tarik ibn Ziyad Square.

We also used scrap from obsolete factories to create original shapes of artistic value. Among the finest of these is *The Bicycle* made from the remains of a factory which had been established by the late Mohammed Bin Laden.

The *Chimney Form* on the Corniche was also assembled from old factory scrap, as were the *Sails Formation* in front of the seaport's pilgrim terminal and the two pieces inspired by a Koranic verse about the attributes and uses of iron (*Al-Saroukh*). These were among the first sculptures in Jeddah in which an artist used waste materials to create works of art.

Although the emphasis in building Jeddah's collection of sculptures was on large original pieces, the Italian artist Giovanni showed us how small ornaments might sometimes be used as models for larger scale works.

One example of this is to be found in a sculpture near the Old Airport. This piece was inspired by an ornamental cube standing on the desk of my friend Said Amin, Director of International Airport Projects. The cube, which has the Arabic name of God on each of its sides, is a copy of a trophy won by King Abdul Aziz Airport under the Aga Khan Award for Islamic Architecture scheme. The award was made to architects Skidmore, Owings and Merrill for their design for the Haj Terminal at the airport.

Another desktop ornament which was used as a model for a larger work was a wire sculpture (about 30 cm high) which I bought in France. This piece represented the motion of waves upon the shore. The larger version of this work now stands on the North Corniche facing the sea and the waves. *The White Horse* sculpture was similarly inspired by a small ornament.

The two *Water Jars Fountains* were derived from the designs of small flower vases which I had bought at Harrods in London. My friend Yusuf Naghi, a leading Jeddah businessman, took the vases to Italy where much larger versions were made in marble, together with marble slabs decorated with Islamic phrases in relief.

The squares and roads around the university have been adorned with sculptures symbolising the many branches of learning. The first were *The Pen*, made in iron and stainless steel and the *Structure of the Atom* which shows the structure of matter.

There are many other examples of large scale representations of everyday items, including *The Censer, The Coffee Pot, The Sweet Box, The Treasure Trove*, and *The Candles*, all were presented to the city by private patrons. Apart from beautifying the city, these monuments also act as landmarks.

In the course of building Jeddah's collection I made many trips to Europe looking for works which would be sympathetic to our Islamic heritage and traditions. In 1982 I made a visit to Ghent in Belgium, meeting city officials there and hearing about their achievements in maintaining and restoring old buildings.

One of the consequences of this visit was that it was agreed that an exhibition – *Jeddah, Yesterday and Today* – should be staged in Brussels in 1984. The exhibition, which was put together as the result of great efforts by Saudi and Belgian officials alike, was inaugurated by H.R.H. Prince Albert

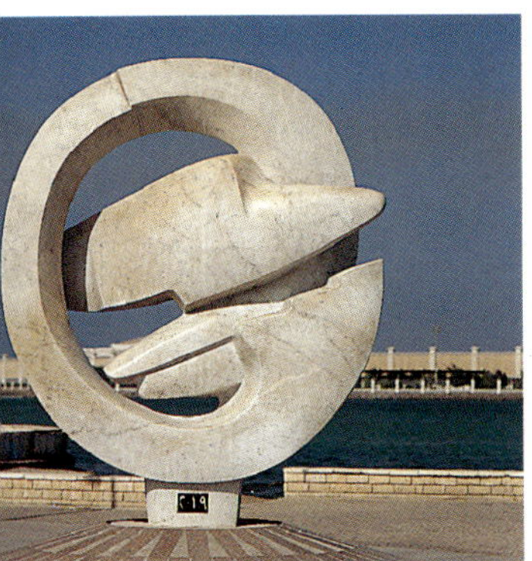

▲ A dolphin dancing within a circle, typifying the contribution of the Belgian artists.

the Belgian Crown Prince in the presence of Arab Ambassadors and many of Belgium's Arab community. Exhibits included Islamic Arab art and handicrafts, ranging from a complete wooden bay window (*rawashin*) to Saudi textiles and traditional dresses to examples of the work of Saudi coppersmiths and silversmiths. We also displayed archive photographs which depicted Saudi Arabia's past, together with more recent photographs illustrating the Kingdom's tremendous development in all walks of life.

As a mark of appreciation of this outstandingly successful exhibition the Belgian Crown Prince presented Jeddah with a special commemorative medal, and it was agreed that Belgian experts would visit Jeddah to help us in the preservation of the historic buildings in the old part of the city.

We also used the occasion of the exhibition in Brussels as an opportunity to acquire some new works, in white marble, for the Jeddah collection. Most of these are now on display at the Al-Hamra Open Air Museum. One looks like a cascading waterfall; another represents a dolphin dancing within a circle, and a third looks like someone playing the saxophone. Each reflects a wonderful clarity which typifies Belgian art, displaying harmony and symmetry. These Belgian artists took some of our ideas and designs and reinterpreted them in white marble specifically for the Jeddah collection. An example of this treatment is *The Heart*, which was designed by Salah Abdulkarim, and which can now be seen in Al-Hamra opposite the Al-Salam Palace.

SOME MAJOR ARTISTS AND THEIR WORKS

Abdulhalim Radwi (*b.* 1939)

Works in Jeddah:

The Bird's Wing
The Bracelet
Harvest of the Sea
Koranic Verse: *'And we became friends.'*
The Balance between Science, Art and Life
Birds
Koranic verse: *'Man can only achieve what he has worked for.'*
Silent Formation
The Globe of Knowledge and Life
Inkwell, Pen and Paper
The Bean Pot
Stone and clay works in the Poets' Garden.
Jeddah Past and Present
The White Minaret
Balancing Cube

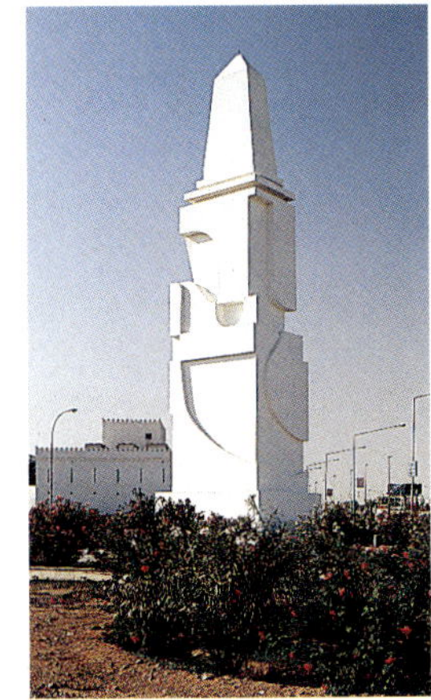

▲ The White Minaret

A native of Makkah, Abdulhalim Radwi was the first artist to create sculptures for the beautification of Jeddah, where he has long been resident. Born in 1939, he worked as an art teacher before turning to serious sculpture in his late twenties. It was the Mayor of Jeddah, Mohamed Said Farsi, who, in 1968, encouraged Radwi to try his hand at producing works of art to stand in the open air at prominent sites around the city.

In the early stages of his career his favourite media were clay and cement, although he subsequently expanded his range to produce works in marble and iron. In those pioneering days, when he worked in clay and cement, Radwi used to work on site, erecting a rough sunshade to protect himself and the sculpture from the worst of the sun's glare. Today, having learned from bitter experience that the materials which he used in the late sixties were not durable enough for Jeddah's harsh climate, he often uses marble and iron as his media and works in the relative comfort of a studio.

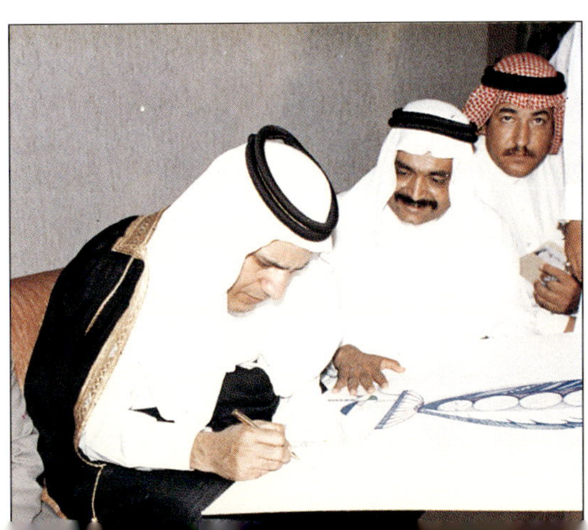

► Abdulhalim Radwi and Mohamed Said Farsi.

Mohamed Said Farsi *writes*:

"Abdulhalim Radwi was the first person to contribute works of art to the city and his first was a mural reflecting his interest in drawing on textiles and paper. Two relatively small sculptures (2.5 metres high, including bases) followed, and Radwi was later to say that he considered them to be his best works. The first – a bird's wing abstraction – expresses sublimity; the second represents the harvest of the sea. When, later, major redevelopment of this part of Jeddah took place, the two works were preserved.

The first of Radwi's large works was a monument erected in front of the Ministry of Foreign Affairs on the occasion of the Islamic Summit Conference in 1973. It is a double-sided concrete mass with two Koranic verses. One side is adorned with olive branches symbolising peace; the other side has sea waves and birds, symbolising the peacefulness and amity in the heart of every true Moslem.

That year also saw the start of landscaping and the creation of parks and gardens such as the Poets' Garden (Hadikat Al-Shuara) which was laid out on some empty ground overlooking Al-Bayah Square. From this beginning, landscaping became an important and integral part of our beautification programme.

The plaster used in Radwi's first two works proved to be susceptible to Jeddah's weather conditions and they both required a certain amount of restoration. This experience prompted us to favour the use of natural materials in subsequent works so as to ensure durability. For example, the wall of Poets' Garden was replaced using marble donated by the Abbas Nour Factory. Later, as the result of vandalism (which upset us greatly), it became necessary to replace this, and use the much cheaper local material, Riyadh Stone. Subsequently, this material was widely used as a facing material in preference to the then current vogue of plastering in contrasting colours. In later park and garden projects wood and palm branches were used as finishing materials.

Three other sculptures by Radwi were faced in Saudi marble, the work carried out by expert workmen from the Mineral Wealth Resources Department under Radwi's close supervision. These works were: *The Bean Pot, Jeddah Past and Present* (at King Abdul Aziz Square) and *Inkwell, Pen and Paper* on the North Corniche.

On a completely different level Radwi contributed to the beautification of the cityscape by designing screens to enclose rooftop water tanks. His design for a carved screen, with deeply incised relief decoration which created interesting patterns of light and shade, served the dual purpose of hiding the obtrusive and unsightly tanks while at the same time enhancing the urban skyline.

From the beginning, Radwi was one of the most co-operative artists with whom we worked. He was able to give artistic form to our ideas and displayed a particular gift for exploiting the potential and qualities of the materials."

Abdulhalim Radwi *comments*:

"The artistic significance of my work in Jeddah is the search for the artistic, intellectual, aesthetic, traditional, historic and human connections between the past and present of the Kingdom. Outsiders in the field of art have long been unaware of the human values of this region.

For me, being an artist from this country, the most important artistic goal is to combine traditional Arabic heritage with modern artistic trends."

Shafiq Mazloum (*c.* 1951-1986)

Works in Jeddah:

Recycled Iron (3)
The Letter "J"
Balance
Sails Formation
The Arch and Waterspouts Fountain
The Baghdadi Fountain

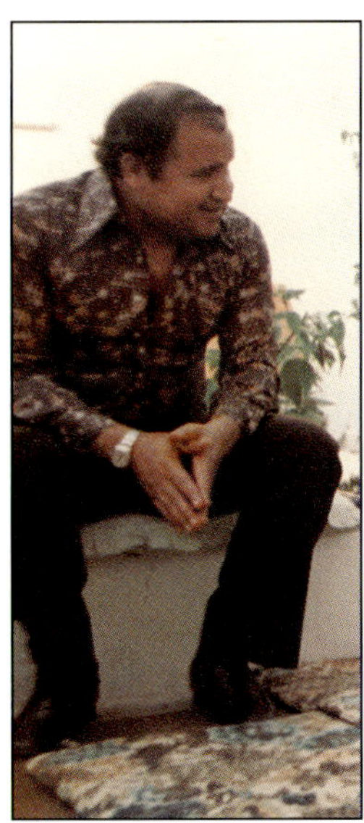

A Palestinian by origin, Shafiq Mazloum was educated in Egypt where he attended the Cairo Art School. He was top of his class, receiving a special prize from President Nasser, and achieved widespread recognition in Egypt as an oil painter. He went to Saudi Arabia in the late sixties and worked in the Planning Office of Jeddah Municipality. Many of his sculptures made use of local materials, particularly scrap iron. He was killed in a car crash while on his way to a wedding in Taif.

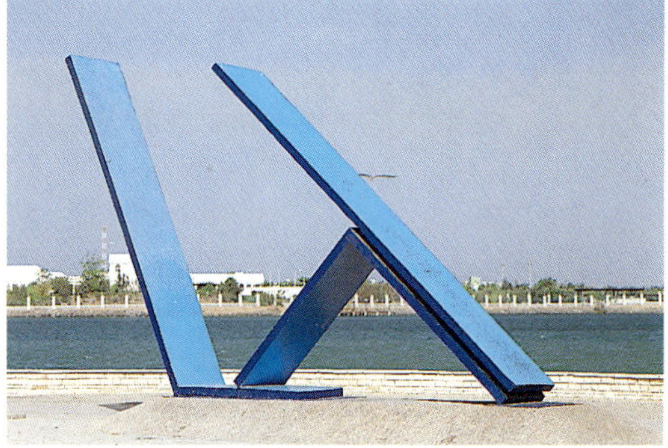

► Balance

Mohamed Said Farsi *writes*:

“ I ask God's mercy upon my friend Shafiq Mazloum! Some acquaintances are beacons of light forever shining bright and some, after ephemeral brilliance, quickly pass away.

Twenty years ago, Shafiq – a Saudi of Palestinian origin – became one of my colleagues in the Planning Office. He was a sensitive artist in whose hands colours became like strings playing delightful tunes representing plains, valleys and mountains.

From 1973 onwards, he shared with Radwi the responsibility of beautifying the first sites in Jeddah. Although different in style, they shared the same philosophic outlook – that the beauty of art should be available to all. Shafiq used materials which were available locally, such as sheet steel which he imbued with life and meaning. His first work in Jeddah, completed in 1973, was the *Sails Formation*. This particular sculpture has been removed recently.

Since suitable sites were in short supply in the early seventies, Shafiq's second work was placed on a wall at the junction of the Medinah-Jeddah North/South roads. Here the concept was to use symbols portraying Jeddah's natural features. As a background, marble of different colours was selected to portray clouds in the upper part and the sea in the lower part. We spent many hours at the factory of Abbas Nour with its manager Ahmad Ali selecting the marble so as to ensure colour harmonisation. The marble 'backcloth' then had superimposed, in wrought iron, an abstraction of the sun, fish and boats to represent Jeddah.

Below this sculpture a fountain was installed, and, subsequently, a work by the artist Pomodoro was erected there. In 1974, Shafiq designed a garden on empty ground in front of the Jeddah Palace Hotel. He made extensive use of Riyadh Stone in decorating the garden and created a sculpture in steel which expressed the spirit of that period.

Among other works by Shafiq is the monumental *Arch and Waterspouts Fountain* (*Al-Ukood and Al-Mayazeeb*) at one of the junctions on Khalid ibn Al-Walid Street. This is in the form of an abstract based on the finest elements of Old Jeddah's houses – window arches, bay windows and projecting gutters. Made of reinforced concrete, it cost $375,000 in 1985.

In that year Shafiq created his last work – the Arabic letter J (to represent Jeddah) shaped to resemble a gazelle lifting its head to scan anticipated horizons of development and restoration in Jeddah's Golden Age. The base was designed in black marble overlaid with local sea shells. It was his last contribution to Jeddah: he passed away like a sudden and unexpected shaft of lightning. But his works of art remain to remind us of the man and his dedication to artistic endeavours.❞

Darwish Ali Salamah (*b.* 1933)

Works in Jeddah:

A collection of model buildings representing the traditional architecture of the Arabian Peninsula.

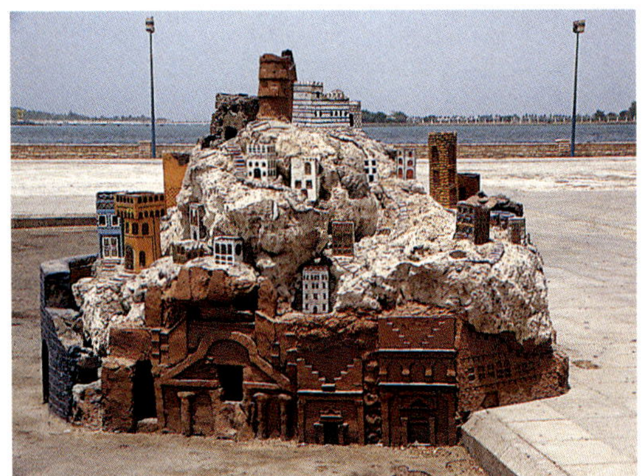

A former fighter pilot, Darwish Salamah is known for his model houses which form a record of traditional Saudi Arabian architecture. Since his childhood he has always been in love with the distinctive shapes of the traditional houses, forts and mosques of the region, and as a hobby he began to build models of his favourite buildings.

As his collection grew, it spilled out from his garden into the street in front of his house in Jeddah, arousing the curiosity of passers-by. Occasionally people would come to his door, thinking that the house was a museum of Saudi Arabian architecture.

Eventually, word of his work reached Mayor Mohamed Said Farsi who, constantly on the look-out for sculptures and other open-air art forms, went to view the collection. Impressed by what he saw, the mayor invited the pilot to display examples of his work on the corniche.

As a Jeddah resident, Darwish Salamah was pleased to accept the invitation and made a number of models in reinforced concrete which now stand on the Corniche as a permanent record of Saudi Arabia's traditional forms of architecture.

Mohamed Said Farsi *writes*:

❝ Darwish Salamah, a Saudi who collaborated with us in 1986, is an artist of great spontaneity and sensitivity. He placed many of his sculptures, which took the form of attractive replicas of traditional Saudi houses and towers, on the pavement outside his home in the Al-Hamra district. These models, representing styles of indigenous architecture from all parts of the Kingdom, have since been brought together to form a local museum to the south of the Coast Guard station on the Corniche. This is not to be confused with the Open Air Museum on the Corniche at Al-Hamra.

Among the works in Salamah's collection are a model of Medain Saleh sculpted from a single large piece of coral rock and a model of the Ajiad Fort in Makkah. These early works came at the beginning of our efforts to beautify Jeddah. Salamah and other artists gave unstintingly of their best, and already we had begun to feel that we were involved in something wonderful and unique which would bring beauty and happiness to our city.❞

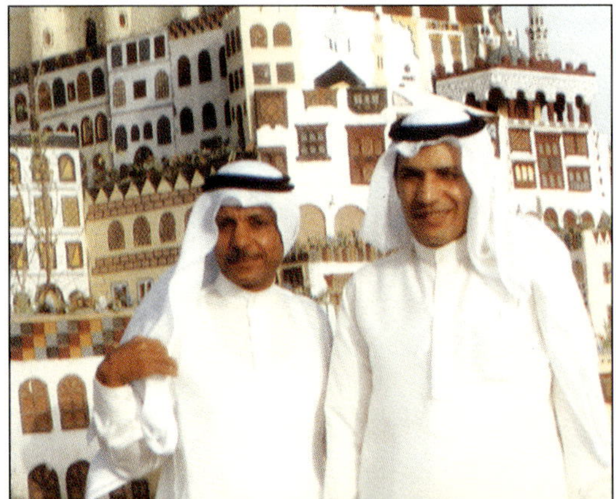

► Darwish Ali Salamah and Mohamed Said Farsi.

Henry Moore (1898-1986)

Works in Jeddah:

Three-piece Reclining Figure
Large Spindle Piece
Oval with Points
Upright Motive

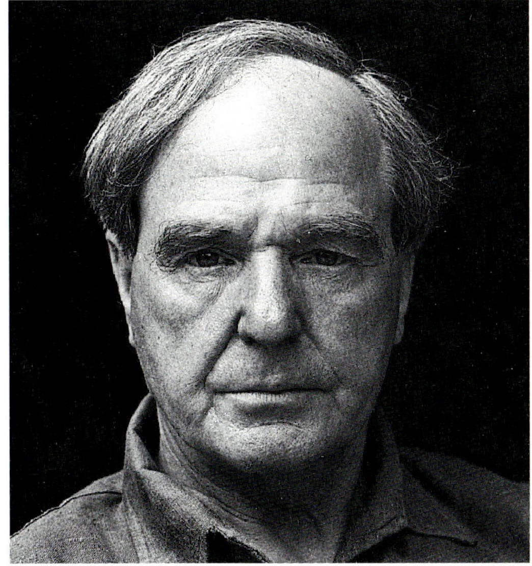

The son of a Yorkshire coalminer, Henry Moore discovered the work of Michelangelo at the age of 14 and was so inspired by that "greatest sculptor in the world" that he longed to become a sculptor himself.

However, he trained as a teacher before serving on the Western Front where he was gassed. In 1919 he made use of an ex-serviceman's grant to study at the Leeds School of Art, where he was a contemporary of Barbara Hepworth. He won a scholarship to the R.C.A. in London in 1921 and subsequently had periods of study in France and Italy.

He had his first solo exhibition in 1928 and by the forties was an international figure. He experimented with quasi-geometrical abstraction during the thirties, but throughout his career his abiding concern was with humanity and the human figure, constantly exploring the fusion of man and nature. He was also at pains to preserve the integrity of the materials he worked with.

In 1932 he carved his first piece with a hole through it, explaining: "The hole connects one side to the other, making it immediately more three-dimensional."

As he became busier during the late forties he did less work in stone, turning more towards modelling and, in particular, working in bronze. "The whole of my development as a sculptor is an attempt to understand and realise more completely what form and shape are about," he said. "Sculpture is a never-ending discovery."

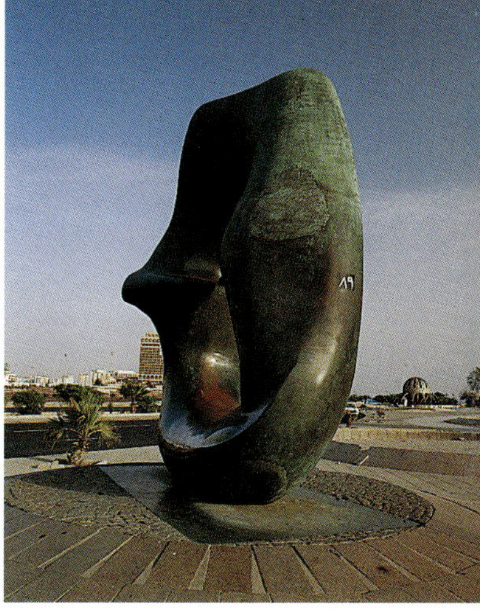

► Oval with Points

Mohamed Said Farsi *writes*:

" Meeting Henry Moore was a seminal experience for me. I got to know him during the course of my search for an international artist who was producing work which eschewed conventional human representation, in conformity to our traditions and cultural values. In Henry Moore – with his abstractionist works characterised by the softness of their lines and the lucidity of their formation – I found such an artist.

Our first meeting in 1977 in his studio took place in the presence of Sir Lesley Martin, Professor of Architecture at Cambridge, and Dr Omer Azzam, Professor of Planning and Architecture and a United Nations adviser. Our talk in that first meeting focused on his experimentation on the balance between mass and space, and how he used these two concepts to symbolically express states of mind. Jeddah boasts four of his works which represent the most important stages in the development of his artistic thinking which completely rejected human representation. The first of these works was installed on the Al-Arbaen Bridge in 1979, but it was afterwards moved to the Open Air Museum on the Corniche to stand alongside other international works.

Bronze was his preferred medium, although he also used marble, wood and limestone occasionally. Through his use of bronze and other metals, Henry Moore was able to accentuate the voids within a piece, thereby enhancing its freshness and subtlety. The use of bronze also enabled him to achieve a wide range of textures – from a coarse rock finish to a bright metallic sheen.

I invited him to come to Jeddah and gave him some pictures and books on Islamic art and architecture in the hope that he might produce some work inspired by our heritage. However, by this time he had given up experimenting with new forms and his advanced age precluded any long journeys, so he was never able to visit Jeddah.

Even before I visited him I had seen photographs of some of his works and had decided to buy a number of them. However, when I met Moore at his studio and looked closely at the works I changed my selection, rejecting my original choices out of a fear that the abstractionist tendency of his modern art might be misinterpreted. The work which I chose instead is now part of the Open Air Museum on the Corniche.

In my several discussions with Henry Moore I found him to be wise and generous of spirit. When he saw photographs showing how we had placed his sculptures in the open air, in a context of sea and sky, he was very pleased, since this was how he felt his work should be viewed. He was intrigued to know how the people of Jeddah had reacted to his work since this was the first time, to his knowledge, that his work had been displayed in the Middle East.**”**

Julio Lafuente (*b.* 1921)

Works in Jeddah:

Water Jars Fountain (3)
Rotation of the Crescent and Moon
Coffee Pots Fountain (2)
The Pomegranate Fountain
The Market Fountain
The Condenser (2)
The Mameluke Mosque Lanterns *(Al-Qanadeel)*
The Bicycle
The Illuminated Globe
Globe in scrap iron
Gathering of the Ships at Night
Accident!
Clouds (DC3 aircraft)
Banners in the Wind
Science and Religion
Al-Kibla *(The Direction of Prayer)*
Shahadat Al-Tawheed *(The Oneness of God)*
Holy Koran
The Censer
Waxing and Waning Moons
The Rose-water Sprinkler
Warships Square
The Treasure Trove
Spanner and Bolt
Verse Boat
Verse in White
"Surely thou art upon a mighty morality" (calligraphy)
Kufic Inscriptions (2) (calligraphy)

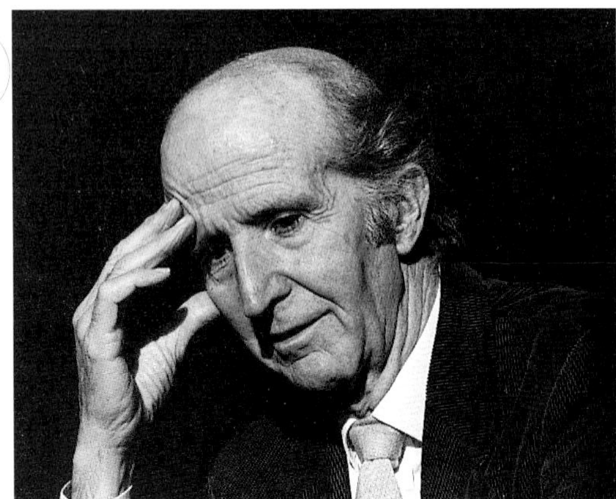

The creator of some of Jeddah's most distinctive monuments, Julio Lafuente first came to the city in the early seventies not as an artist but as an architect. However, rather than working on the new buildings of the growing city, the Spanish architect was charged with responsibility for planning and supervising the urban beautification programme.

Mayor Mohamed Said Farsi was concerned that as the new infrastructure for the rapidly expanding city was put in place the new roads and roundabouts would be anonymous, featureless components of a vast, confusing labyrinth. Many of the new roads were unnamed and there were few buildings to act as landmarks on the outskirts of the city. It was decided that large scale monuments erected on major intersections would fulfil two roles – creating highly visible and recognisable landmarks and stimulating the imagination of the city's inhabitants.

While, as an architect, Lafuente was kept busy planning and supervising landscaping projects throughout the city – creating public gardens; arranging for hundreds of thousands of trees and bushes to be planted alongside the main roads; turning

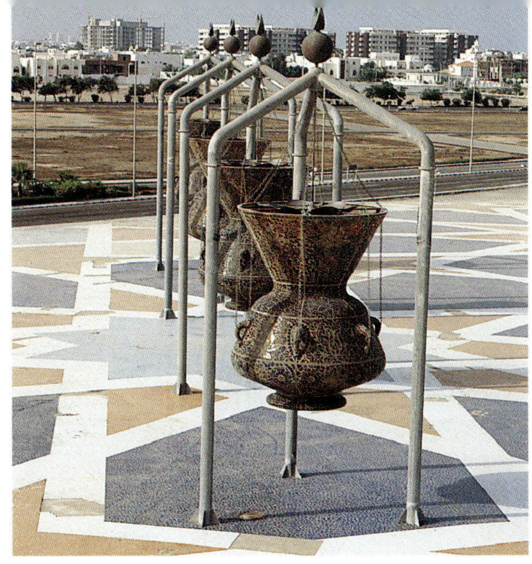

reclaimed land into an elegant corniche – he also wanted to put his mark on the city in a more personal way. Thus in 1975 he designed a fountain – the first of more than a score of fountains and monuments which he was to create for Jeddah over the next twelve years.

Lafuente's work in Jeddah includes some of the city's best-known large monuments – *The Bicycle*, the *Mameluke Mosque Lanterns*, *The Illuminated Globe*, *The Condensers* and *Science and Religion* – and although not an Arabic speaker he also produced notable works based on Arabic calligraphy.

▲ The Mameluke Mosque Lanterns

Mohamed Said Farsi *writes*:

“ When I first met Julio Lafuente, in the early seventies, I recognised him as a most remarkable architect and artist. Although he could not speak Arabic and I could not speak his native Spanish, we have somehow always managed to communicate with each other. After a few hours, or sometimes a whole day, and after a discussion on form, content, size, site, meaning and space, he would show me conceptual drawings which brought to life his wonderful comprehension of the essence of traditional forms – of how to incorporate such forms into contemporary works of art.

No other artist showed the same degree of understanding in creating works of art for Jeddah. He designed the three sculptures made from pieces of the Turkish condenser which provided Jeddah with its drinking water between 1905 and 1946. Appropriately, these sculptures stand at the junction of the road which leads to the massive new desalination plant. His theory was that, by using scrap bits and pieces (at no cost whatsoever for materials), he could demonstrate that art should not be measured or evaluated in purely monetary terms.

Julio designed various fountains, including the *Water Jars Fountain*. He drew his inspiration for this and others from the various traditional pots and vessels still in everyday use. Julio subsequently produced his *Coffee Pots Fountain* and *The Censer* and the *Gathering of the Ships at Night* on the Corniche at Al-Hamra.

Copies of the *Coffee Pots Fountain* were presented to the cities of Taif and Tabuk as gifts from the Jeddah Municipality.

Julio created several sculptures in the form of Koranic inscriptions. For example, the bronze piece which is a Koranic verse in the rough shape of a boat (near the gateway to the Royal Terminal at King Abdul Aziz Airport) weighs 20 tonnes. A special computer programme was written to define the ratios of height, width and depth of the Arabic letters to ensure that the moulds designed to cast the bronze would yield an accurate and beautiful inscription.

Julio also created several sculptures incorporating glass and ceramics which could be illuminated at night, to great effect. During one of our discussions I observed that Holy Makkah is the centre of the world and this prompted him to conceive the idea of a gigantic globe of coloured glass in a steel frame. Engineered to allow for expansion and contraction in the heat of Jeddah's summer, the globe is skilfully lit from within and radiates harmony and vigour. The surface area of *The Illuminated Globe* is 600 square metres. It was fabricated in Italy at a cost of $1.2 million (excluding the base). The four magnificent *Mameluke Mosque Lanterns* in the square facing the Al-Salam Royal Palace use the same materials as *The Illuminated Globe*.

Although they are all the same size and shape, the decorative pattern of each one is unique.

Julio Lafuente's contribution to the city was not limited to specific works of art, but included advice on the selection of appropriate sites for sculptures by other artists and supervision of their erection. It was he who was responsible for determining the site and layout of the Open Air Museum at Al-Hamra, and he designed many of the pedestals and plinths for the city's sculptures.

In short, harmony rather than dissonance prevailed in every aspect of his generous contribution to the beautification of Jeddah.❞

Julio Lafuente *comments*:

❝ My involvement with the Jeddah project lasted six years – a period of passion and intensity which was made possible by the understanding, friendship and encouragement of the Mayor of Jeddah and his extremely efficient colleagues.

I worked on many sites in Jeddah: one of the first was Al-Bayah Square, with a monumental fountain which one could walk under, surrounded by the noise of the water. I created other fountains using objects from everyday life, from Islamic culture and from the collective memory of Saudi Arabia.

Of all the the many facets of Islamic culture an unquenchable source of inspiration was Arabic calligraphy. I transformed verses from the Koran into sculptures – either in relief or in three dimensions – and this greatly increased the plastic and spiritual value of the monuments. This revival of ancient tradition by giving a new expression to the spiritual values was for me the greatest contribution that I could make to Jeddah.❞

Maurice Malsia

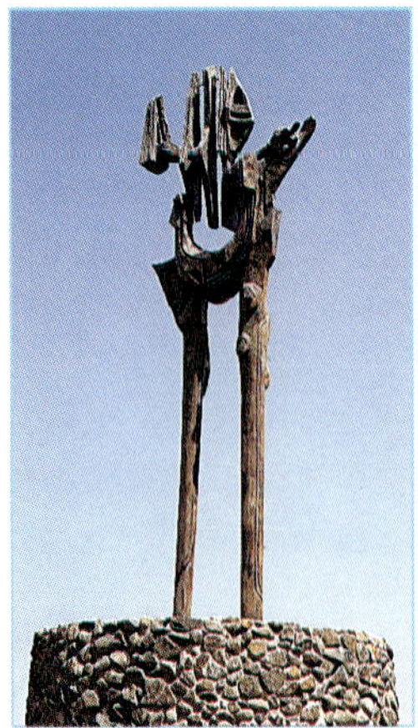

Works in Jeddah:

Various calligraphic representations of the phrase: "There is no God but God" in fossilised wood.

Born in Borneo, Maurice Malsia came to the attention of Mohamed Said Farsi in 1978 when, during the course of a visit to Jakarta, the Mayor saw examples of furniture which this craftsman had made out of fossilised wood. This unusual medium – found deep in the heart of Borneo's jungle – was very hard and difficult to work. In consequence Malsia tended to restrict himself to producing smallish items, but at the urging of Mayor Farsi he agreed to create a number of large sculptures for Jeddah's collection.

Mohamed Said Farsi *writes*:

❝ I have never seen anyone as pleased as this old man was when I told him that I came from Makkah and that I wanted him to make a piece to beautify a square in Jeddah – the gateway to the Holy City.

For several months after commissioning him, I heard nothing, since the artist had vanished into the jungle in search of the petrified wood he needed. Finally, through my friend Said Abu-Al-Saud, who had business interests in Indonesia, I heard that the sculptures had been completed. However, there was a problem: given the great size and weight of the pieces, the artist was having difficulty trying to arrange transportation from his mountain village to the coast. This obstacle was overcome after the Governor of Jakarta generously provided a helicopter to fly the pieces out of the jungle.

A team of workers was sent from Indonesia to Jeddah to help install the sculptures at sites on Prince Sultan

Street and at the entrance to Jeddah Islamic Seaport. Installation of these remarkable works of art took six months of hard and continuous work, at the end of which Jeddah had a new set of sculptures in a rare and challenging medium.

Unfortunately, we were never able to re-establish contact with the artist, Maurice Malsia, and could not commission any additional works.❞

Victor Vasarely (*b.* 1908)

Works in Jeddah:

Balance in the Air
Changing Positions
Al-Mafrookah
The Illusion of a Second Cube
Non-Parallel Cubes and Rectangles

Widely recognised as the originator of post-war optical painting, Victor Vasarely was trained in the design aesthetic of the Budapest *Bauhaus* in the late twenties and then worked in Paris as a graphic and commercial artist.

He produced his first optical works during the thirties but did not develop his characteristic geometric abstract style until the early fifties. Moreover, it was not until the sixties that he moved from black and white to colour and started to experiment with three-dimensional effects. Around the same time he also began to create works which were characterised by the systematic repetition of a single image.

Vasarely was not always in agreement with his leading contemporaries, rejecting what he saw as "the old egocentric philosophy" of artists such as Dali and Picasso.

In 1970 he established the Vasarely Didactic Museum in his Renaissance chateau in the Provençal village of Gordes, announcing that it was to form the first stage of a sociological foundation. "We will study and debate here one of the major problems of today: the integration of the arts with society," he promised.

This programme was taken a step further in 1976 when the Vasarely Foundation was established in Aix en Provence to explore the application of the artist's theories to the field of urban development. Vasarely has exhibited all over the world and collections of his work are to be found in cities such as Paris, Chicago, Rotterdam, Washington and São Paolo.

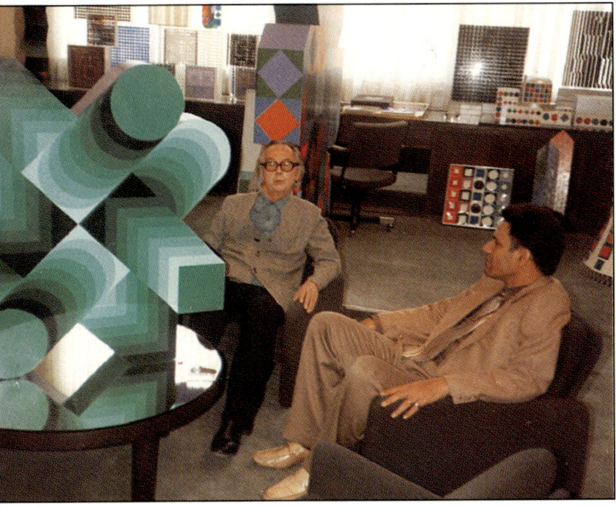

▲ Artist and Mohamed Said Farsi with a model of Al-Mafrookah.

Mohamed Said Farsi *writes*:

❝ Many art critics and historians consider Victor Vasarely the first master of a new class of visual art which depends on the viewer's reaction to differences in colour.

In 1981, after seeing examples of his work in many European cities, I visited Vasarely in his studio in a small town near Paris. From our first conversation, I sensed his youthful, vigorous and enterprising spirit. He was enthusiastic about continuously presenting new ideas so as to keep pace with our fast-moving world, and believed that as new art materials became available they should be used – on advertising hoardings at subway stations, bus stops and the like. Popular culture, he argued, should be seen by the people – wherever they might be.

He explained that visual art depends on geometric shapes which are abstract but divided by primary colours according to mathematical proportions. I was surprised by his rejection of the human form in his art, but I admired him and was glad to choose some of his works for Jeddah.

He used different designs to create optical illusions, creating strikingly three-dimensional effects from flat 'paintings'. I told him that this art form had much in common with the decorative and calligraphic art which flourished during the golden age of Islamic civilisation.

The fruit of this discussion was the creation of Vasarely's *Al-Mafrookah* painting – a turquoise and violet painting erected at the intersection of Al-Andalus Street and Al-Seif Street. This work was positioned with particular care so as to ensure that it could be seen by people approaching from any direction.

We selected several of Vasarely's works for the Open Air Museum on the Corniche at Al-Hamra and a further ten large paintings for Jeddah's museum. Although Vasarely is known as a painter rather than as a sculptor, he was persuaded to design some sculptures for Jeddah. The steel sheets from which these sculptures are made were enamelled so as to make them resistant both to the weather and to the effects of children climbing over them!”

César (*b.* 1921)

Works in Jeddah:

The Fist
The Eye
The Thumb *(Private Collection)*

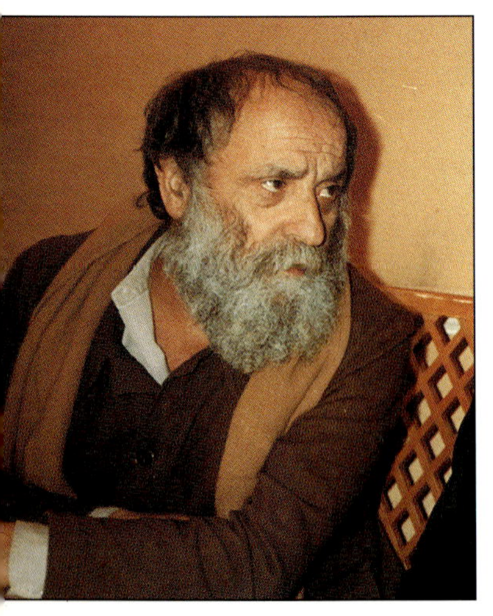

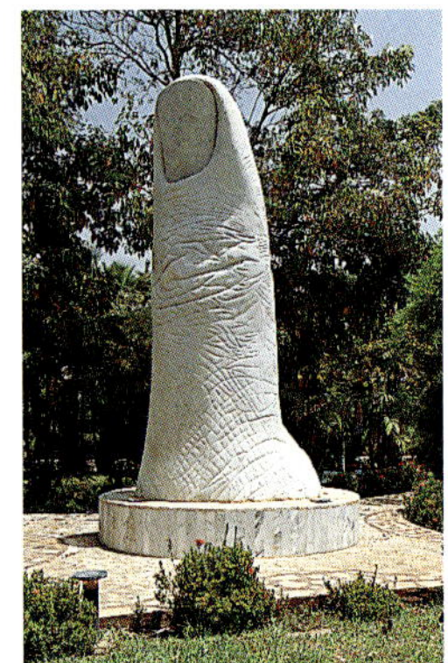

Born in Marseilles, César Baldaccini studied at the *École des Beaux Arts* in Paris during the Second World War, graduating in 1943. He staged his first show in 1954 at the Galérie Lucien Durand in Paris. At about the same time, César started to create synthetic sculptures – which he called *amalgames* – from bits of scrap metal.

In 1959 he won the Carnegie Prize and was the winner of a silver medal at the International Expo at Brussels. During the sixties he became known chiefly for the sculptures which he made by crushing old cars in an hydraulic press. Perhaps the most famous of these *compressions dirigées* was his *1955 Yellow Buick*.

A major retrospective of his work was staged in Rotterdam in 1976.

Mohamed Said Farsi *writes*:

“César is representative of those artists whose work reflects an age of wars and social destruction – factors which eventually led to the degeneration of industrial man into a mere component . . . a tiny cogwheel in a vast soulless machine. In this harsh environment great artists were driven to create beauty out of ugliness, transforming scrap iron and other waste materials into works of art which stand as prominent landmarks in the history of contemporary art.

I met him for the first time in the late seventies, intending to ask him to create some works for Jeddah in a style in keeping with our civilisation and culture. Subsequently I visited him on a number of occasions, partly to get to understand him better but also in order to acquaint him with our own heritage and past achievements.

Our first collaboration was inspired by a verse in the Holy Koran which refers to God's ability to create unique finger prints for each and every human being. This extraordinary fact was addressed in Islam more than a thousand years before it was taken up by Western science. We decided that the concept could best be embodied in the form of a thumb and set out to create this in marble. A single piece of marble weighing 70 tonnes was sculpted into a 34 tonne monolith in which the lines of the thumbprint are clearly delineated.

Despite the clarity of the work's meaning in the context of the Koranic verse, there were some who raised questions and objections at the time.

The monument was erected at a site about four kilometres inland, since it was feared that the details of the thumbprint would not last long in the saline environment of the Corniche, and it is no longer on view to the public.

Later, César created two bronze pieces for Jeddah – *The Fist*, which symbolises strength, and *The Eye*. The sites for these two works were carefully chosen so as match their themes to the areas which they were to grace. Thus *The Fist* monument was erected on the approach to the palace of H.R.H. Prince Sultan ibn Abdul Aziz, the assistant Deputy Prime Minister and Minister of Defence and Aviation.

Similarly, it had been intended to site *The Eye* near the TV station or near Dr Akif Maghrabi's Eye Hospital, but lack of suitable space at these locations resulted in the work eventually being erected at the Open Air Museum.

Jeddah has a number of excellent and carefully selected works by César – a man who uses his skills and materials to express the spirit of an era in which beauty and ugliness are both found.❞

Ottmar Hollmann (*b.* 1915)

The works of this German artist were brought to the attention of Mohamed Said Farsi by a German landscape architect who was involved in Jeddah's beautification programme. Hollmann was commissioned to produce a dozen pieces for Jeddah and, since his preferred medium was cast alloy, the sculptures were all made in Europe before being shipped to Saudi Arabia. Hollmann met Mohamed Said Farsi in Europe on several occasions to discuss his commissions, but did not visit Jeddah until after his works had been installed.

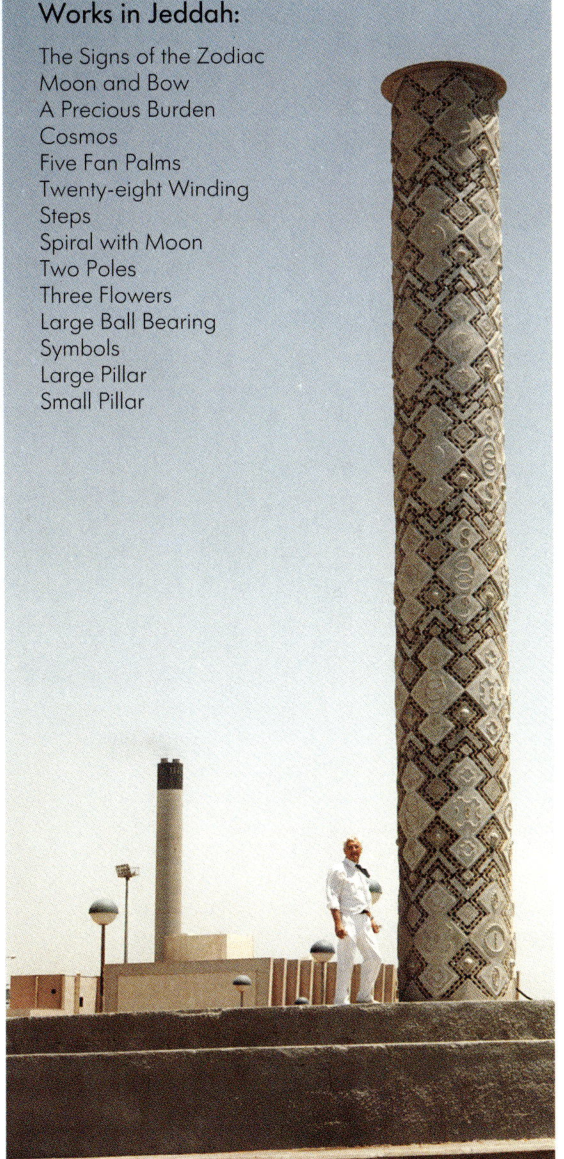

Works in Jeddah:

- The Signs of the Zodiac
- Moon and Bow
- A Precious Burden
- Cosmos
- Five Fan Palms
- Twenty-eight Winding Steps
- Spiral with Moon
- Two Poles
- Three Flowers
- Large Ball Bearing
- Symbols
- Large Pillar
- Small Pillar

◀ Hollmann standing alongside the Large Pillar.

Mohamed Said Farsi *writes*:

❝ I met the German artist Ottmar Hollmann quite by accident while visiting the Paris office of my friends Hiram and David Corm, the Lebanese architects. Following that meeting, Hollmann became a permanent friend of Jeddah, creating several distinctive works. These works embodied ideas which we selected to express Arab Islamic culture and sciences, or to exploit our Arabic calligraphy.

The first in his series of calligraphic works was based on a poem by the Saudi poet Kindil and represented the twelve zodiacal signs of the year. This series of sculptures can be seen on the Corniche to the north of the desalination plants, not far from another Hollmann work – a pillar decorated with lacework engravings.

All the expenses involved in these two projects (including the fees of the poet and sculptor) were paid by Mohammed Said Tayib in his capacity as managing director of Tihama Company. The company's calligrapher also prepared the calligraphy for the projects. The abstraction of *The Signs of the Zodiac* is an excellent example of modern art and such abstraction is the goal of any contemporary artist. It is also worth mentioning that the verses of the poem relate to the name Jeddah.

Other works by Hollmann include another ornamental pillar (in front of the Jeddah Dome at the junction of Prince Fahd and Falesteen Roads; *Three Flowers* (on the Corniche at Al-Hamra) and *Two Poles*, which comprises two circles – the upper of which represents the part of life remaining with the advancement of age in a measured balance controlled by God.

Hollmann also created *Cosmos* which symbolises power lying in the depth of the desert; *Spiral with Moon*; and *Twenty-eight Winding Steps*, inspired by the drawings in the book by Avicenna and symbolising the human life cycle. This work has, at its top, a crescent to symbolise Islam and an astrolabe to signify Arab scientific achievements.

Cosmos, which rises 36 metres above an 8.5 metre high base, making it one of the world's largest works of art. This great work is made of steel and aluminium, its soaring tubes symbolising the galaxy. The upper sphere constitutes a part of the orbit and ties together the two parts of the work. The two lower enormous galaxies seem to float by themselves within the curving tubes. The overall design of the base was conceived by Salah Abdulkarim while the detailed drawings were prepared by the artist Lafuente.❞

Ottmar Hollmann *comments*:

❝ Before I ever executed these works for the Mayor of Jeddah, I was already interested in Islam, its tradition, its habits and its religion, but my knowledge of the subject was not vast and I have to say that Mohamed Said Farsi was of great help to me in finding the inspiration for my works. He introduced me to many aspects of the Islamic world previously almost unknown to me and we had great pleasure discussing my work and its progress during our many meetings in Europe.❞

Sylvestre Giovanni (*b.* 1933)

More a craftsman than a sculptor, Giovanni was born in the Alpine area of Northern Italy. He met Mohamed Said Farsi at the Milan International Show where he was exhibiting examples of his work. The Saudi admired the Italian's sense of design and persuaded him to visit Jeddah and to turn his hand to larger scale works.

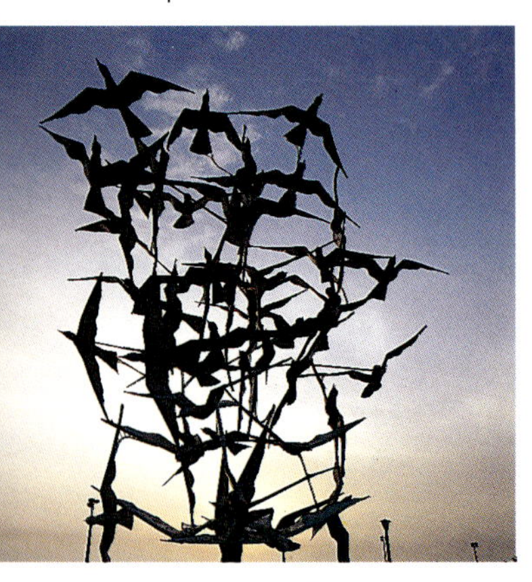

Works in Jeddah:

Aloe Flowers
Sails (2)
Migrant Birds
Light and Shade
The Flower Basins
Sea Harvest Trellis
Sea Fountain

◄ Migrant Birds

Mohamed Said Farsi *writes*:

❝ Giovanni is an artist of the Italian countryside who finds inspiration in the peaks and glaciers of the Alps. I first met him at the Milan International Show while attending an international conference which brought together mayors and chief executives of the world's great cities. I have regularly attended this annual event since 1972 and on this occasion was part of a Saudi delegation led by the late Abdullah Arif, the then mayor of Holy Makkah.

Never in my life have I known an artist of such remarkable simplicity. Giovanni's works are characterised by simple, but subtle artistic lines which are sure to touch the heart of anyone who admires and appreciates painting and other arts. I have always greatly admired his simple pieces, which take the form of beautiful toys, and the *jardinières* which he designs for use in private gardens.

All of the works by this creative artist were designed to conform to the precepts of our Islamic faith.

Among the sculptures produced by Giovanni for the Jeddah collection is *Aloe Flowers*, a bronze and copper piece on a small base which can be seen at the north-west corner of the Crown Prince's palace. Other Giovanni works in the city include *Migrant Birds* on the Corniche at Al-Hamra; *The Sails*, a scrap iron sculpture in front of the Telecommunications Office at Al-Nozla, and the *Sea Fountain* on University Street.

His *Flower Basins* consists of ten square iron planters stacked together to form a column which is topped by a crescent. After discussions with the late Abdul Rahman Tunisi, director of the Thaqer School, this monument was placed outside the Thaqer School as a landmark for that institution.”

Mustafa Senbel (*b.* 1946)

Works in Jeddah:

Dialogue
The Oil Lamp
The Ramadan Lantern
Builder's Plumbline
The Seagull (Al-Nawras)
Sails
Allah – In Arabic, readable from both sides
Sunrise
The Fisherman's Net
Desalination Pipes (3)
Beach Themes
Iron Palm
Sign for the Fish Market
The Wave
The Samovar
The Fountain of Shells
Obsolete Coastguard Vessels
Obsolete Motor Launches
The Fisherman's Net *(Large)*
Two Vases
The Plaza of Missiles
Chimney Form
The Sail
Sail Formation
Gravity

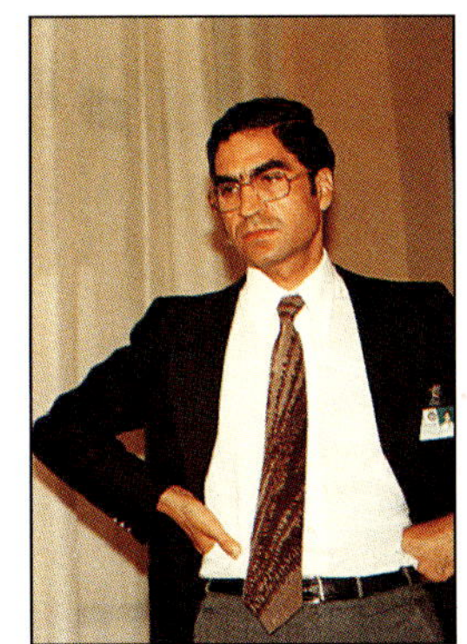

A classmate of Mohamed Said Farsi at Alexandria University, Senbel left Egypt after graduating to continue his studies in France. He completed a Ph.D. in urban planning and design at the *École des Beaux Arts* in Paris and then returned to Egypt to work with a French firm of consulting engineers. When Mohamed Said Farsi became mayor of Jeddah and started to build the team which would be responsible for the transformation of the city he was eager to recruit such a well-qualified old friend.

Senbel joined the Municipality in 1978 as a town planner and worked in the city for nearly a decade before retiring to Egypt. Although he had no previous experience as a sculptor, Mayor Farsi encouraged him to produce some designs. Some of these were among the city's most modest and inexpensive sculptures (e.g. the various *Worked Iron Formations*) but Senbel also designed the massive *Seagull*. Senbel now lives in Alexandria.

Mohamed Said Farsi *writes*:

“Mustafa Senbel's involvement in the beautification of Jeddah dates from 1979 and was to extend over a period of eight fruitful years. What distinguished Senbel from the other artists who contributed to the beautification of Jeddah was his intense awareness of the relationship between mass and space and his sensitivity to their environmental context. He used to amaze me with his preliminary sketches which were complete works of art in their own right. His *Worked Iron Formations* are the truest expression of his sensitivity. Situated on the Corniche, these sculptures express the inherent life and environment of the coast without obscuring the vision of sea and sky.

Each of these works cost only $5,500 because they were made from steel reinforcing rods. The works were fabricated in a Jeddah workshop where laser beams were used as a cutting tool so as to ensure clean edges.

Among his finest works are *The Ramadan Lantern* – inspired by

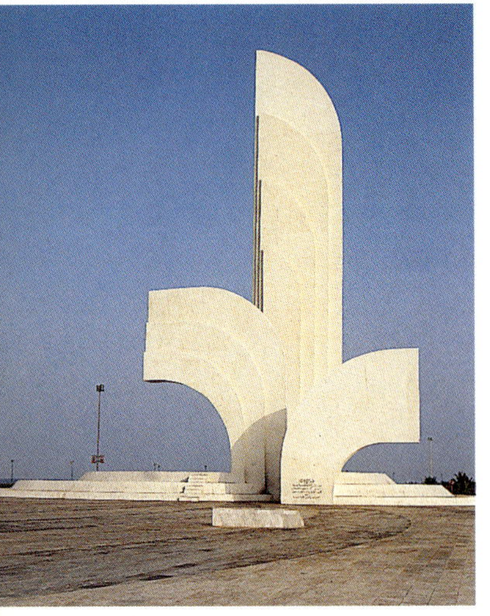

traditional forms and now to be seen on a small island off the North Corniche – *The Wave* and the marble hot water pot or *Samovar* on King Abdul Aziz Street, Old Jeddah.

The most important of Senbel's works is *The Seagull* on the North Corniche. Its towering 55 metres represent the wing of a seagull, a bird which is constantly gliding above the waves scanning the sea below for signs of food. When it sees a fish it folds its wings and dives into the water leaving a white splash on the surface to mark its point of entry. This entry into the water is represented in the sculpture's base which consists of white and dark green marble whorls.

Another important work is his *Desalination Pipe Fountain* – an assemblage of blue-green water pipes which symbolises the development and progress made in the field of desalinating water. The work derives some of its inspiration from the external spiral staircase of the Samarra Minaret.

The fountain at the Red Sea Palace Hotel on the Arbaen Lagoon is also one of Senbel's works.❞

Salah Abdulkarim (*b.* 1928-1989)

Works in Jeddah:

Various Koranic Inscriptions
Scrap Iron
The Mameluke Minarets
The mosaic base to Hollmann's Cosmos
The Heart
Formation of Ships (2)
The Pendentive *(Al-Mukarnasat)*
Rosewater Censers
Stalks of Wheat
Sails
Solidarity *(Al-Tadamun)*
Al-Saroukh (2)
(Iron – its strengths and benefits)

Salah Abdulkarim, who was educated in Egypt, France and Italy, was already well-established as one of the leading sculptors of the Arab world when he was commissioned by Mohamed Said Farsi to produce some works for Jeddah's collection. Dean of the Fine Arts School at Cairo University, this Egyptian artist was used to working on a fairly modest scale with his collaborator, Halem Yacoub (*b.* 1939), but welcomed the opportunity to create some of Jeddah's largest monuments. Thus his *Scrap Iron* – an abstract animal form which was created before he received his commission from the Mayor – stands less than two metres tall, whereas those works produced specifically for Jeddah include some of the city's largest sculptures such as *The Mameluke Minarets, The Pendentive* and the two *Al-Saroukh* monuments.

▼ Salah Abdulkarim talking to Mohamed Said Farsi.

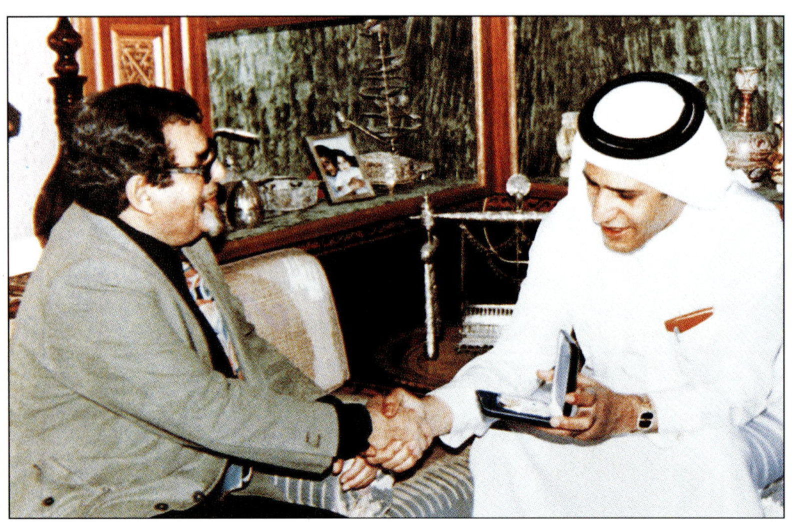

Mohamed Said Farsi *writes*:

❝ Salah Abdulkarim, one of our contemporary Arab artists, is distinguished by his creativity and sensitivity and I want to record his outstanding contribution to the story of art in Jeddah.

Salah began his work in Jeddah in 1978, collaborating with Dr Abdulbaki Ibrahim, Instructor of Islamic Architecture and Planning and publisher of the architecture and planning magazine *Alam al-Bina*, and formerly United Nations town planning consultant to the Ministry of Municipal and Rural Affairs.

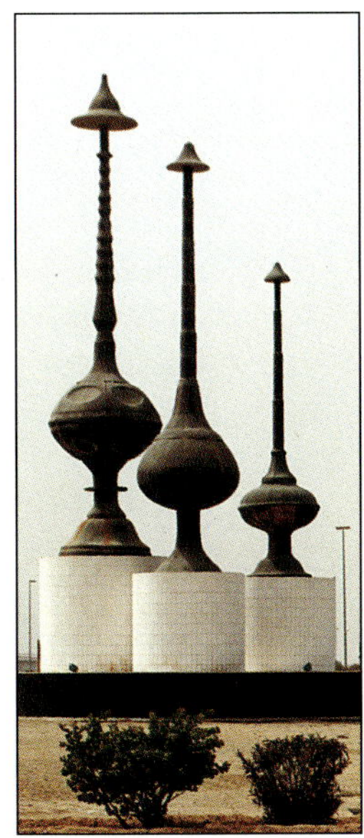

▲ The Rosewater Sprinkler shows the influence of the Mameluke period. Located in front of the Naval Base to the south of the city.

I impressed upon Salah and Dr Ibrahim our wish to further art in Jeddah through works which would reflect our deep-rooted Islamic traditions and, in response, the artist interpreted a verse from the Holy Koran in a most beautiful form. This work – the *Stalks of Wheat* formation on the Corniche – was fabricated using steel posts and bronze sheets, and was his first piece on such a large scale.

Our next discussions focused on another Koranic verse which praises the strength and usefulness of iron. Salah responded by offering designs for two huge and very unusual pieces (*Al-Saroukh*), inviting me to select one for implementation. Both dealt with the importance of iron and its uses in industry and manufacturing, but, unable to choose between them, I decided to go ahead with both.

Salah's designs for these two works incorporated the Golden Ratio of human proportions which was used by Arab artists in the design of the minarets of the Prophet's Mosque some 500 years ago, as well as in the calligraphy of the *thuluth* period.

In the course of our discussions we analysed the beautiful proportions of the Mameluke minarets (also an example of the Golden Ratio) and these discussions prompted the artist to design the monument, based on these minarets, which now stands at Al-Bayah Square. By any standards, the beauty of these minarets makes this a truly outstanding achievement.

The base and facing of this work are of brown granite in a pattern known as *ablaq* which was the main feature of Islamic architecture within the Mameluke period. In my day-to-day trips around the city I often go out of my way to pass Al-Bayah Square so as to have added opportunities to savour the unusual beauty of this work.

Salah designed *The Heart*, which can be seen in the Open Air Museum. This, like another work in the abstract shape of an animal (known as *Scrap Iron*), was fabricated in Italy.

The last of his works in Jeddah was *Al-Mukarnasat* (*The Pendentive*) which was first conceived in 1983 and took nearly three years to complete. This marvellous work, inspired by our own heritage, ingeniously and effortlessly transforms a square shape into an octagon and then into a circle which becomes the base of a dome or the balcony of a minaret. This very large monument – a gift to the city from Khalid ibn Mahfouz – stands in front of the National Commercial Bank.

Like the Statue of Liberty in New York it is of copper sheets on a steel framework. Some 11 tonnes of steel and 14 tonnes of copper were used.

In my opinion, this monument and that of *The Mameluke Minarets* in Al-Bayah Square represent an outstanding achievement in the history of urban beautification and art in Arab Islamic cities.

Thus, our dialogue with this great artist resulted in expressions of art which highlight our traditional Islamic values such as strength and benevolence. Not by accident, but by thought, prayer and discussion over many days and nights, sometimes sitting together and sometimes apart – but always in communion. Throughout, we shared a common understanding and love for our work by brotherhood and joint endeavour and enjoyed the warm feeling of true friendship.**”**

Section Two
The SCULPTURES and MONUMENTS

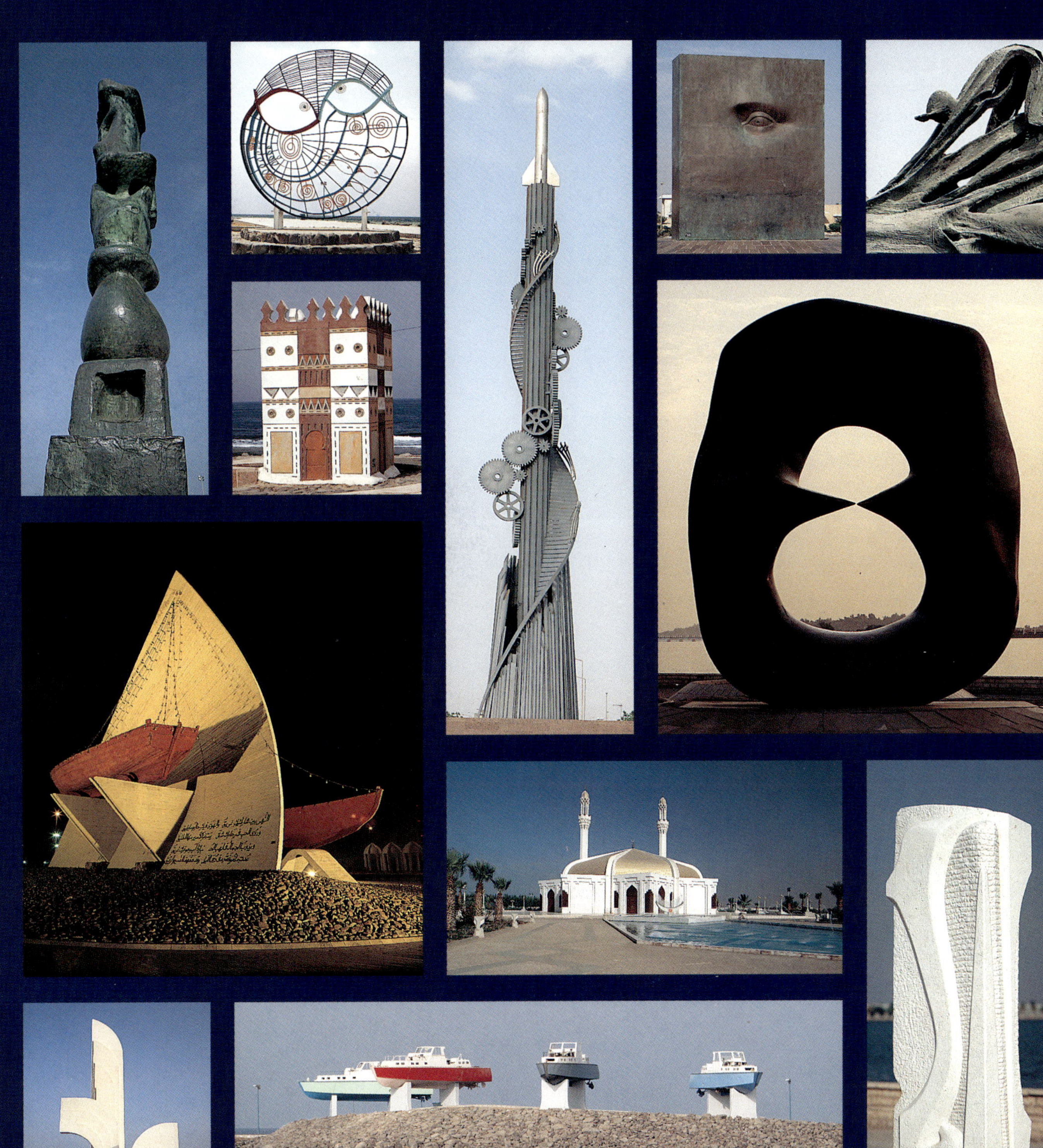

THE LOCATION OF THE PRINCIPAL SCULPTURES AND MONUMENTS

1 King Fahd Fountain **D7**
2 Cosmos **B5**
3 Sunflower Fountain **D4**
4 The Pendentive **C8**
5 The Seagull **D5**
6 Peace **C7**
7 Water Jars Fountain **C6**
8 Al-Kibla **C6**
9 The Ramadan Lantern **D4**
10 The Oil Lamp **C8**
11 Gathering of the Ships at Night **C7**
12 Warships Square **C8**
13 Old Motor Launches **D4**
14 Sails **C9**
15 Boat and Sail **B1**
16 Sails **B4**
17 Worked Iron Formation **D4**
18 Jeddah, Bride of the Sea **D4**
19 Shahadat Al Tawhid **D4**
20 The Supplication **D5**
21 The Name of Allah **D4**
22 The Name of Allah **D3**
23 Verse in White **D3**
24 Koranic Verse **D3**
25 Stalks of Wheat **D3**
26 El-Wakil Mosque **D3**
27 Fisherman's Net **D4**
28 Dialogue **D4**
29 School of Dolphins **A9**
30 At Sea **C7**
31 Sea Harvest Trellis **C8**
32 Abstract I **D3**
33 Sublimity **D3**
34 Invocation **D3**
35 Abstract II **D3**
36 Cross-Section of the Heart **D3**
37 Accident! **D4**
38 The New Wave of Cars **C8**
39 Traditional Arabian Architecture **D5**
40 Builder's Plumbline **D3**
41 Chimney Form **C8**
42 Moon and Bow **D4**
43 Large Pillar **D6**
44 The Signs of the Zodiac **D5**
45 Three Flowers **C7**
46 Five Fan Palms **C7**
47 Two Poles **C7**
48 The Fountain of Shells **C8**
49 The Shell **C6**
50 Fossilised Nautilus Shell **D5**
51 The Mameluke Mosque Lanterns **D6**
52 Two Vases **D3**
53 Al Anani Mosque **C7**
54 Rotation of the Crescent and Moon **C7**

Al Hamra Open Air Museum C7/D7

55 The Eye
56 Three Piece Reclining Figure No. 1
57 Large Spindle Piece
58 Oval with Points
59 Upright Motive No. 2
60 The Essence is Gold
61 Large Ball Bearing Symbols
62 The Solar Clock
63 The Traveller's Post
64 Cube
65 Flame of Life
66 Scrap Iron
67 Al-Mafrookah* **C6**
68 Balance in the Air
69 Changing Positions
70 The Illusion of a Second Cube
71 The Fisherman's Net
72 Flexibility of Balance
73 Balance
74 Arrangements
75 Alterations in Space
76 The Guitar of Love
77 Waiting

1 2 3 4 5

A B C D

Ring Road Expressway (Al Haramain Road)
KING ABDUL AZIZ INTERNATIONAL AIRPORT
Obhur Creek
Al Malek Road
North Corniche
Al Madinah al Munawarah Road
Al Amir Sultan Street
Al Nuzhah Street
Al Makarounah Street
Al Amir Fahd Street
Al Amir Majed Street
Al Amir Met'ab Street
Hera'a Street
Quraysh Street
Sari Street

N

78 Swirl
79 Pure Abstraction
80 Circle and Square
81 Telephone
82 Symmetry
83 Rotation and Balance
84 Music
85 Family
86 The White Horse* **C3**
87 Arab Knight
88 Symbols of Victory
89 Unity is Strength
90 Crescent and Moon
91 The Semsemiah
92 Early Cubism
93 A Step Forward
94 Personage I
95 Personage II
96 Frustration
97 Migrant Birds
98 Pomegranate Fountain **C6**
99 The Bicycle **B6**
100 Spare Wheel **B6**
101 Verse Boat **C3**
102 Twin-engined Aircraft **B5**
103 Personal Aircraft of King Abdul Aziz **B8**
104 Fighter Aircraft and Trainer **C5**
105 Clouds **B6**
106 Ratchet Spanner **B7**
107 Arch and Waterspouts Fountain **C7**
108 Dallah Fountain **C7**
109 Coffee Pots Fountain **C5**
110 The Treasure Trove **C8**
111 Sack Fountain **C7**
112 The Rose-Water Fountain **C8**
113 Water Skins Fountain **A9**
114 Water Jars Fountain **C7**
115 Water Jar Fountain **C8**
116 Aloe Flowers **C7**
117 Calligraphy **C9**
118 The Mameluke Minarets **C8**
119 The Market Fountain **C8**
120 The Bean Pot **C8**
121 Inkwell, Pen and Paper **D5**
122 Birds **C8**
123 Traditional Jar **C8**
124 The Globe of Knowledge and Life **A8**
125 Silent Formation **C9**
126 And We Became Friends **C8**
127 Horse and Jockey **B10**
128 Swords of God **B7**
129 The Fist **C5**
130 The Condenser I **D6**
131 Banners in the Wind **D6**
132 The Condenser II **D6**
133 Twenty-eight Winding Steps **B6**
134 A Precious Burden **B7**
135 Spiral with Moon **C8**
136 Small Pillar **C8**
137 Desalination Pipes I **D6**
138 Desalination Pipes II **A6**
139 Desalination Pipes III **A7**
140 The Letter J **C6**
141 Recycled Iron I **C8**
142 Recycled Iron II **C8**
143 Recycled Iron III **C8**
144 Science and Religion **D4**
145 Calligraphic Discs **C9**
146 Holy Koran **C6**
147 Calligraphic Disc **C8**
148 The Illuminated Globe **C3**
149 Globe in Scrap Iron **C6**
150 Al-Saroukh I **C5**
151 Al-Saroukh II **D4**
152 Balancing Cube **B9**
153 Structure of the Atom **B9**
154 The Atomium **B9**
155 Gravity **B9**
156 Engineers' Tools **B7**
157 Spanner and Bolt **C10**
158 Astrolabe **D5**
159 Fountain Pen **B9**
160 Knowledge **A9**

*NOTE: These two monuments are not in the Al Hamra Open Air Museum.

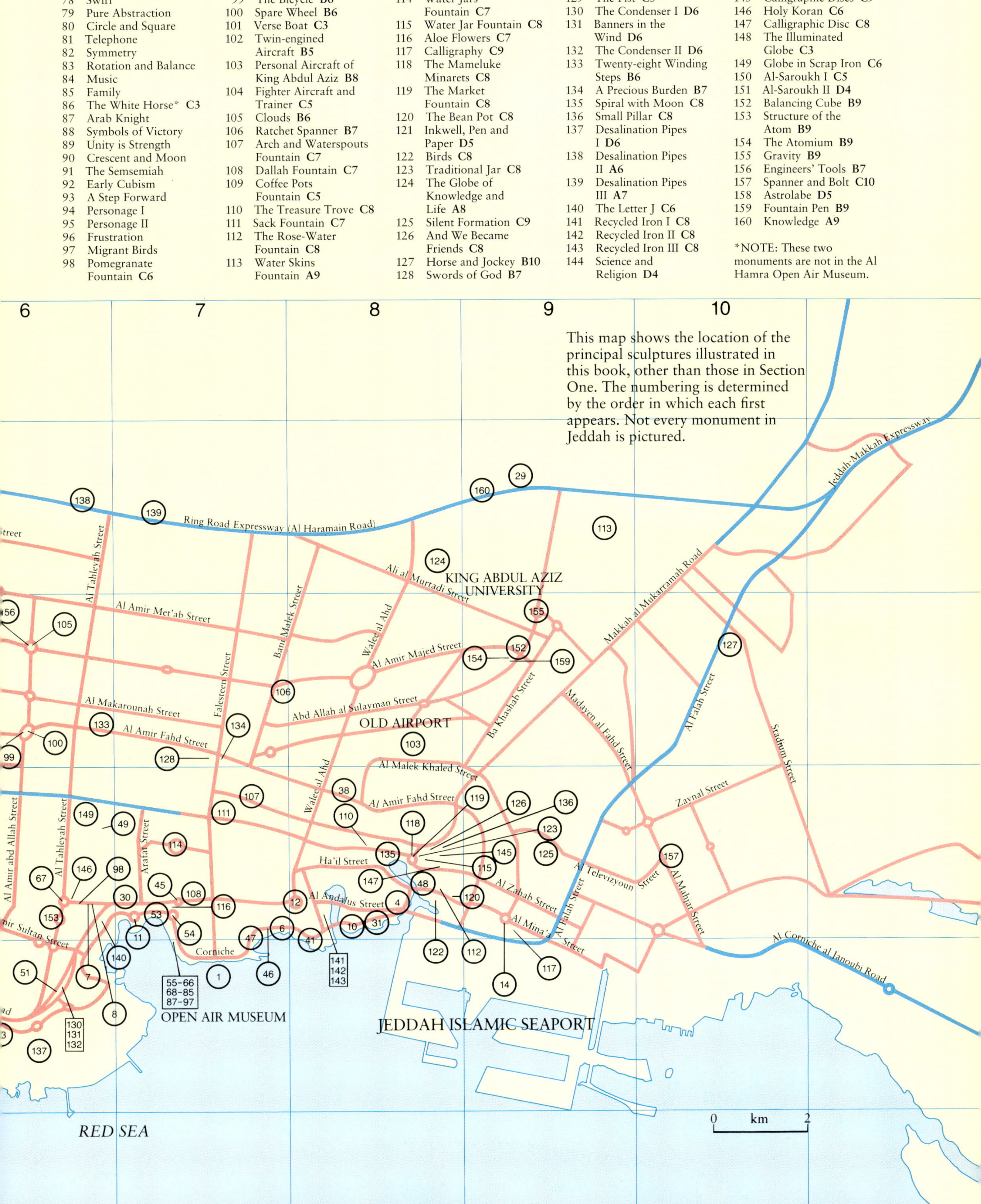

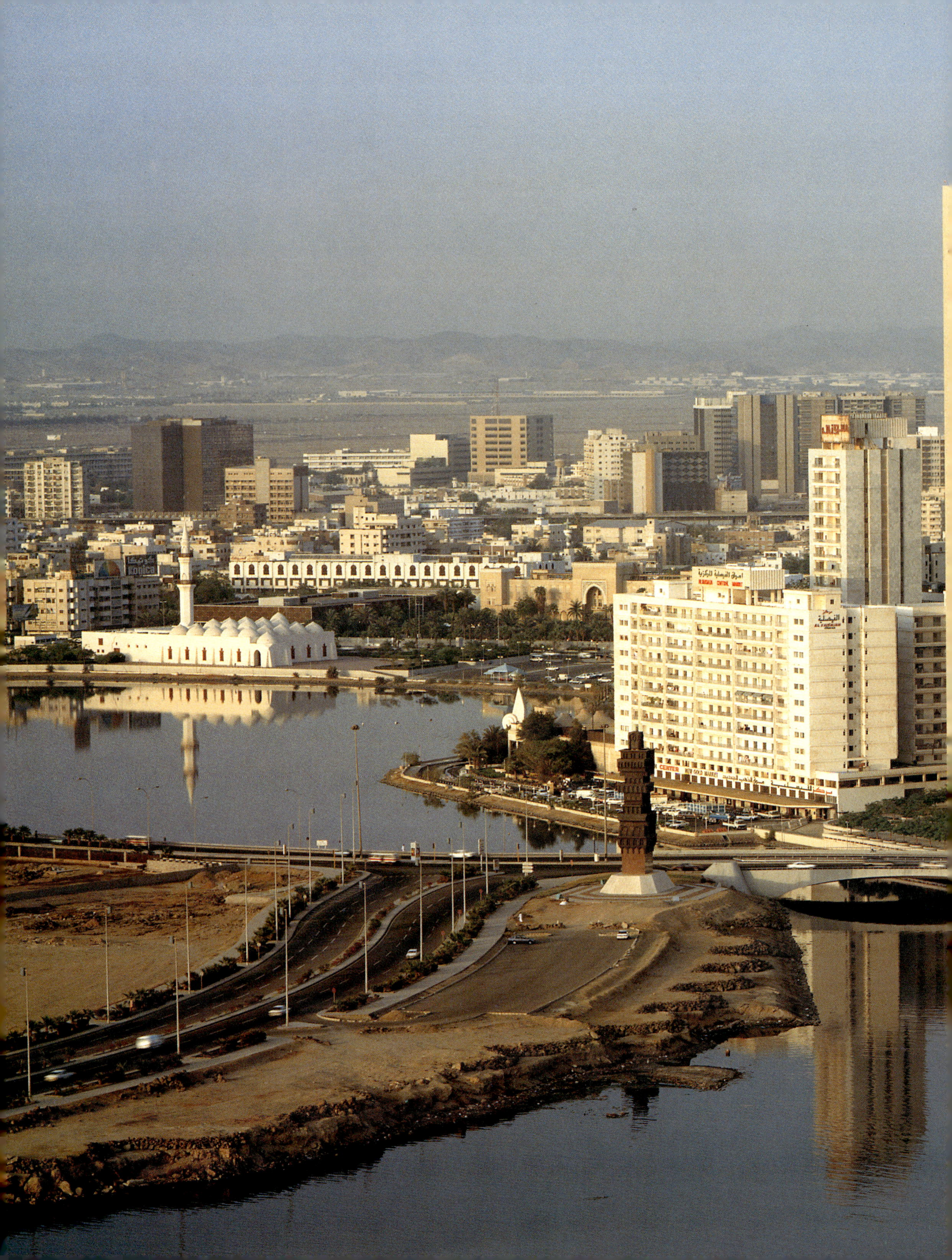
أسواق الفيصلية المركزية
CENTRAL MARKET
الفيصلية
CENTER
NEW GOLD MARKET

The CORNICHE

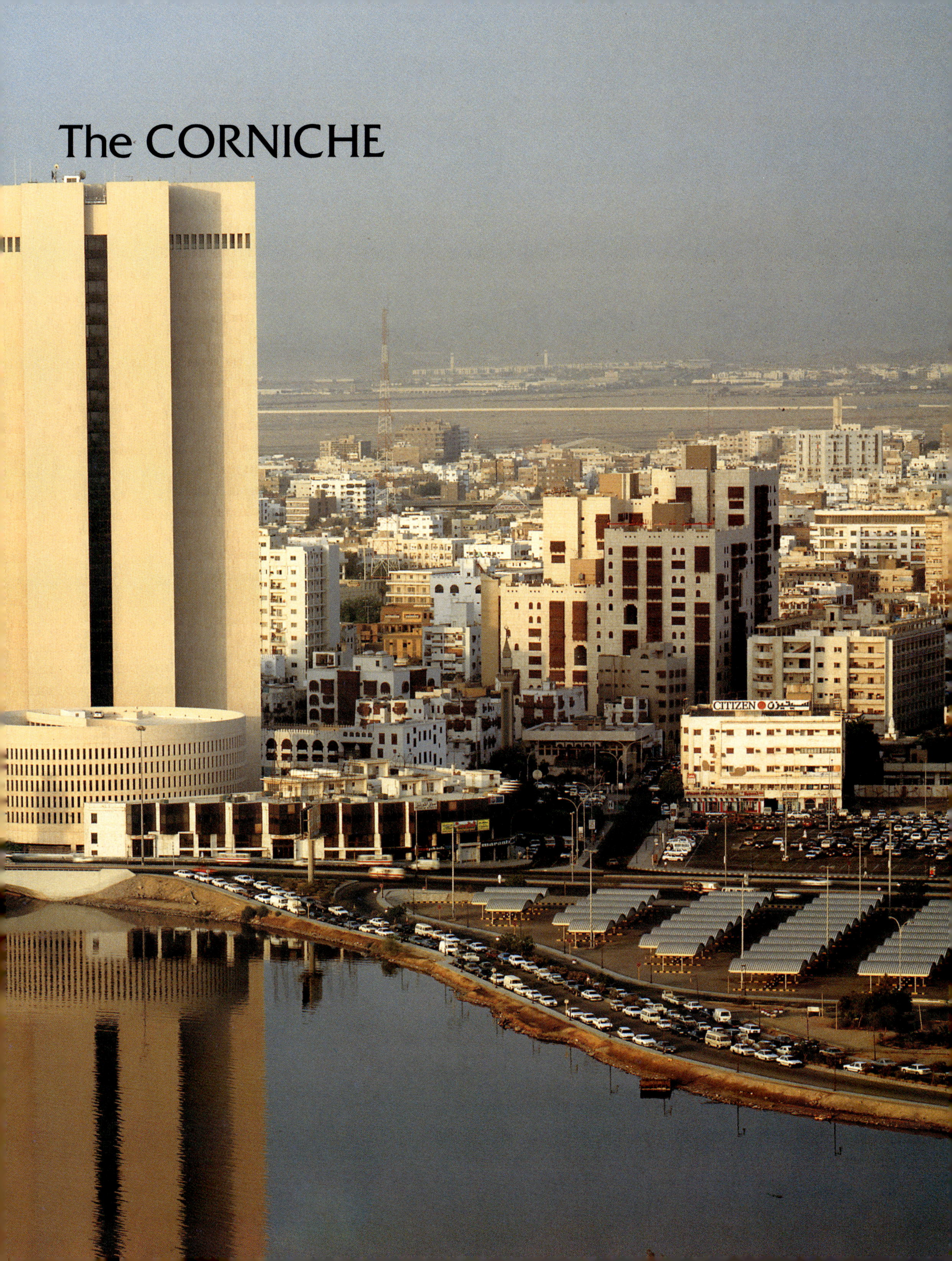

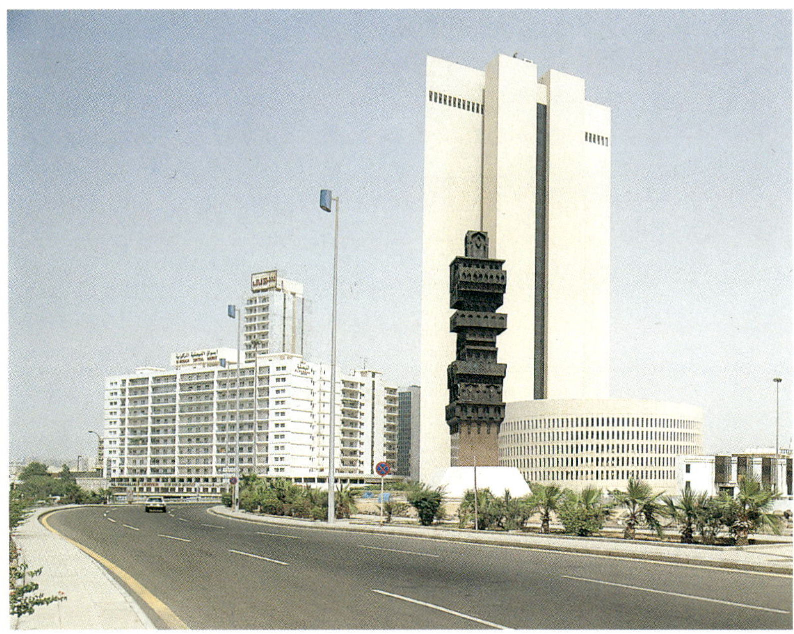

◄ The monolithic bulk of Skidmore Owings and Merrill's National Commercial Bank looms above Salah Abdulkarim's *Pendentive* (*Al-Mukarnasat*). While the bank building (winner of a major American architectural award) represents the modern face of Jeddah, the sculpture stands as a monument to centuries of Arab architectural achievement.

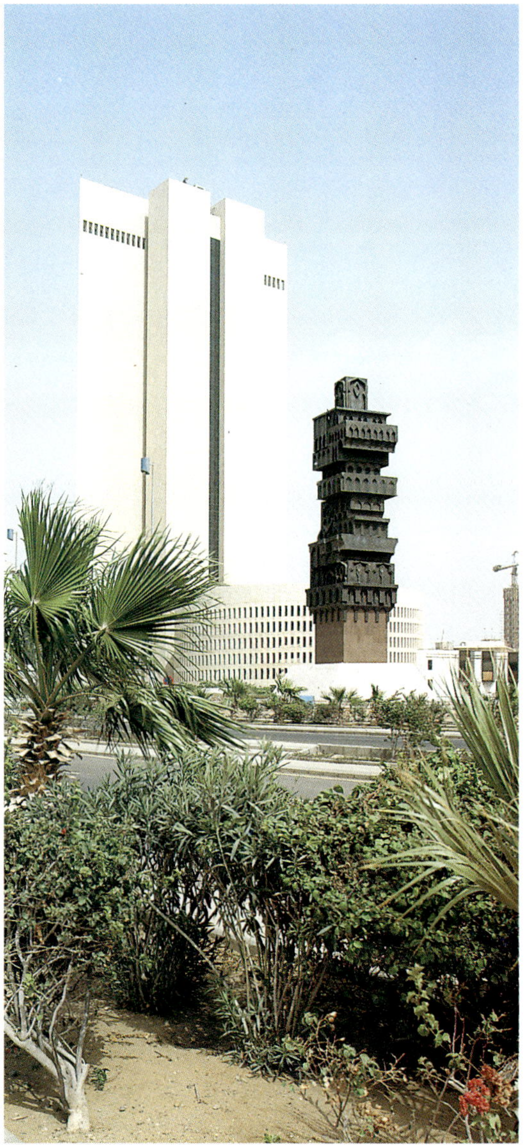

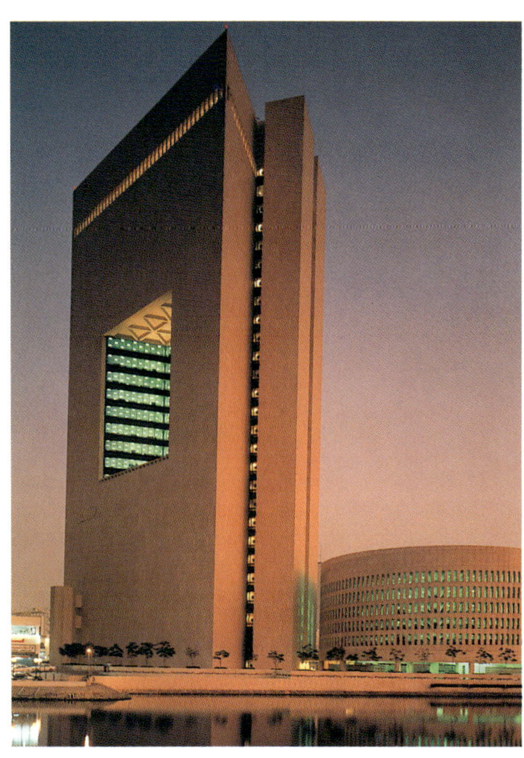

◄◄◄ Ancient and modern styles of architecture stand starkly contrasted by the side of Jeddah's Arbaen lagoon.

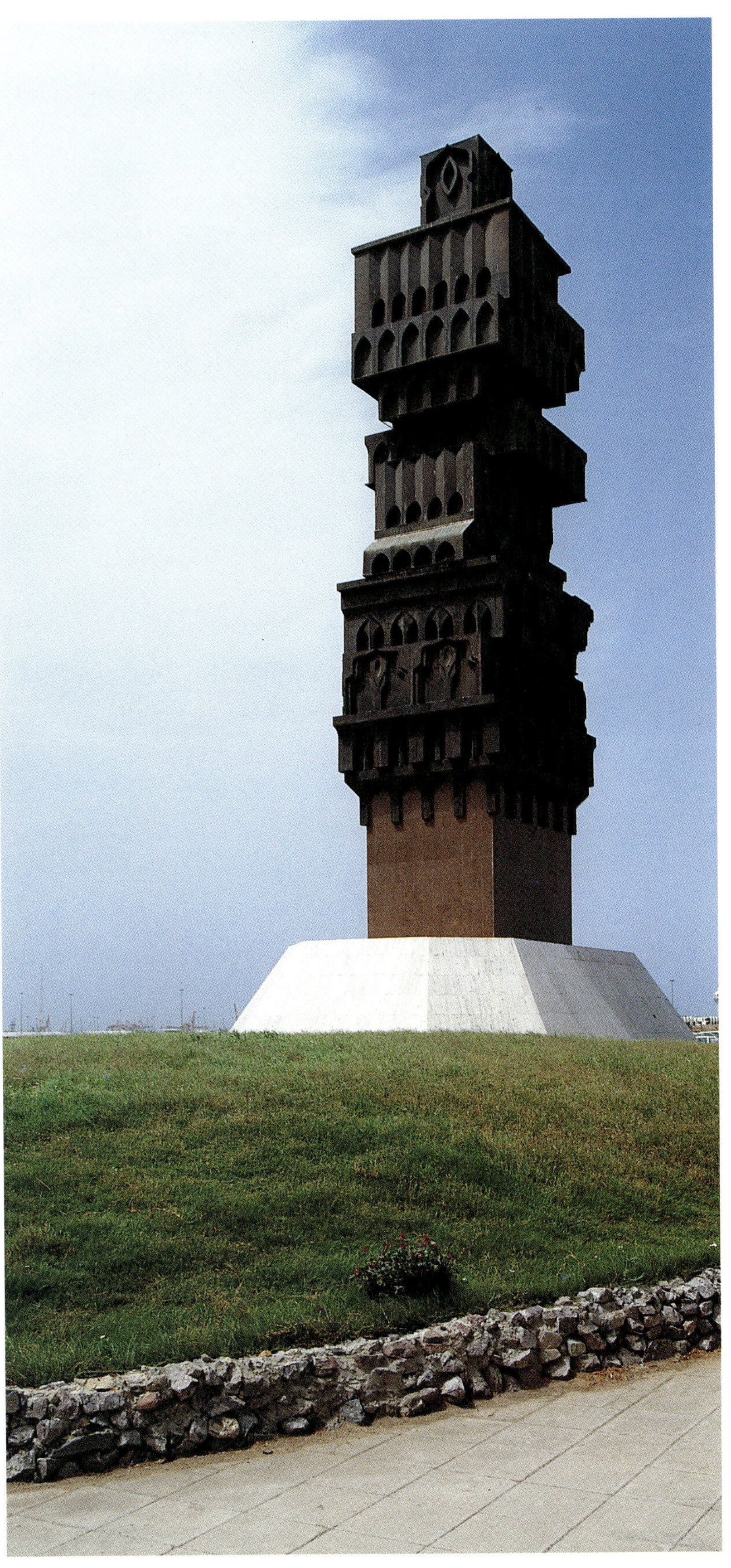

◀ **THE PENDENTIVE** (Al-Mukarnasat) (4)
Salah Abdulkarim
Copper sheets on a steel frame

Mohamed Said Farsi describes *The Pendentive* as "an outstanding achievement in the history of urban beautification and art in Arab Islamic cities". It celebrates an architectural device which made possible the soaring domes and minarets of classical Islamic architecture. Structurally, this large monument is similar to New York's Statue of Liberty, consisting of a steel frame clad with copper sheets.

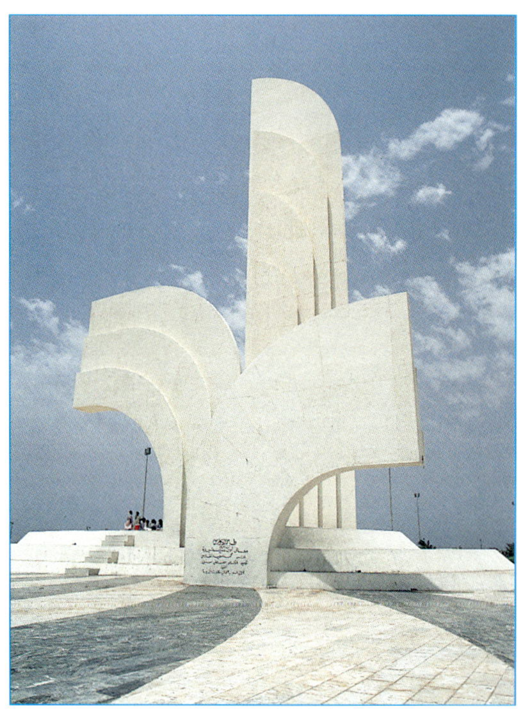

□ **THE SEAGULL** (Al-Nawras) (5)
Mustafa Senbel
Reinforced Concrete

One of the world's largest abstract sculptures at 55 metres tall, *The Seagull* took three years to build. It was a gift from the Ministry of Post, Telegraph and Telephone and cost over $1 million. Senbel, the Egyptian artist had been at University with Mohamed Said Farsi. He also worked on a much more modest scale, creating a series of works from steel reinforcing rods.

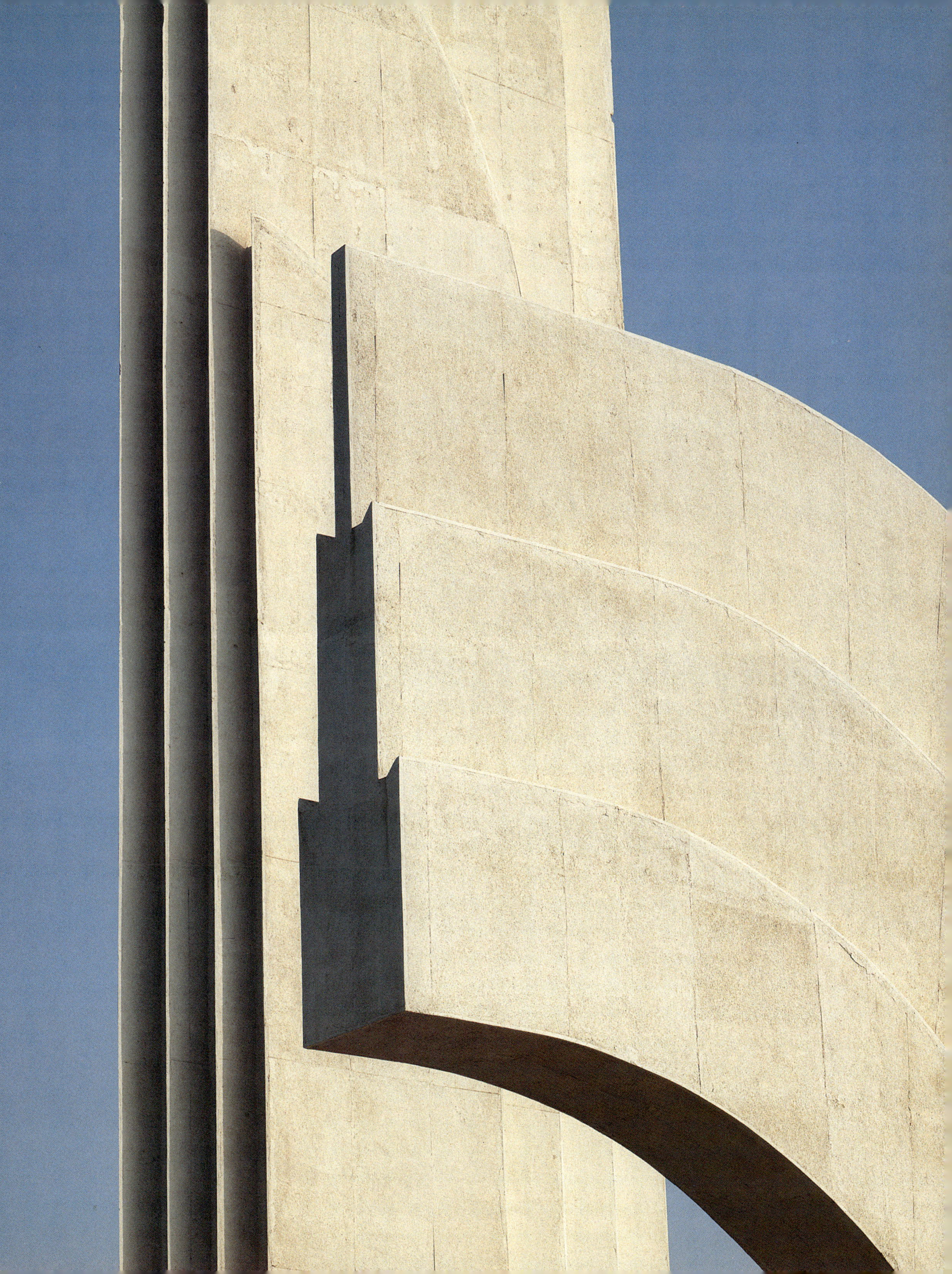

□ The painted design on *The Seagull's* 'wing' not only indicates the symbolism of the piece, but also emphasizes the scale and line of the work. The poetry is a selection of verses celebrating Jeddah from four of the most renowned poets of the western region of Saudi Arabia.

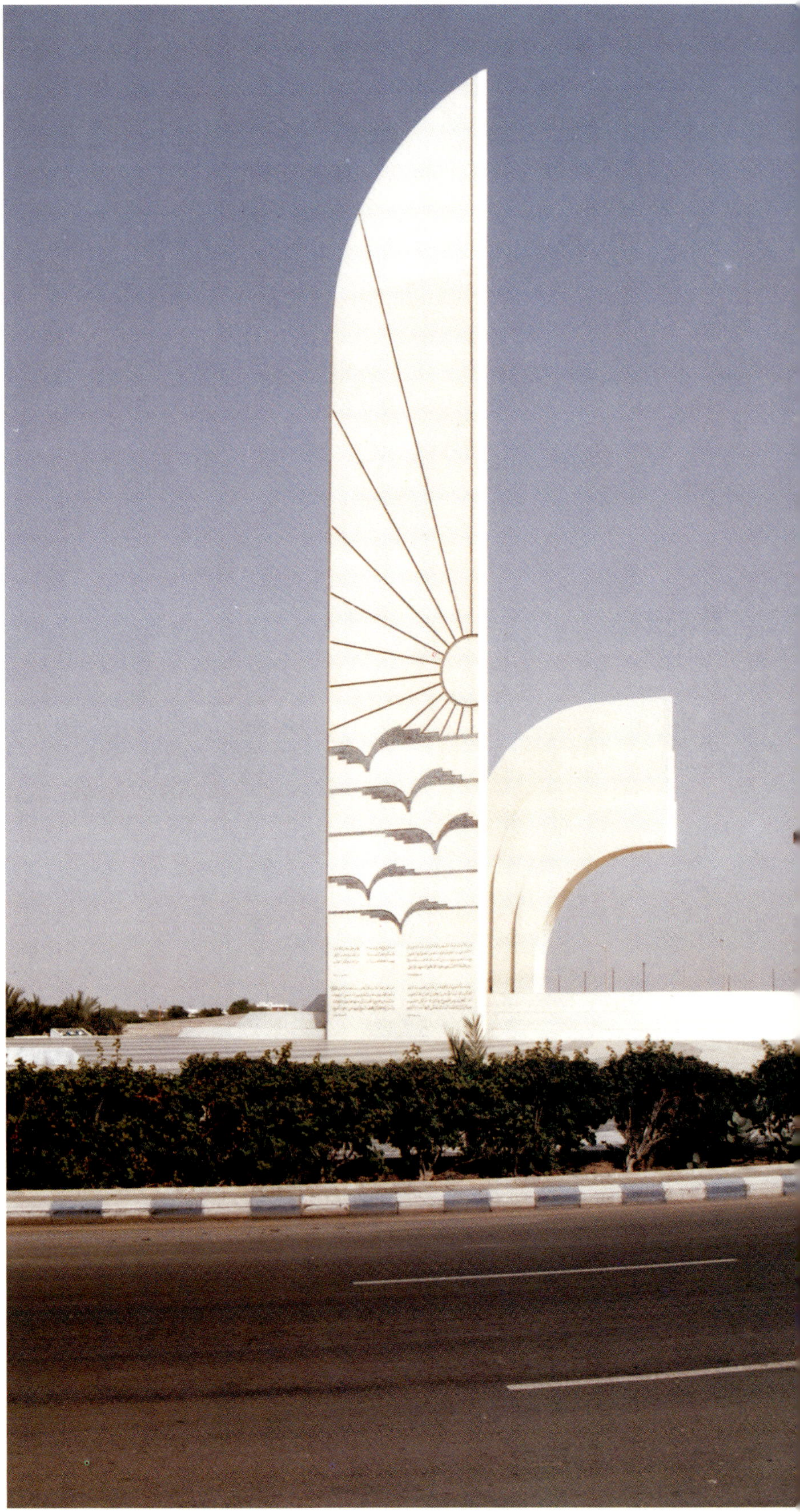

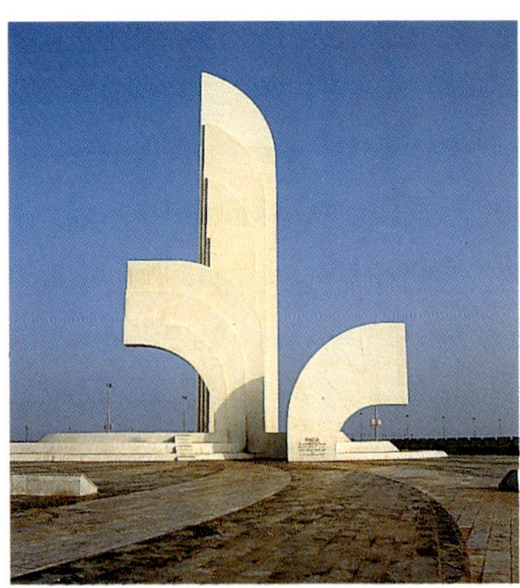

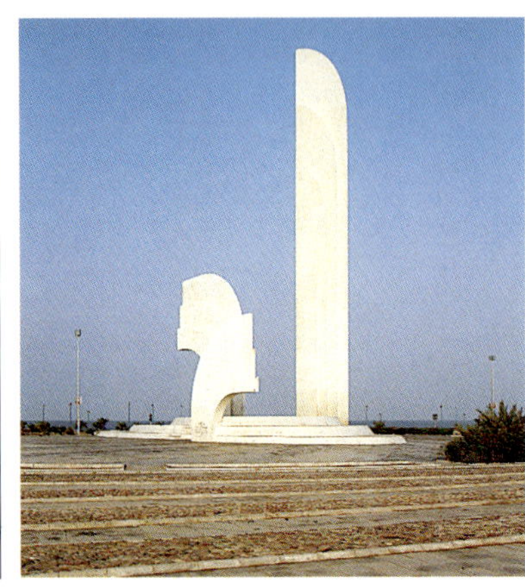

□ **PEACE** (Al-Salam) (6)
Newman
Stainless Steel

This abstract work, shaped with laser beams from a single piece of stainless steel, was a gift from Arabian Cleaning Enterprises which has for many years been responsible for maintaining the city's sculptures.

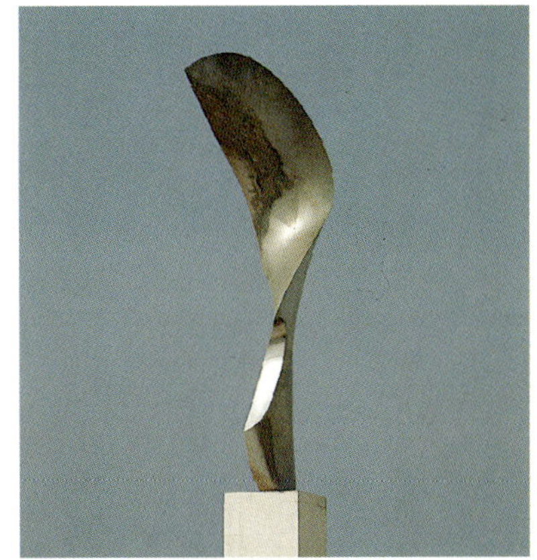

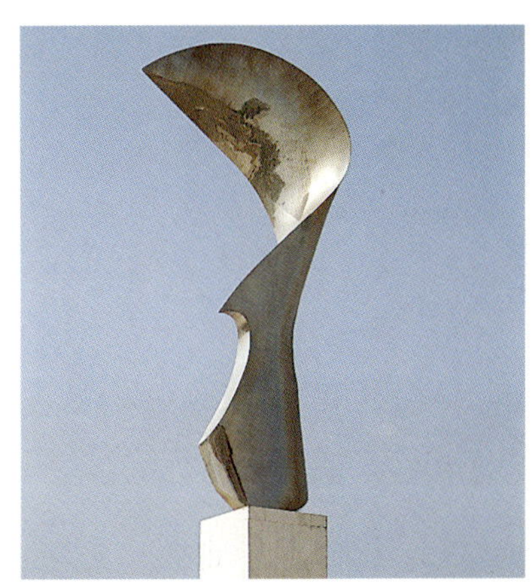

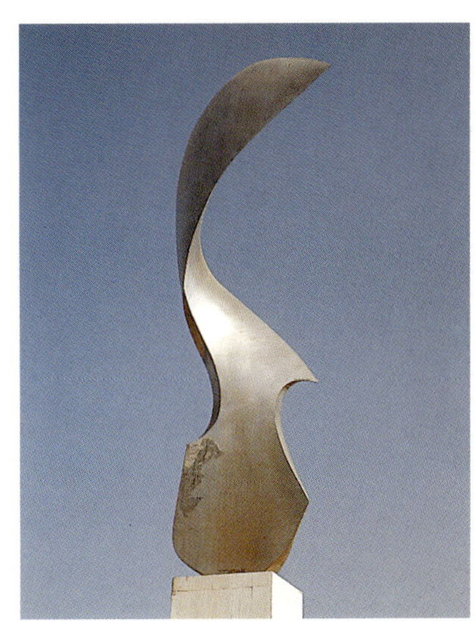

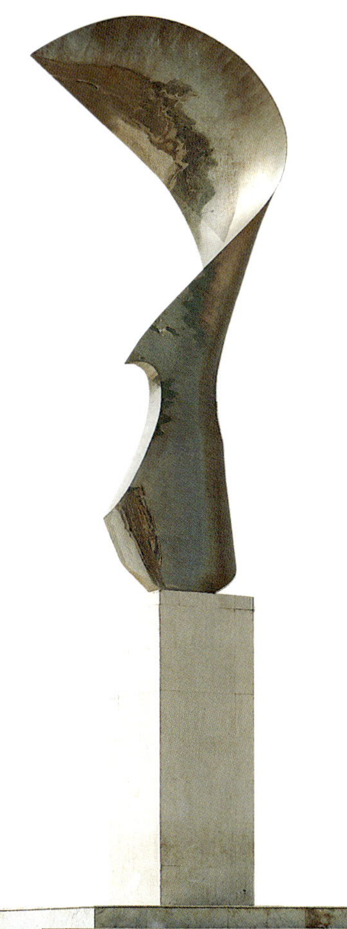

□ A project which took some five years to realise, *Al-Kibla* is one of Jeddah's most starkly imposing monuments. Towering 15 metres above its raised base, it consists of 260 pieces of marble which were carved in Italy before being shipped to Jeddah for assembly. Much of the sculpture's impact derives from its base which is paved with bricks made locally from the red clay of Wadi Fatimah.

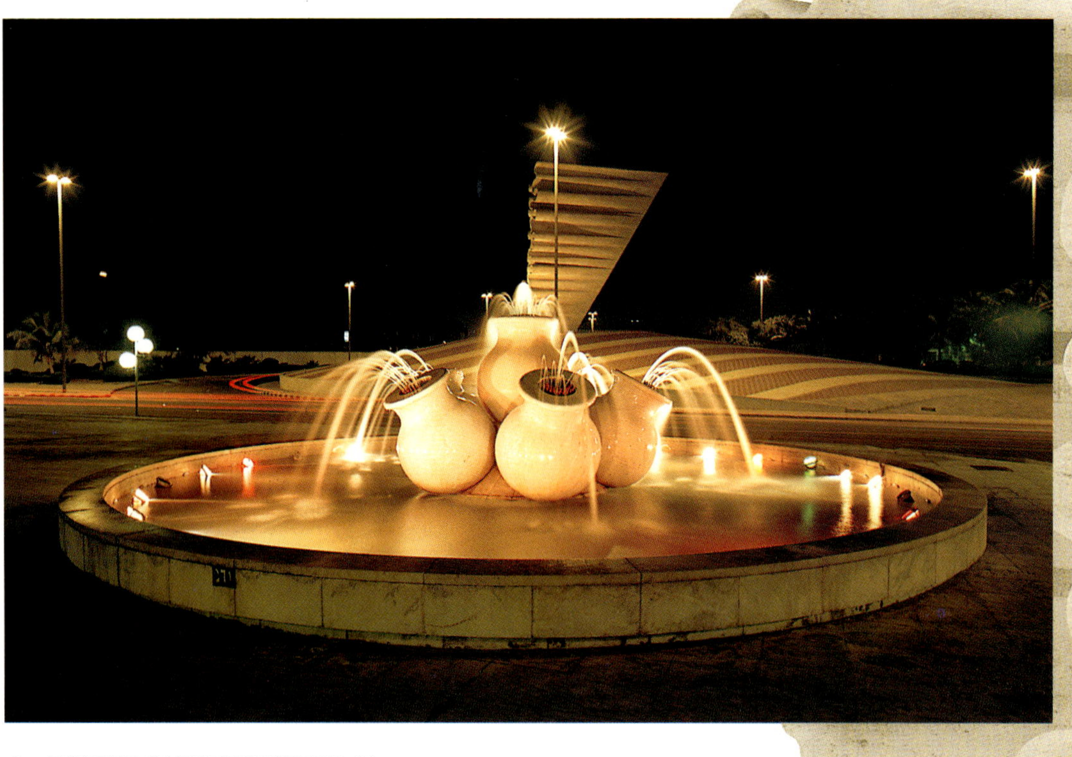

▲ **WATER JARS FOUNTAIN** (7)
Julio Lafuente
Greek Marble

Small flower vases bought by the mayor during a visit to London's Harrods emporium provided the models for these larger versions which were carved in Italy.

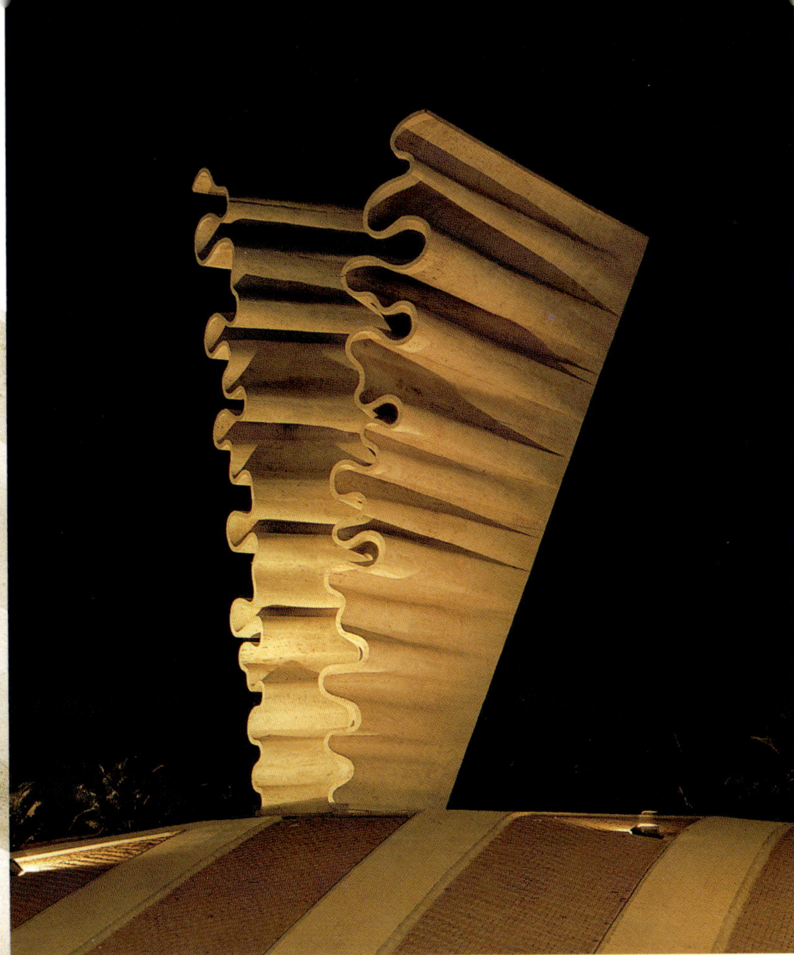

◄ **AL-KIBLA** (The Direction of Prayer) (8)
Julio Lafuente
Travertine Marble

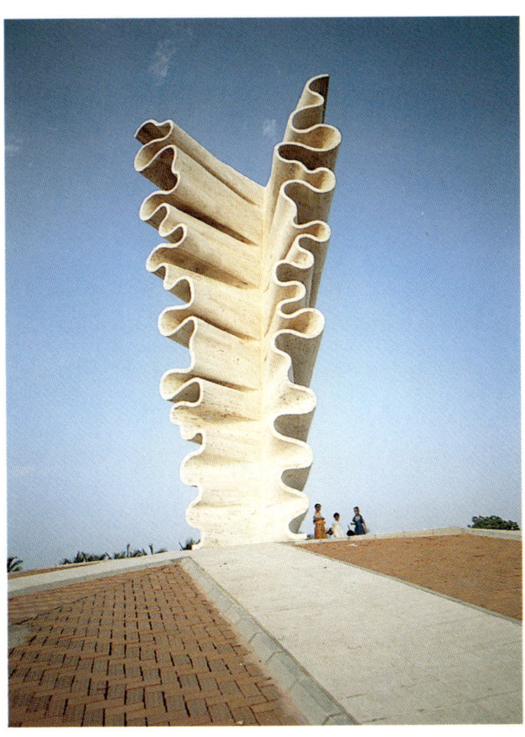

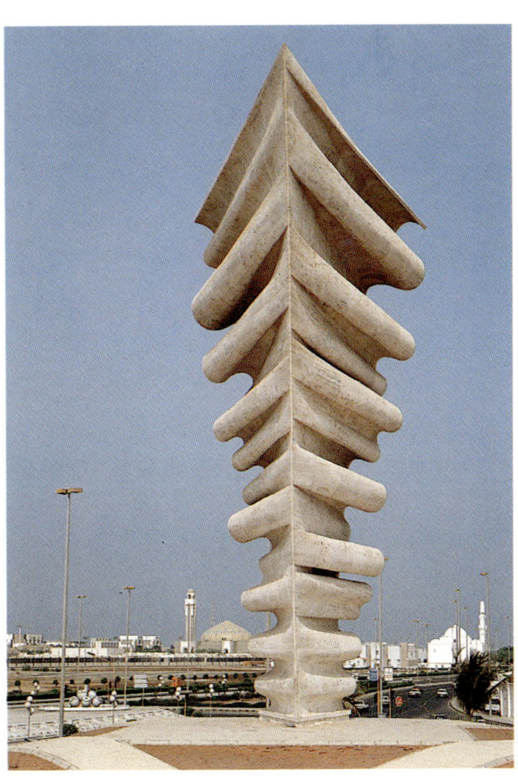

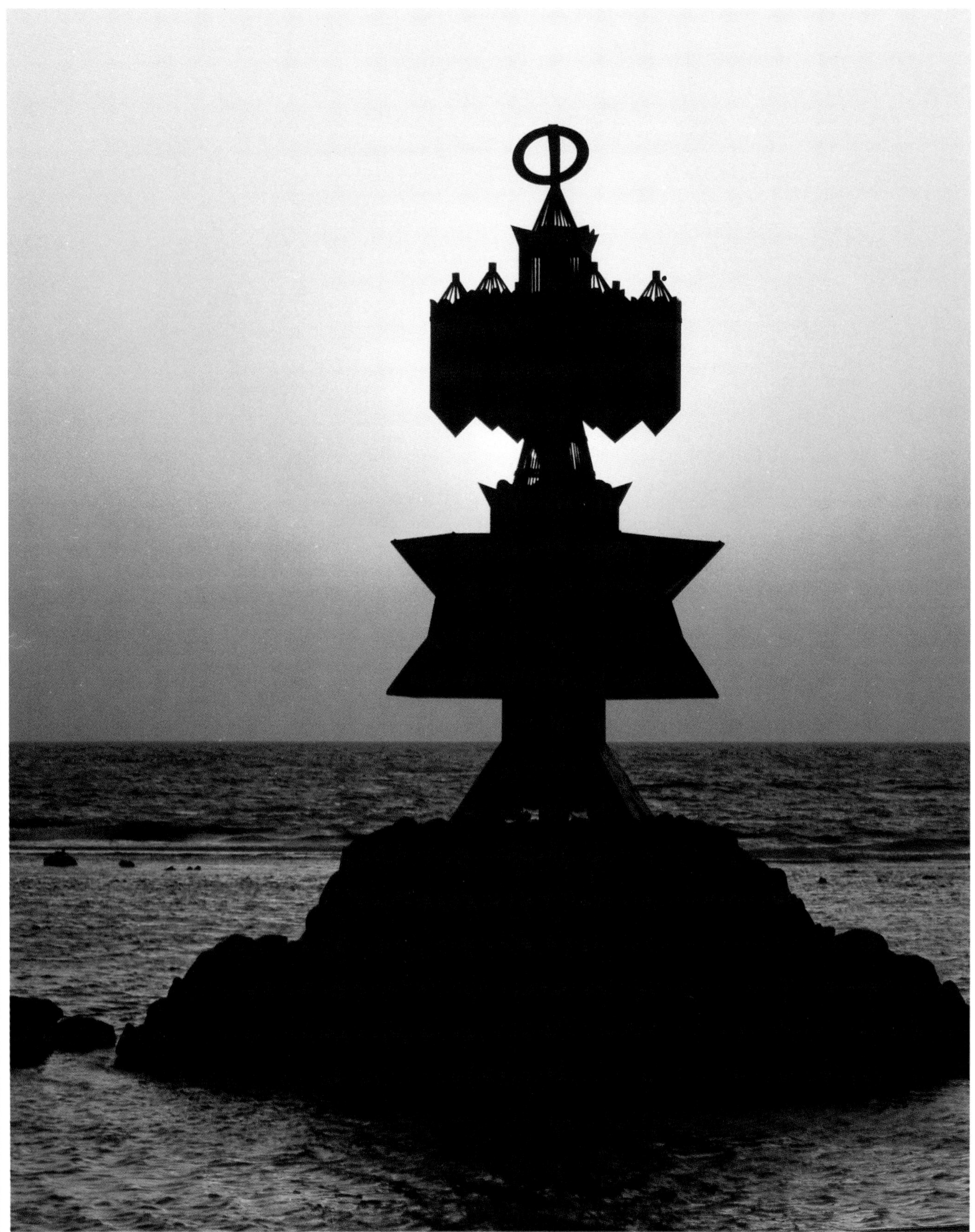

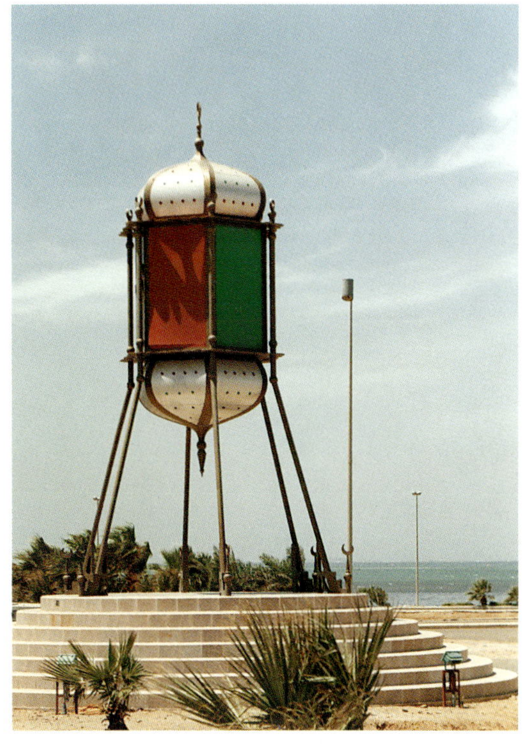

▲ THE OIL LAMP (10)
Mustafa Senbel
Steel and glass

◄▼ THE RAMADAN LANTERN (9)
Mustafa Senbel
Steel and glass

A little island was made for this sculpture just off the Corniche so that when it was illuminated at night its vivid colours would be reflected in the surface of the sea.

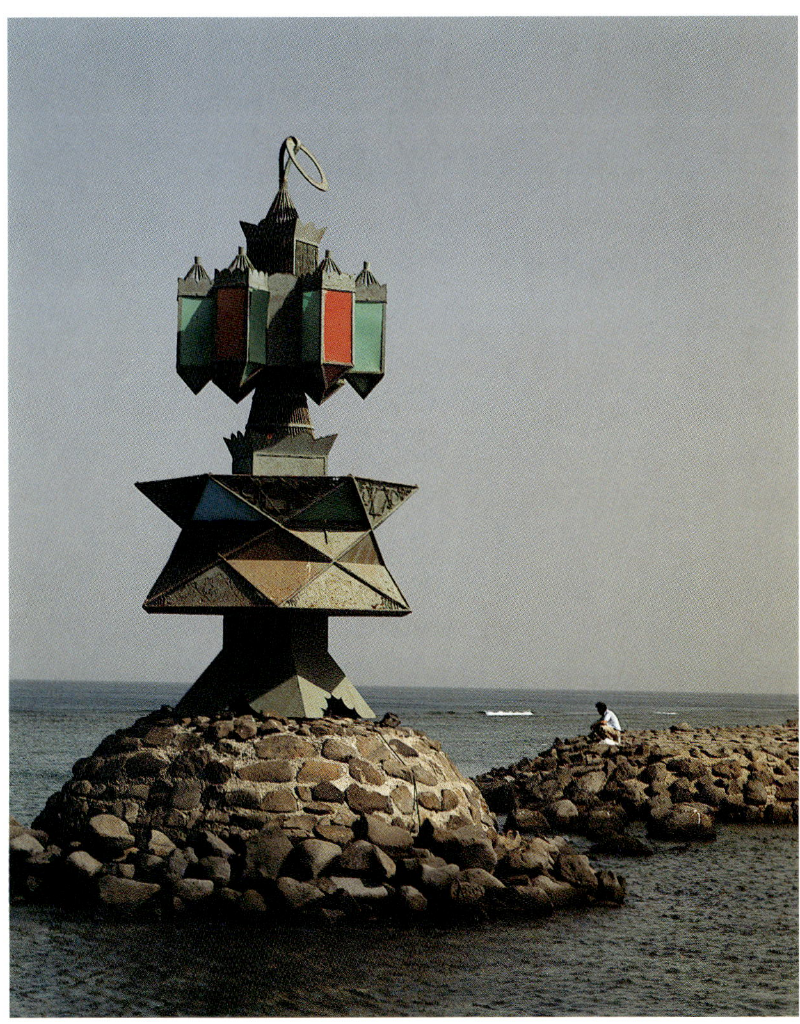

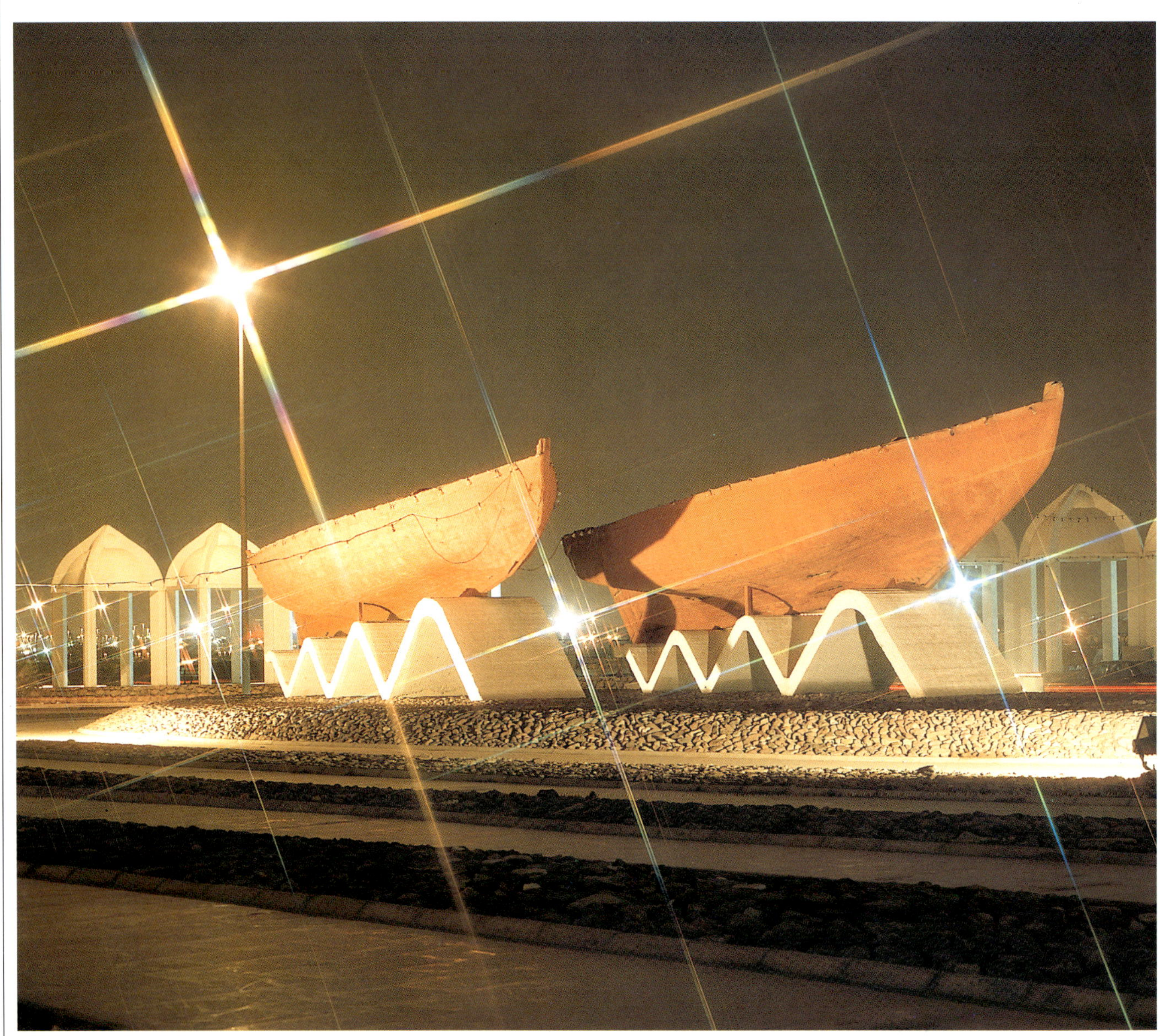

□ GATHERING OF THE SHIPS AT NIGHT
(Tashkeel Al-Saway) (11)
Julio Lafuente
Obsolete boats and reinforced concrete

Skilful lighting of this group of boats gives the work added impact at night. The calligraphic inscription is a verse from the famous Hejazi poet, the late Hamza Shihatta, which evokes the spirit of Jeddah and its relationship with the sea.

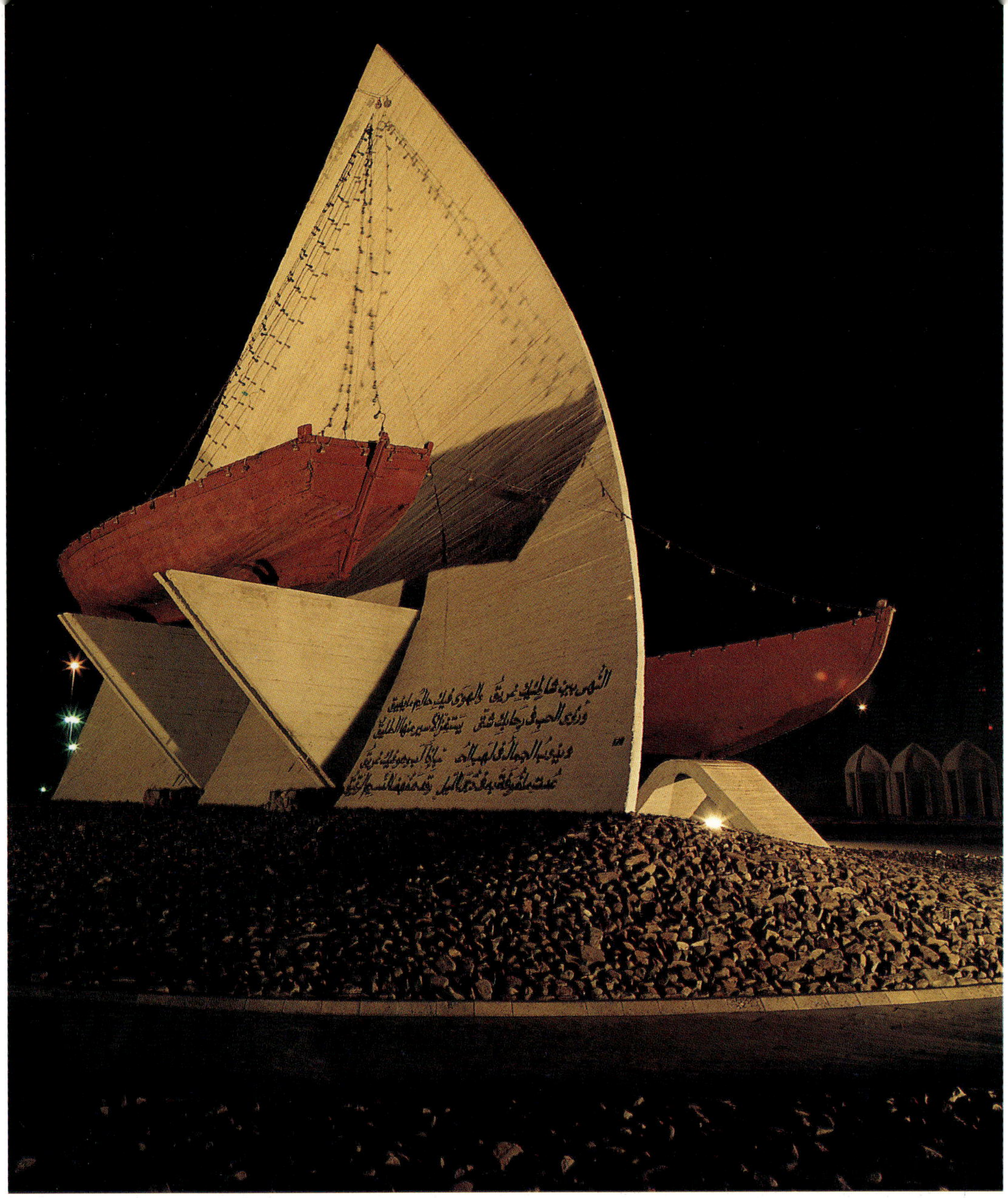

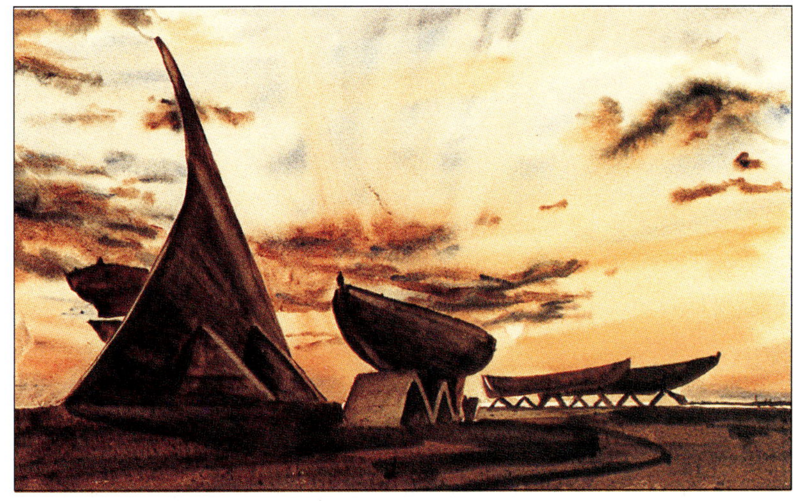

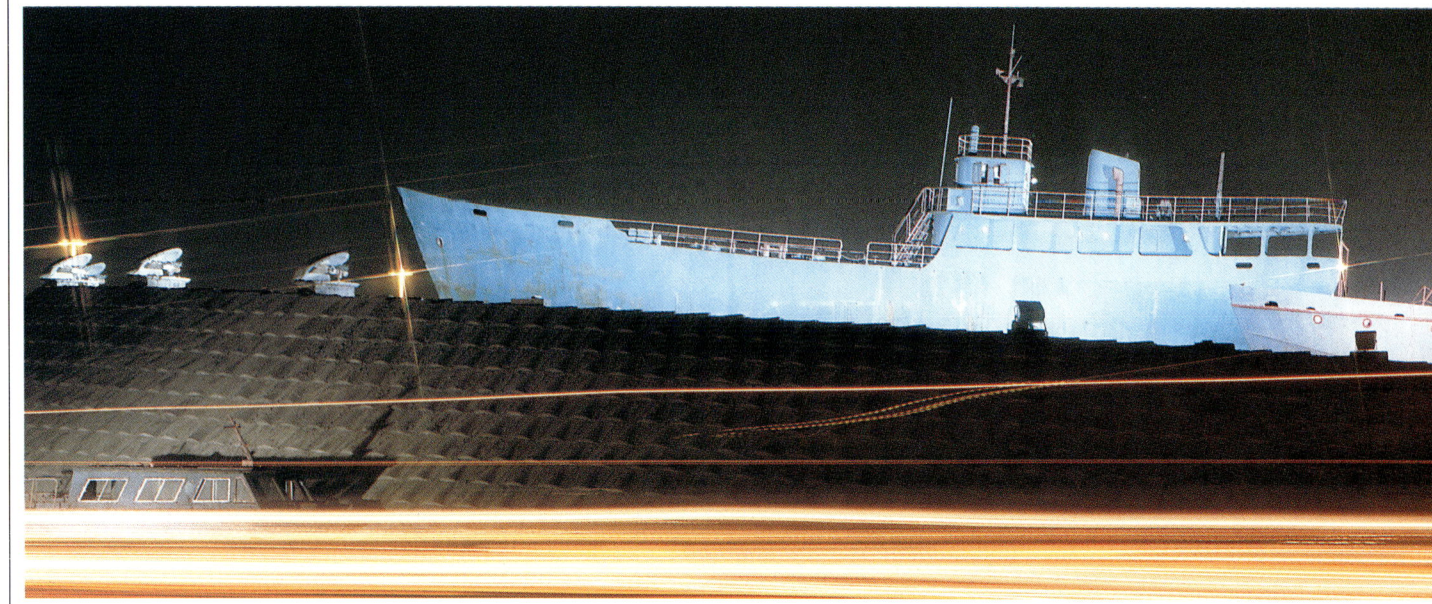

□ **WARSHIPS SQUARE** (12)
Julio Lafuente
Obsolete vessels and reinforced concrete

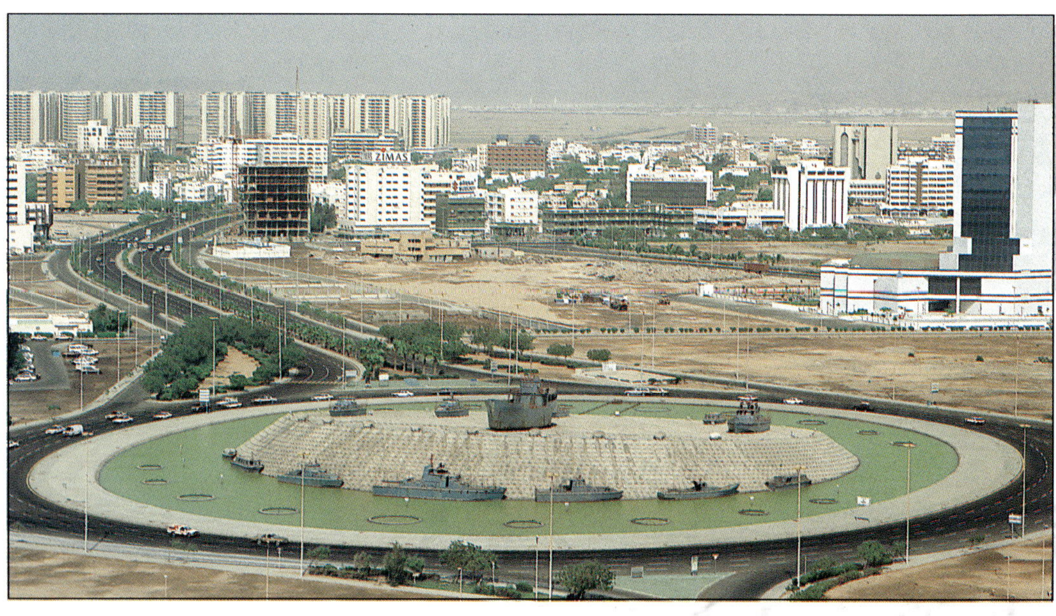

There are twenty-nine vessels in this massive group, ranging from small launches to a ship of nearly 300 tonnes which took two weeks to move from the sea to the site on Andalus Road. This monument required 100,000 cubic metres of earth to be moved, and 1000 tonnes of steel reinforcement were used in the concrete elements of the work.

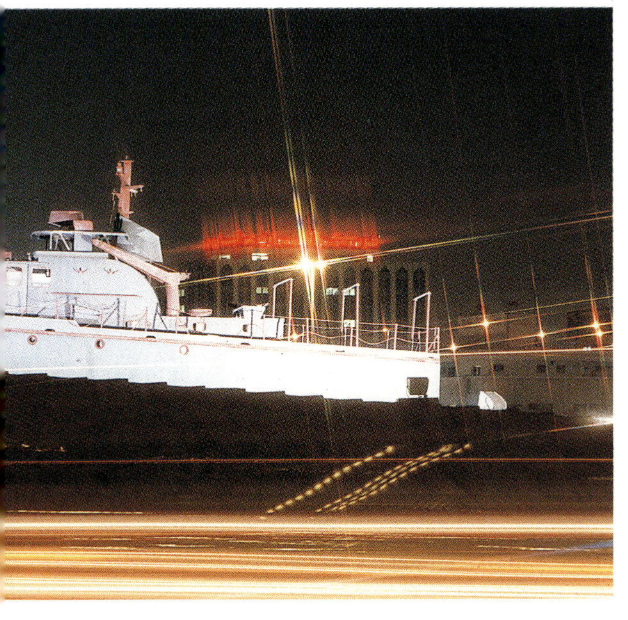

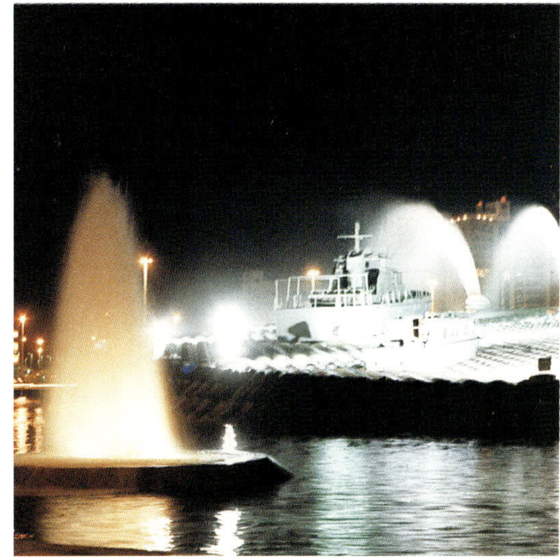

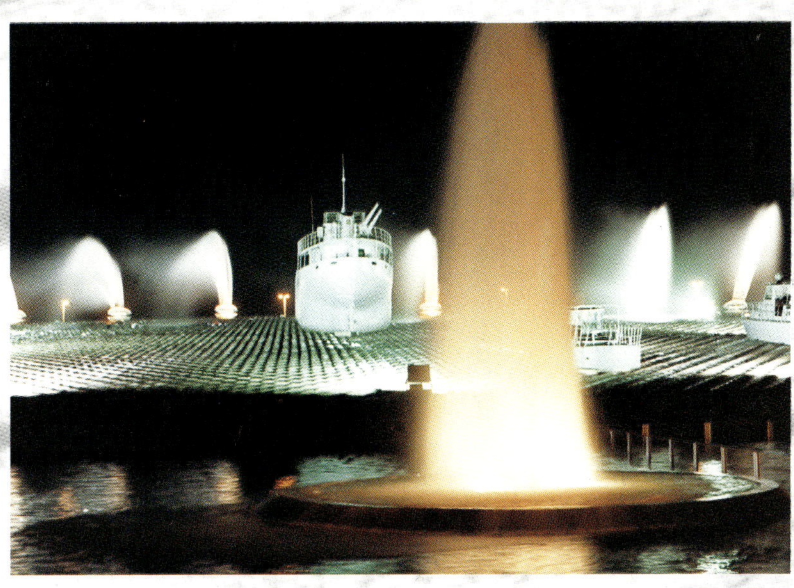

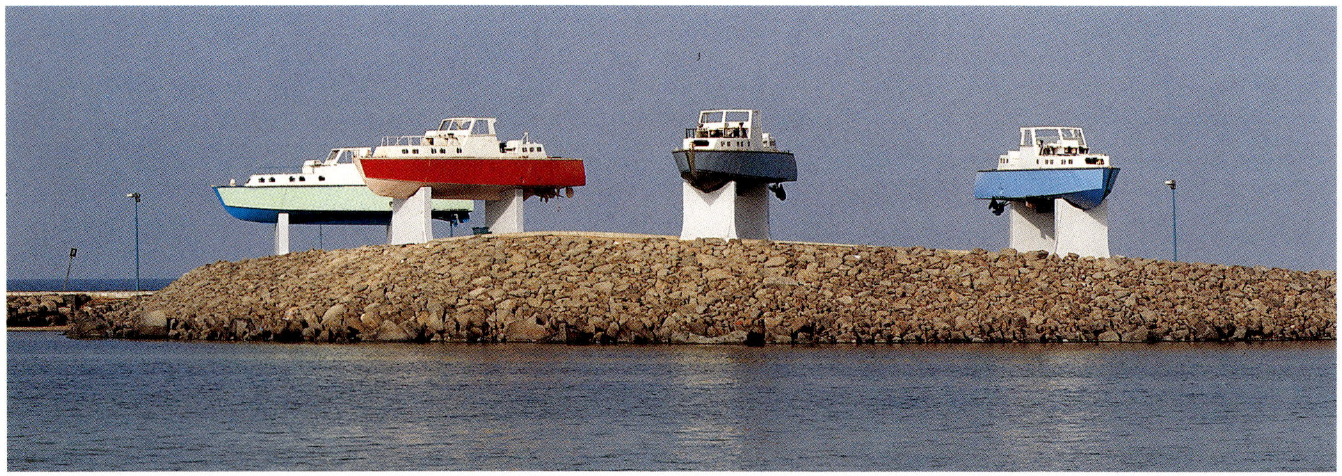

▲ OLD MOTOR LAUNCHES (13)
Mustafa Senbel

□ Not surprisingly, in view of Jeddah's maritime heritage, boats and the sea are recurrent themes in the city's sculpture collection. In the majority of cases real boats – from humble wooden fishing boats to small ships – have been used. In the representation of sails, however, more imagination was called for and artists have used a wide variety of different materials including reinforced concrete, steel and copper.

► BOAT AND SAIL (15)
Artist Unknown
Reinforced Concrete

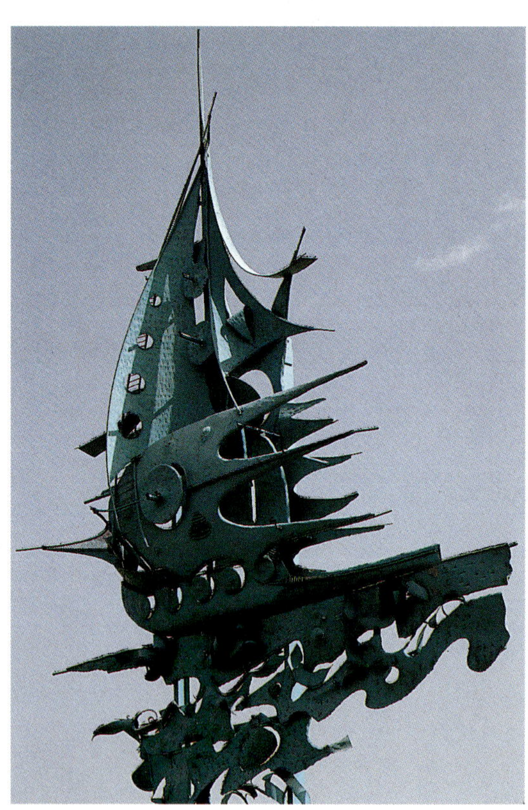

▲ SAILS (14)
Sylvestre Giovanni
Bronze and Steel

In keeping with Mayor Farsi's belief that form should mirror function, this sculpture stands as a landmark at the entrance to Jeddah Islamic Seaport.

This working drawing for one of the boat monuments is a reminder of the fact that the work of the artists was supported by the efforts of architects and civil engineers.

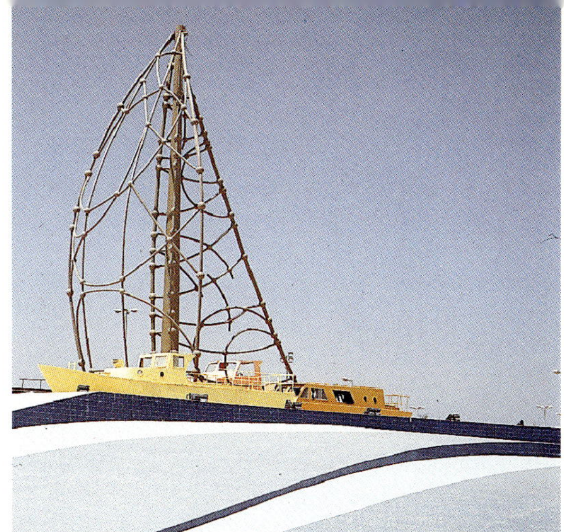

► **SAILS** (16)
Mustafa Senbel
Steel

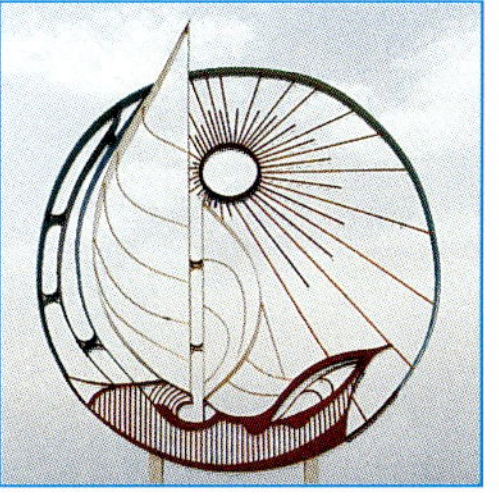

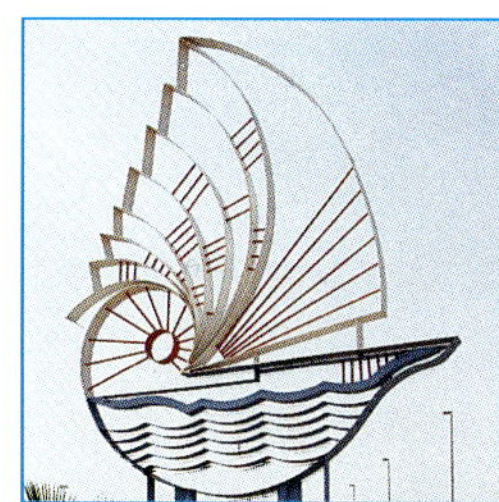

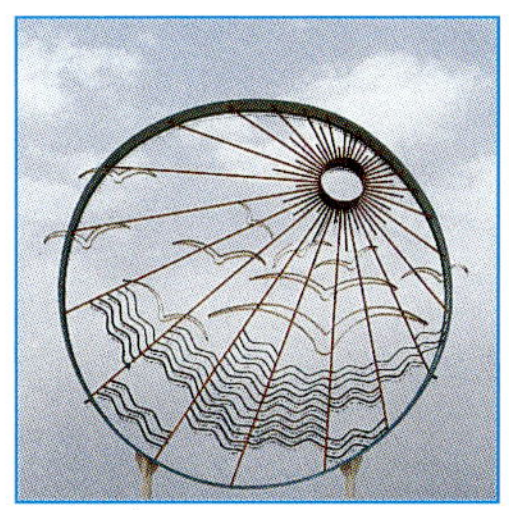

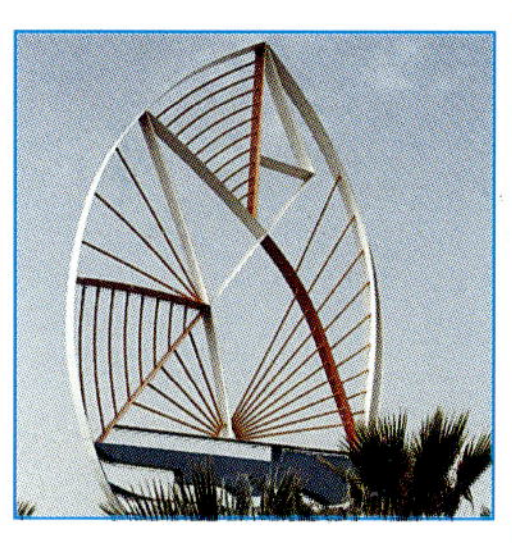

▲ **JEDDAH, BRIDE OF THE SEA** (18)
(Calligraphy)
Mahmoud Banat
Marble

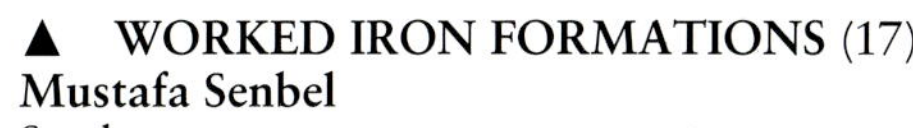

▲ **WORKED IRON FORMATIONS** (17)
Mustafa Senbel
Steel

Works from a series made out of steel reinforcing rods. These examples are: *Sunrise; The Sail; Beach Themes* and *Sail Formation*.

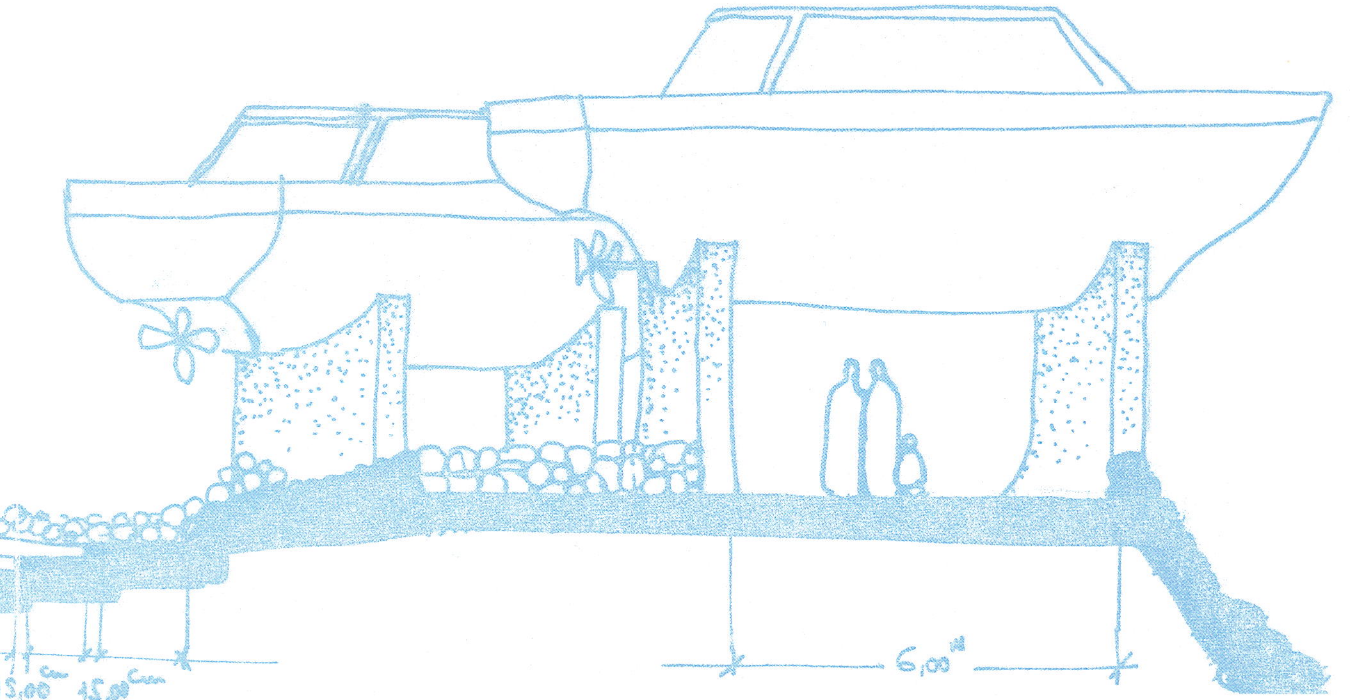

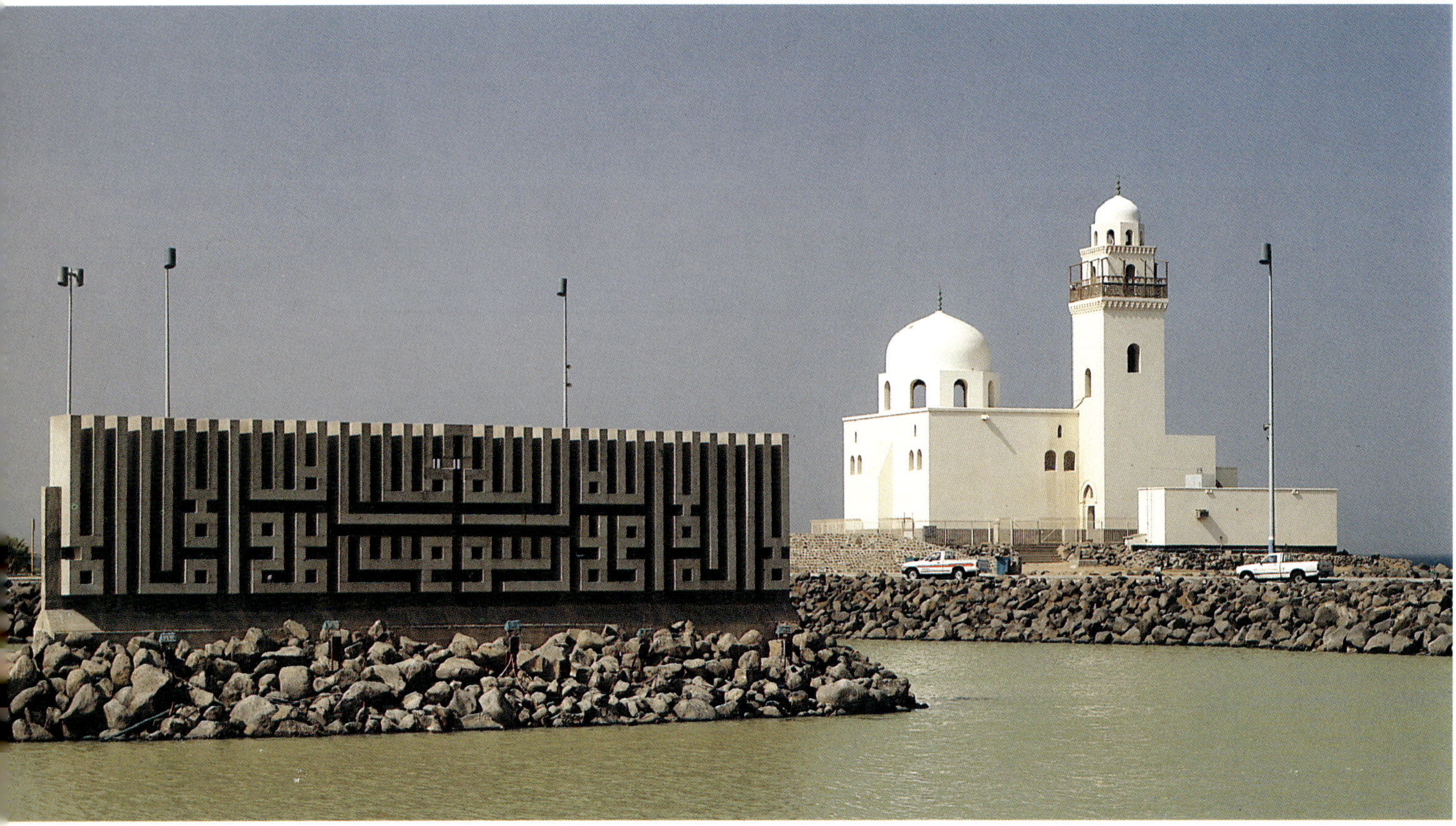

▲ **SHAHADAT AL TAWHID** (19)
(Koranic Verse)
Julio Lafuente
Granite

This sculpture is based on the affirmation of monotheism – that there is no god but God.

Although not an Arabic speaker, Lafuente was eager to exploit the potential of Arabic calligraphy and used Islamic religious themes in several of his sculptures.

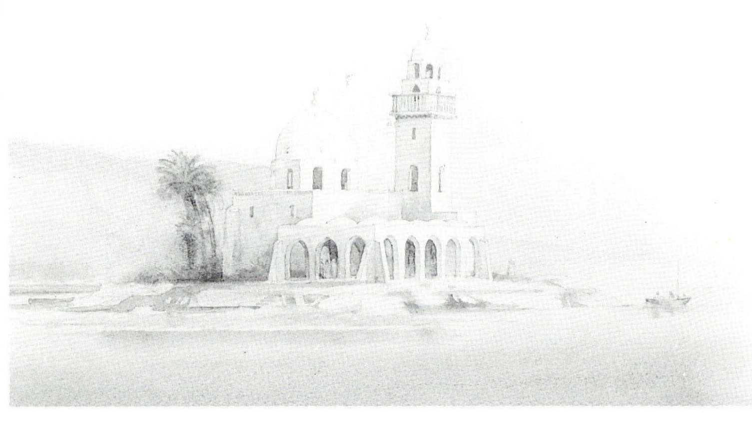

► **AL JAZIRAH MOSQUE**
(The Island Mosque)
Abdel Wahed el Wakil Architect

This is one of four mosques built along the Corniche for prayer and worship by those who have come to use the seashore for peace and recreation.

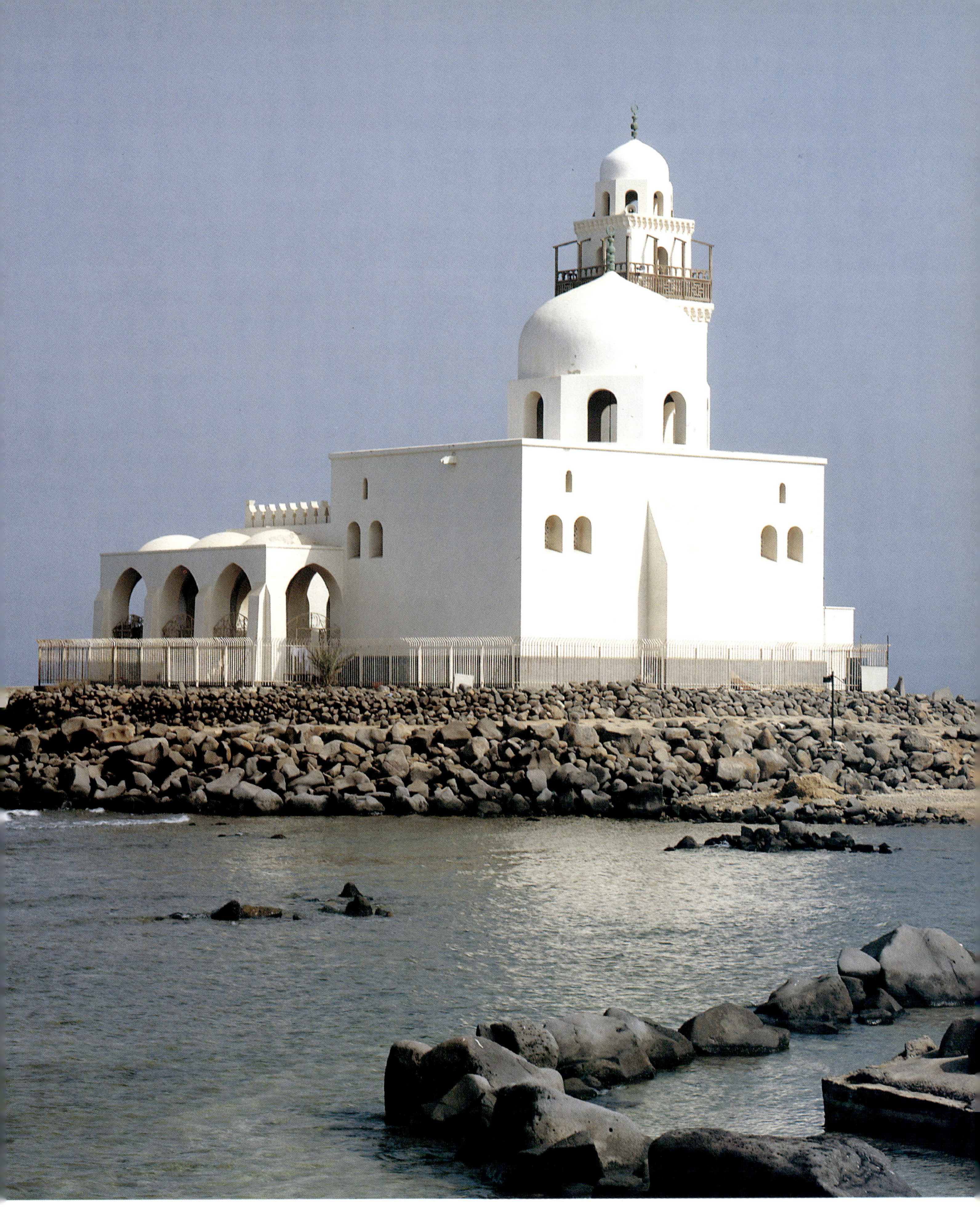

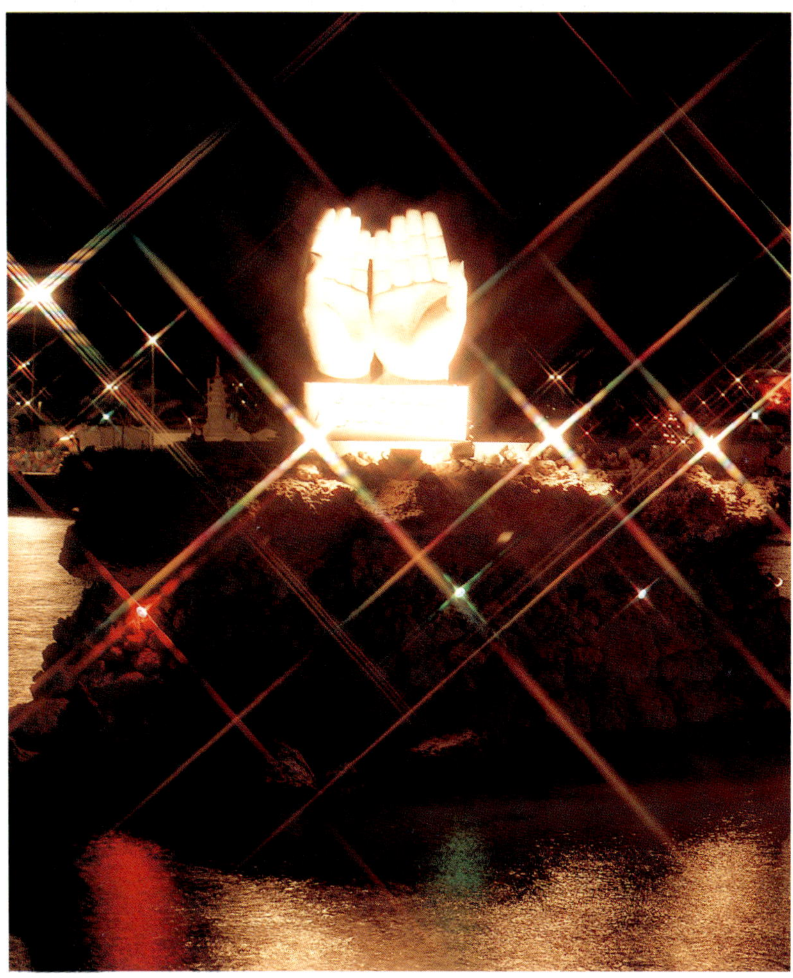

◀ **THE SUPPLICATION** (Al-Doaa) (20)
Mahmoud Banat
Marble

The inscription on the plinth reads: "O my Lord! Expand me my breast; Ease my task for me." (Holy Koran 20:25)

▼ **THE NAME OF ALLAH** (21)
Cook
Steel

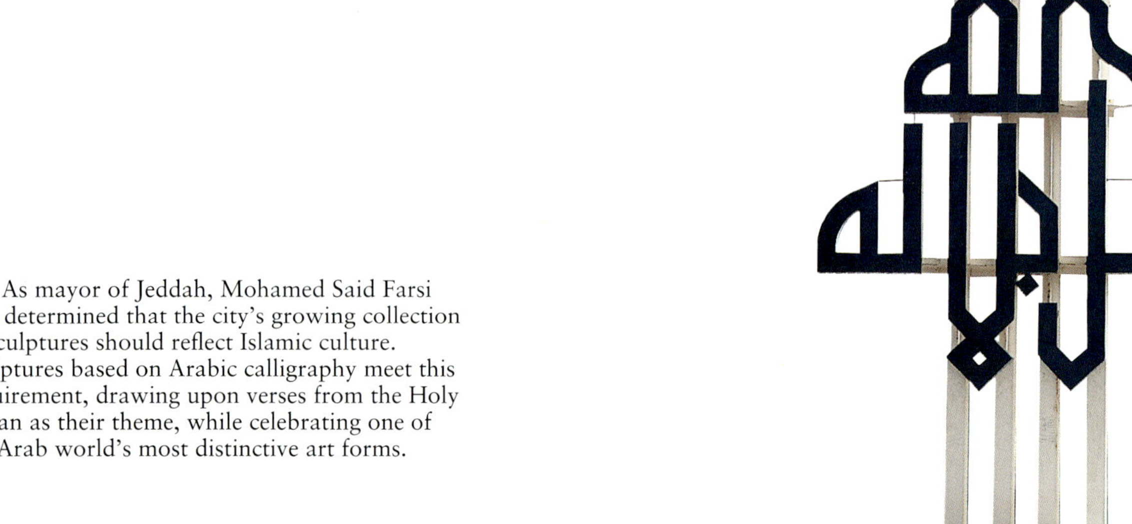

□ As mayor of Jeddah, Mohamed Said Farsi was determined that the city's growing collection of sculptures should reflect Islamic culture. Sculptures based on Arabic calligraphy meet this requirement, drawing upon verses from the Holy Koran as their theme, while celebrating one of the Arab world's most distinctive art forms.

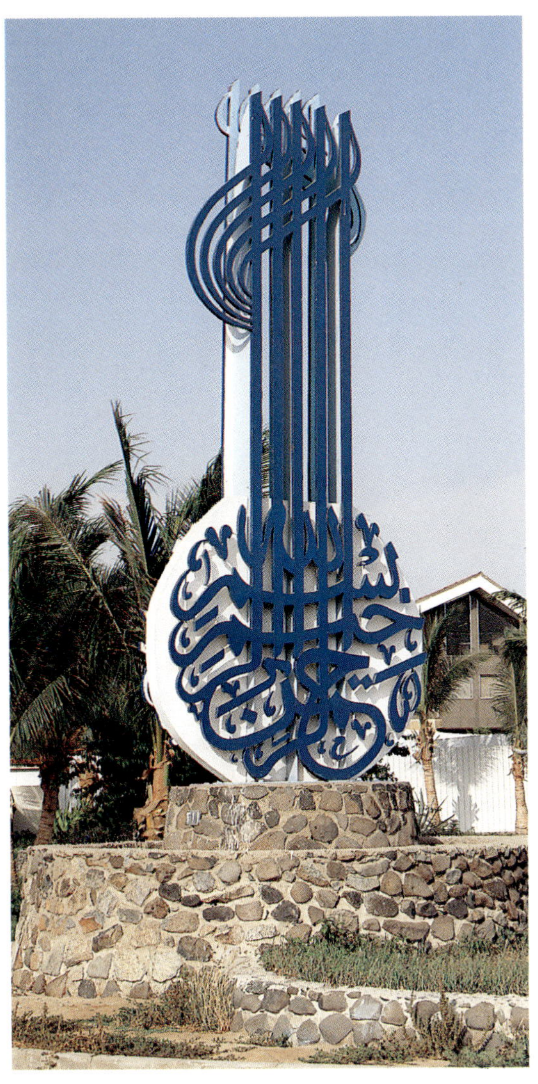

▲ **THE NAME OF ALLAH** (Kufic) (22)
Julio Lafuente
Bronze

▼ **VERSE IN WHITE** (23)
Julio Lafuente
Marble

"God is the light of the Heavens and the Earth."
(Holy Koran 24:35)

▼ **KORANIC VERSE** (24)
Julio Lafuente
Bronze

"Surely thou art upon a mighty morality."
(Holy Koran 68:4)

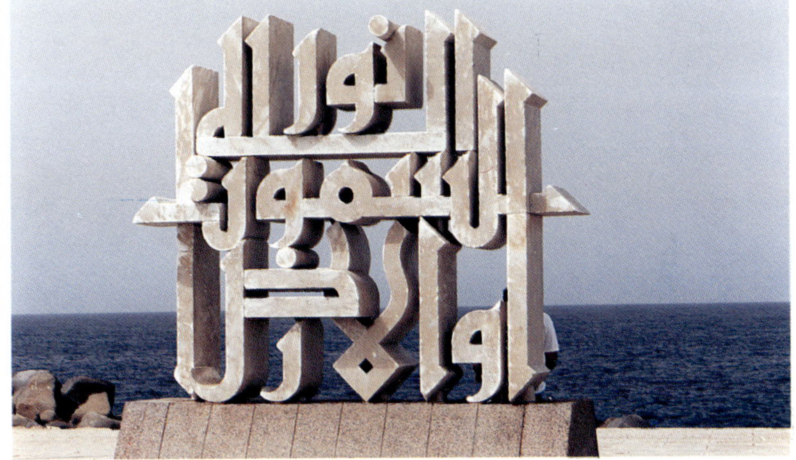

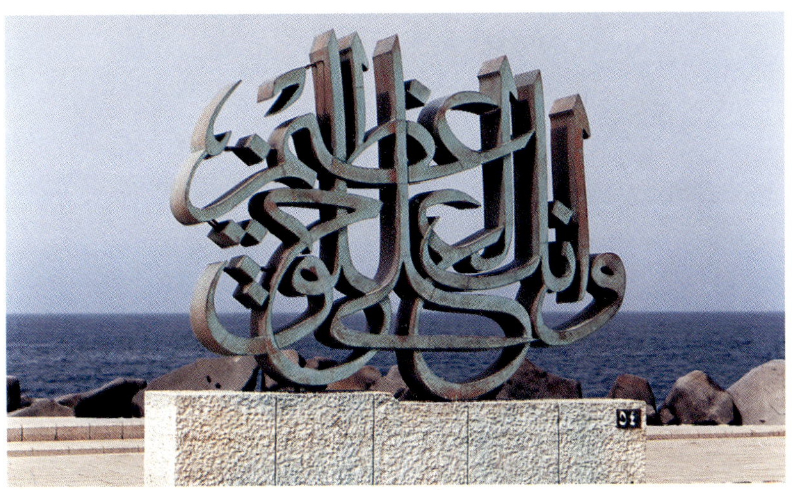

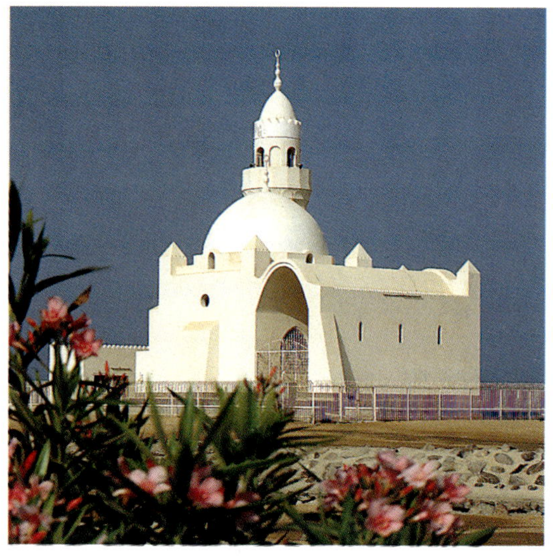

▲► **EL-WAKIL MOSQUE** (26)
(Municipality Mosque)
Abdel Wahed El-Wakil Architect

Winner of the Aga Khan Award for Islamic Architecture in 1989, this mosque was commended for "its effort to compose formal elements in ways that bespeak the present and at the same time reflect the luminous past of Islamic societies".

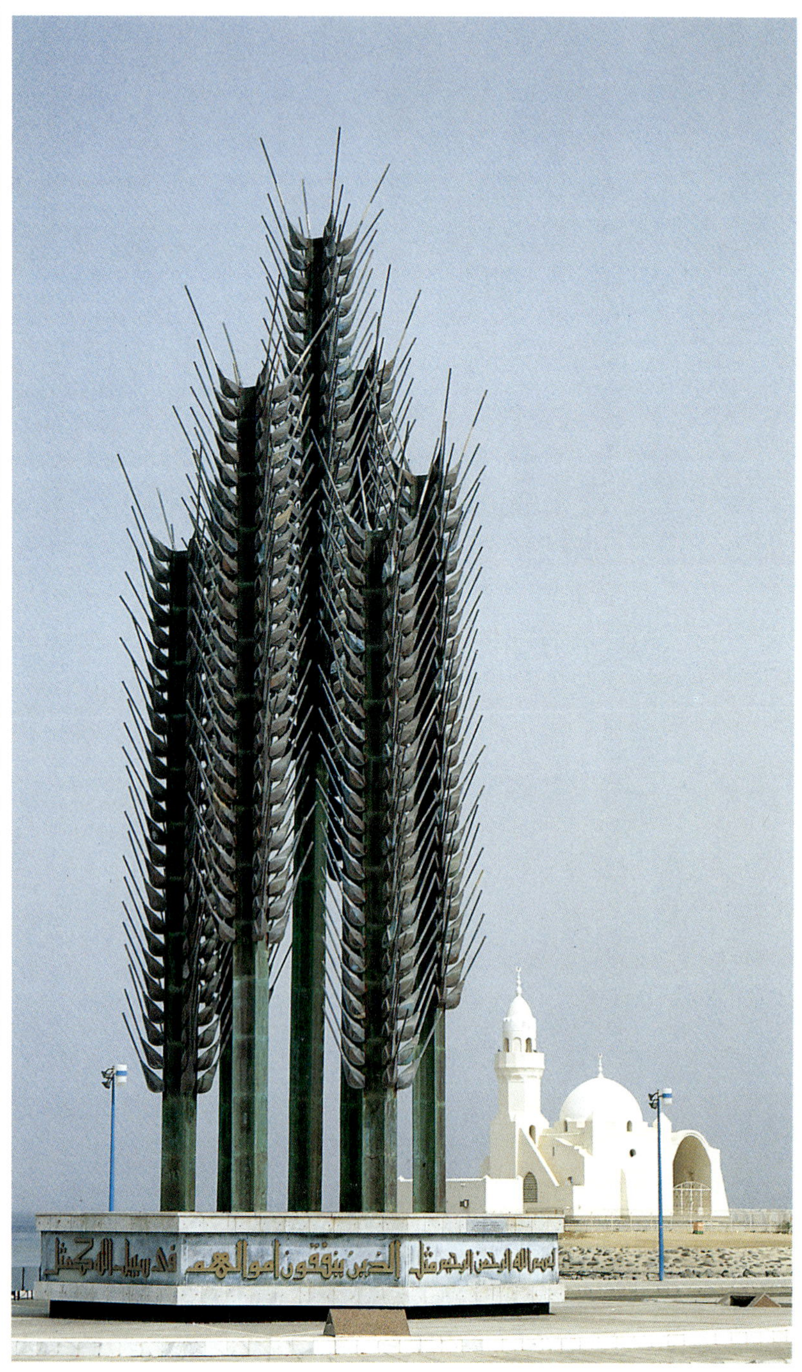

◄ **STALKS OF WHEAT** (Al-Sanabel) (25)
Salah Abdulkarim
Steel and bronze

This group is one of many works inspired by verses from the Koran.
"The likeness of those who expend their wealth in the way of God is as the likeness of a new grain of corn which sprouts seven ears."
(Holy Koran 2:261)

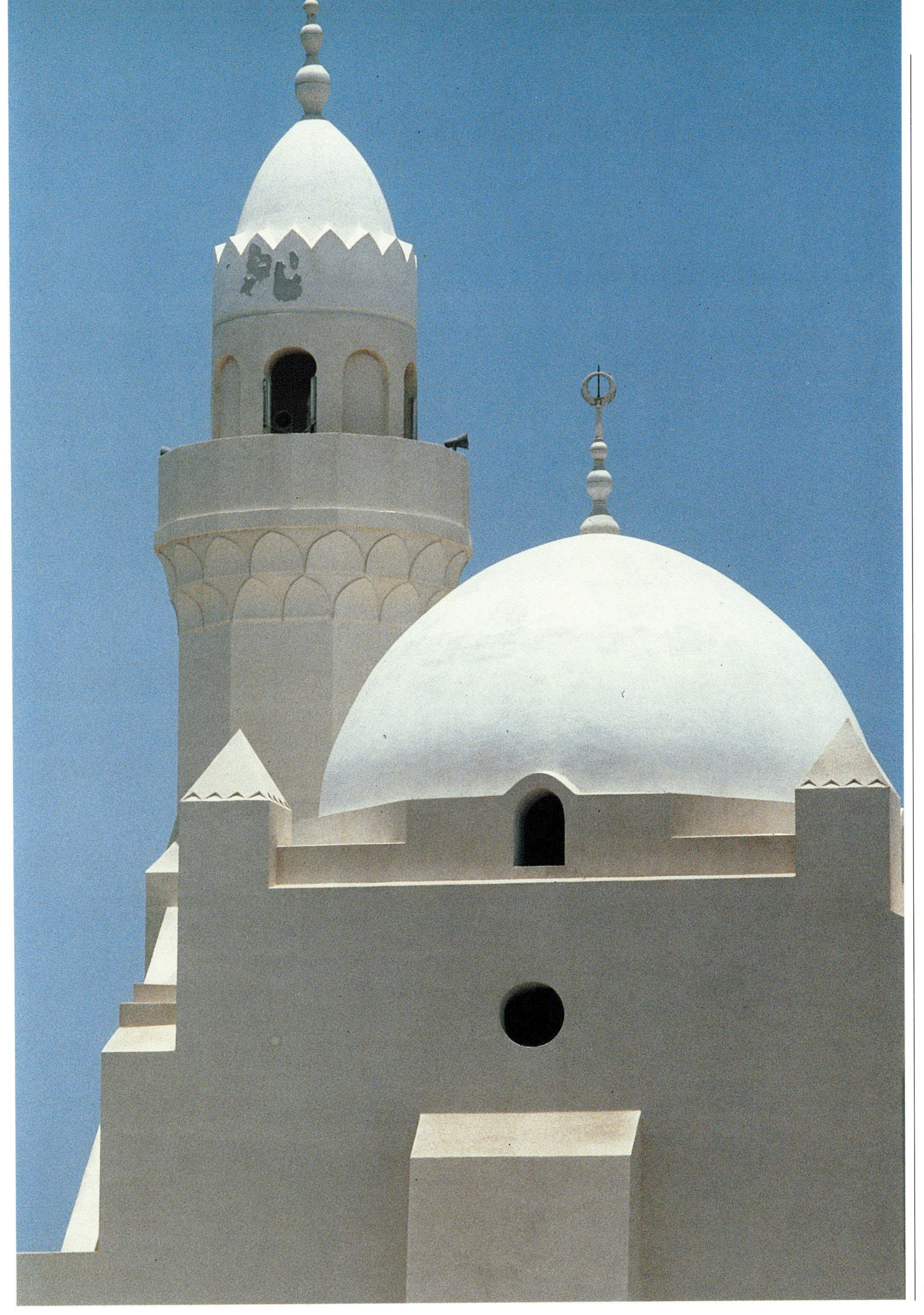

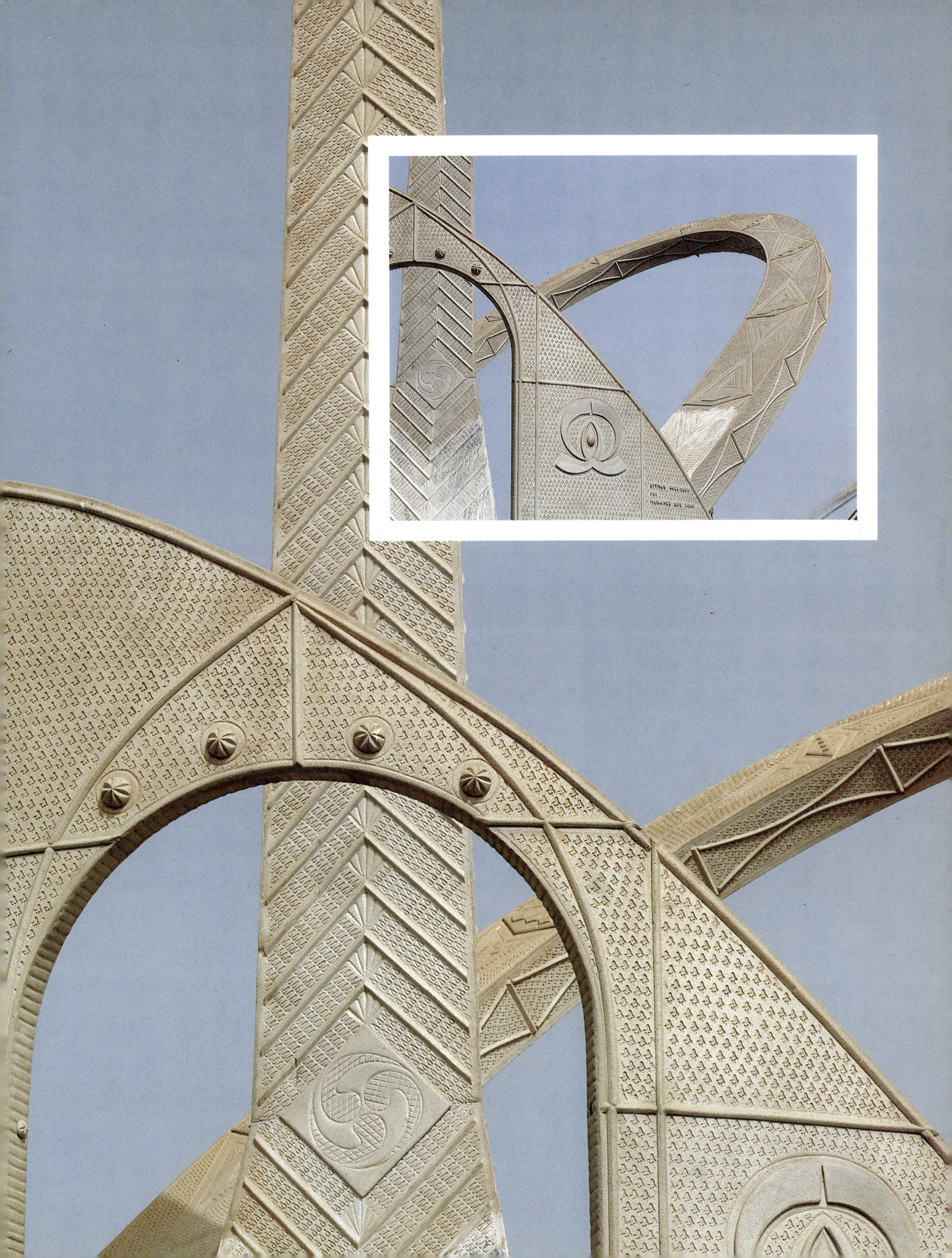

▶ **FISHERMAN'S NET** (27)
Mustafa Senbel
Scrap Iron

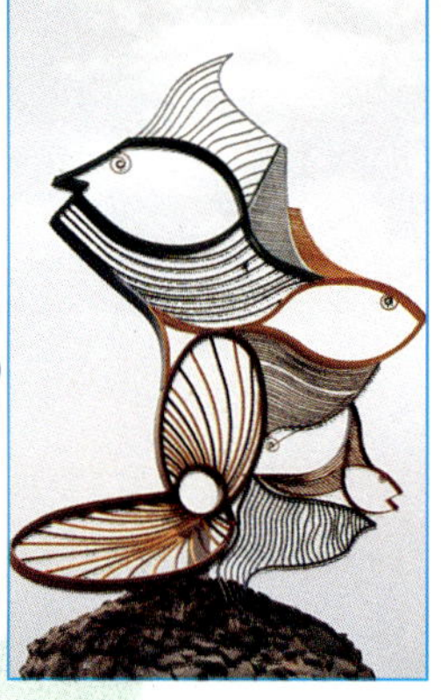

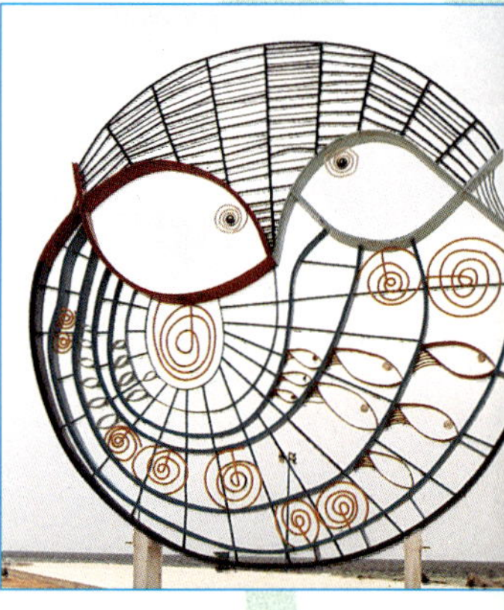

▲ **DIALOGUE** (28)
Mustafa Senbel
Scrap Iron

▼ **SCHOOL OF DOLPHINS** (29)
Artist Unknown
Scrap Iron

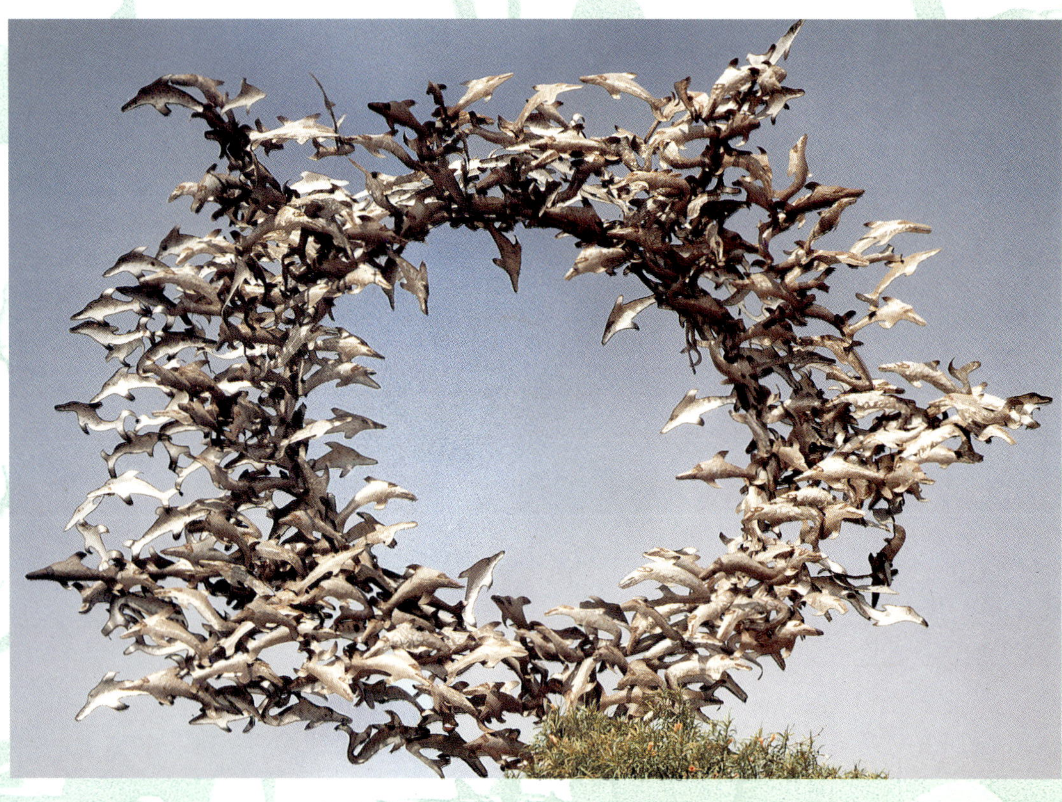

◀ **AT SEA** (30)
Artist Unknown
Concrete

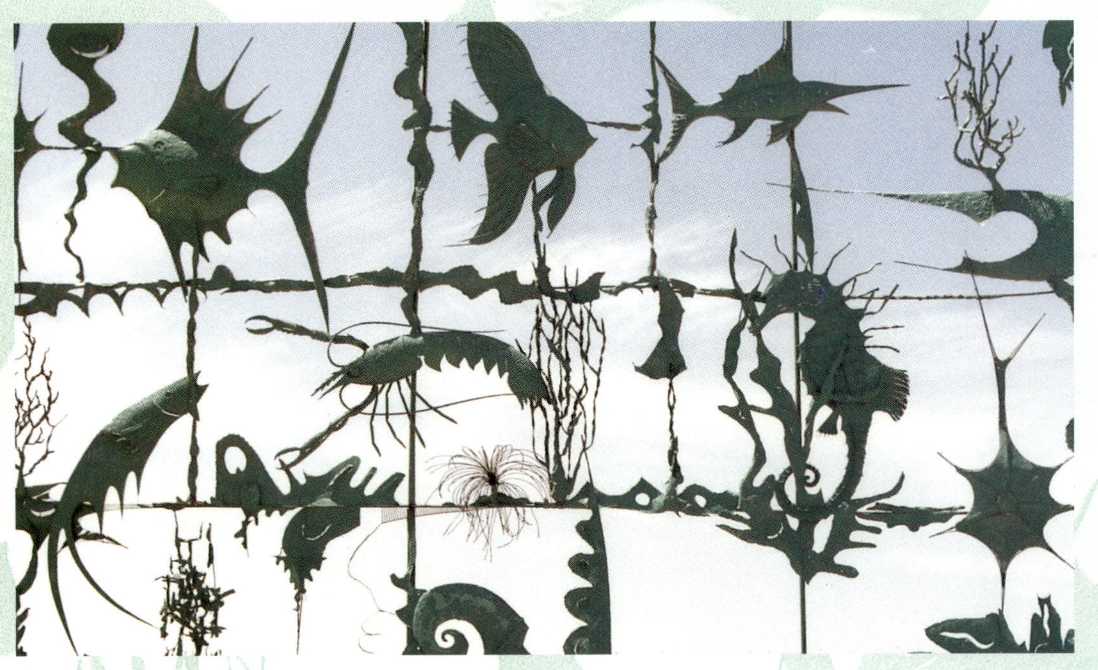

▲ **SEA HARVEST TRELLIS** (31)
Sylvestre Giovanni
Steel

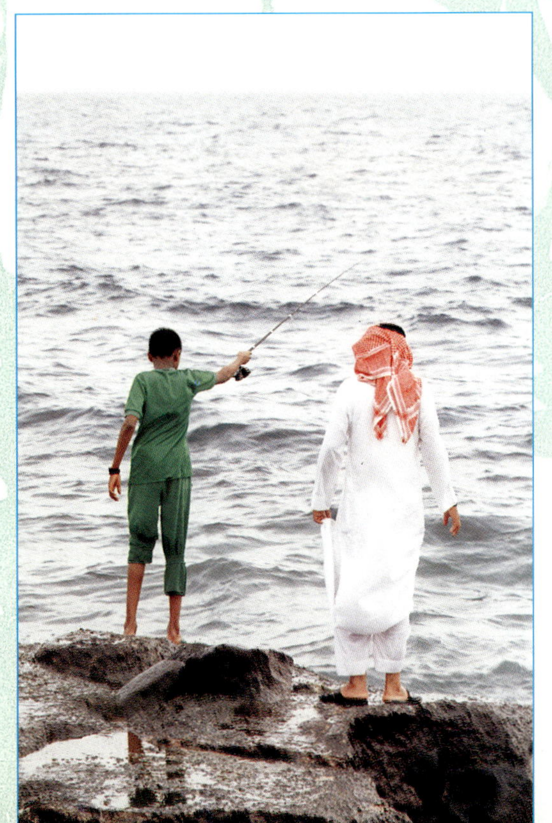

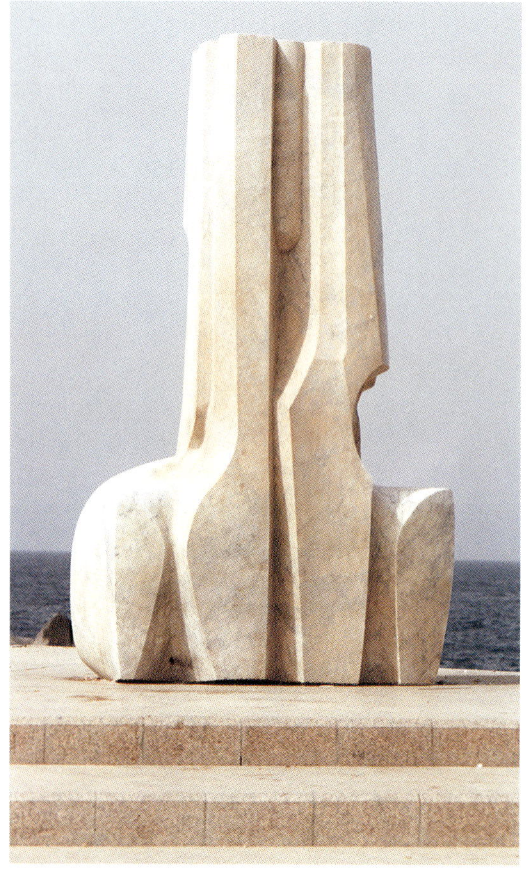

▲ ABSTRACT I (32)

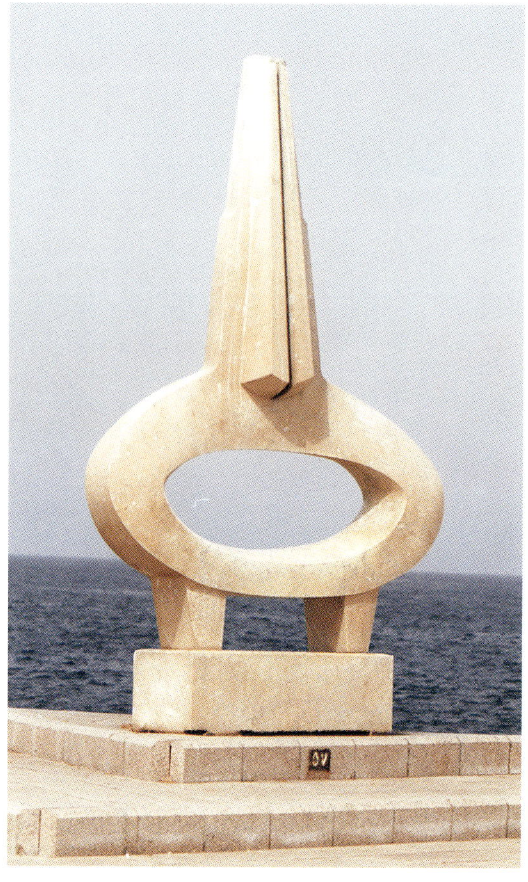

▲ SUBLIMITY (33)

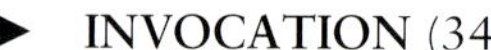

► INVOCATION (34)

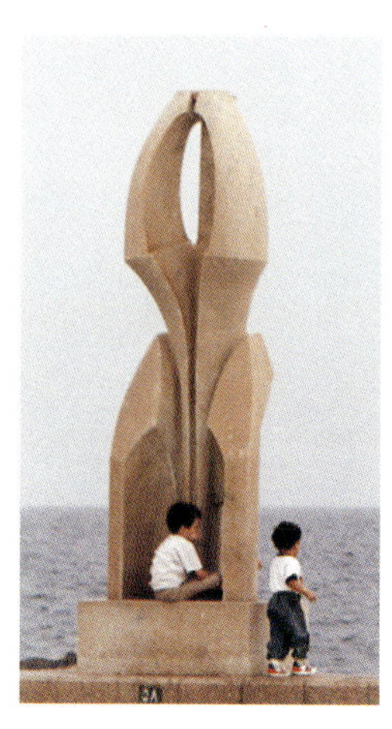

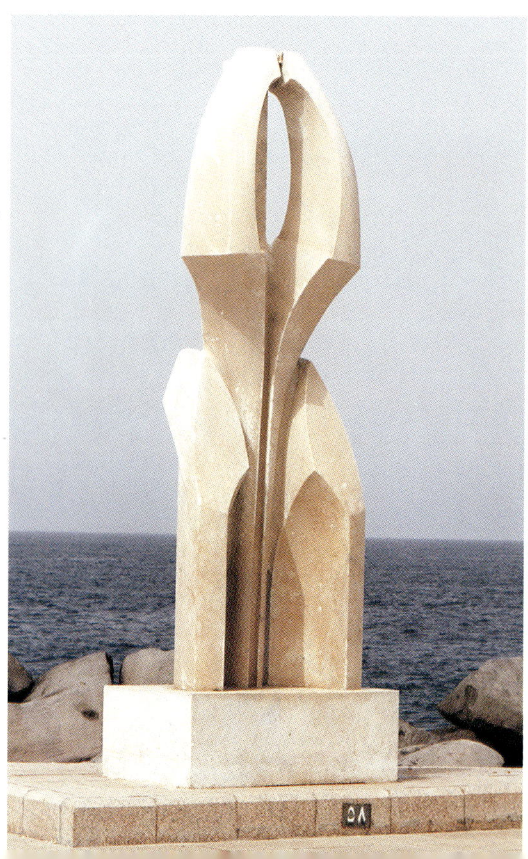

□ **VARIOUS ABSTRACTS**
A group of Belgian artists
Marble

These monuments were commissioned as a result of Mohamed Said Farsi's visit to the Belgian town of Ghent in 1982. This led to the exhibition *Jeddah, Yesterday and Today* staged in Brussels in 1984 and following which a group of Belgian experts visited Jeddah to help with restoration work.

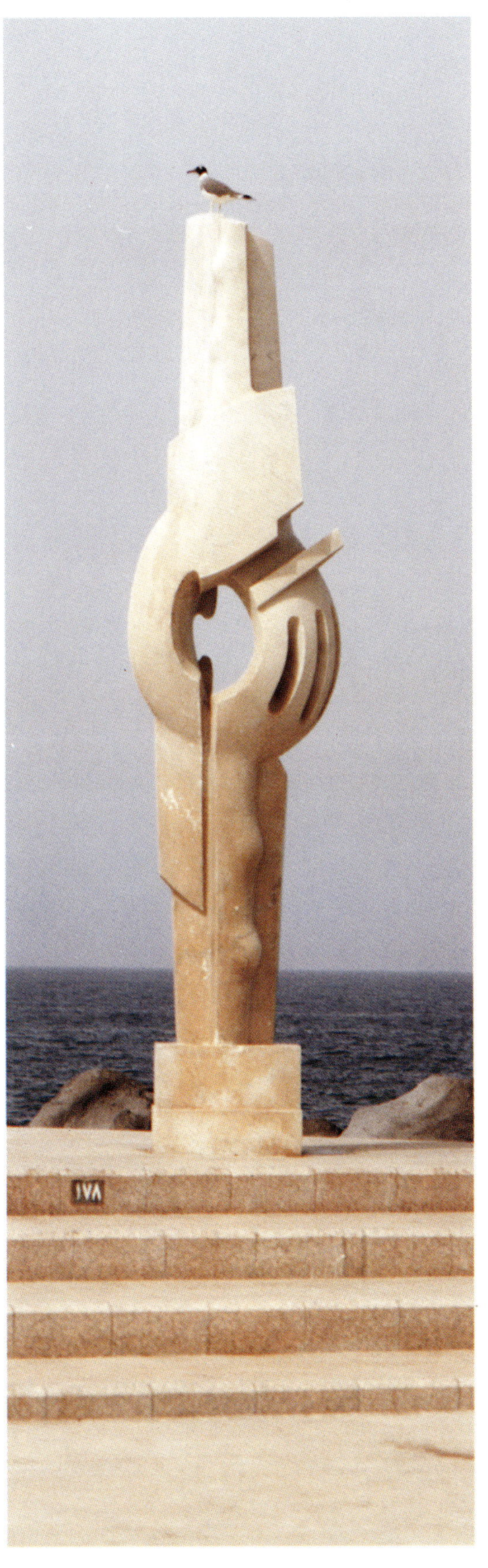

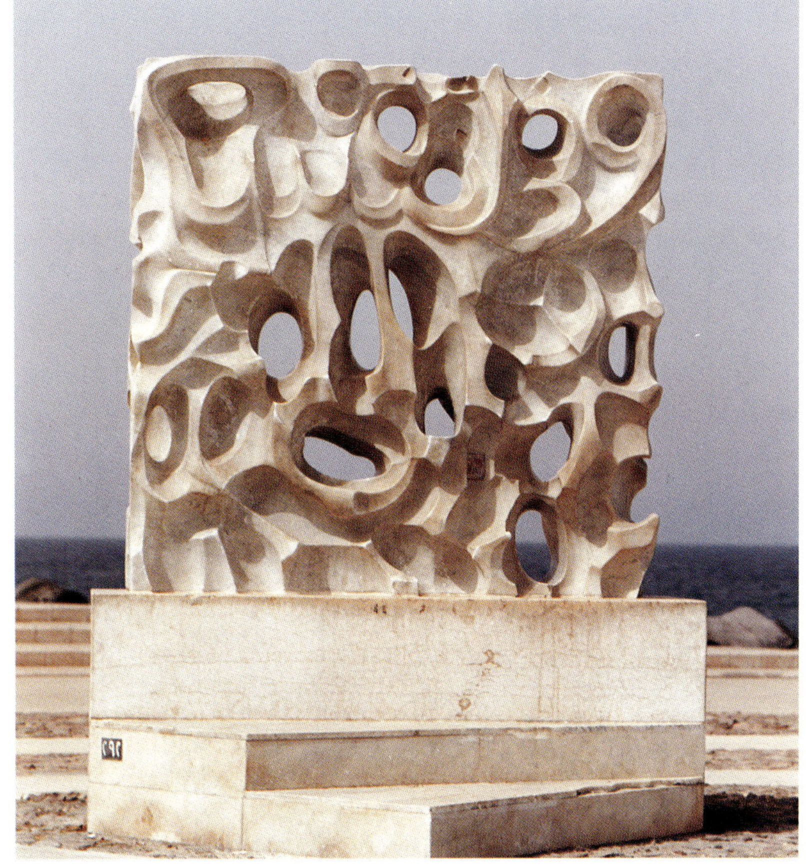

▲ CROSS-SECTION OF THE HEART (36)
Collaboration: **Aref el Rayess and a Belgian artist**
Marble

Erected after Mohamed Said Farsi had undergone heart surgery, this monument was a collaboration between the Lebanese el Rayess and a Belgian artist who was also a doctor of medicine. The Arabic lettering, which was later highlighted with paint, is a quotation from the Koran referring to the mysteries of the inner being. *"In the earth are signs for those having sure faith; and in your selves; What, do you not see?"* (Holy Koran 51:21)

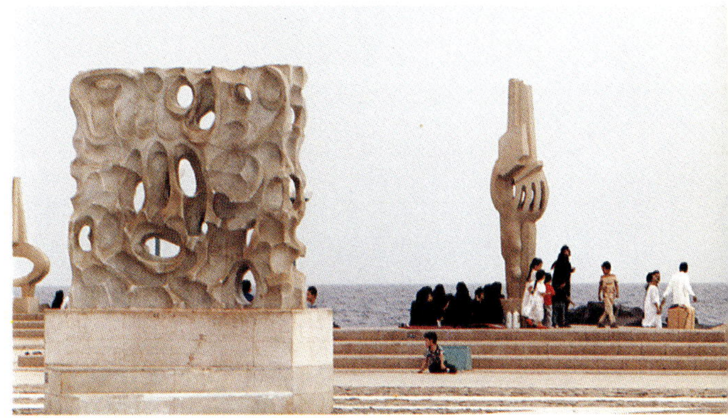

◄ **ABSTRACT II** (35)

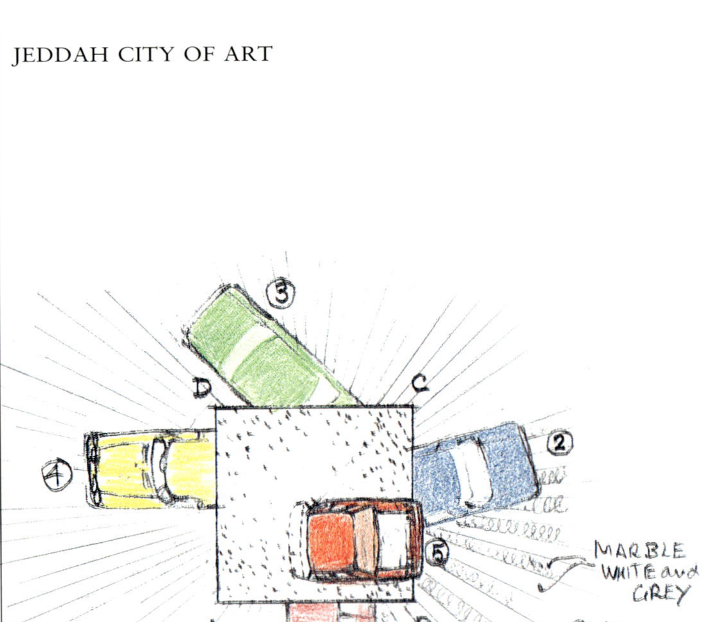

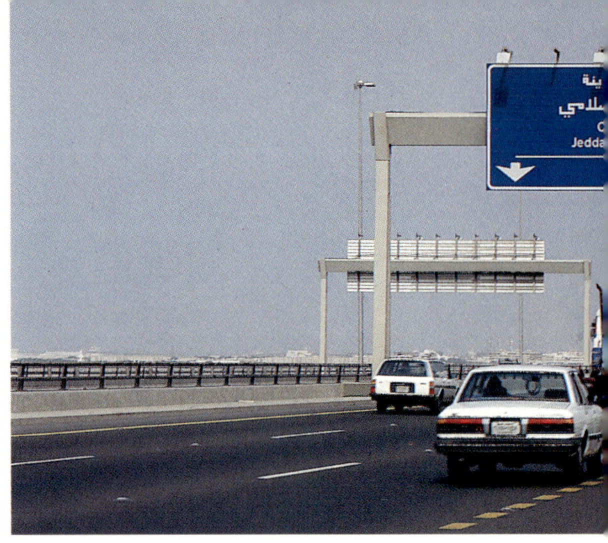

□ Jeddah's road network expanded enormously during the seventies and eighties – a twentyfold expansion over two decades. By 1990 there were more than 600,000 vehicles in the city. The siting of distinctive monuments at intersections helps residents and visitors alike to find their way around the city.

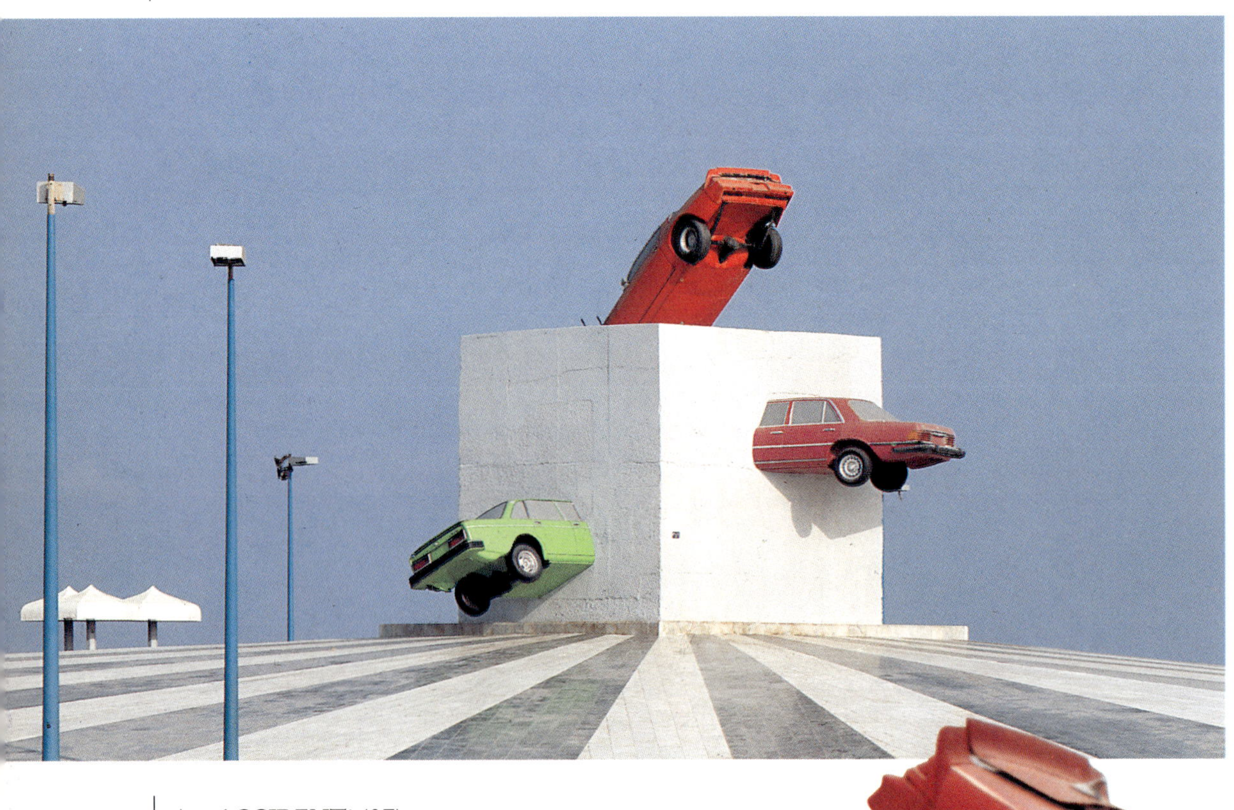

▲ ACCIDENT! (37)
Julio Lafuente
Cars in reinforced concrete

However whimsical the protest against the overexuberance of some of Jeddah's drivers, Julio Lafuente's message is uncompromisingly clear.

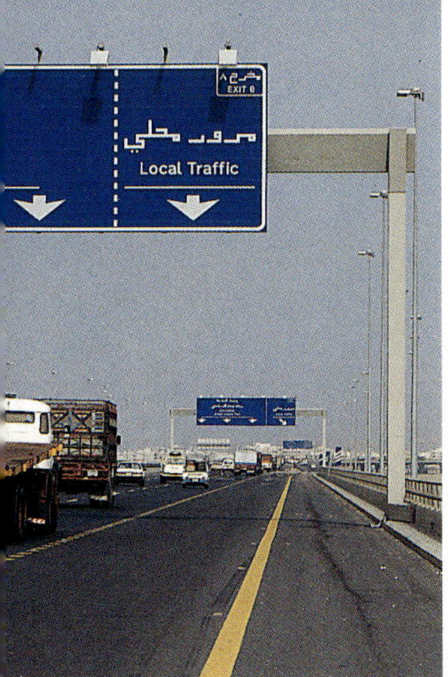

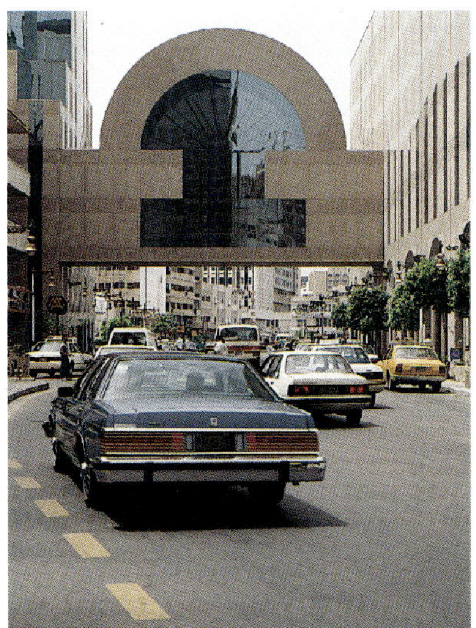

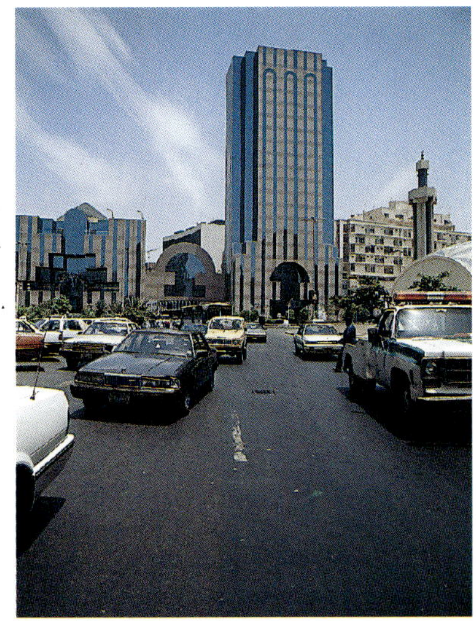

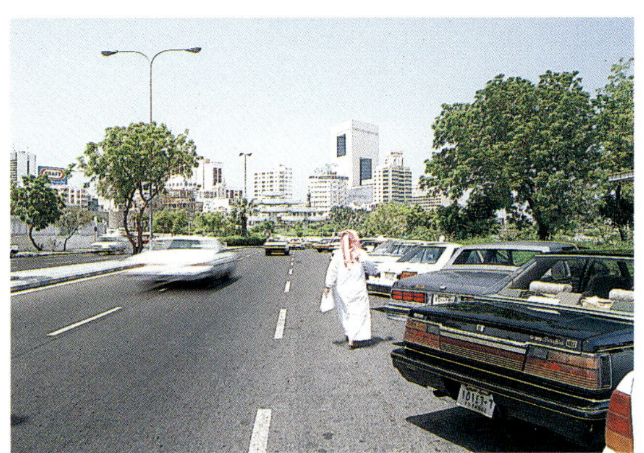

▼ **THE NEW WAVE OF CARS** (38)
Kamal Qummusani

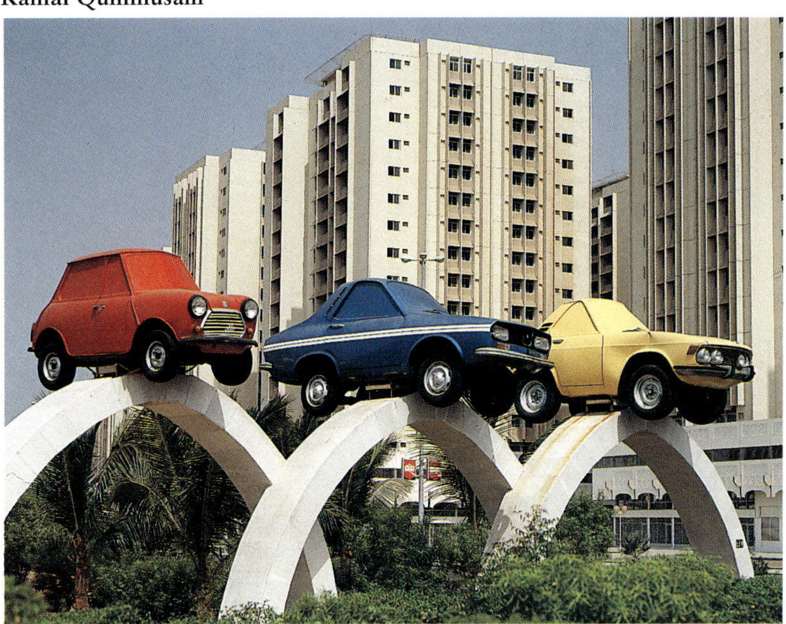

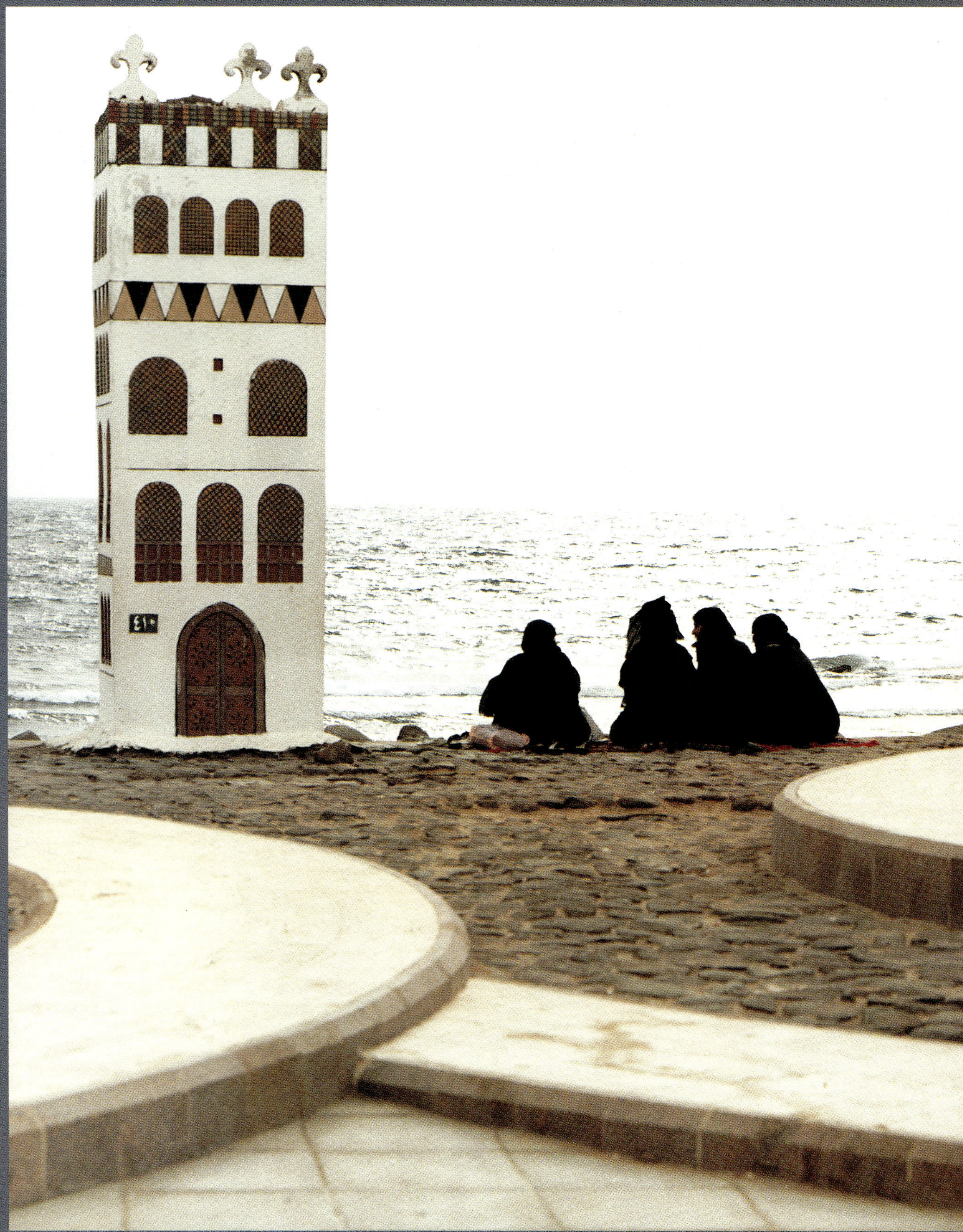
٤١٠

□ **TRADITIONAL ARABIAN ARCHITECTURE**
Darwish Salamah
Reinforced concrete

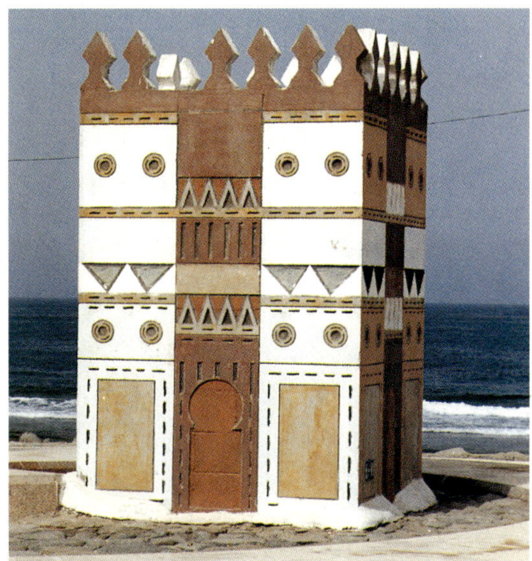

This miniature village is a popular meeting place for Jeddah families: the model buildings depict traditional forms of architecture from various parts of the kingdom. The models incorporate features such as the intricate *rawashin* and decorative roof crenellations.

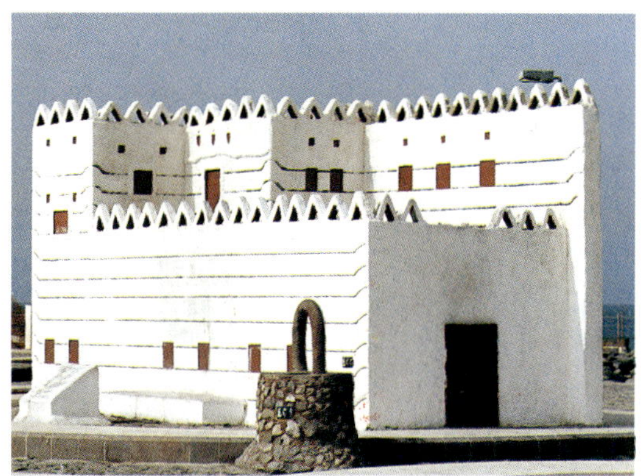

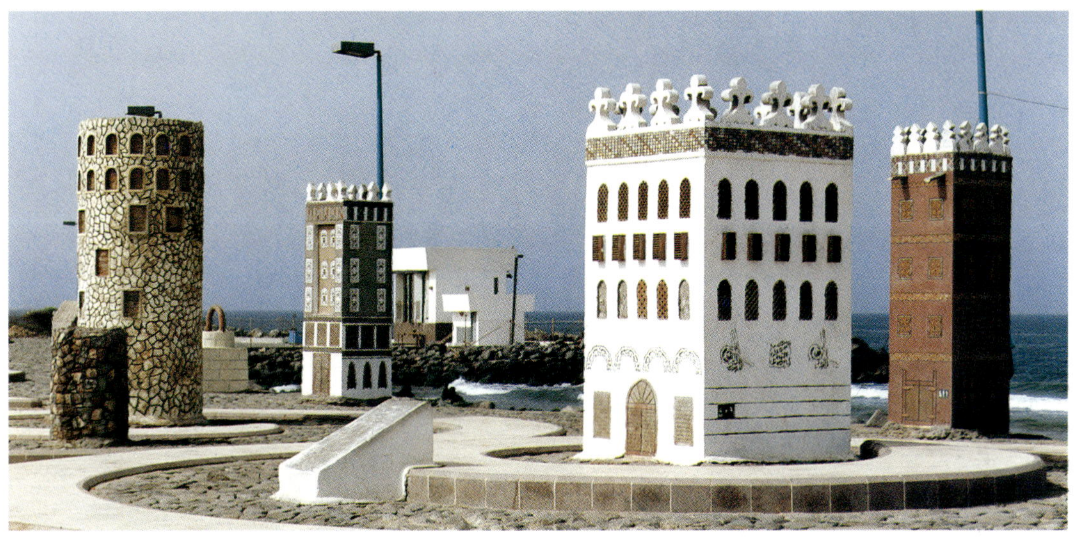

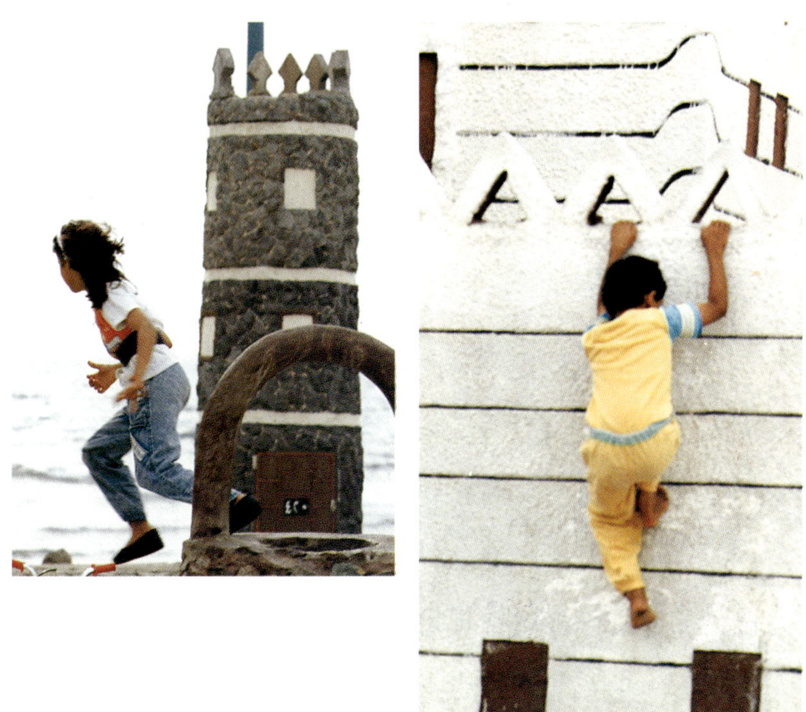

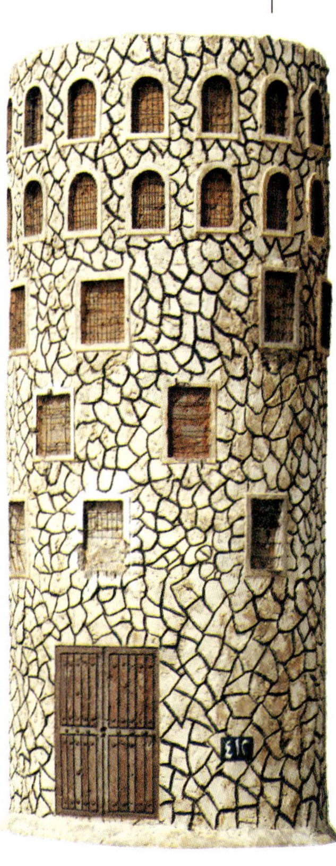

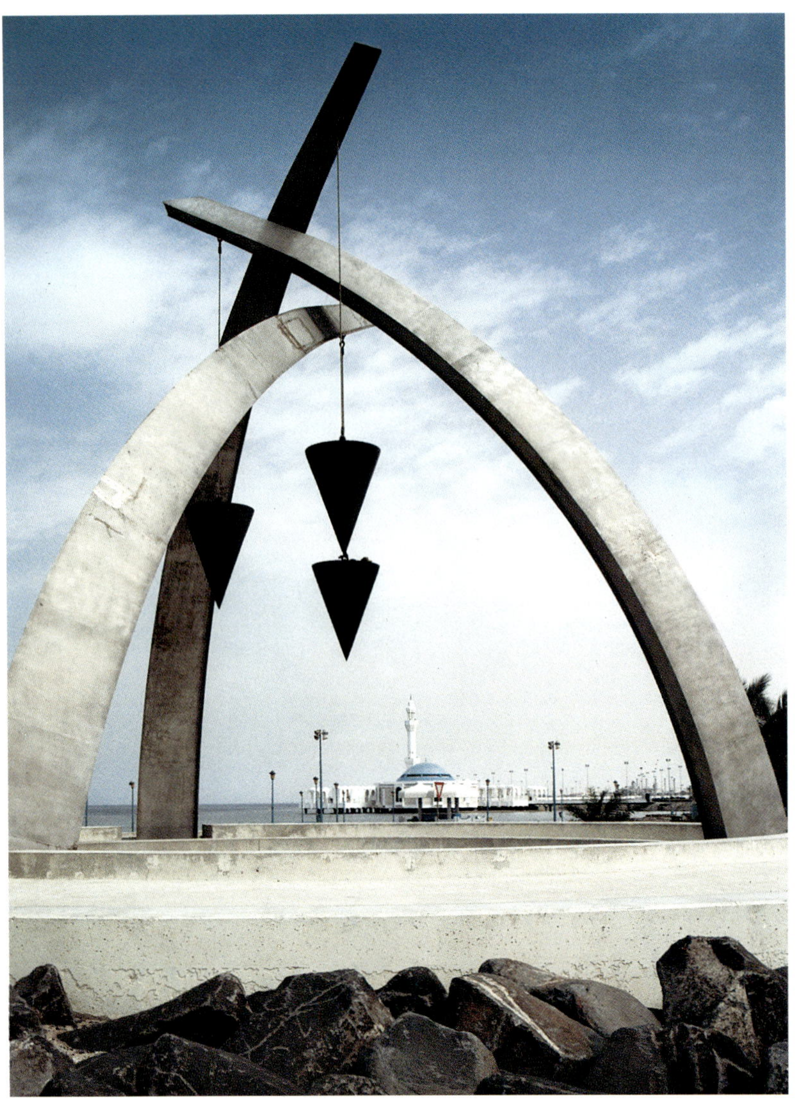

► **MOON AND BOW** (The Sundial) (42)
Ottmar Hollmann
Cast Alloy

This sculpture functions as a huge sundial in which the hours are marked by the shadow of the central spike moving across the encircling bows.

◄ **BUILDER'S PLUMBLINE**
(Shaghoul Al-Binaa) (40)
Mustafa Senbel
Steel

One of many sculptures with a scientific theme, the *Plumbline* is a monument to the achievements of the master builders of the ancient world.

▼ **CHIMNEY FORM** (41)
Mustafa Senbel

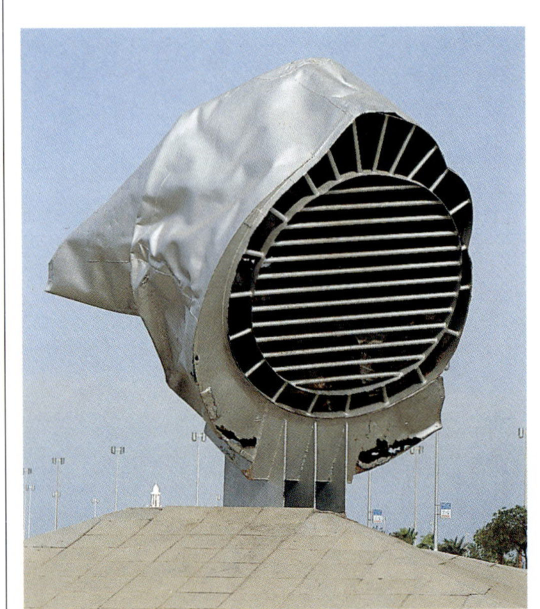

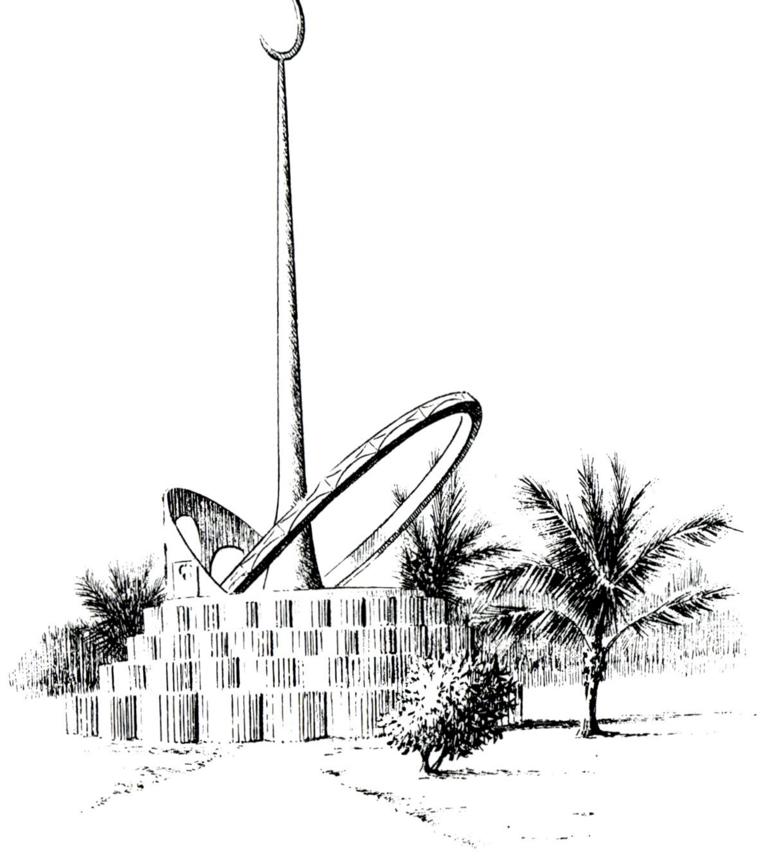

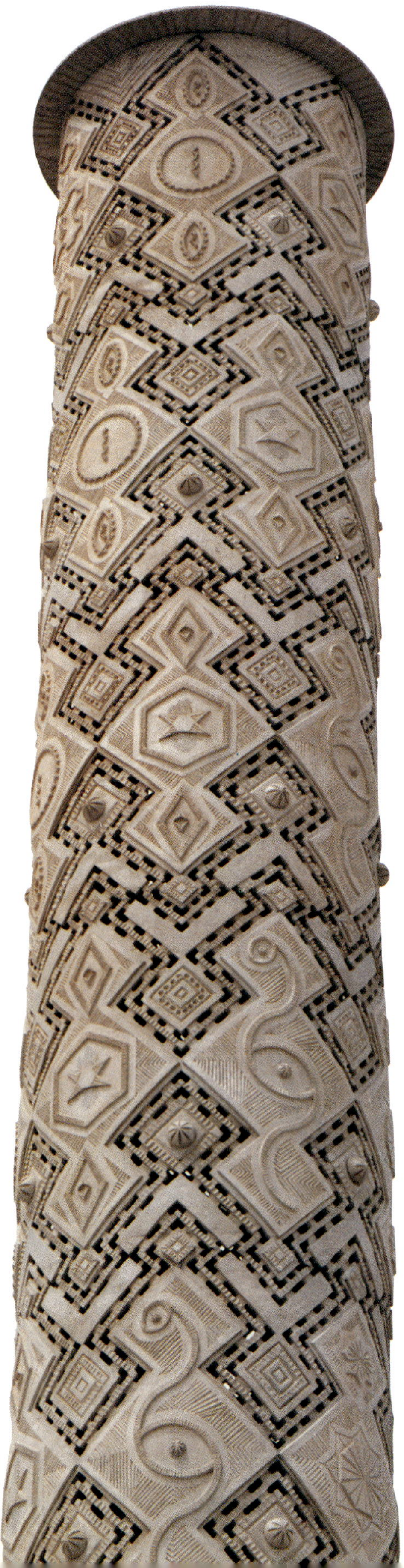

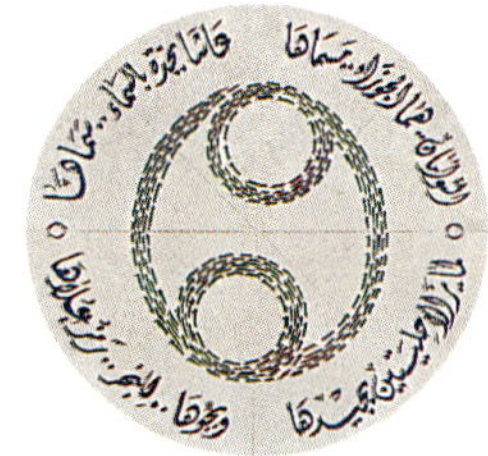

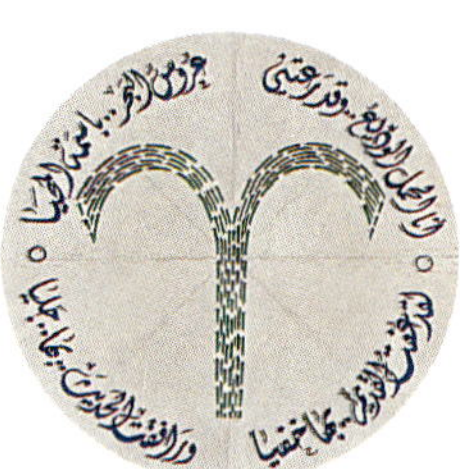

□ Hollmann's works in Jeddah are given their strong texture by the wealth of surface detail and motifs. The motifs are drawn from both Western and Oriental traditions.

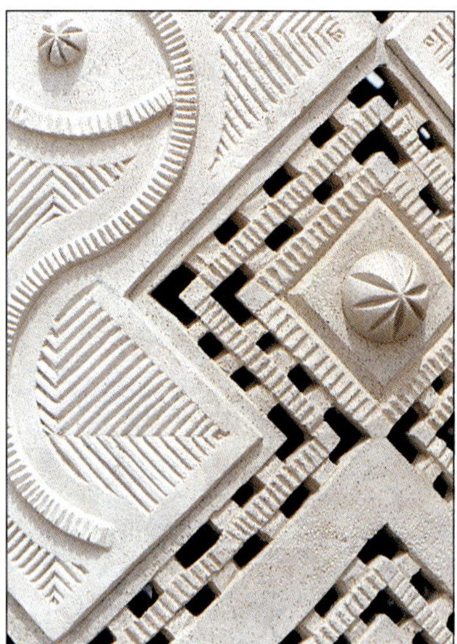

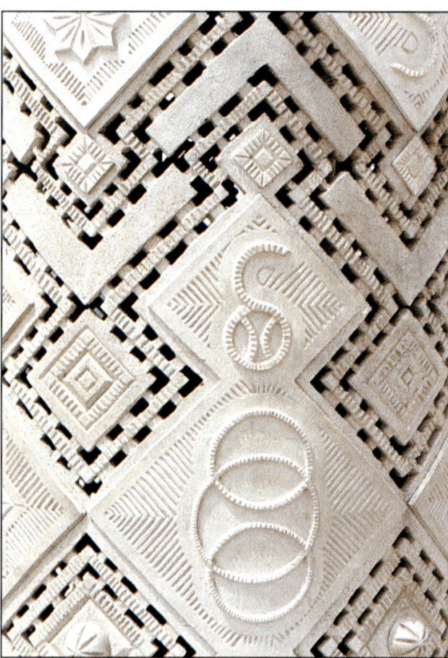

◄ **LARGE PILLAR** (43)
Ottmar Hollmann
Cast Alloy

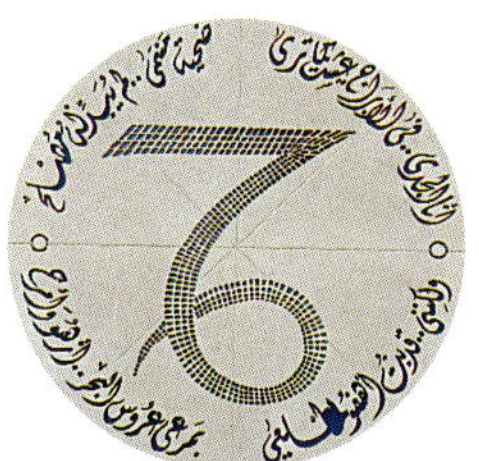
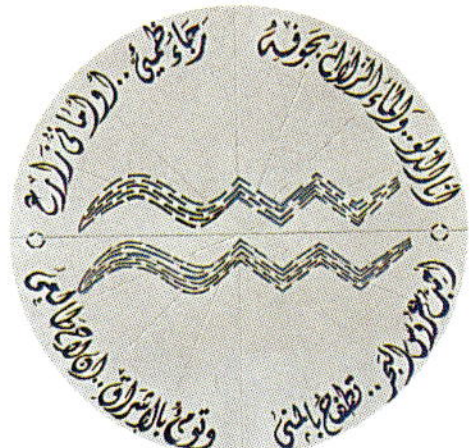
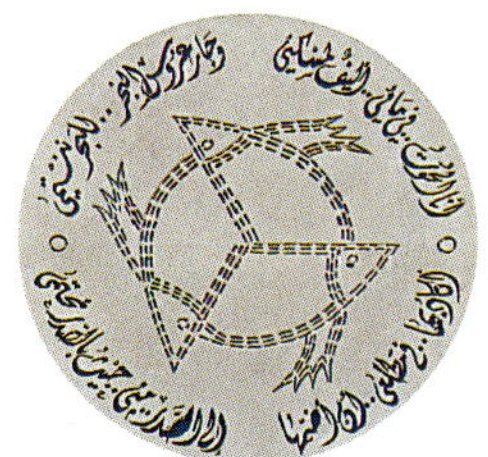
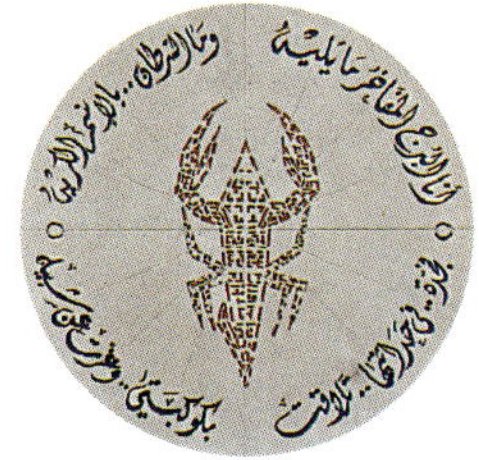
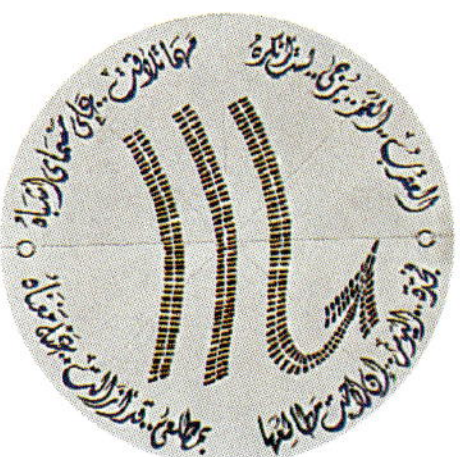

▲ THE SIGNS OF THE ZODIAC (44)
Ottmar Hollmann
Cast Alloy

This series of twelve discs features the signs of the zodiac and poetry by the Saudi poet Kindil.

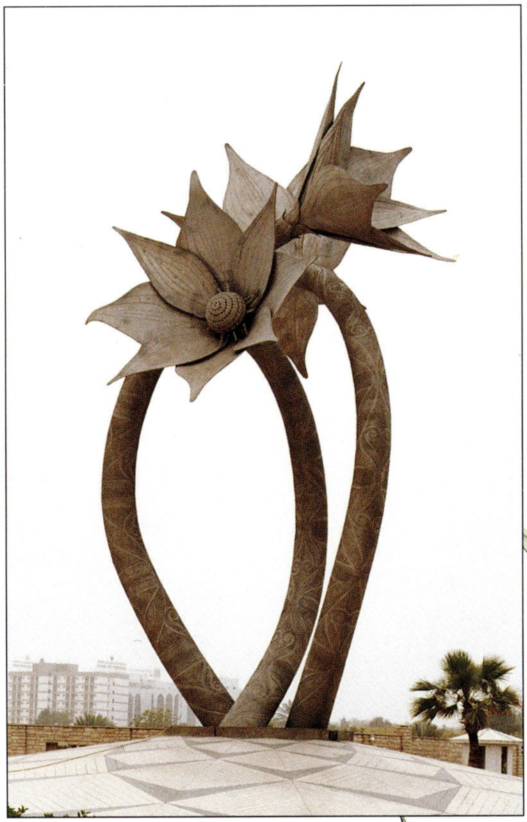

► THREE FLOWERS (45)
Ottmar Hollmann
Cast Alloy

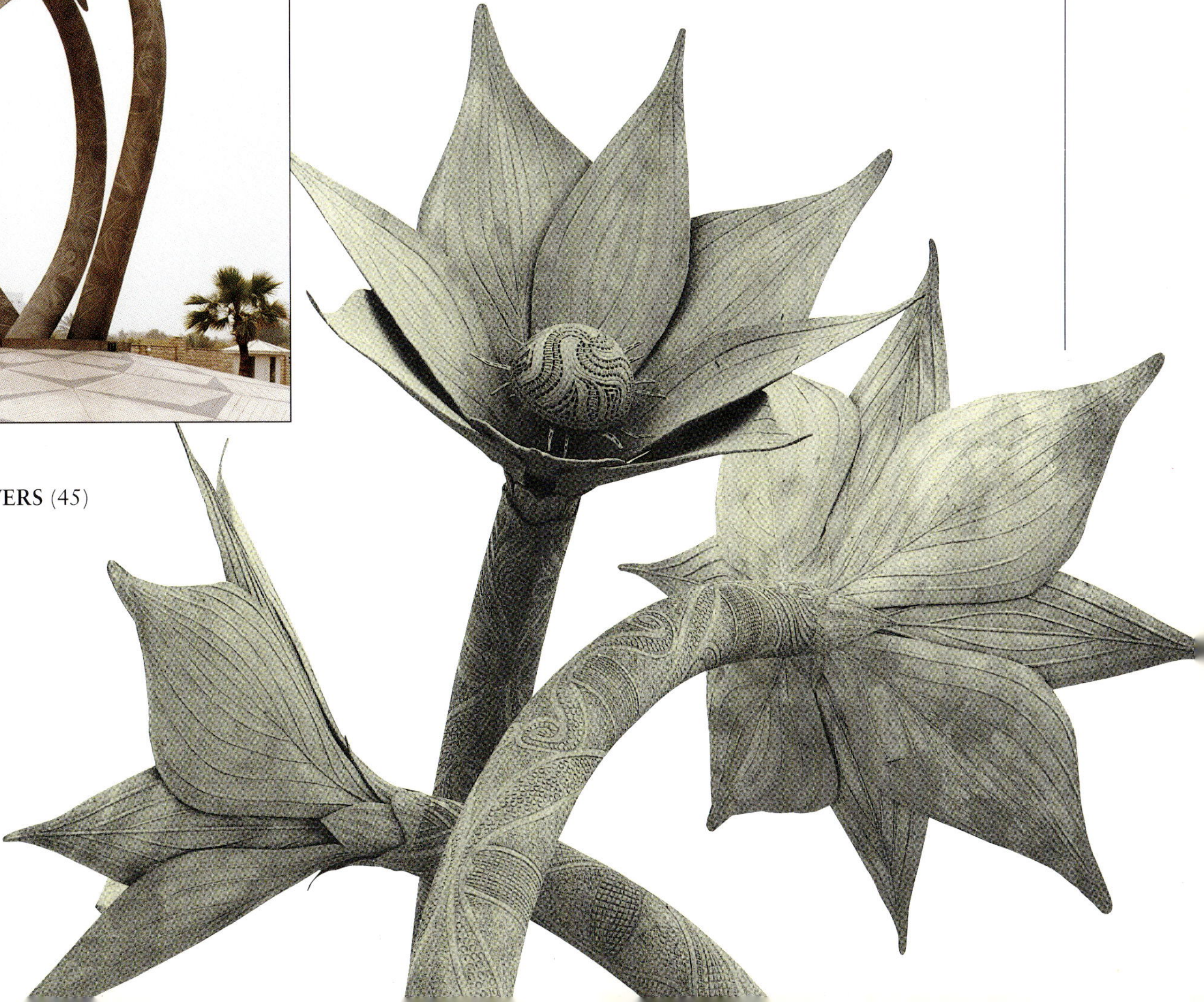

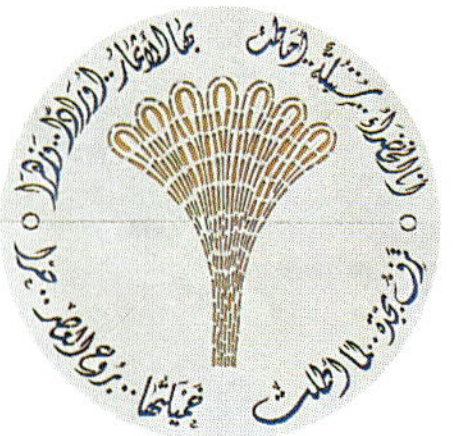

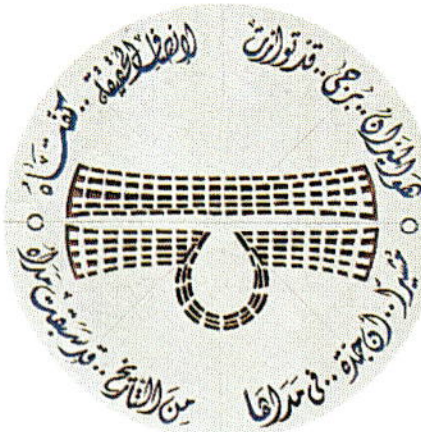

► **FIVE FAN PALMS** (46)
Ottmar Hollmann
Cast Alloy

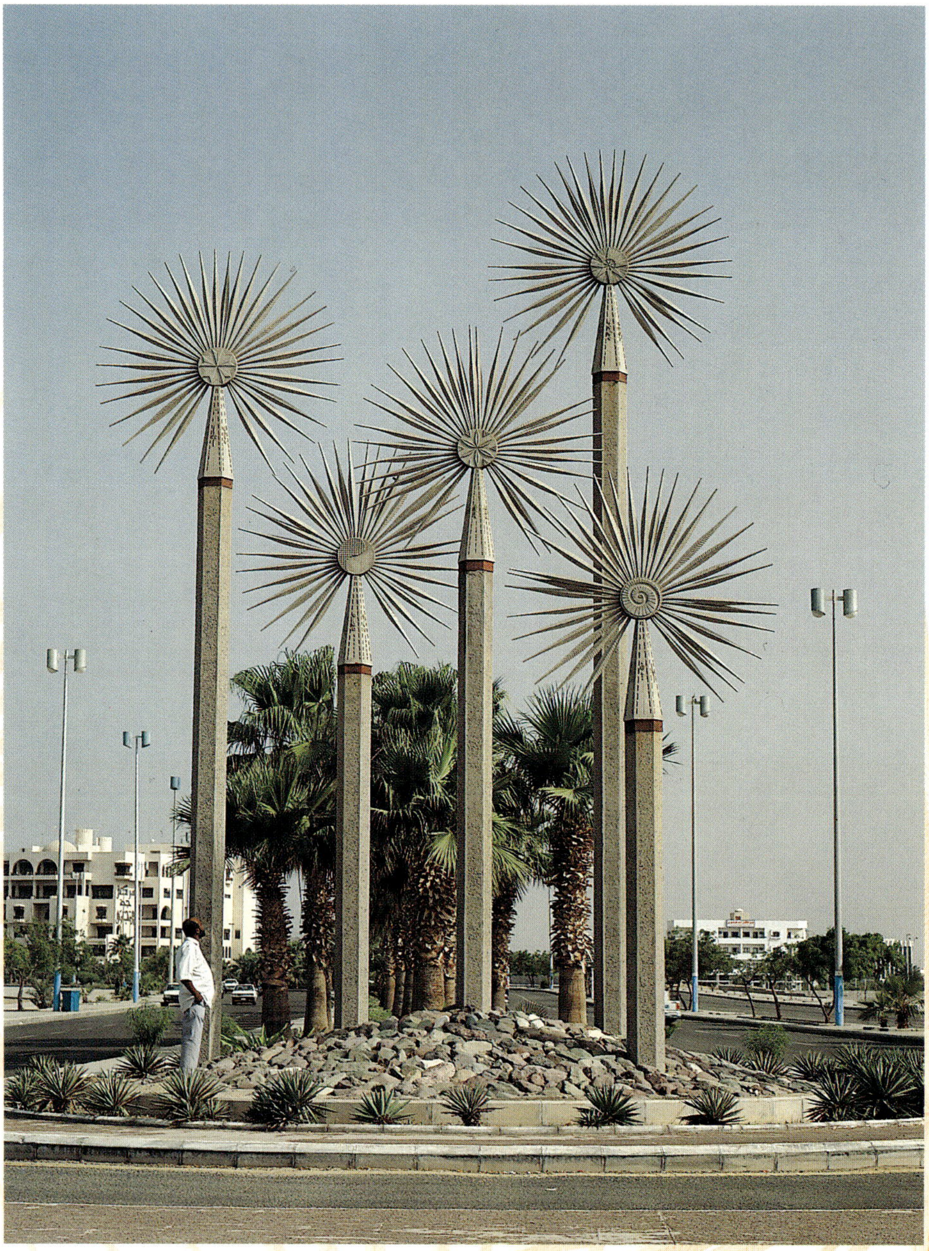

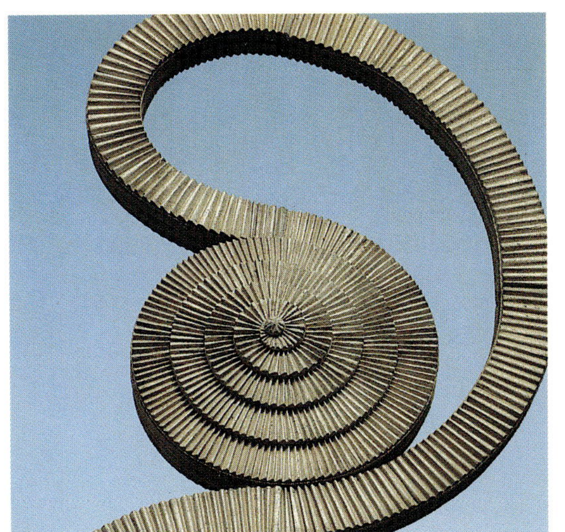

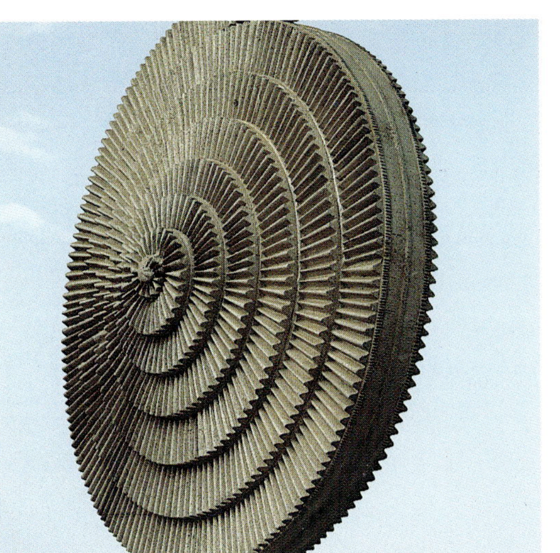

► **TWO POLES** (47)
Ottmar Hollmann
Cast Alloy

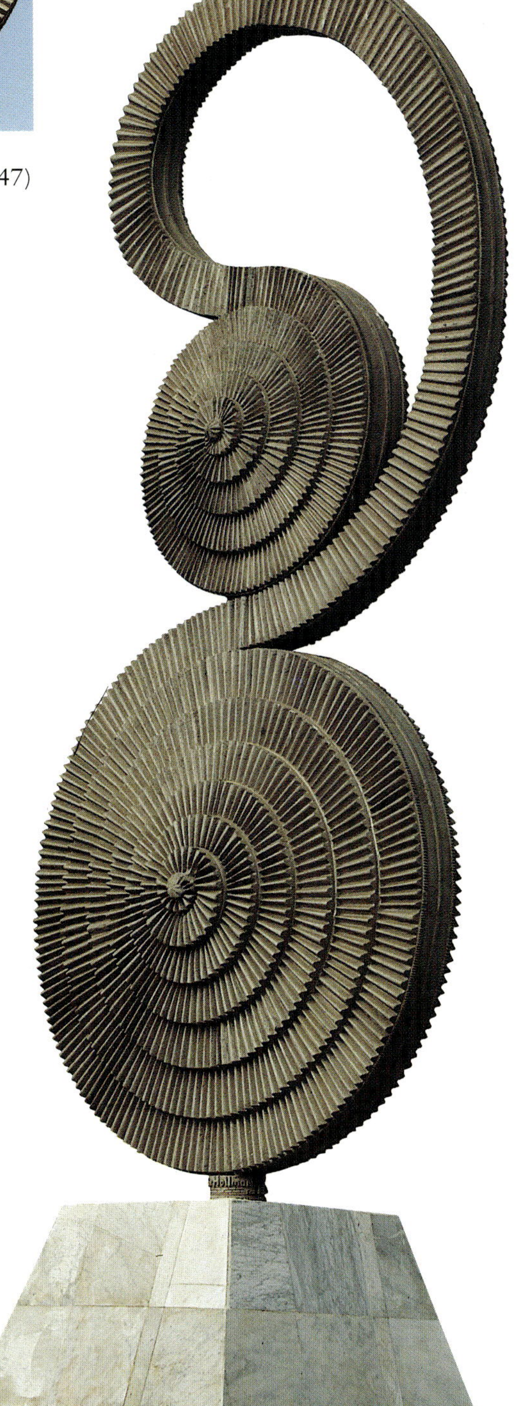

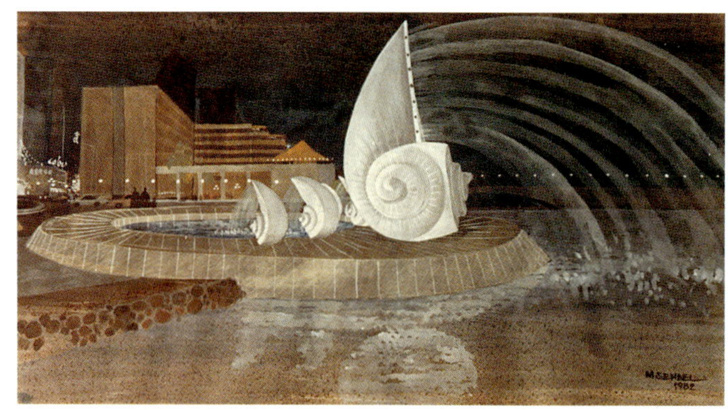

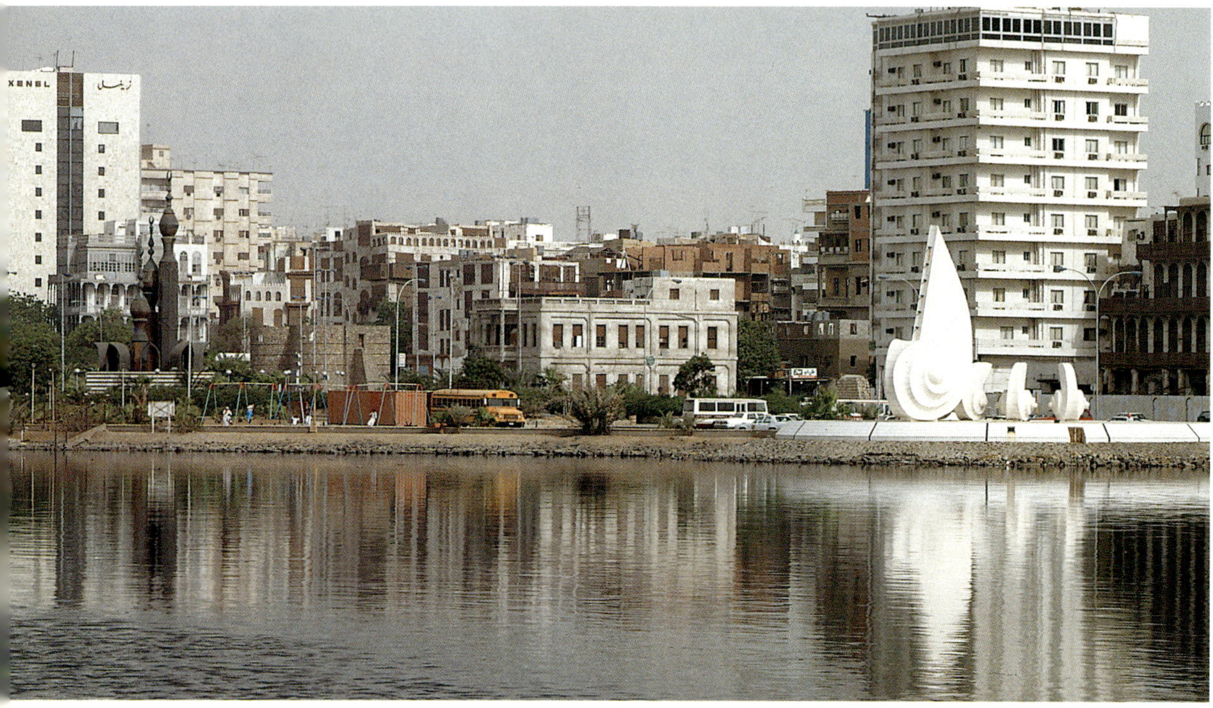

▲ THE FOUNTAIN OF SHELLS (48)
Mustafa Senbel
Marble

A distinctive feature of this fountain is that its jets of water, rather than tumbling over its own sculpture or into its own basin, loop out in elegant parabolae into the lagoon itself.

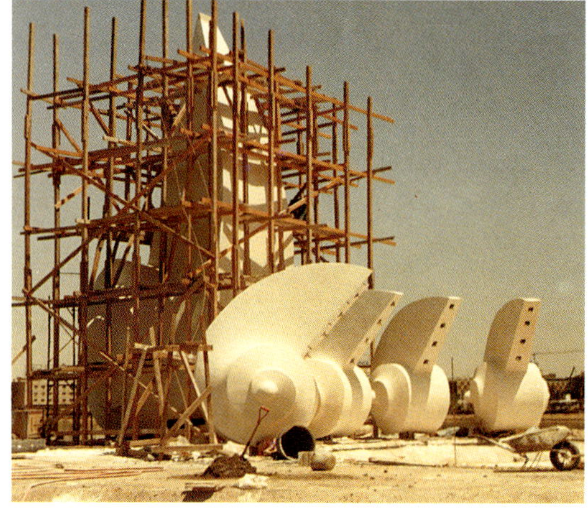

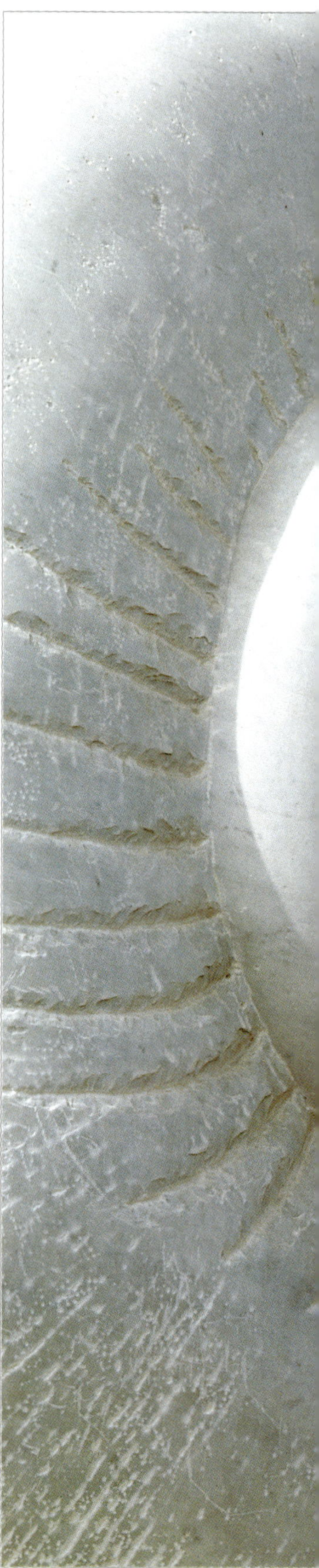

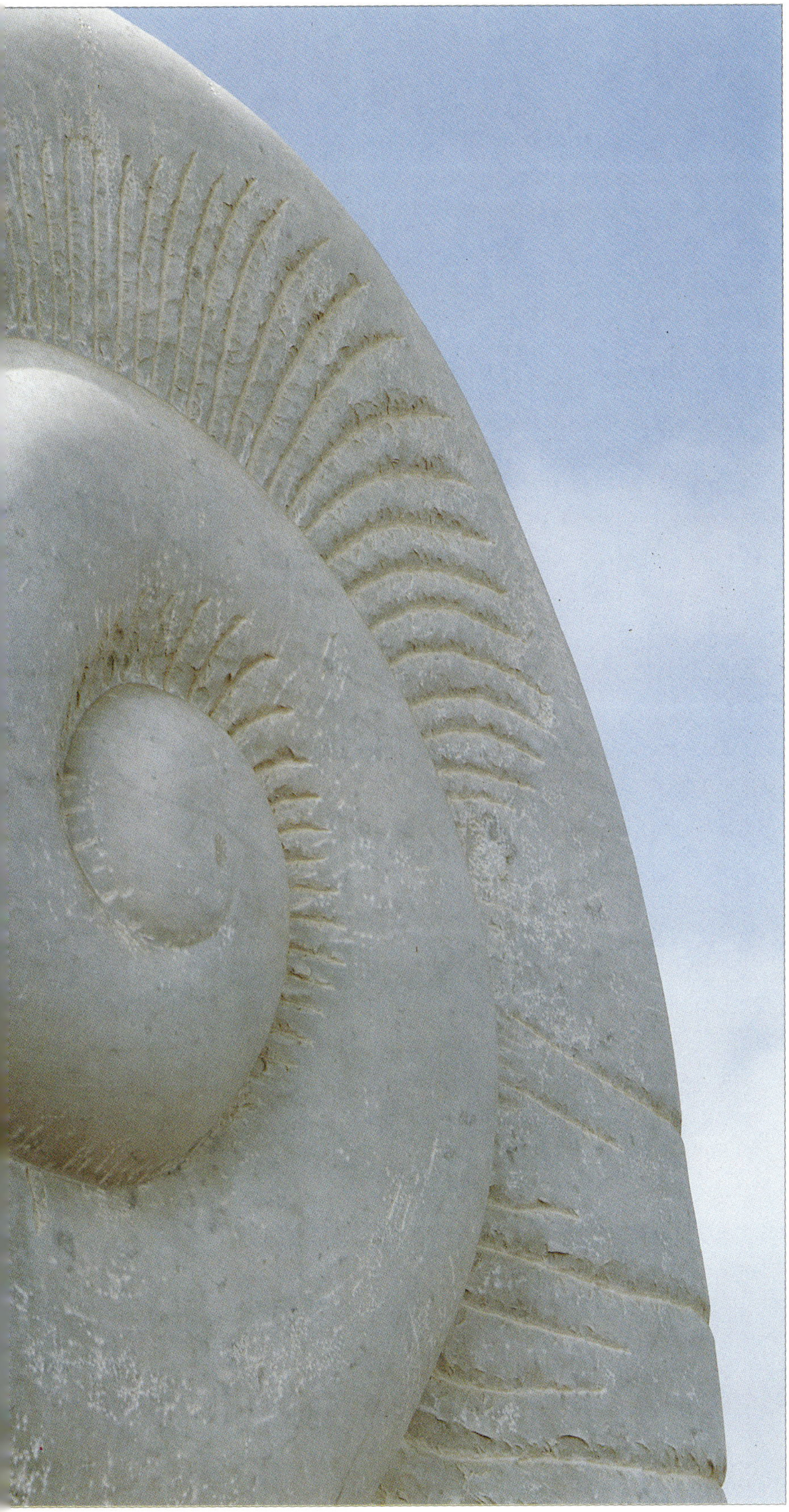

◄▼ **THE SHELL** (49)
Ali Amin
Marble

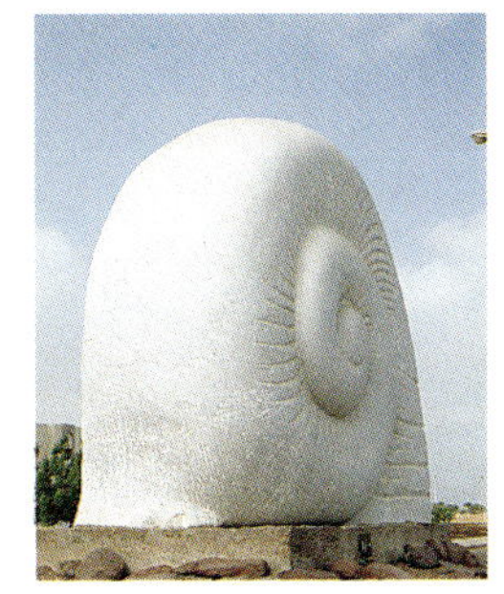

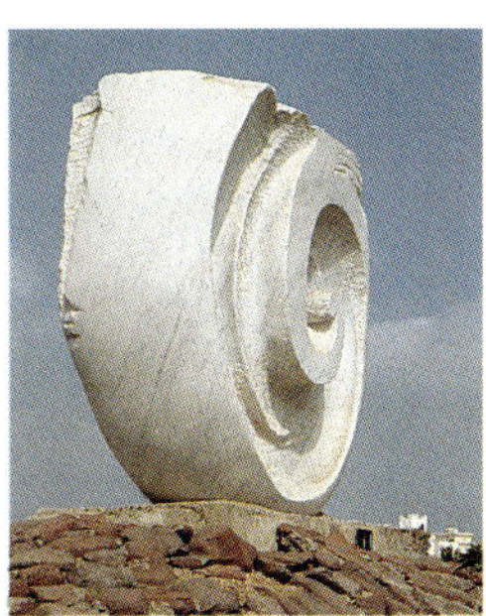

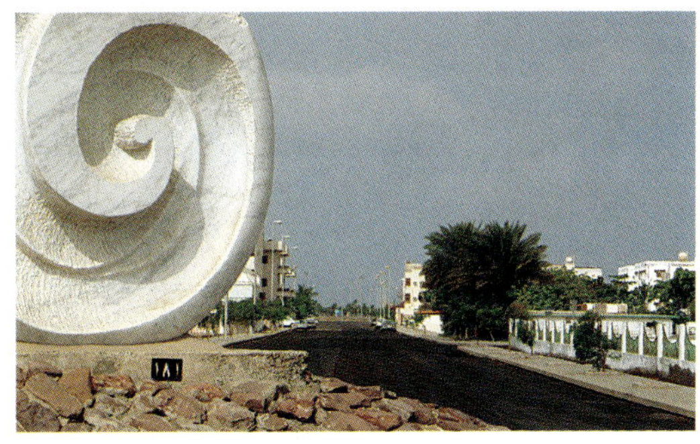

▲ **FOSSILISED NAUTILUS SHELL** (50)
Artist Unknown
Marble

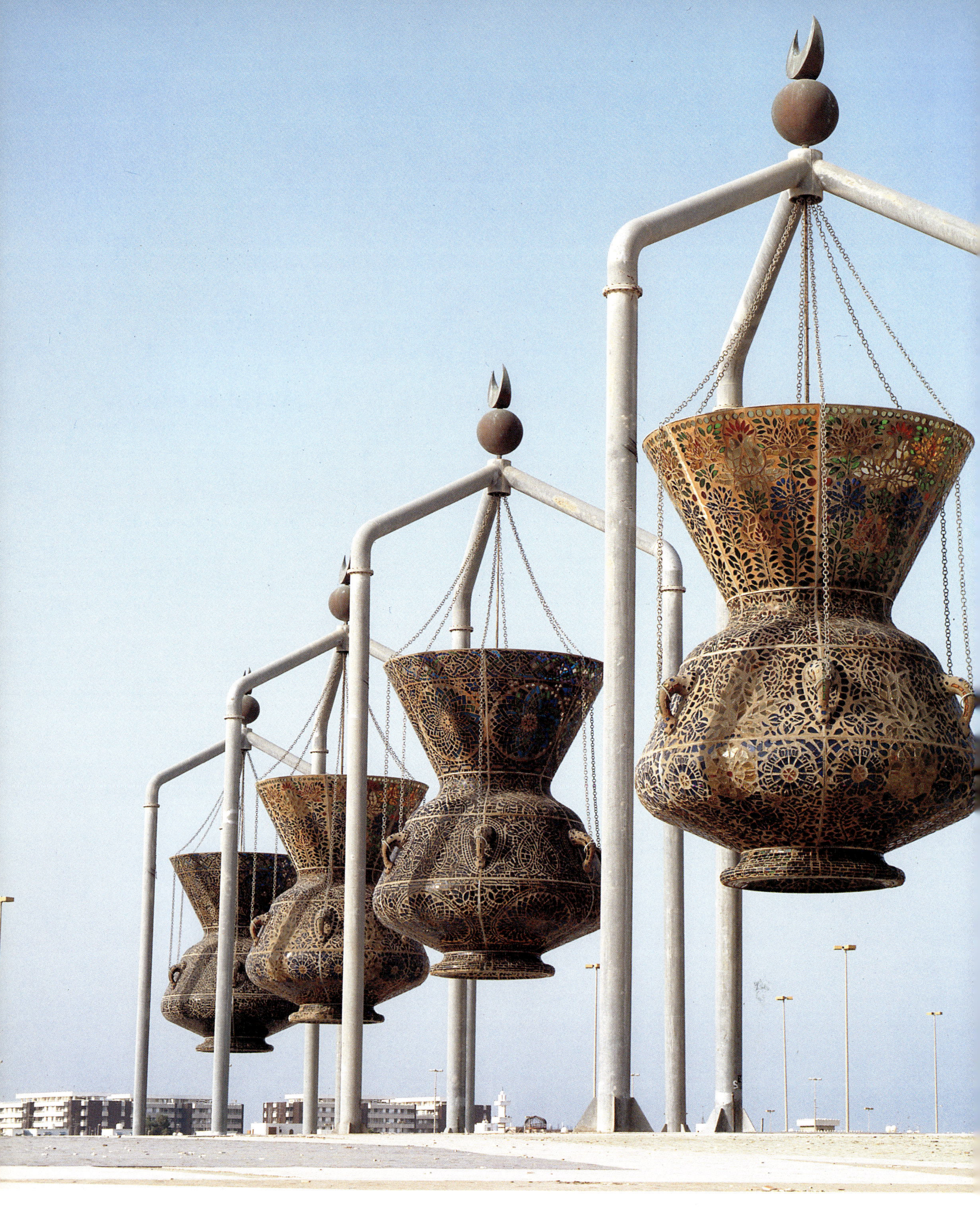

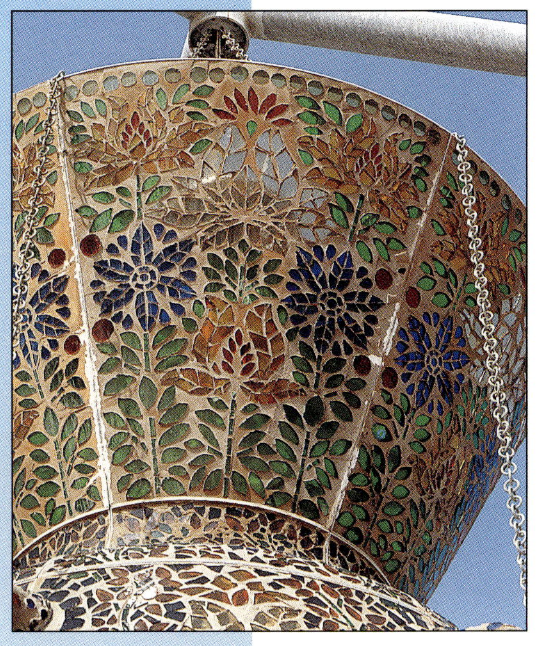

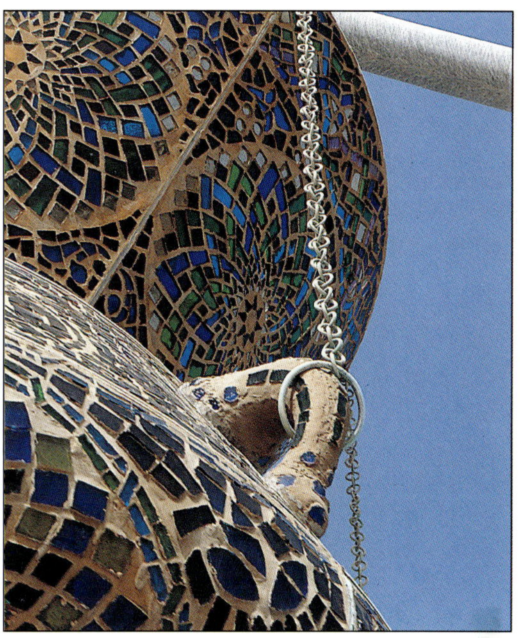

□ **THE MAMELUKE MOSQUE LANTERNS**
(Al-Qanadeel)
Julio Lafuente
Steel and Glass

This group, which is based on a type of lantern commonly used in Mameluke mosques, is best appreciated at night, when the coloured glass panels are illuminated from within. In early stages of the design the four lanterns were to form a square, but an in-line configuration was preferred.

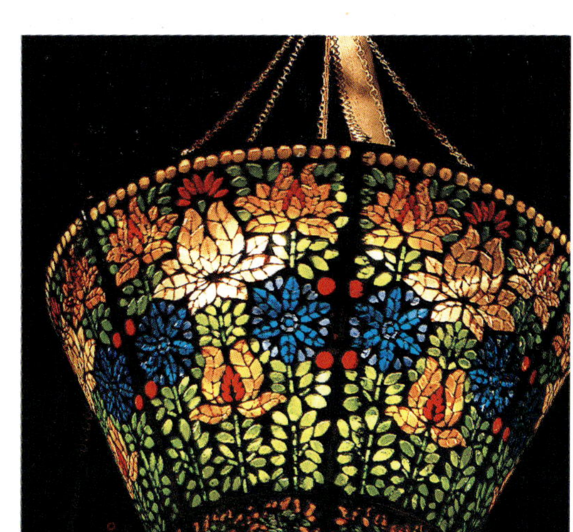

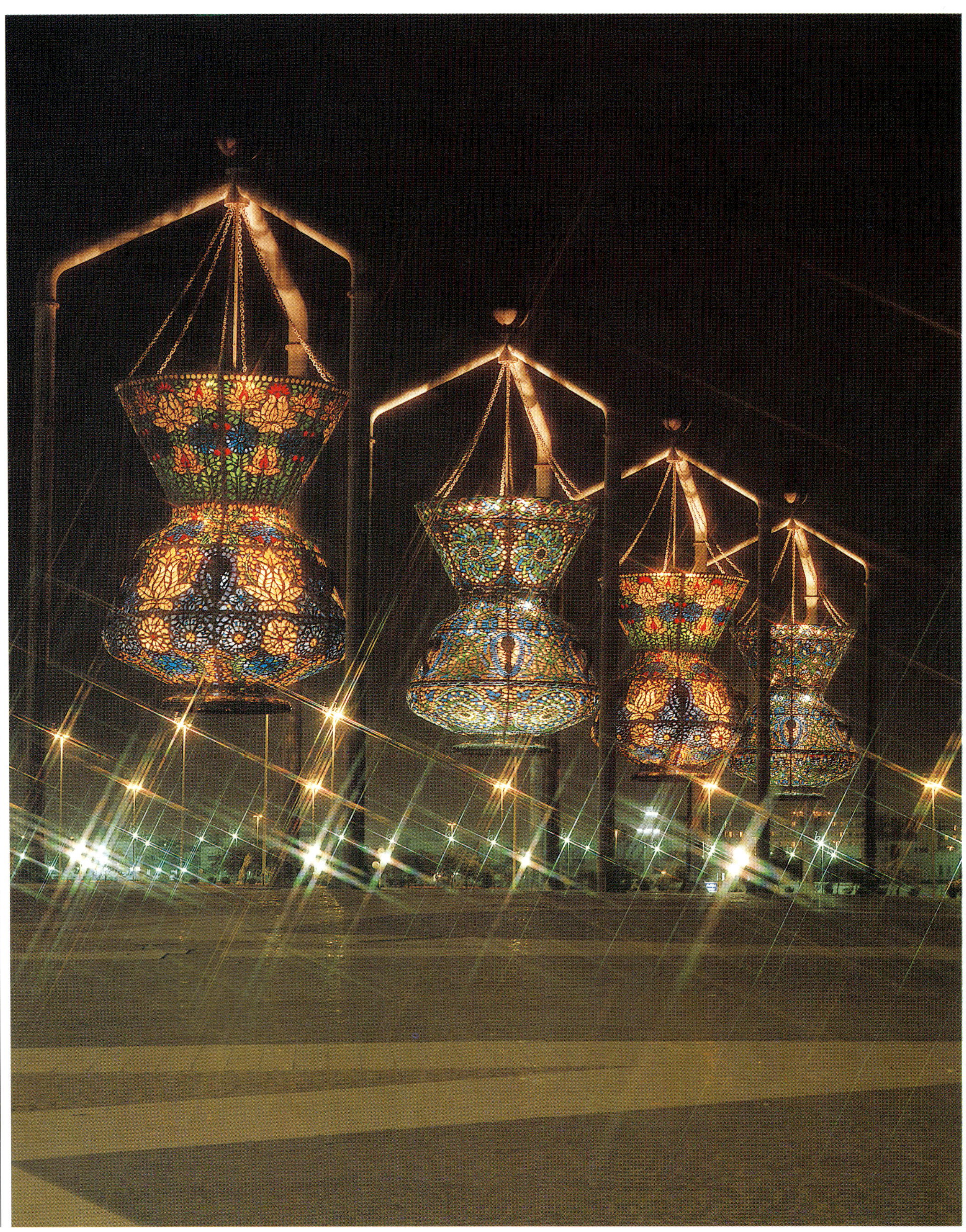

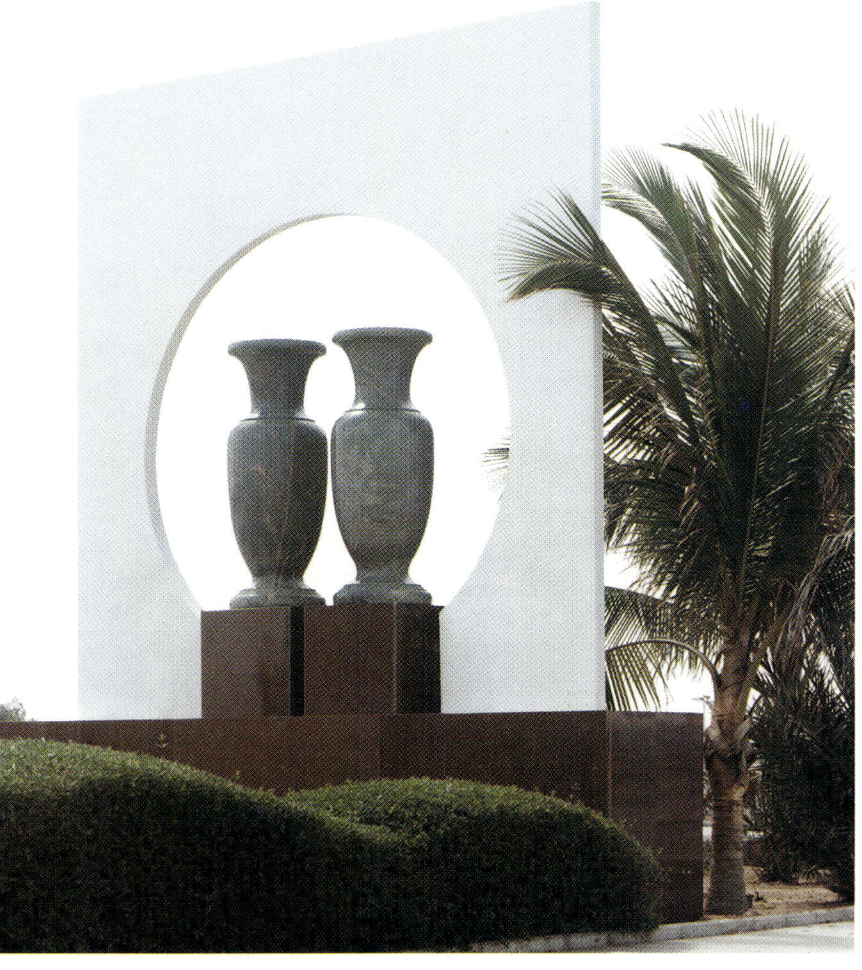

◀ **TWO VASES** (Mazharatein) (52)
Artist Unknown
Onyx

These vases were presented to the city by the late King Khaled ibn Abdul Aziz. The placing of the vases side by side is designed to echo the form of minarets which evolved towards the end of the Mameluke period in Egypt.

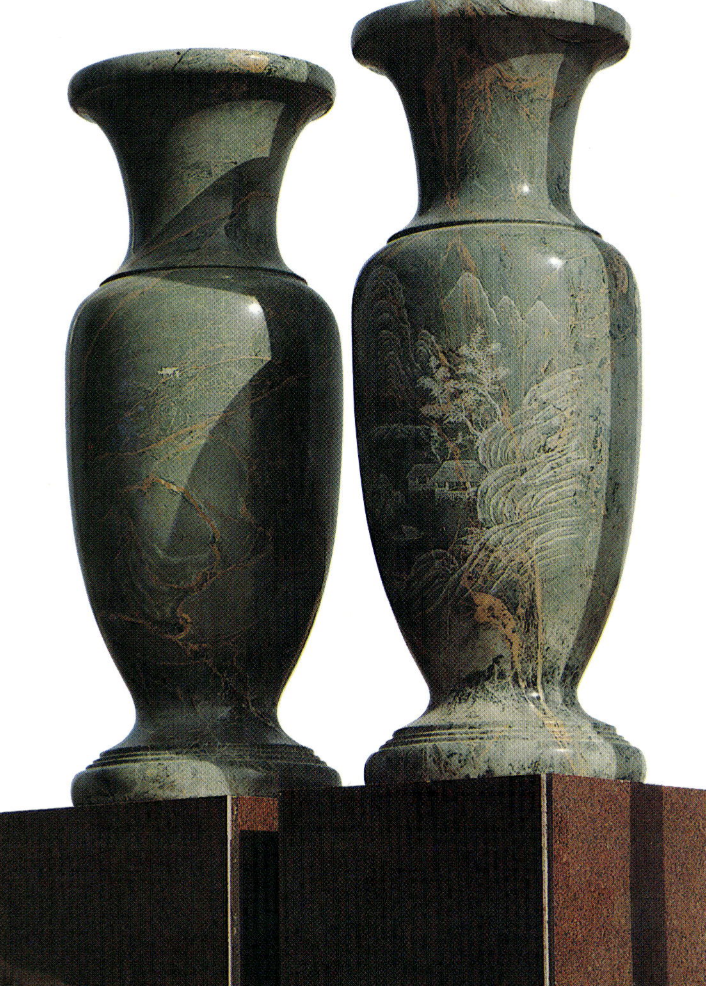

◀ At night Lafuente's mosque lanterns are a brilliant landmark.

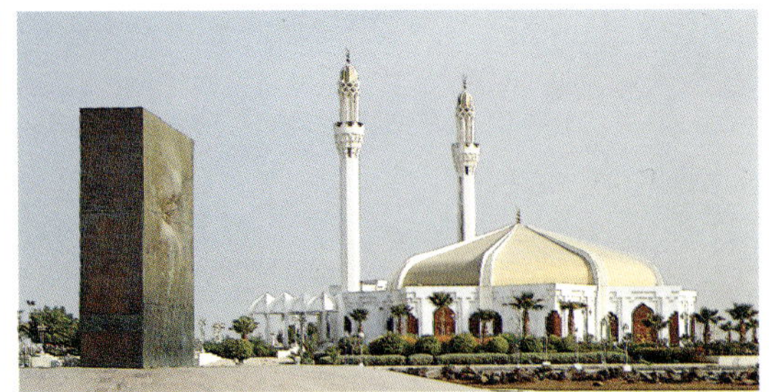

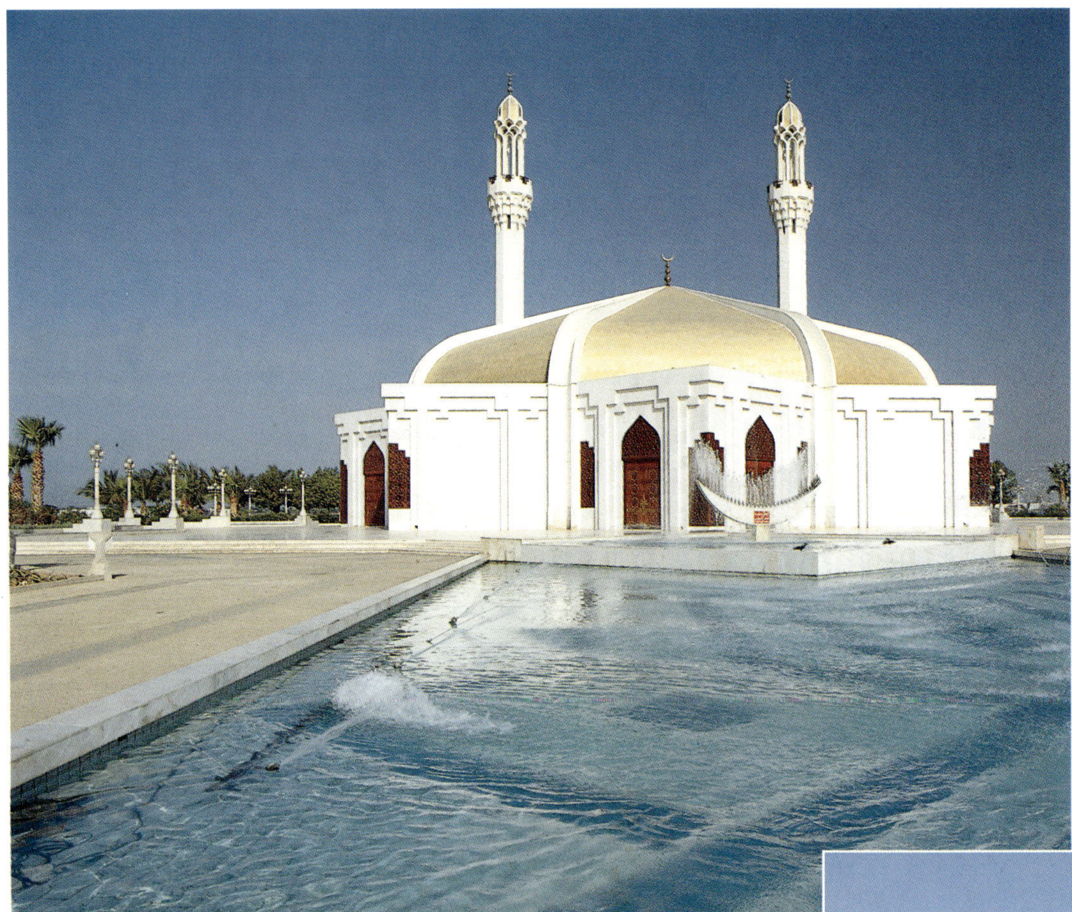

▲ **AL ANANI MOSQUE** (53)
Raouf Helmi Architect

On a site near the Open Air Museum stands one of the largest mosques in the Al Hamra area. It was designed by the architect Raouf Helmi who also turned his hand to sculpture, creating a 'map' of Jeddah's master plan from scrap metal left over from building the mosque.

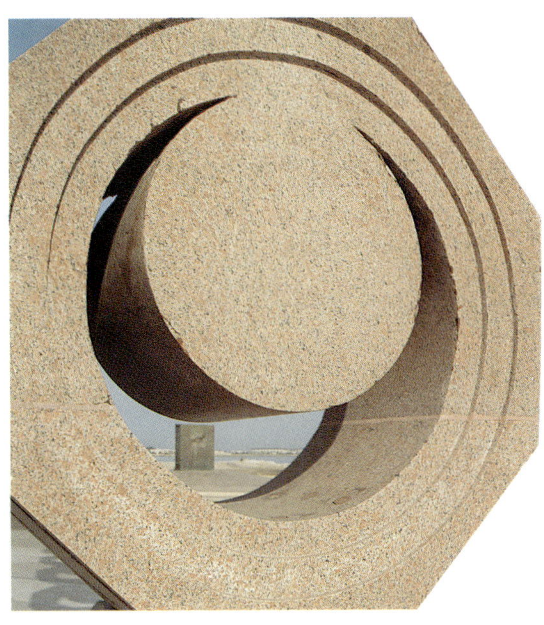

► **ROTATION OF THE CRESCENT AND MOON** (54)
Julio Lafuente
Granite

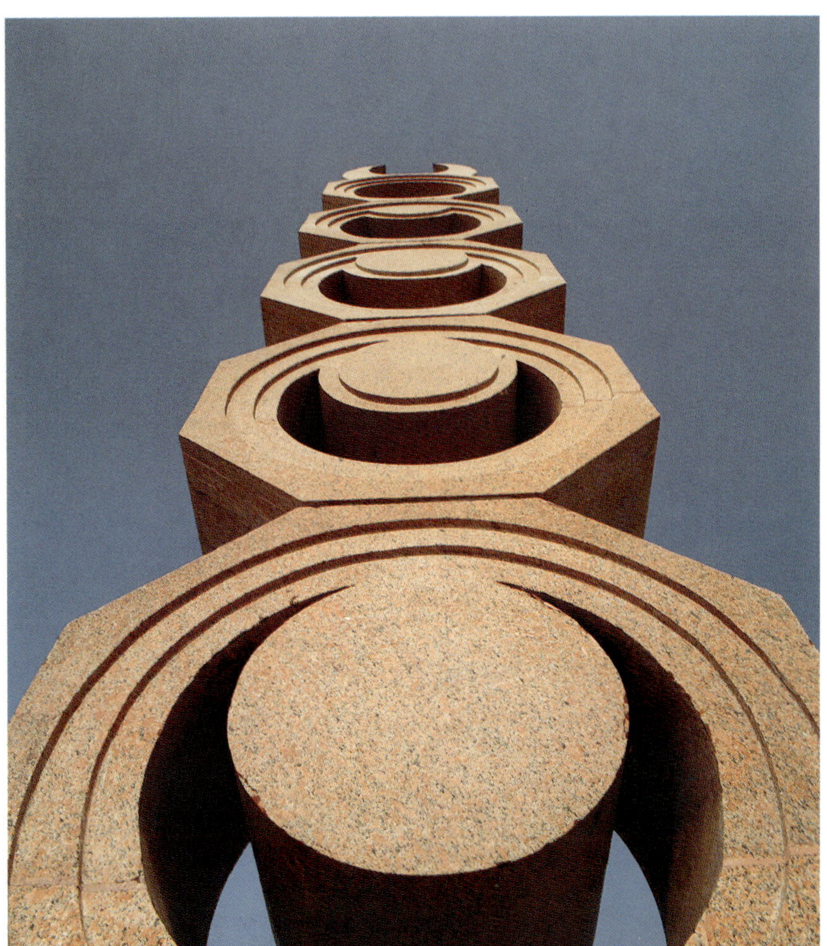

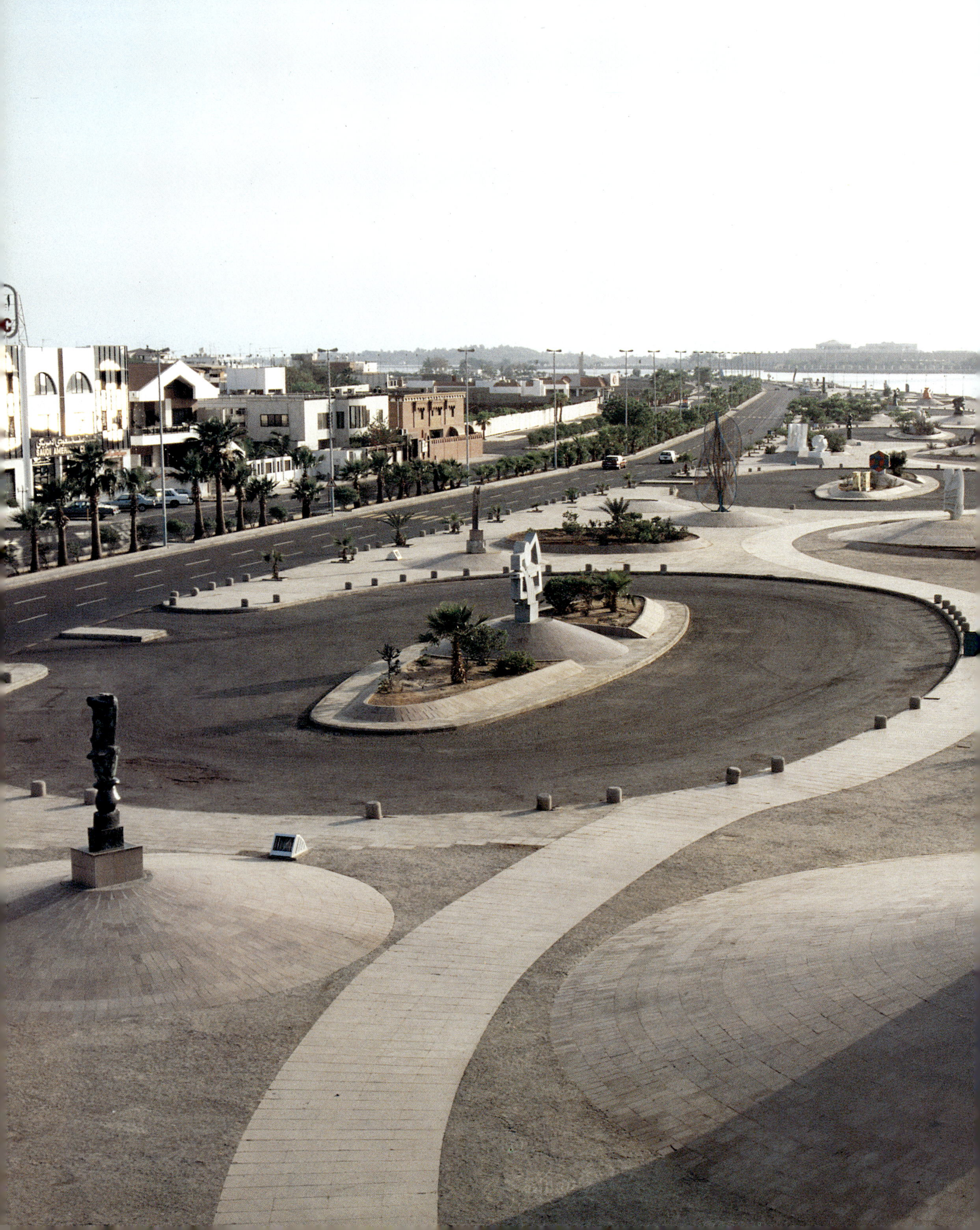

The AL HAMRA OPEN AIR MUSEUM

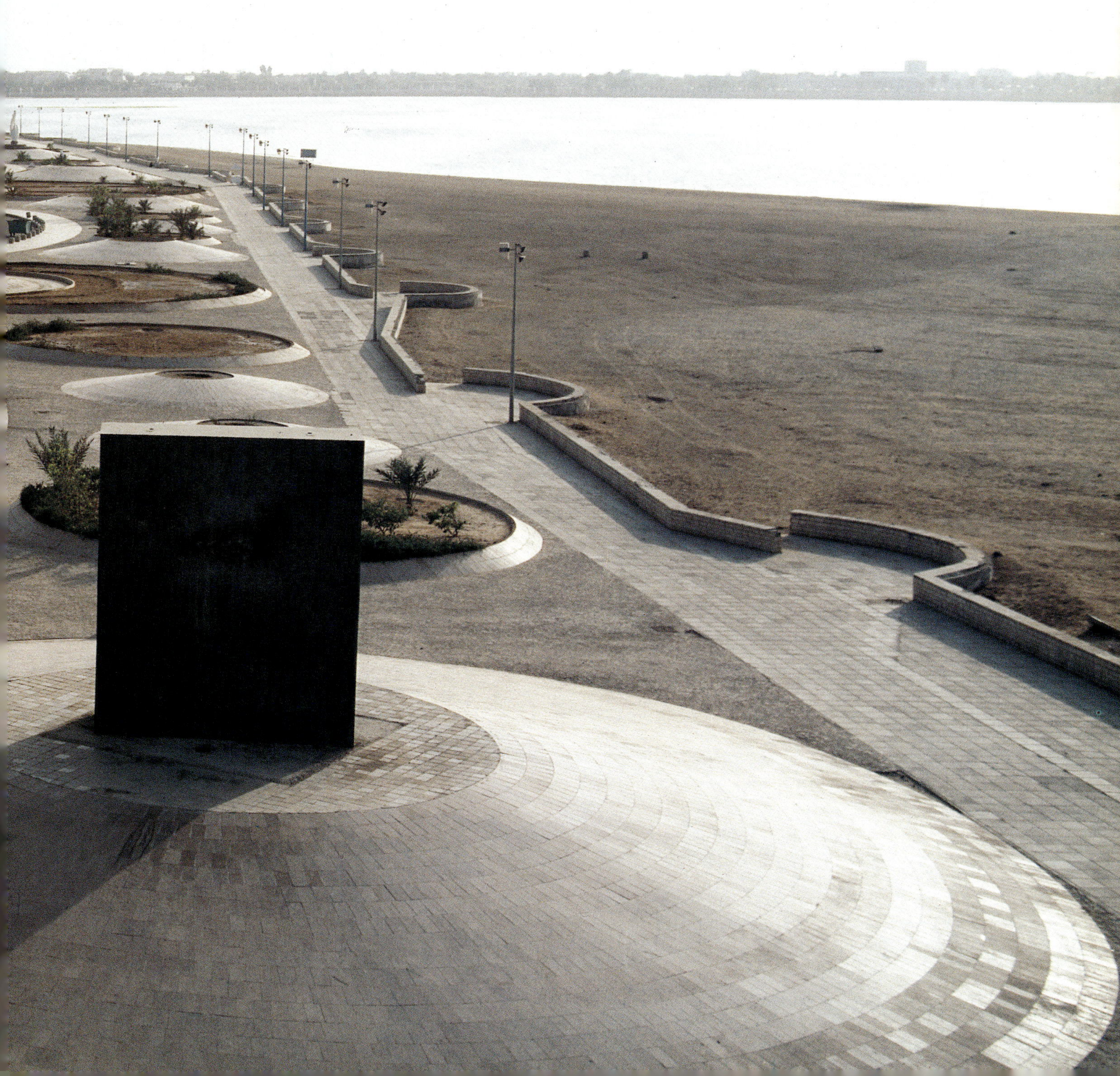

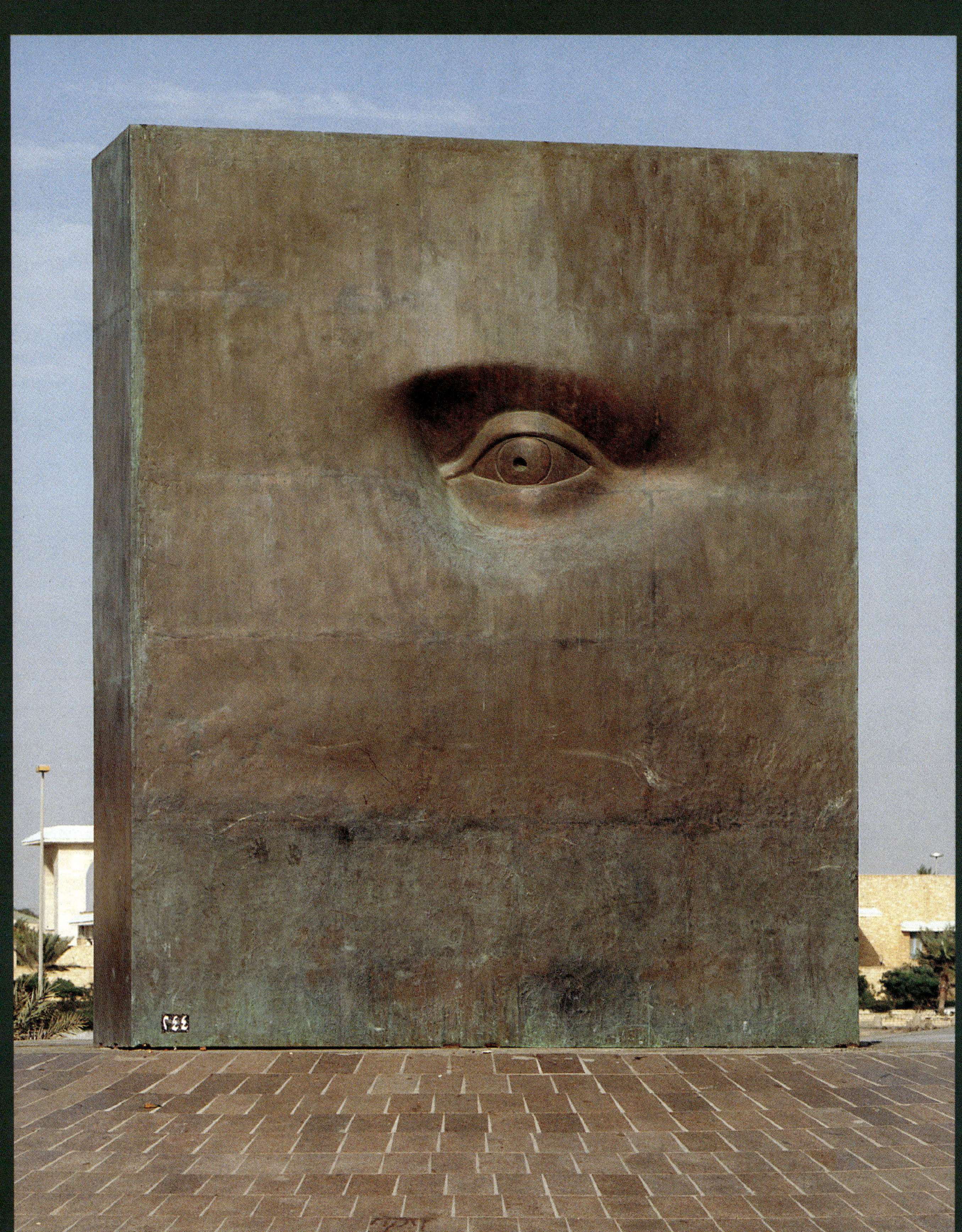

□ **THE EYE** (55)
César
Bronze

Initial plans had called for this sculpture to be sited near Dr Akif Maghrabi's Eye Hospital or outside the television studios, but suitable space could not be found at either of those locations and the work was eventually added to the collection at the Open Air Museum.

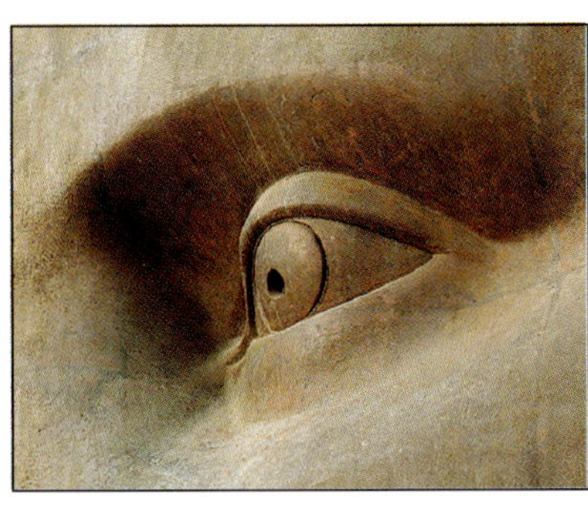
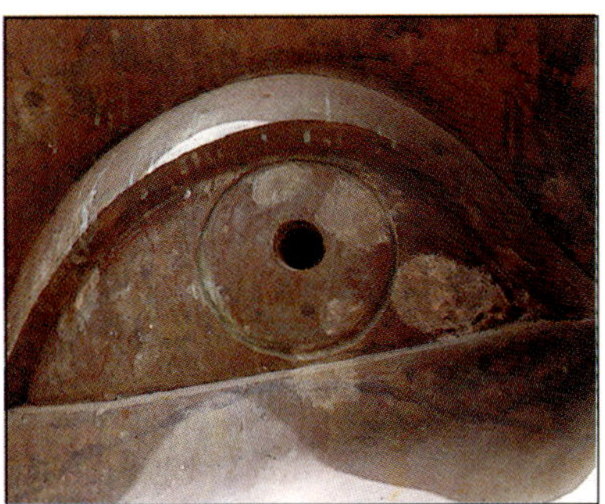
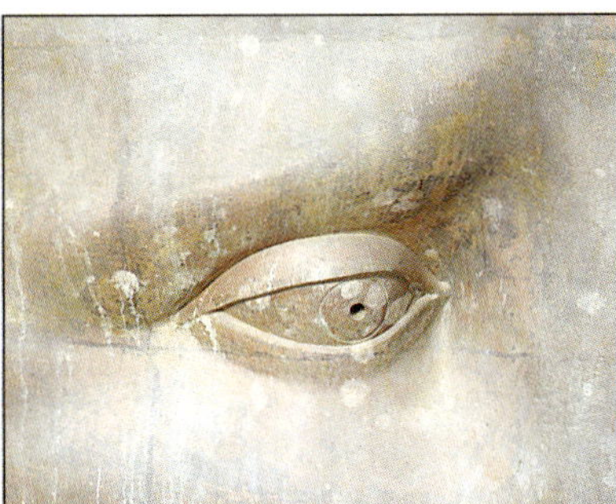
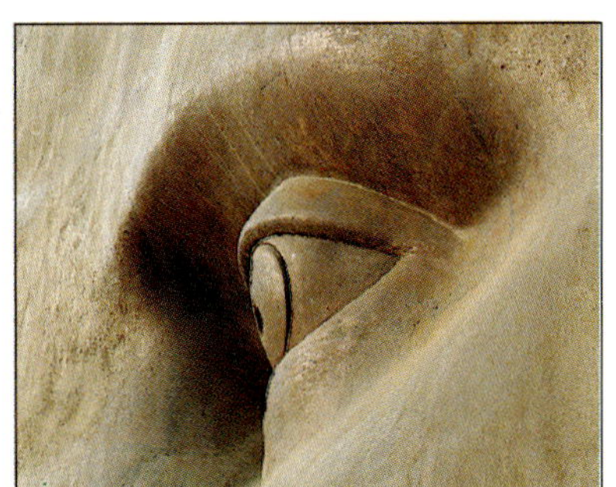

□ **THREE PIECE RECLINING FIGURE** (56)
Henry Moore
Bronze

In the early 1960s Moore produced a number of sculptures in which the body is divided into parts. The elements have been compared to eroded rock formations and are seen by some as being in opposition to one another. Moore's use of bronze, his preferred medium during this period, implicitly associates the craggy forms with elements of a reclining figure.

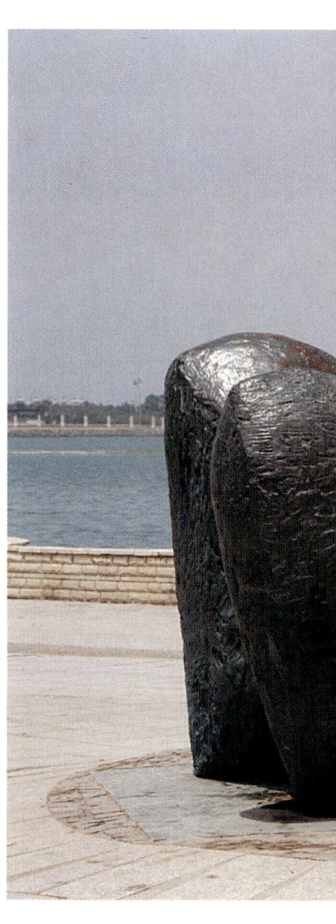

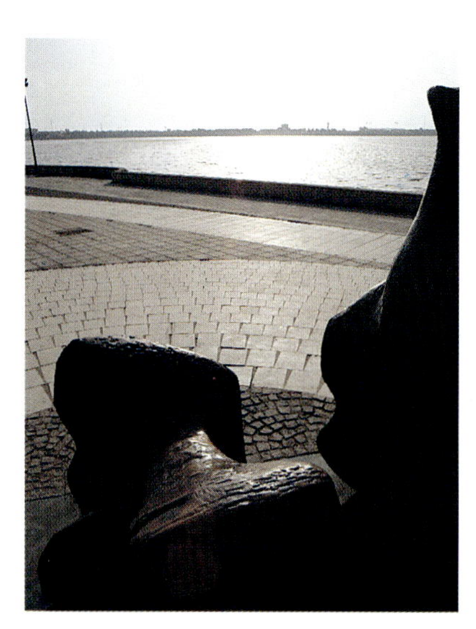

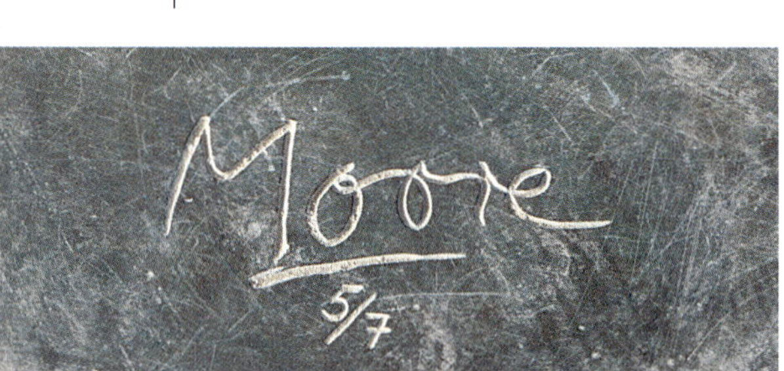

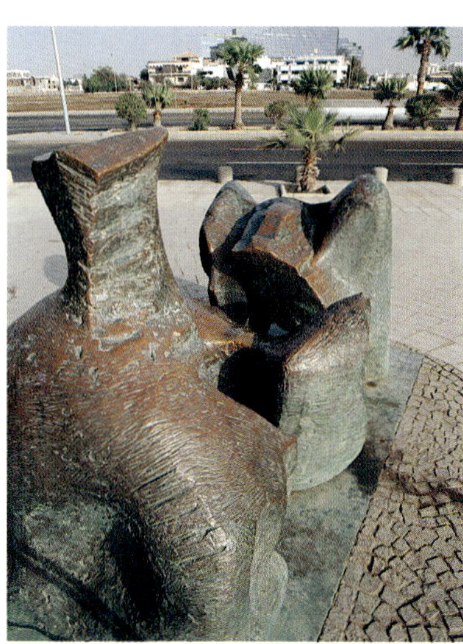

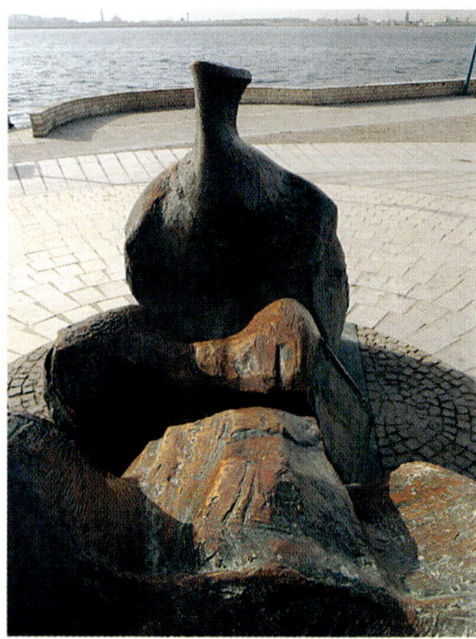

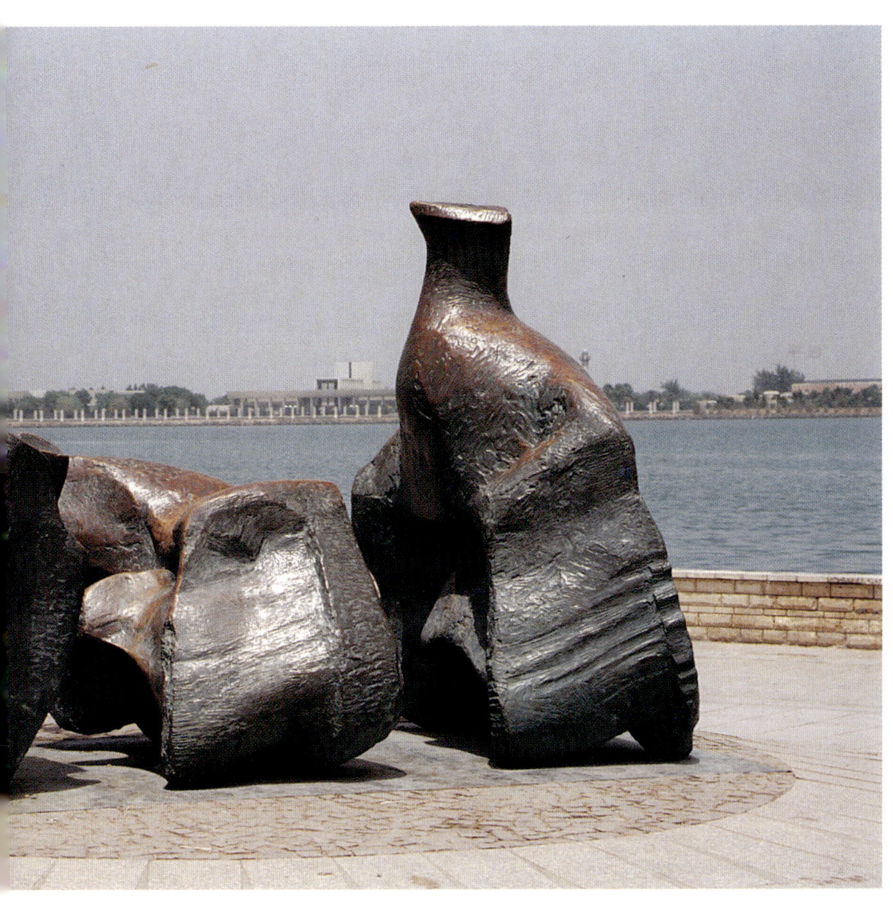

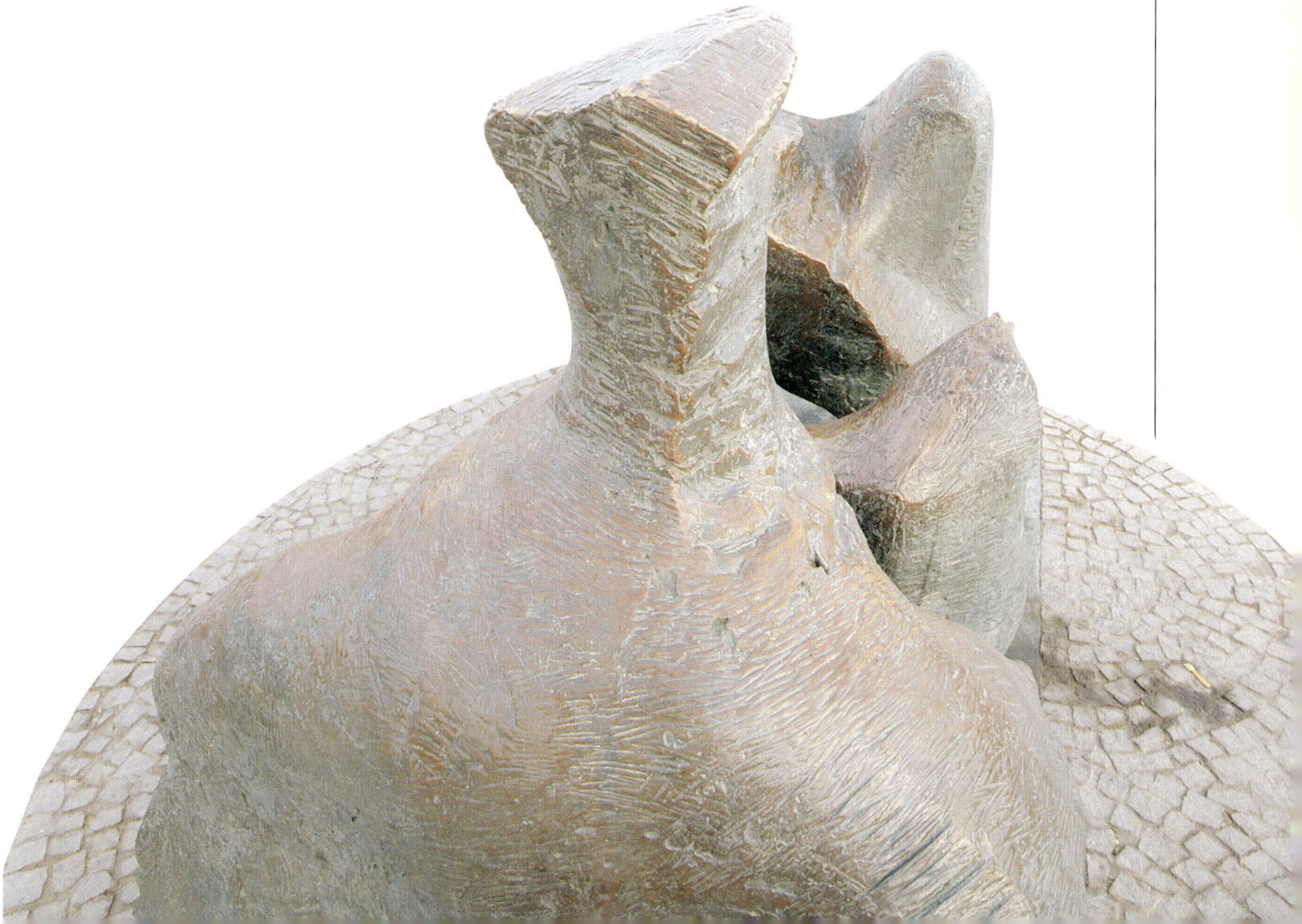

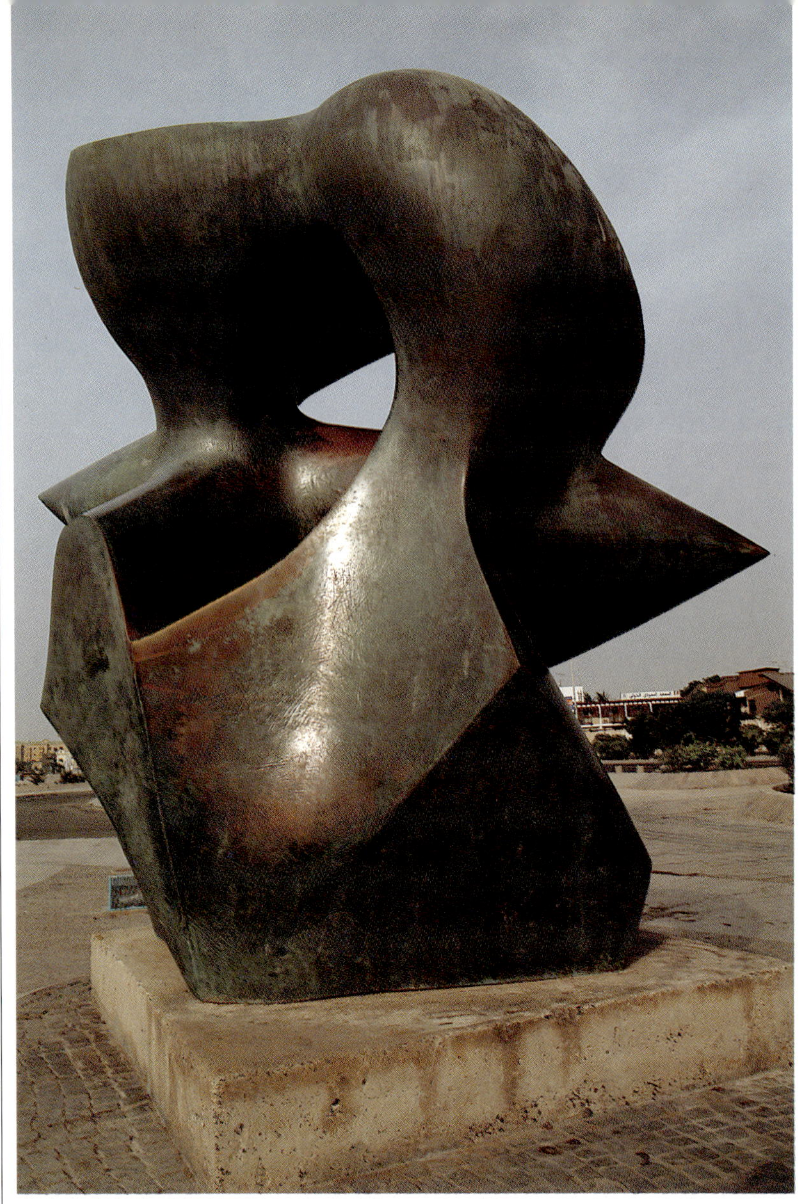

□ LARGE SPINDLE PIECE (57)
Henry Moore
Bronze

This piece evolved over several years and is a fine example of Moore's later abstract work. In some ways it is related to the *'Helmet Heads'* of the 1950s which explore the theme of protection and intrusion.

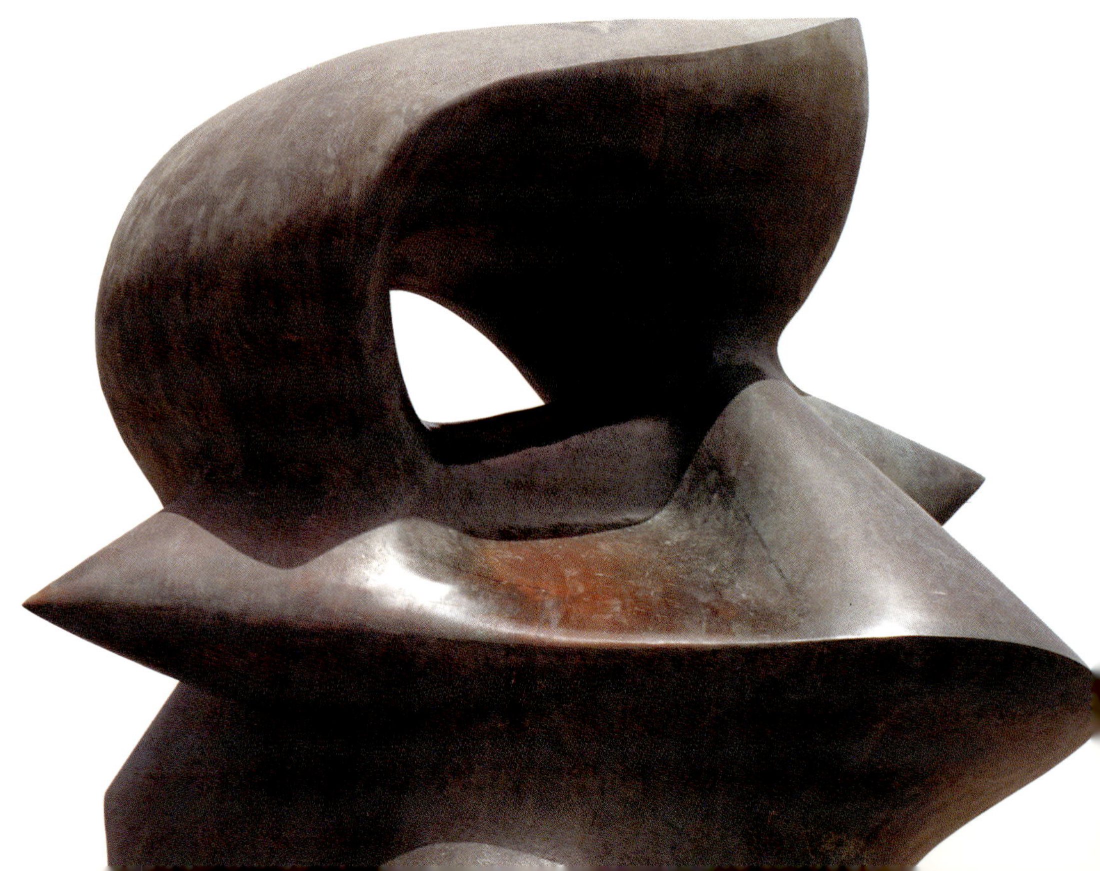

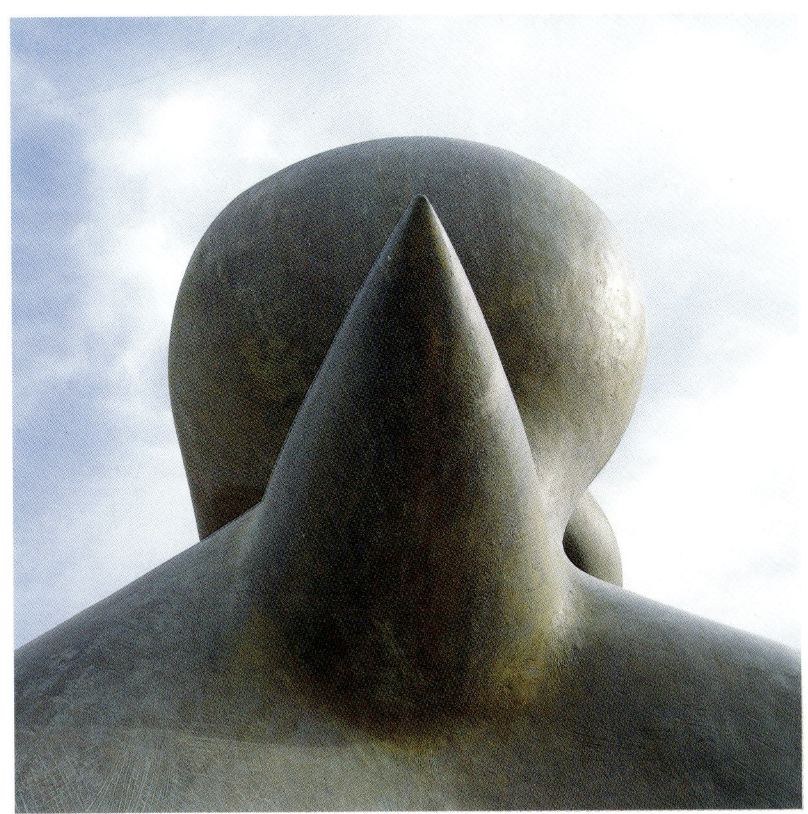

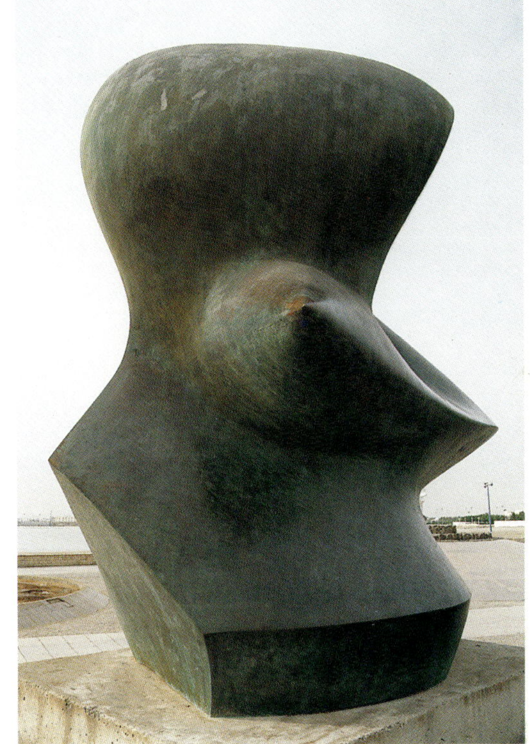

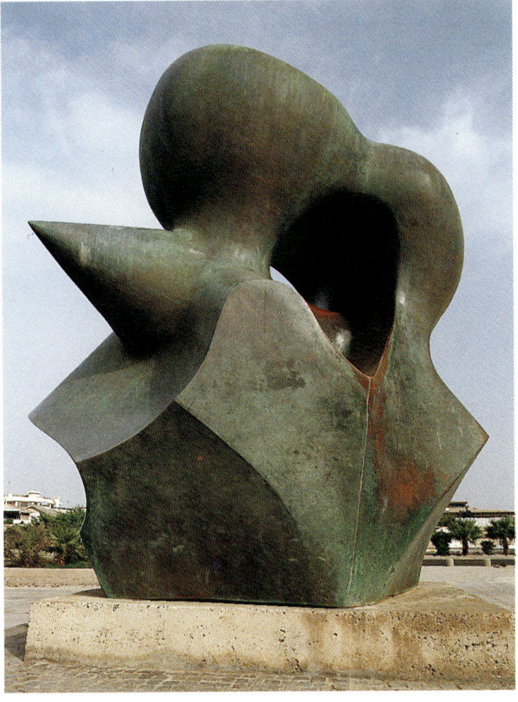

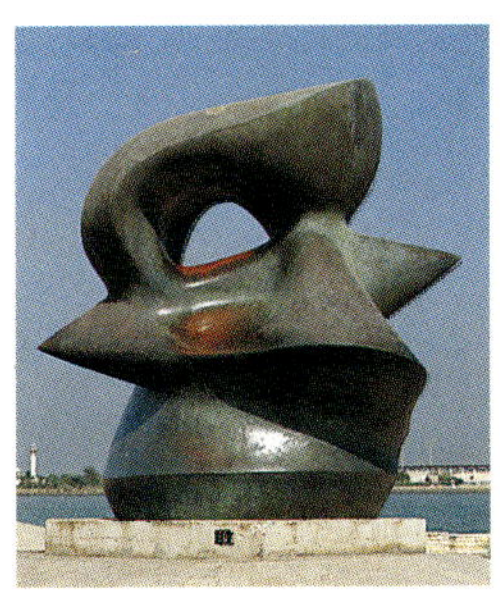

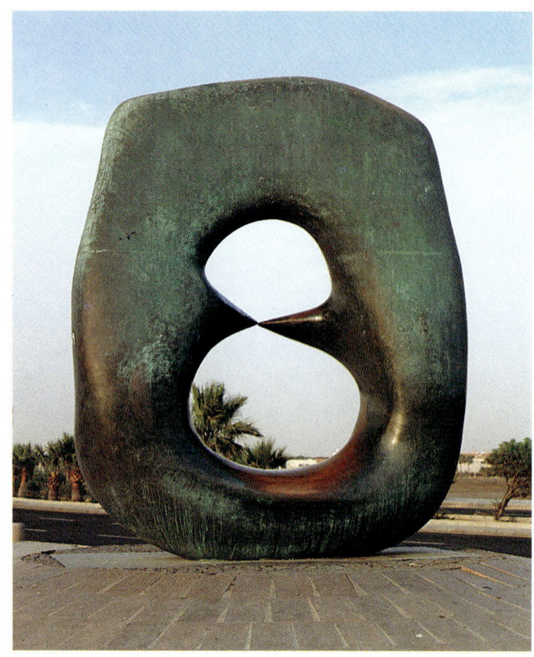

□ **OVAL WITH POINTS** (58)
Henry Moore
Bronze

Dating from the late 1960s, *Oval with Points* is typical of Moore's later work, in its combinations of naturalistic and mechanical forms. The genesis of the idea for this sculpture is found in a drawing dating from c.1938 inscribed 'points practically touching'. Moore himself considered it dangerous to look for a single source for his sculptures. By providing such a generalised title, he has left interpretation to the viewer.

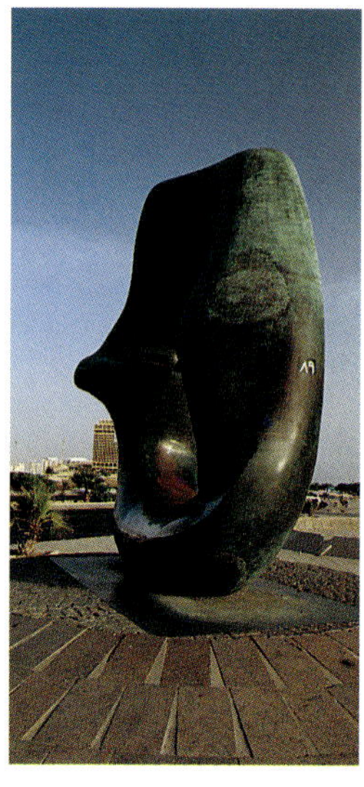

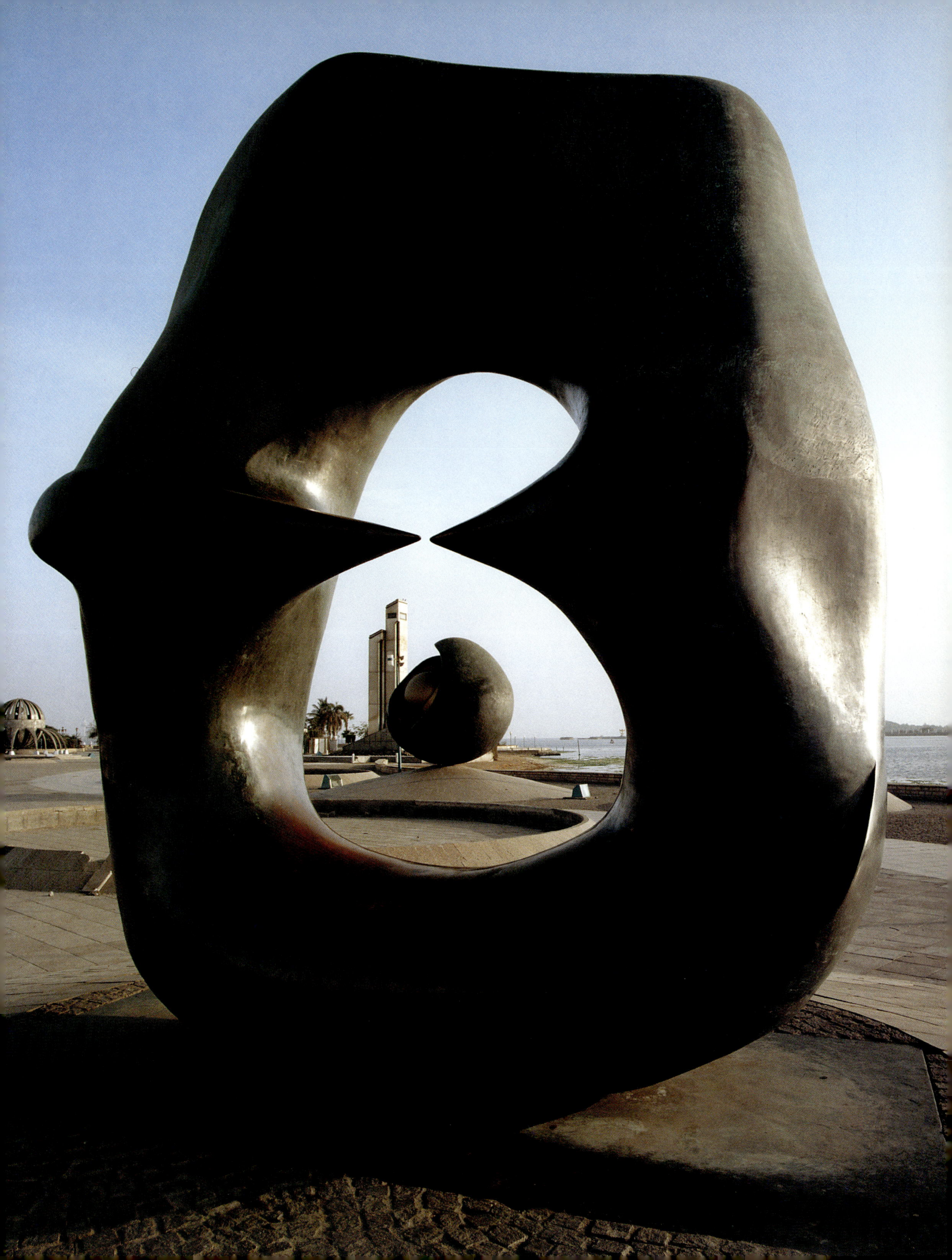

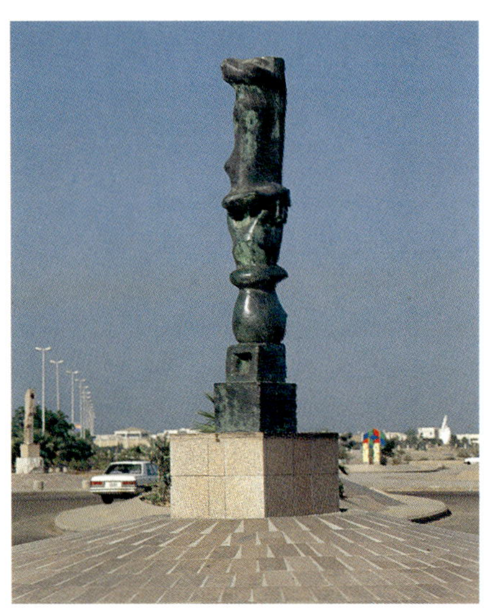

□ **UPRIGHT MOTIVE NO. 2** (59)
Henry Moore
Bronze

This was one of a series of such figures from the mid 1950s. Aside from their totemic character the *Upright Motives* reflect a change in Moore's working method. He said later that he had 'started by balancing different forms one above the other . . . but as I continued the attempt gained more unity, also perhaps became more organic.'

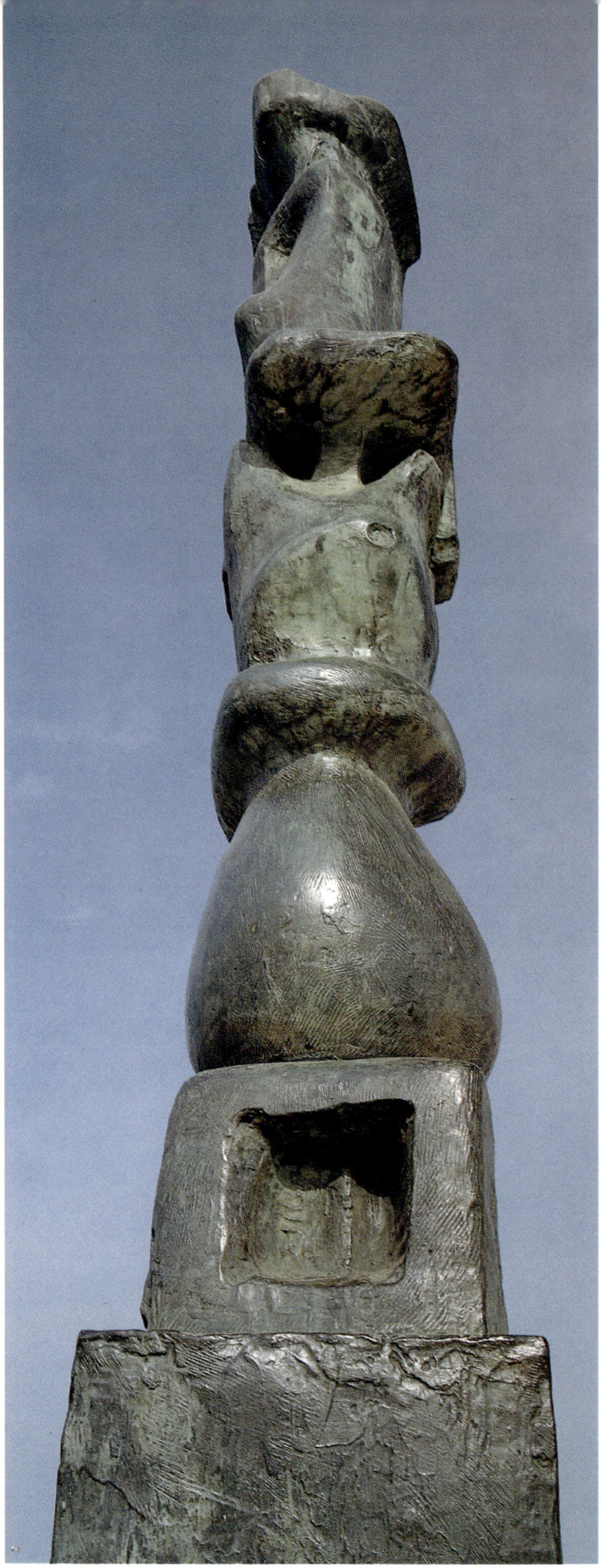

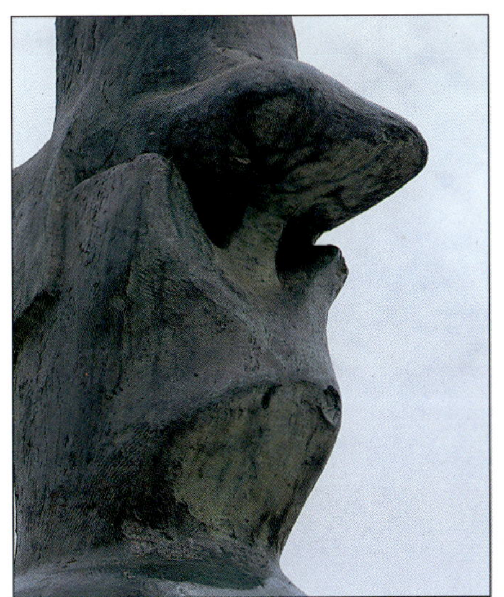

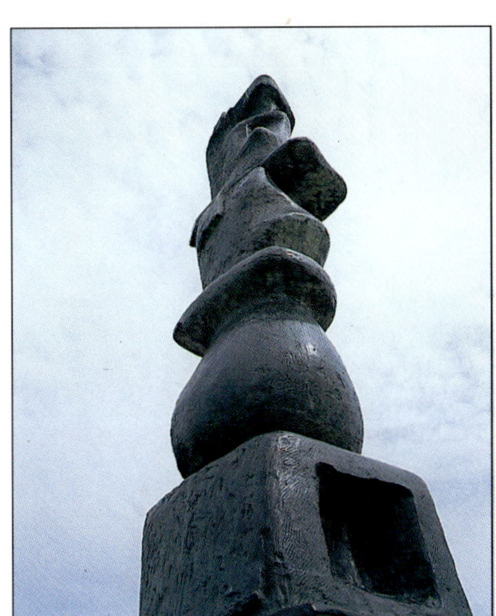

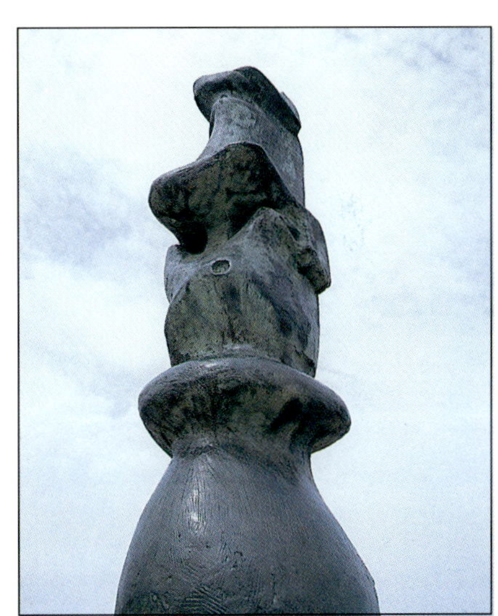

► The richness of the Open Air Museum Moore's *Oval with Points* and the *King Fahd Fountain* are seen here with *The Essence is Gold*.

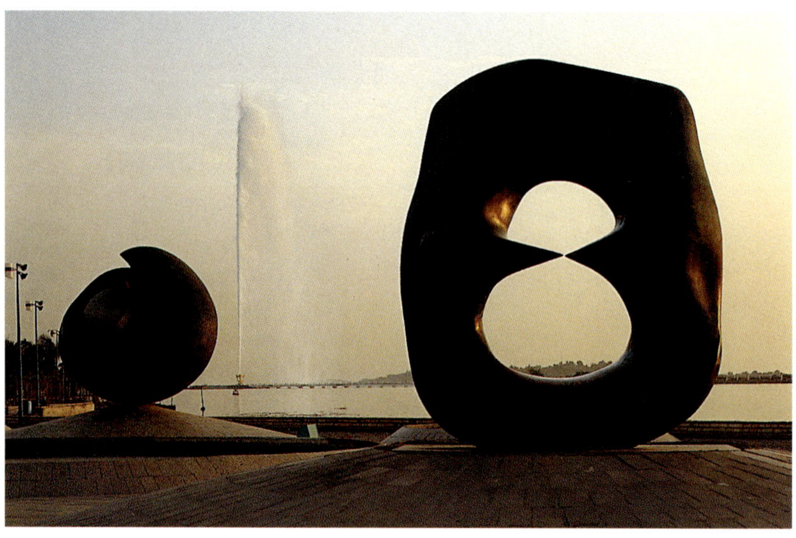

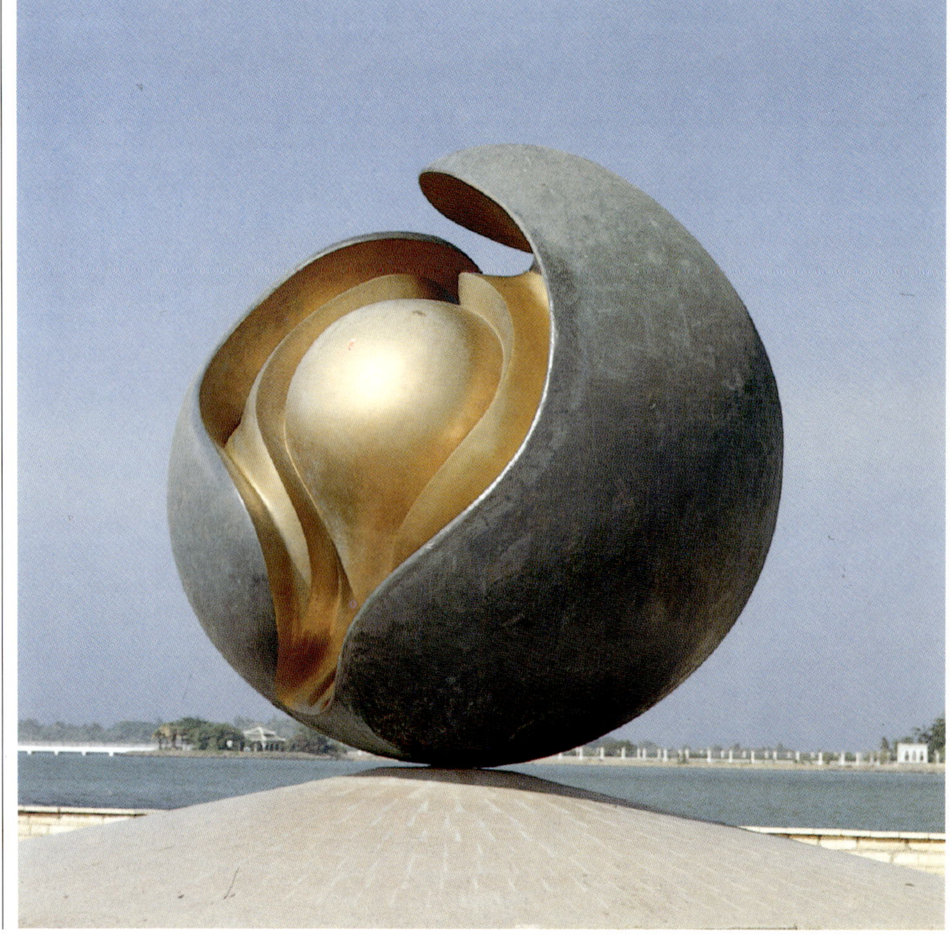

◄ **THE ESSENCE IS GOLD**
(Al-Johar min Dahab) (60)
E Dest
Bronze

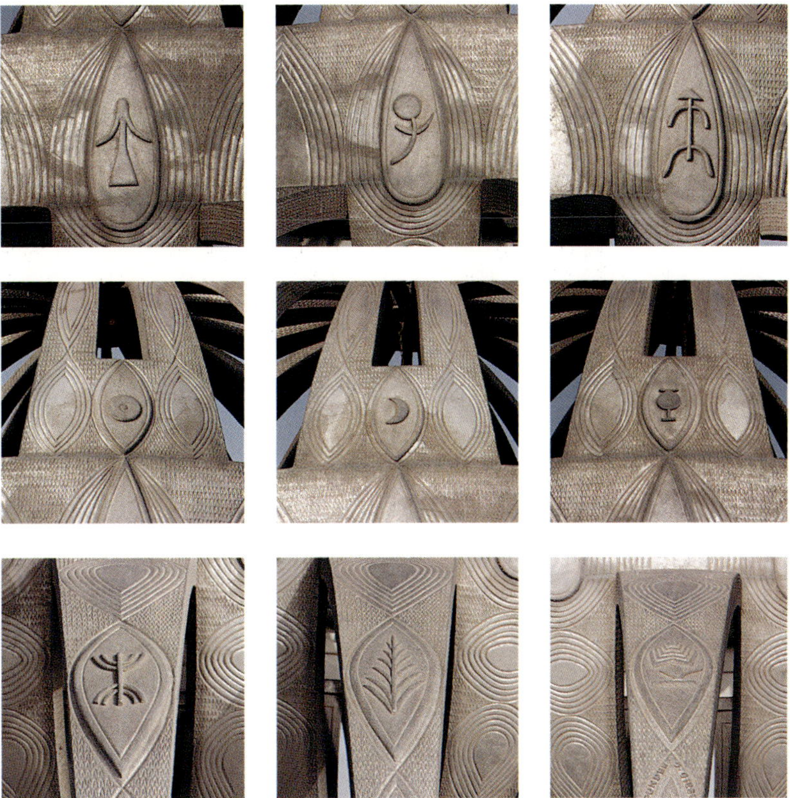

□ **LARGE BALL BEARING SYMBOLS**
Ottmar Hollmann
Cast Alloy

These details from Hollmann's work show how he has enriched his Jeddah sculptures by drawing on symbolic motifs from various sources – from Oriental philosophy to astrology and Western science.

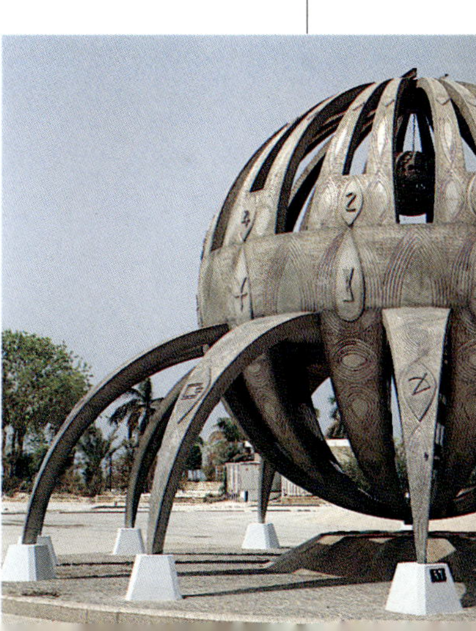

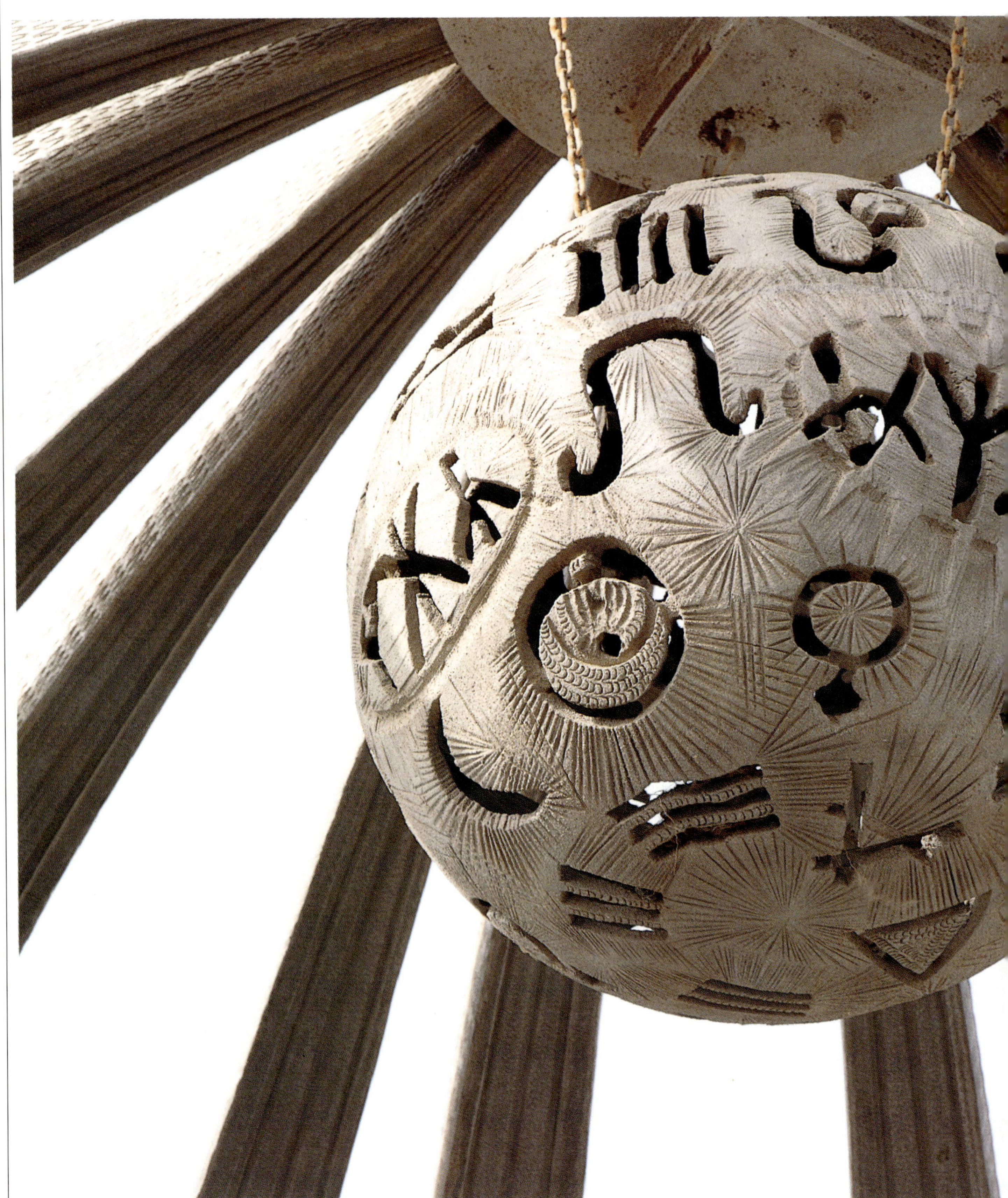

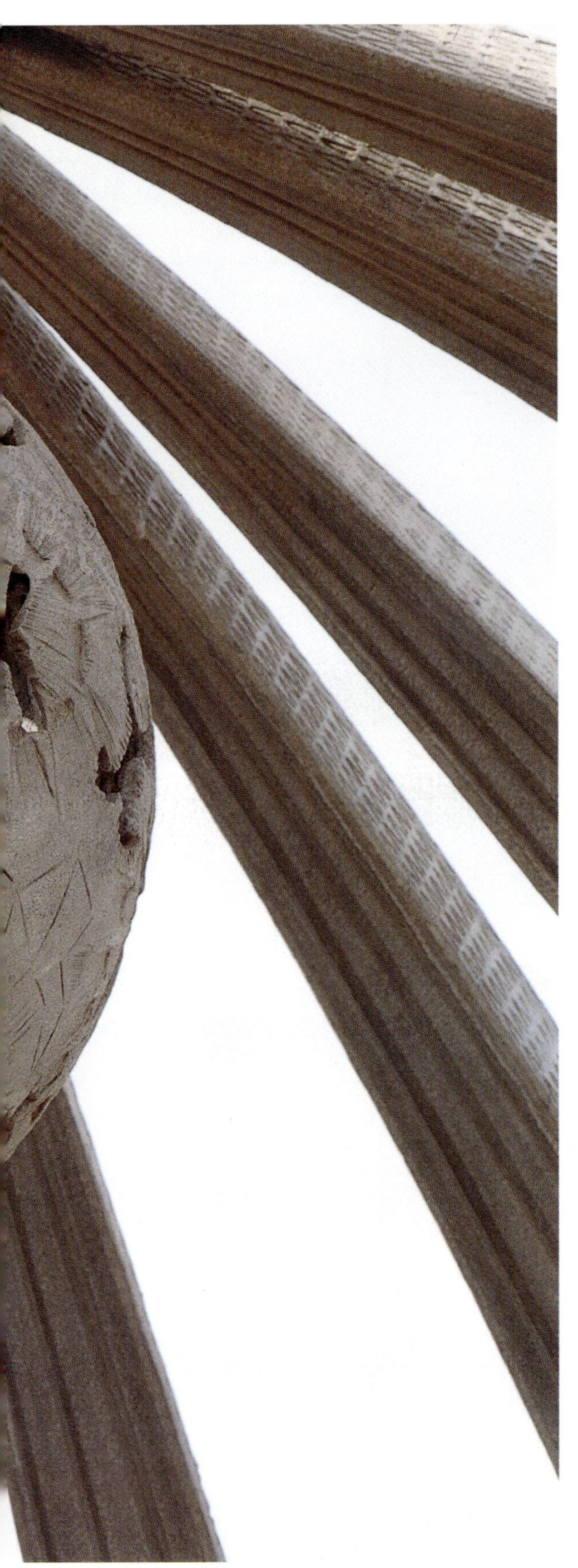

□ LARGE BALL BEARING SYMBOLS (61)
Ottmar Hollmann

Hollmann's only sculpture in the Open Air Museum is his *Large Ball Bearing Symbols* which was placed – at the artist's request – near the Henry Moore sculptures. This abstract work has proved intriguing enough to Jeddah's inhabitants to earn itself nicknames such as *The Spaceship* and *The Octopus*.

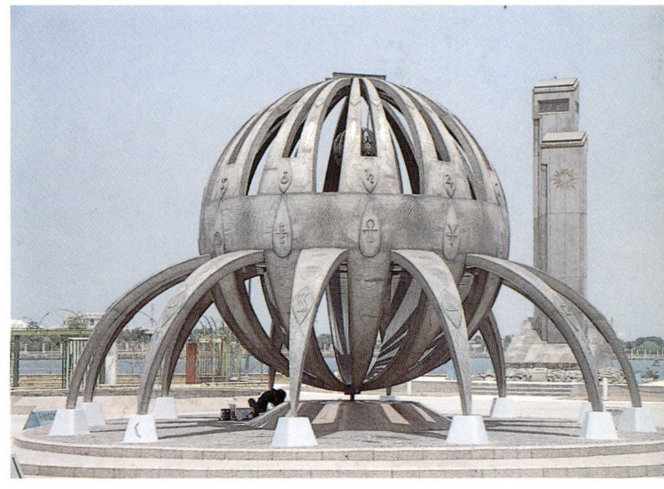

▲ In the background can be seen The Solar Clock designed by the American, Walter Ferro. The monument was a gift from Mobil and operates its time/temperature displays from electricity generated by two photovoltaic panels mounted on top of the taller column.

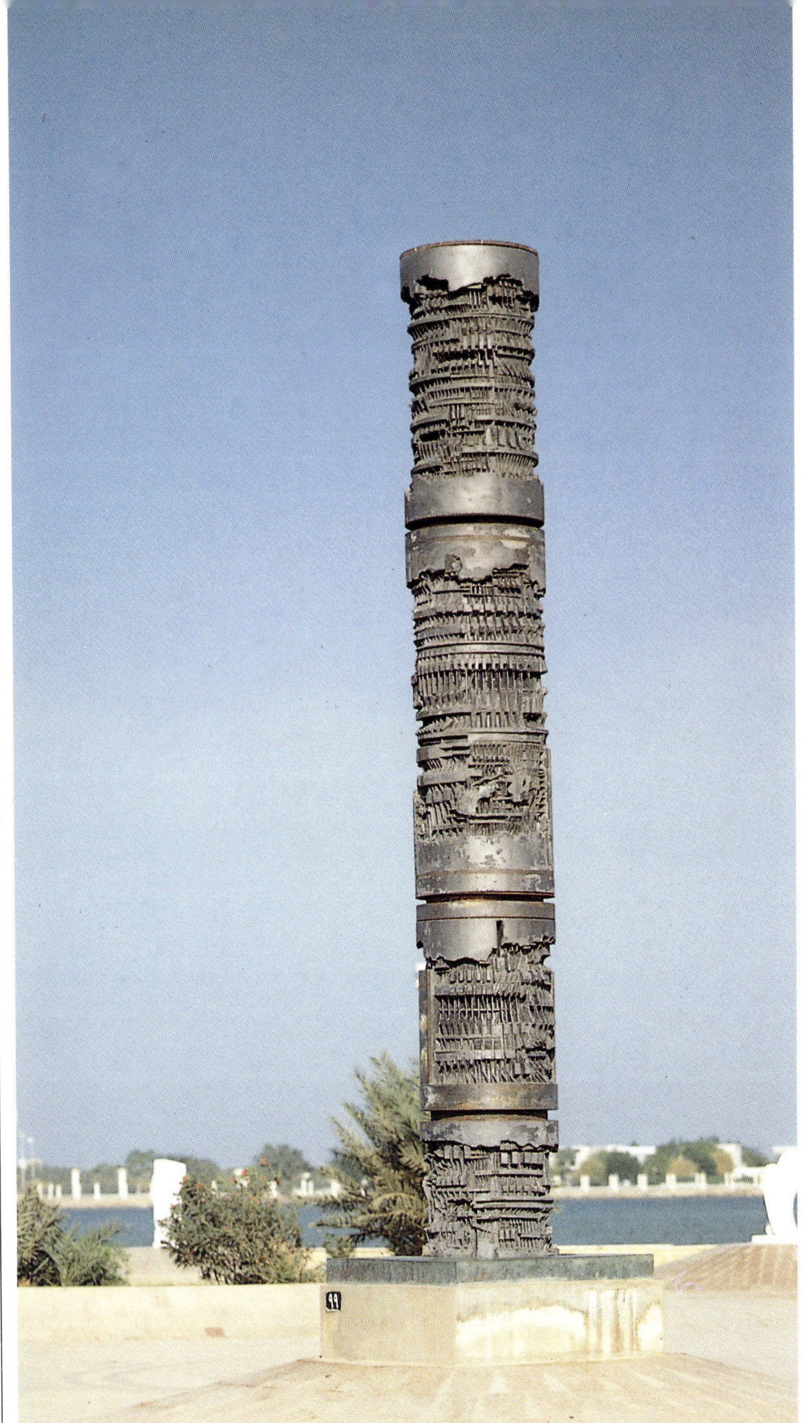

◄ THE TRAVELLER'S POST (63)
Arnaldo Pomodoro
Scrap Metal

▼ CUBE (64)
Arnaldo Pomodoro
Scrap Metal

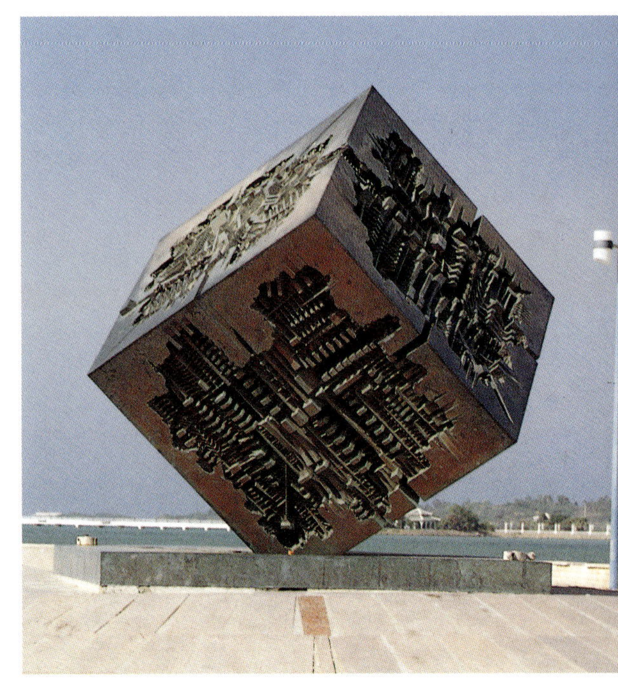

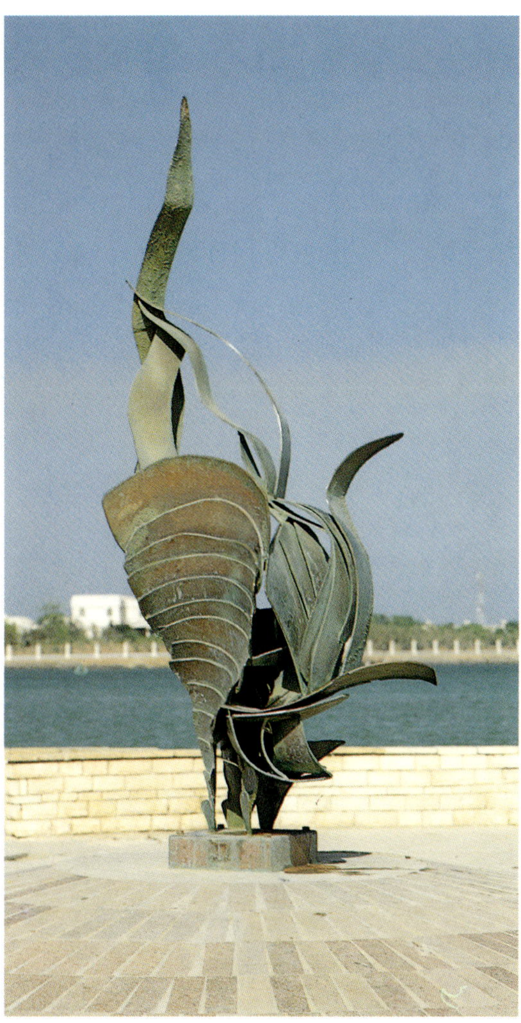

◄ **FLAME OF LIFE** (Shoualah) (65)
Eila Hiltunen
Scrap Metal

To this Finnish artist goes the distinction of being the only female sculptor to have works included in the Jeddah collection. In this particular piece the source of her scrap material was a ship which had been wrecked on the coral reef off Jeddah.

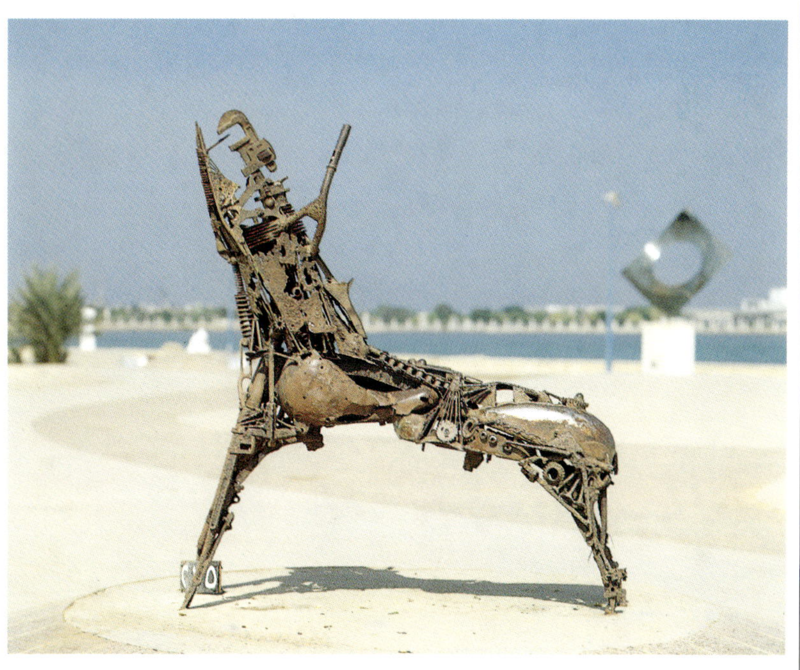

▲ **SCRAP IRON** (66)
Salah Abdulkarim
Scrap Metal

□ Mohamed Said Farsi met Vasarely in Paris in 1981 and commissioned these geometrical sculptures. All are in the Open Air Museum with the exception of *Al-Mafrookah* which was positioned at the intersection of Al-Andalus and Al-Seif Streets so as to be appreciated from both directions.

▼ CHANGING POSITIONS (69)
Victor Vasarely
Enamelled Steel

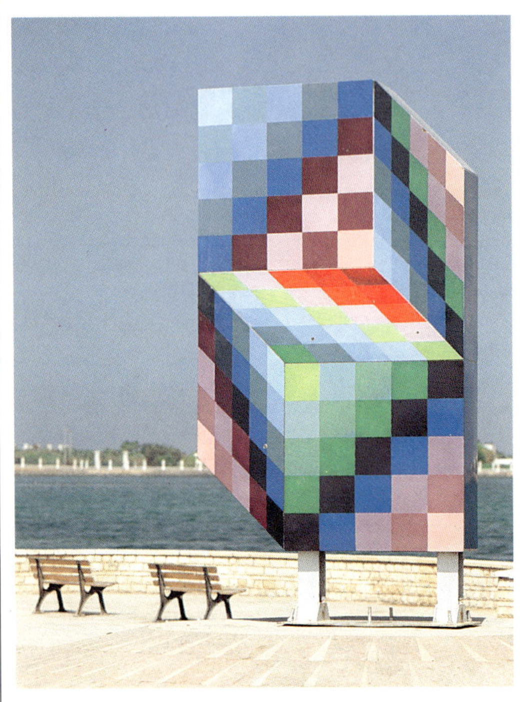

▲ AL-MAFROOKAH (67)
Victor Vasarely
Enamelled Steel

▼ BALANCE IN THE AIR (68)
Victor Vasarely
Enamelled Steel

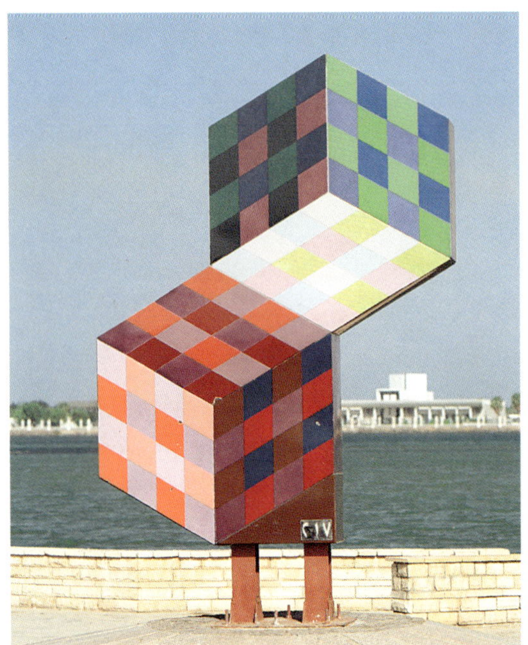

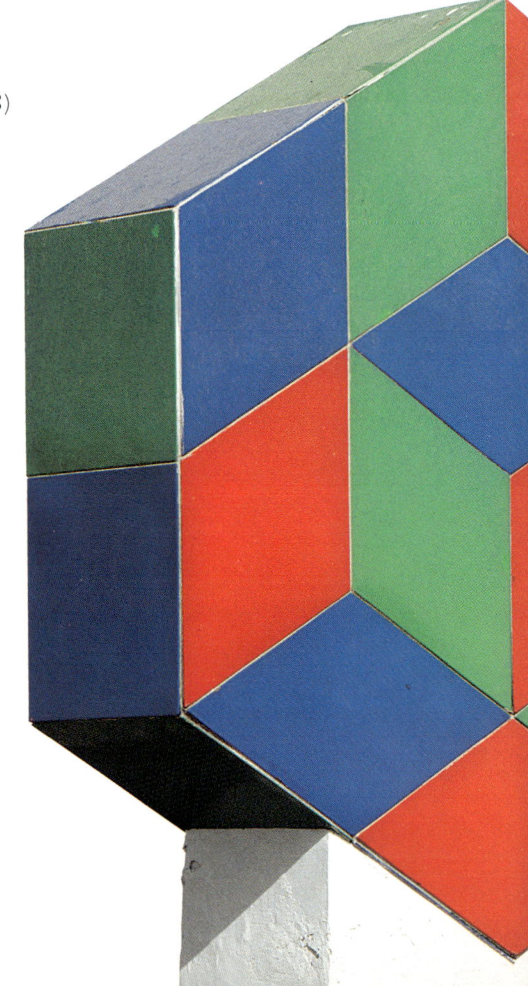

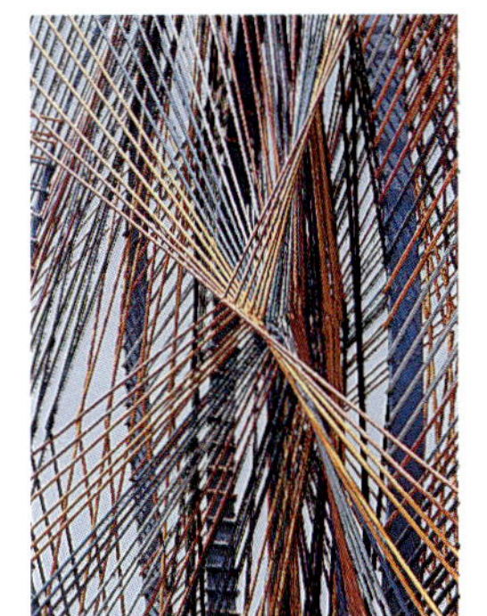

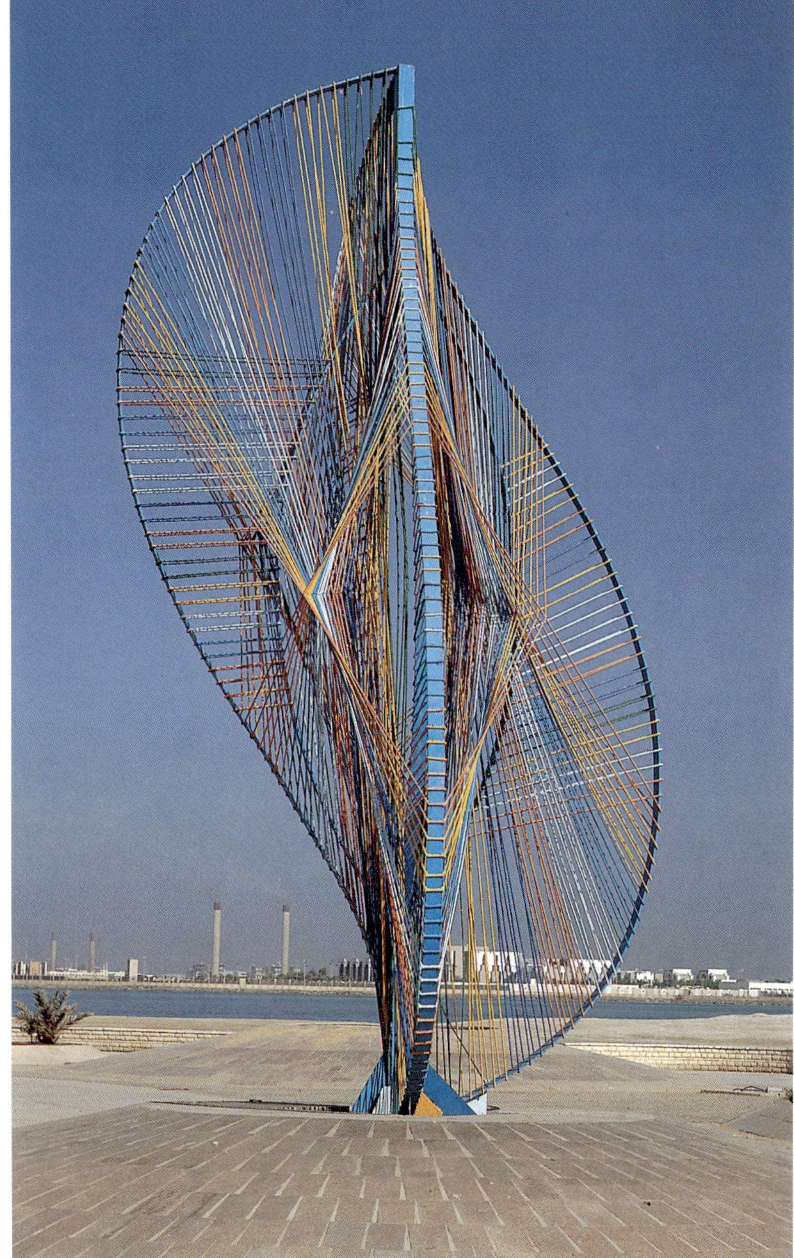

▲ THE FISHERMAN'S NET (71)
Mustafa Senbel
Steel

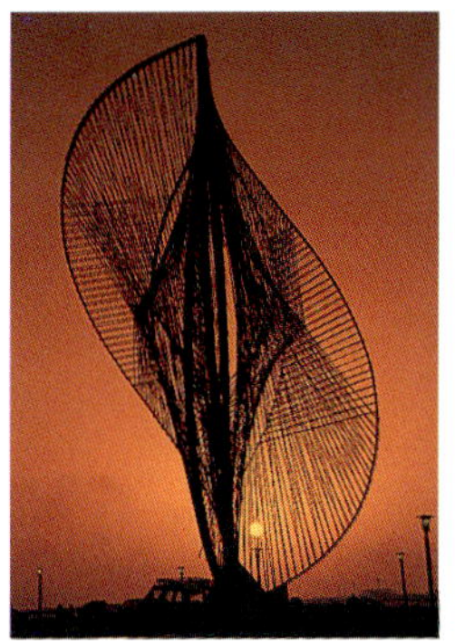

◄ THE ILLUSION OF A SECOND CUBE (70)
Victor Vasarely
Enamelled Steel

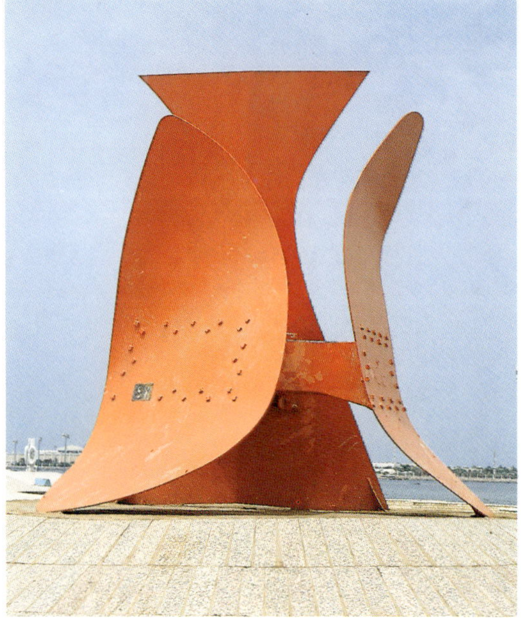

▲ **FLEXIBILITY OF BALANCE** (72)
Alexander Calder
Steel

Although a striking piece, this sculpture is less representative of Calder's work than his better known mobiles. One of his most celebrated works is to be seen in the lobby of New York's John F. Kennedy Airport.

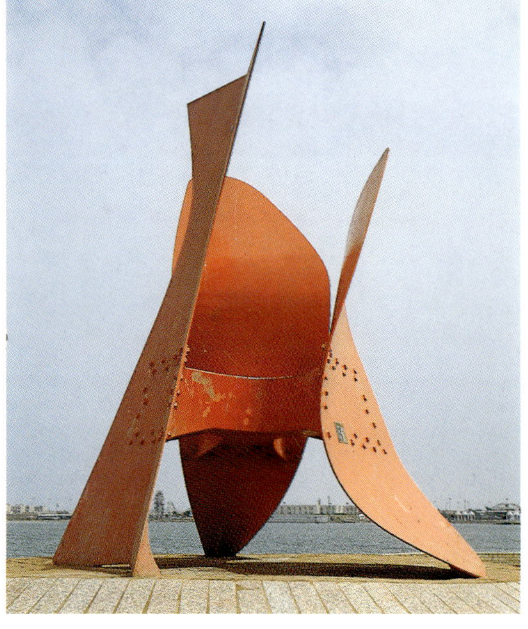

▼ **BALANCE** (Tawazin) (73)
Shafiq Mazloum
Steel

This piece by the late Shafiq Mazloum was one of the first sculptures to be sited on the Corniche.

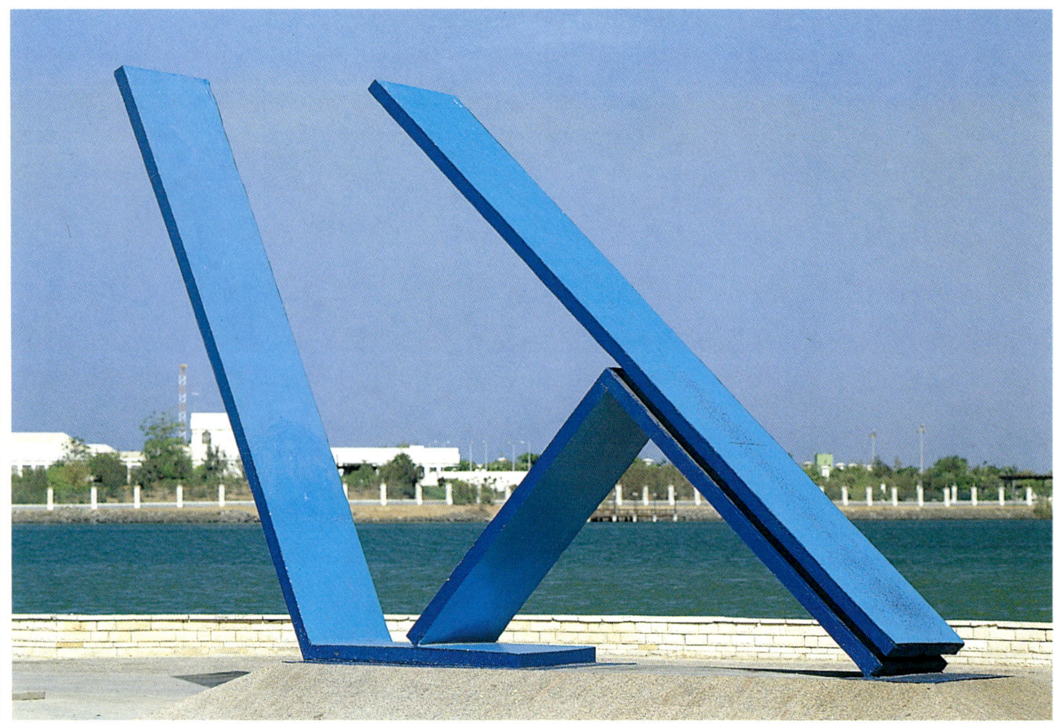

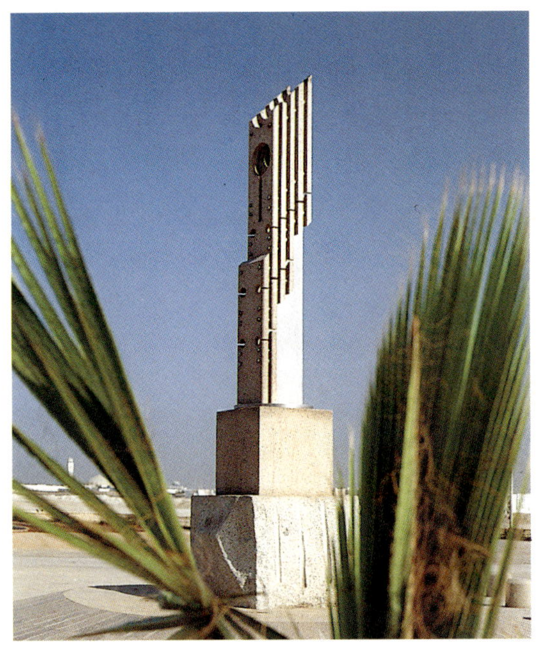

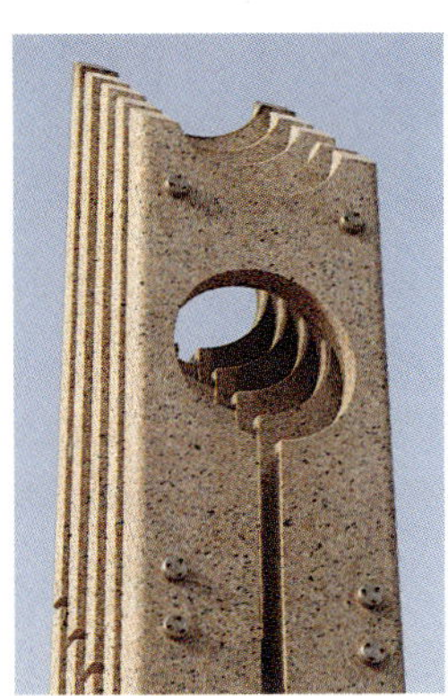

▲ **ARRANGEMENTS** (74)
Cook
Stainless Steel

▼ **ALTERATIONS IN SPACE** (75)
Kofax
Bronze

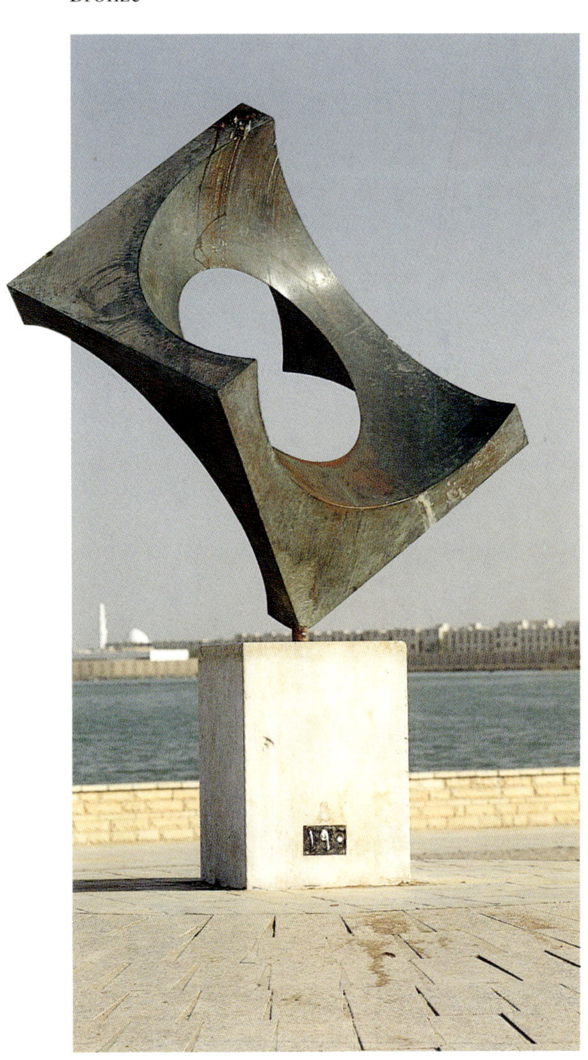

□ The Lebanese artist Aref el Rayess who has studied and worked in Paris and Rome, spent the late seventies in Jeddah. Now based in London, he has described his time in Jeddah as "a period of frenetic activity – it was very exciting to work in that atmosphere". The result was a number of abstract works in a white stone from the Lebanon.

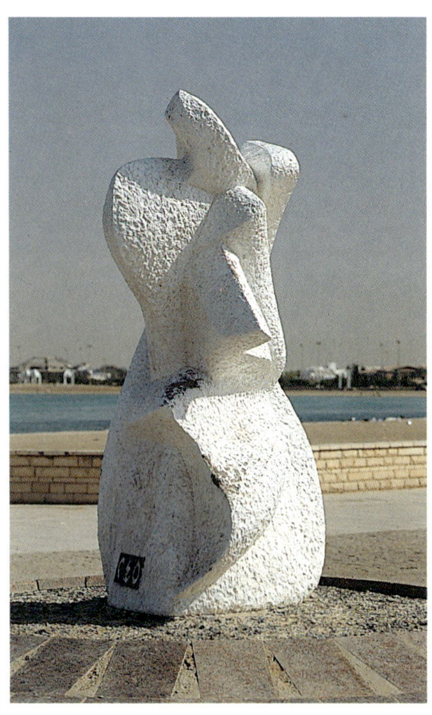

▲ THE GUITAR OF LOVE (76)
Aref el Rayess
Stone

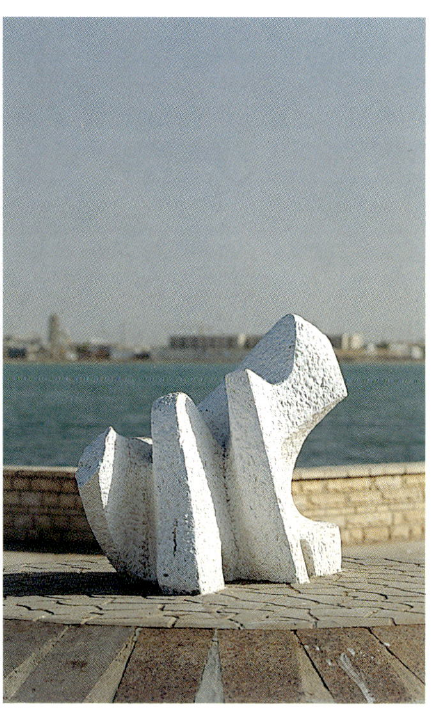

▲ WAITING (77)
Aref el Rayess
Stone

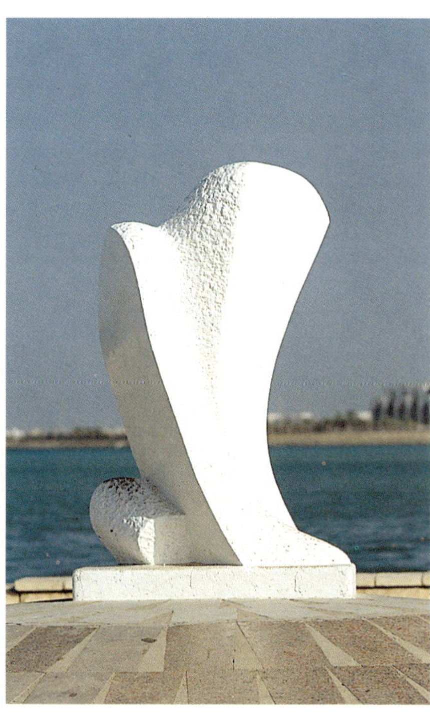

▲ SWIRL (78)
Aref el Rayess
Stone

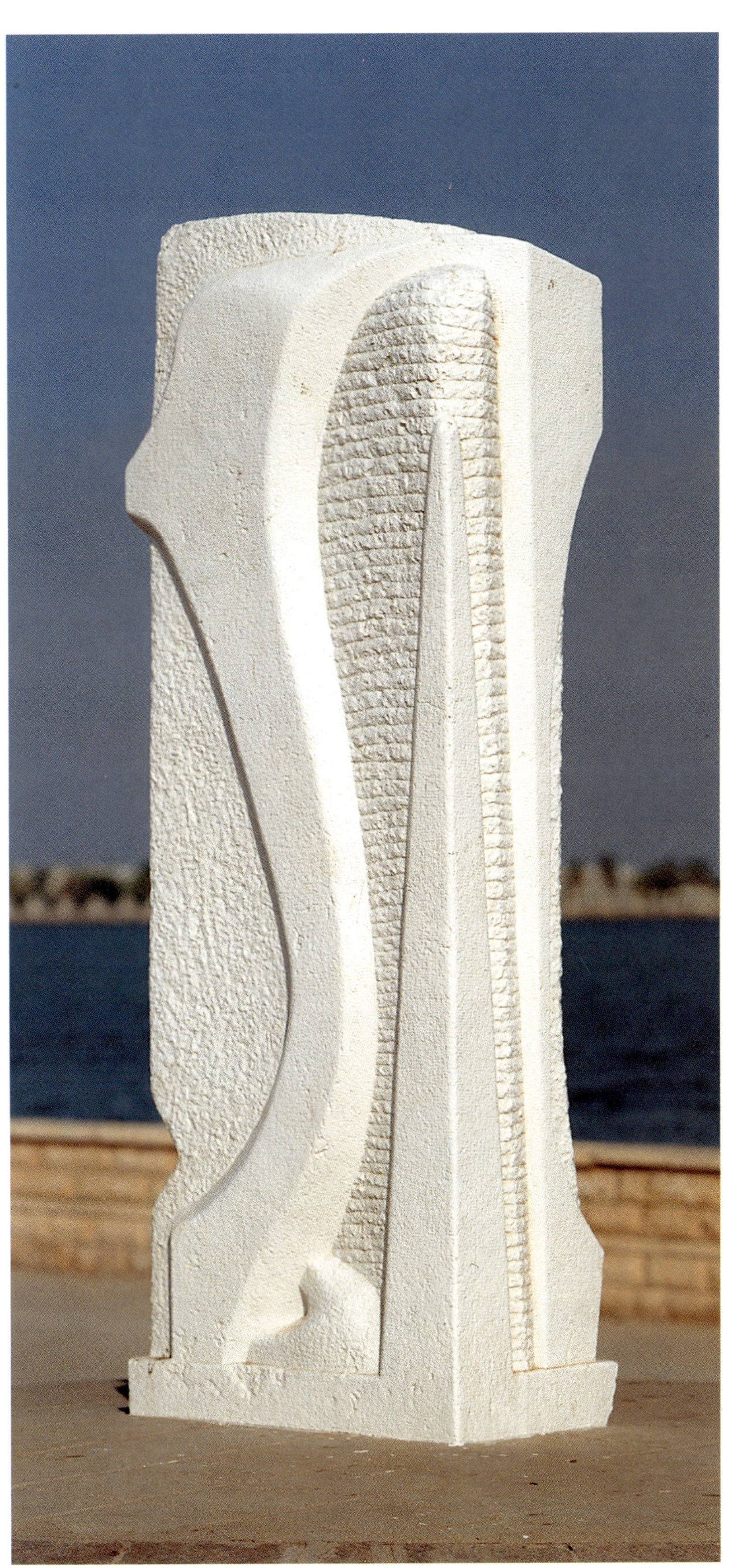

► PURE ABSTRACTION (79)
Aref el Rayess
Stone

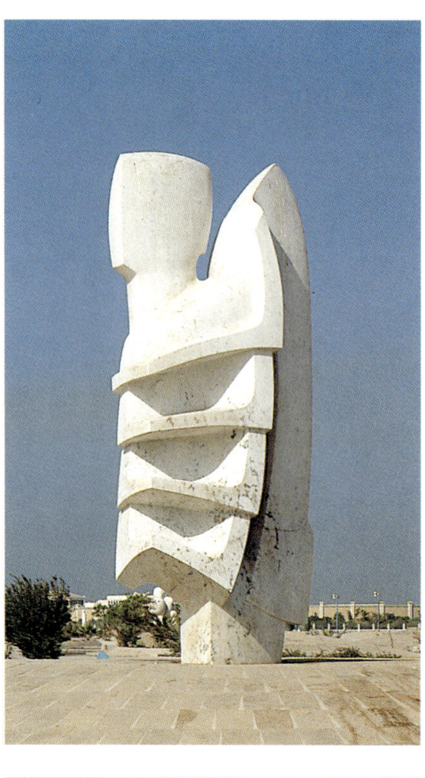

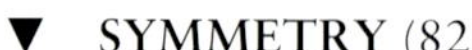

◄ **TELEPHONE** (81)

▼ **CIRCLE AND SQUARE** (80)

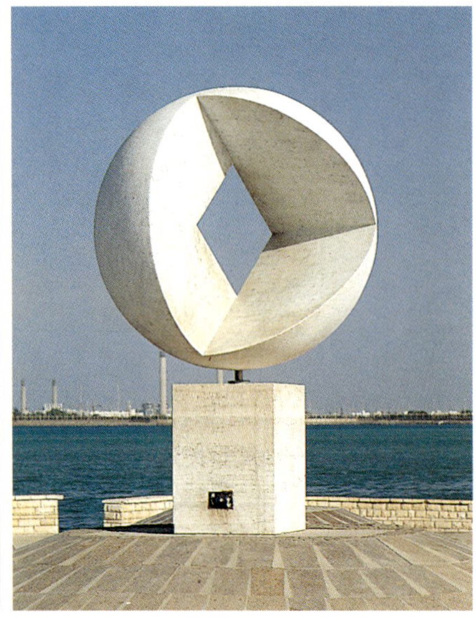

▼ **SYMMETRY** (82)

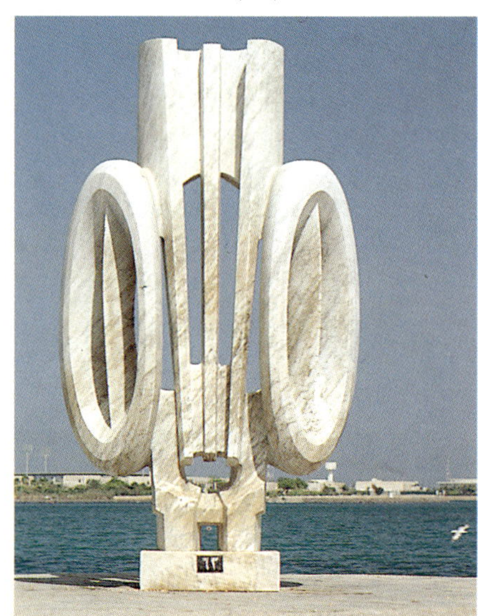

▲ **ROTATION AND BALANCE** (83)

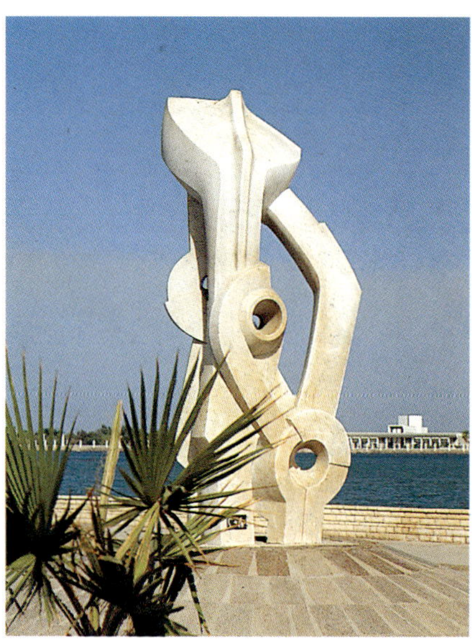

▲ **MUSIC** (84)

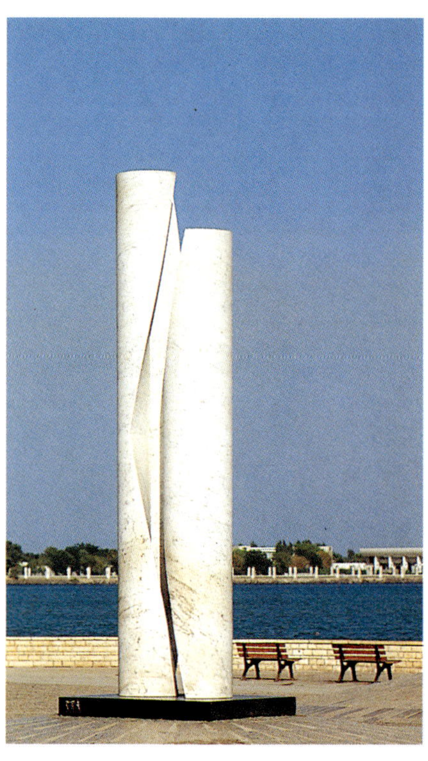

▲ **FAMILY** (85)

□ All of the above works are in marble and were produced by the group of Belgian artists who created sculptures for Jeddah following the 1984 Brussels exhibition: *Jeddah, Yesterday and Today*.

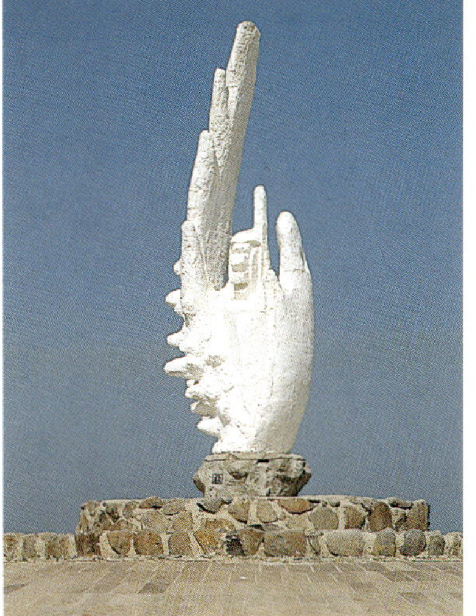

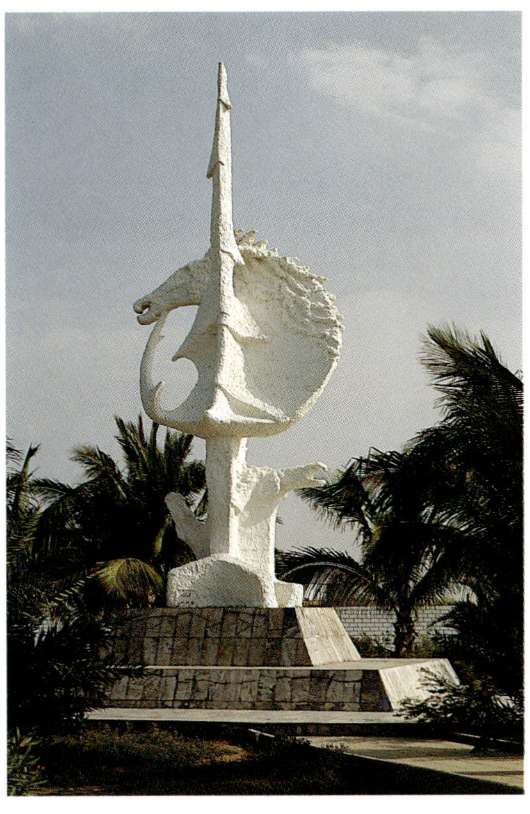

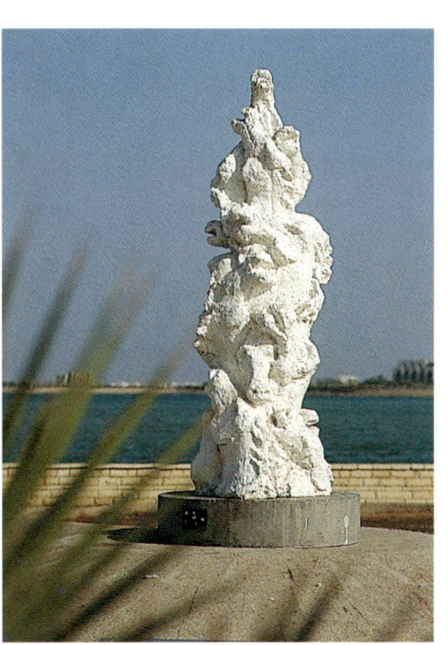

▲ ARAB KNIGHT (87)
Rabi Al-Akhras
Local stone

◄ THE WHITE HORSE (86)
Rabi Al-Akhras
Local stone

► SYMBOLS OF VICTORY (88)
Rabi Al-Akhras
Local stone

▼ UNITY IS STRENGTH (89)
Paul Speld
Veined white marble

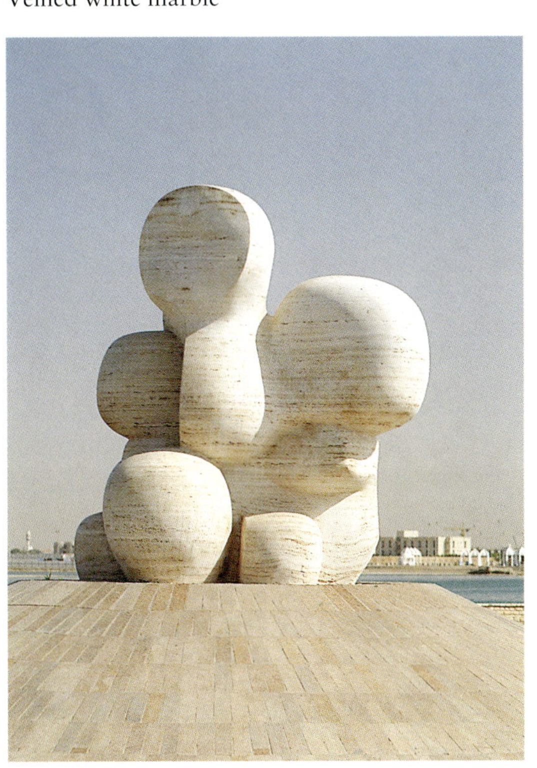

▼ CRESCENT AND MOON (90)
Pietro Cascella
Local stone

This sculpture is one of many in Jeddah which refer to the significance of the moon – particularly the new or crescent moon (*Al-Hilal*) in Arab and Islamic culture.

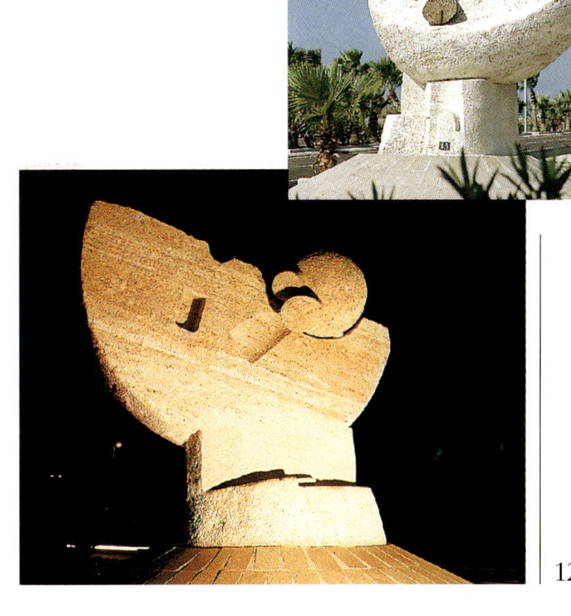

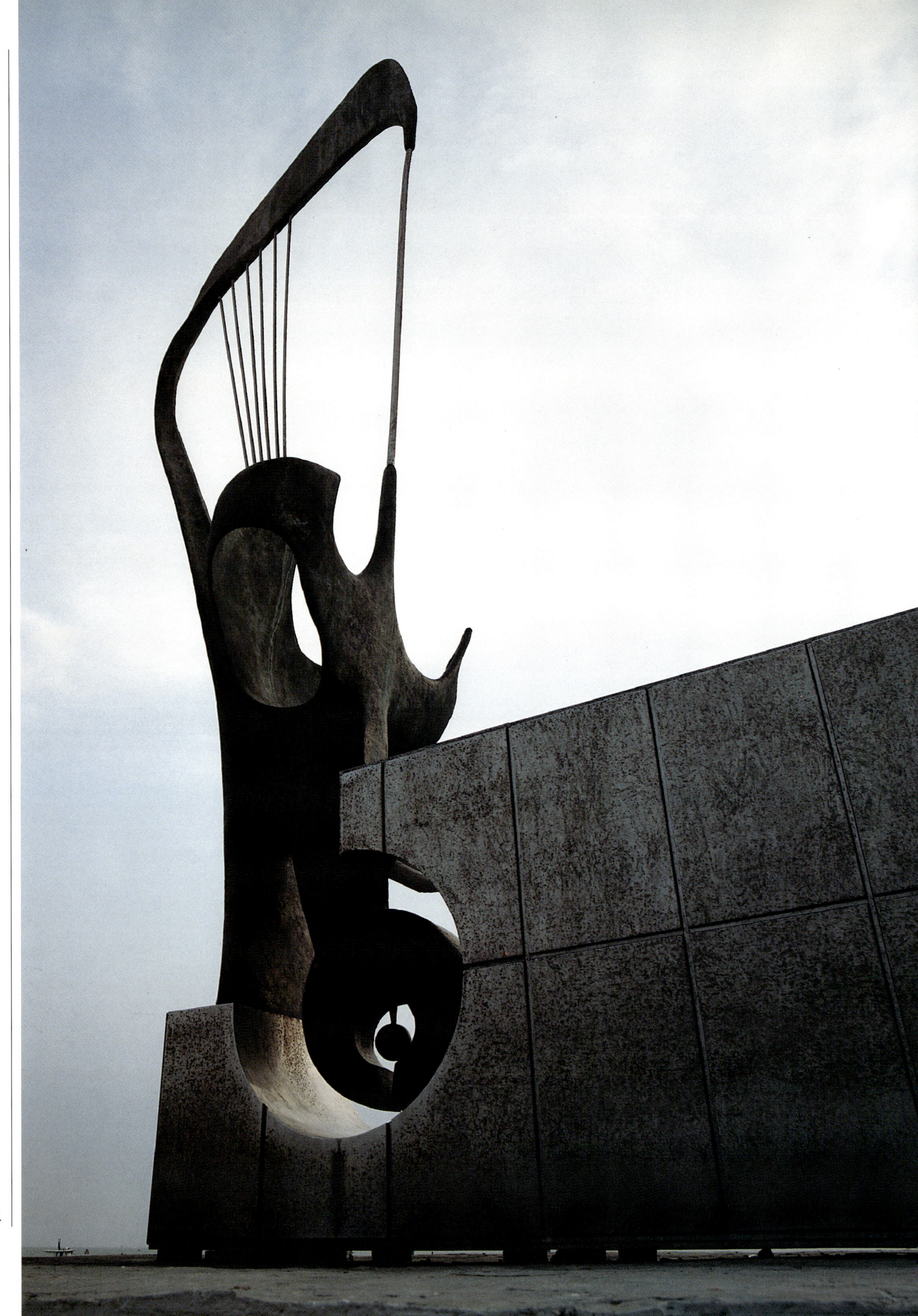

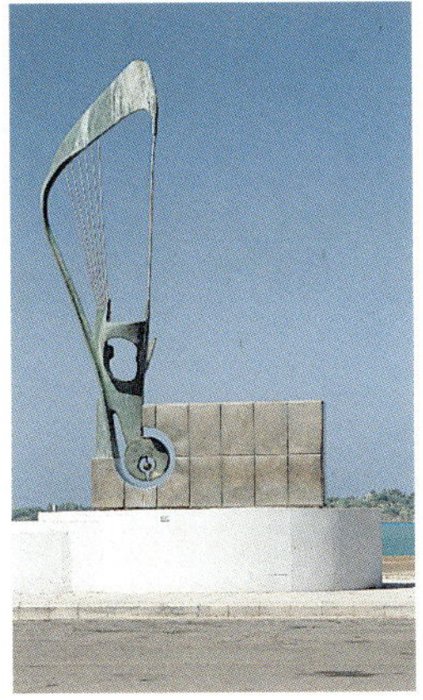

◄ THE SEMSEMIAH (91)
Oscar Estranoma
Steel and Stone

This piece is a representation of a traditional Arab musical instrument which is a combination of a lute and violin. It is particularly popular at festive gatherings and usually accompanies dancing.

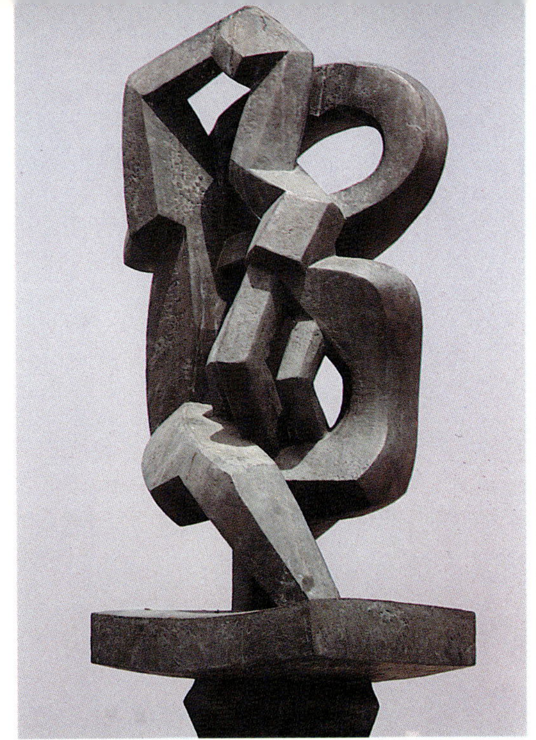

▲ EARLY CUBISM (92)
Jacques Lipchitz
Bronze

This internationally known Lithuanian American (1891-1973) was also known for his transparent sculptures.

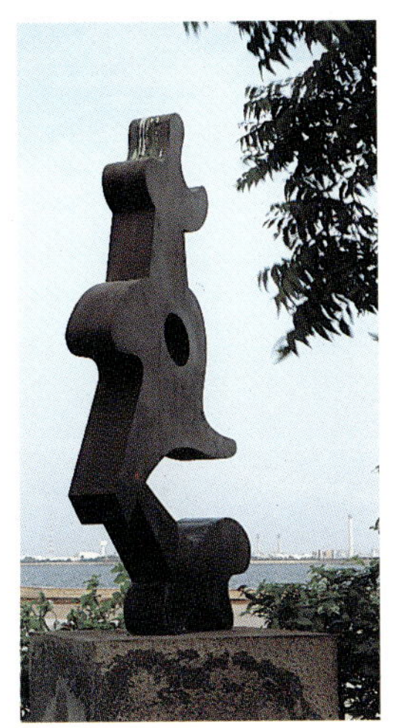

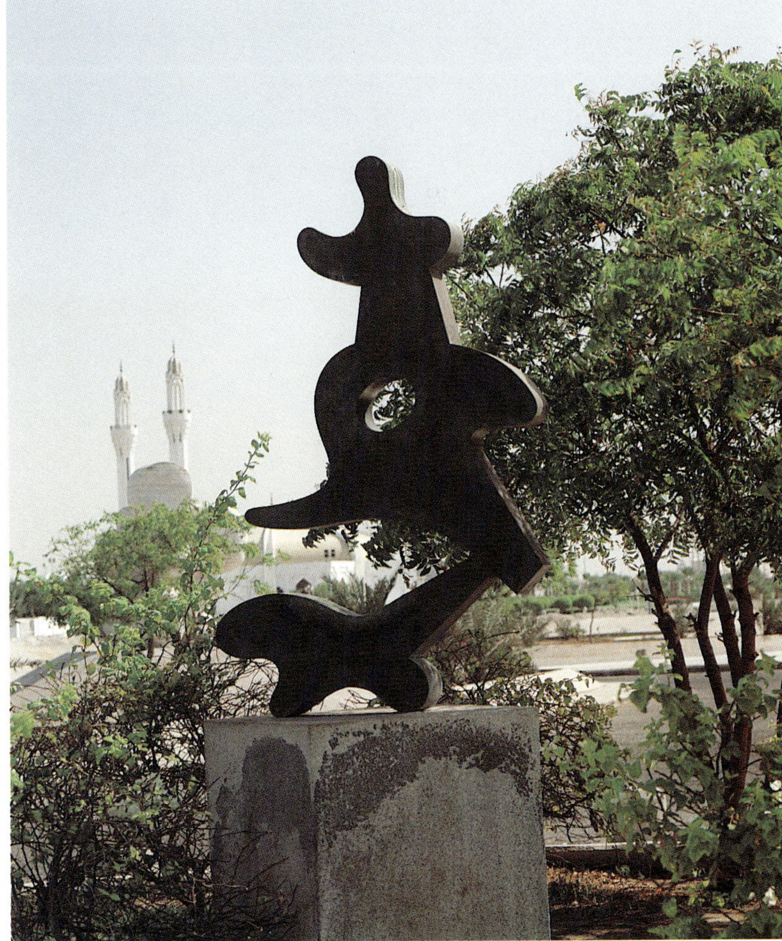

► A STEP FORWARD (93)
Jean Arp
Bronze

Jean Arp (1887-1966), a native of France, helped to found the Dada movement and was also associated with the Surrealists in the 1920s, before founding the group *Abstraction – Creation* in 1931 and directing his efforts towards sculpture.

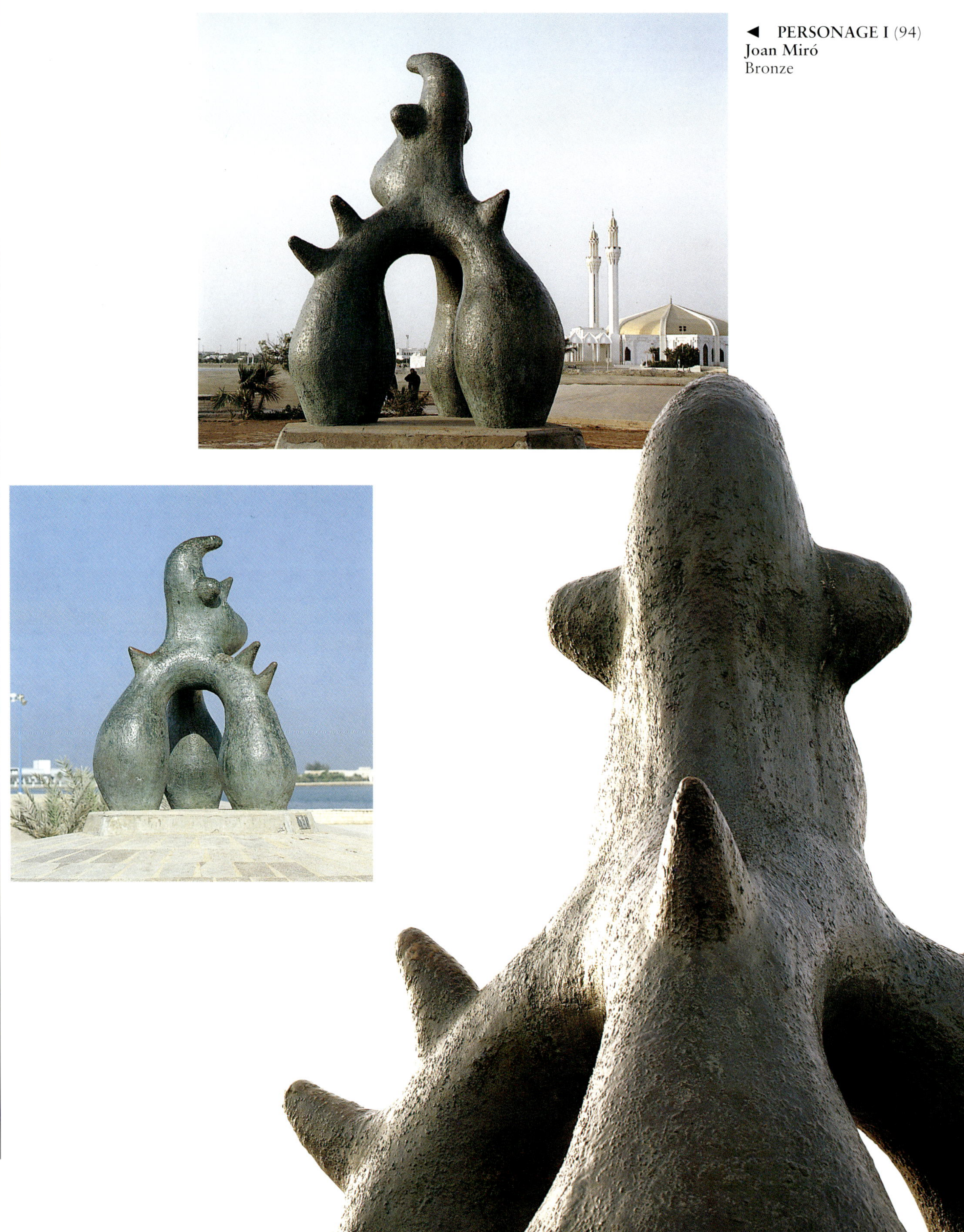

◄ **PERSONAGE I** (94)
Joan Miró
Bronze

□ The early work of Joan Miró (1893-1983) shows the influence of various modern movements such as Fauvism, Cubism and Dadaism, but he is chiefly associated with the Surrealists. Indeed, Breton – one of his fellow Surrealists – described him as "probably the most Surrealistic of us all". He was noted for a playful approach to his work.

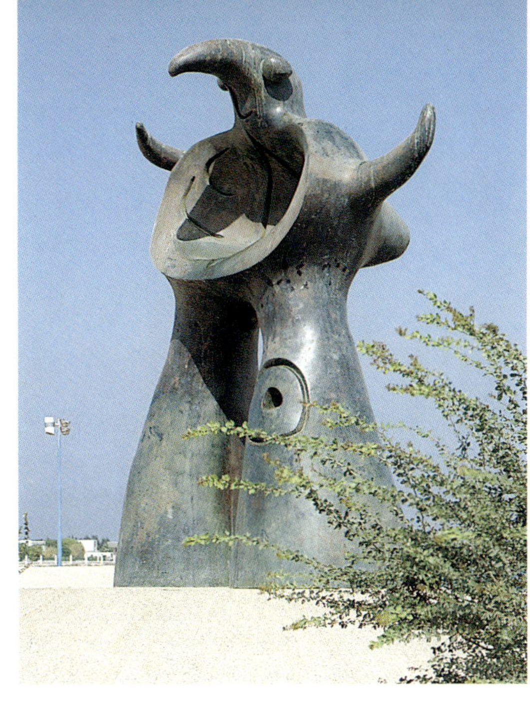

▲ **PERSONAGE II** (95)
Joan Miró
Bronze

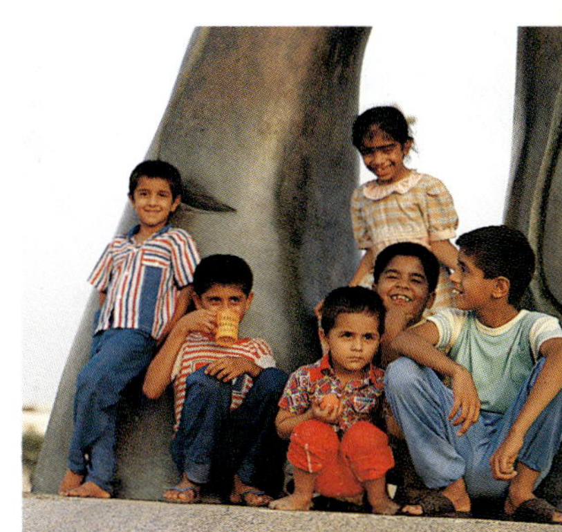

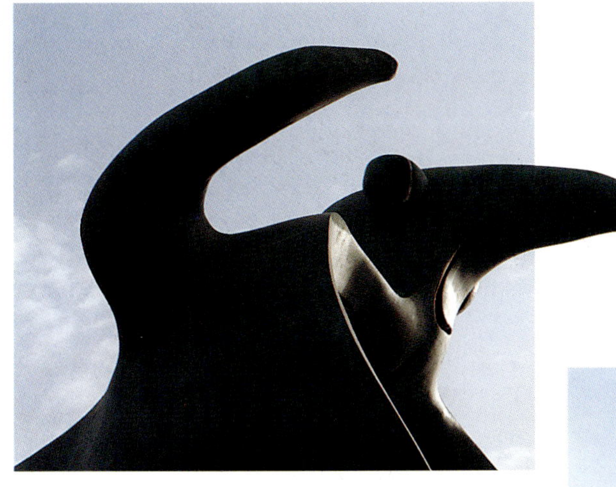

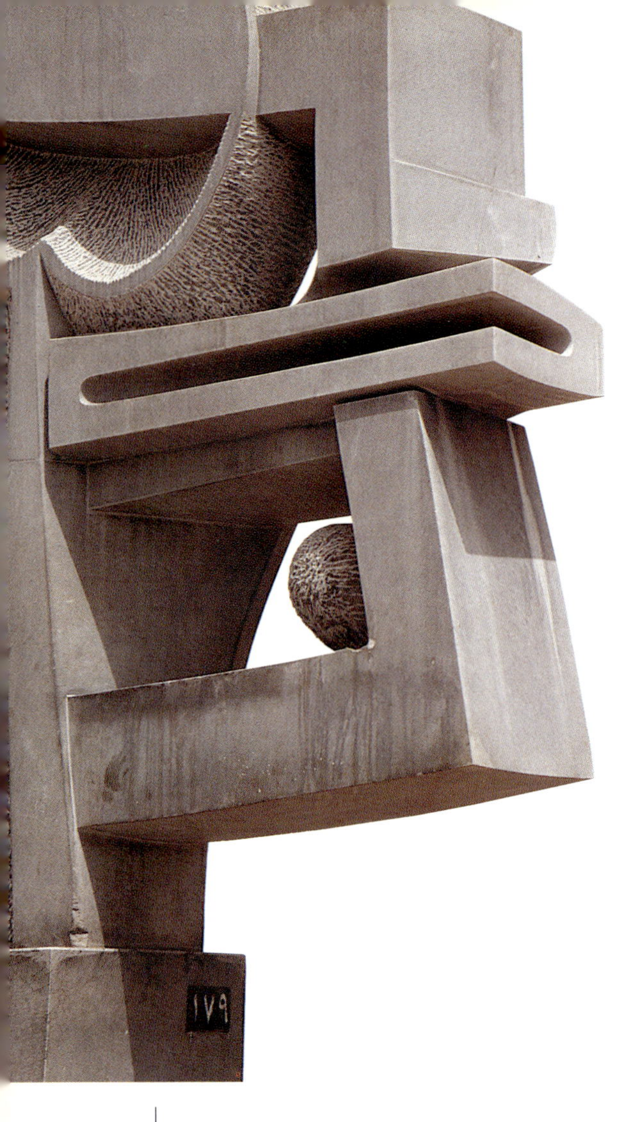

□ **FRUSTRATION** (96)
Unknown Belgian Artist
Concrete

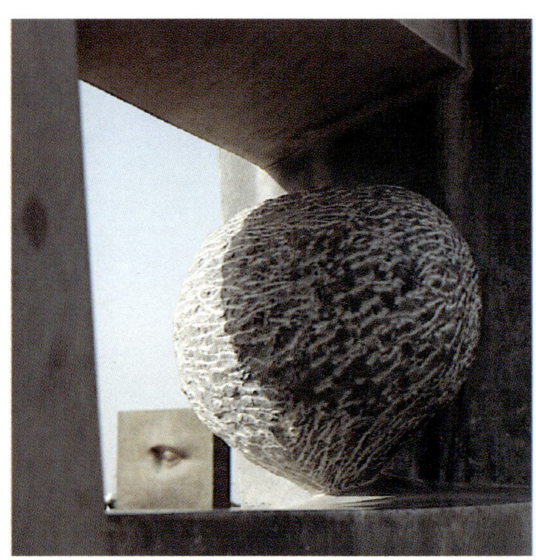

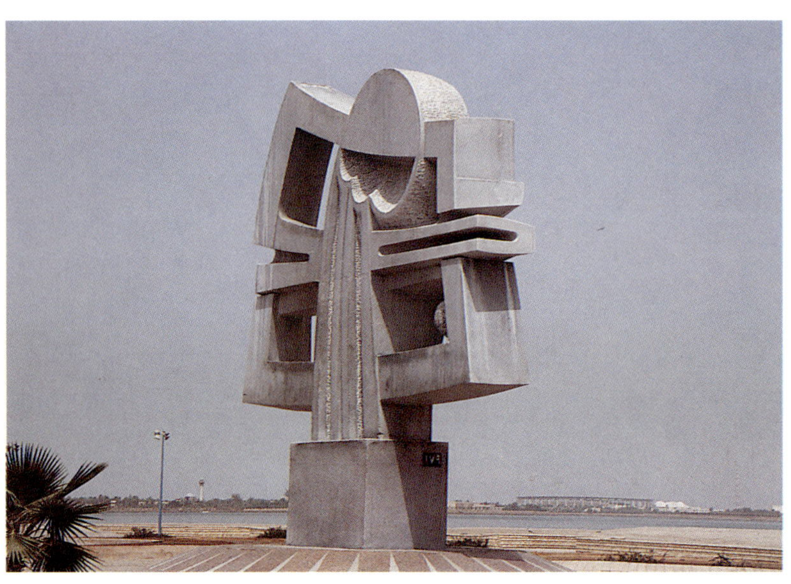

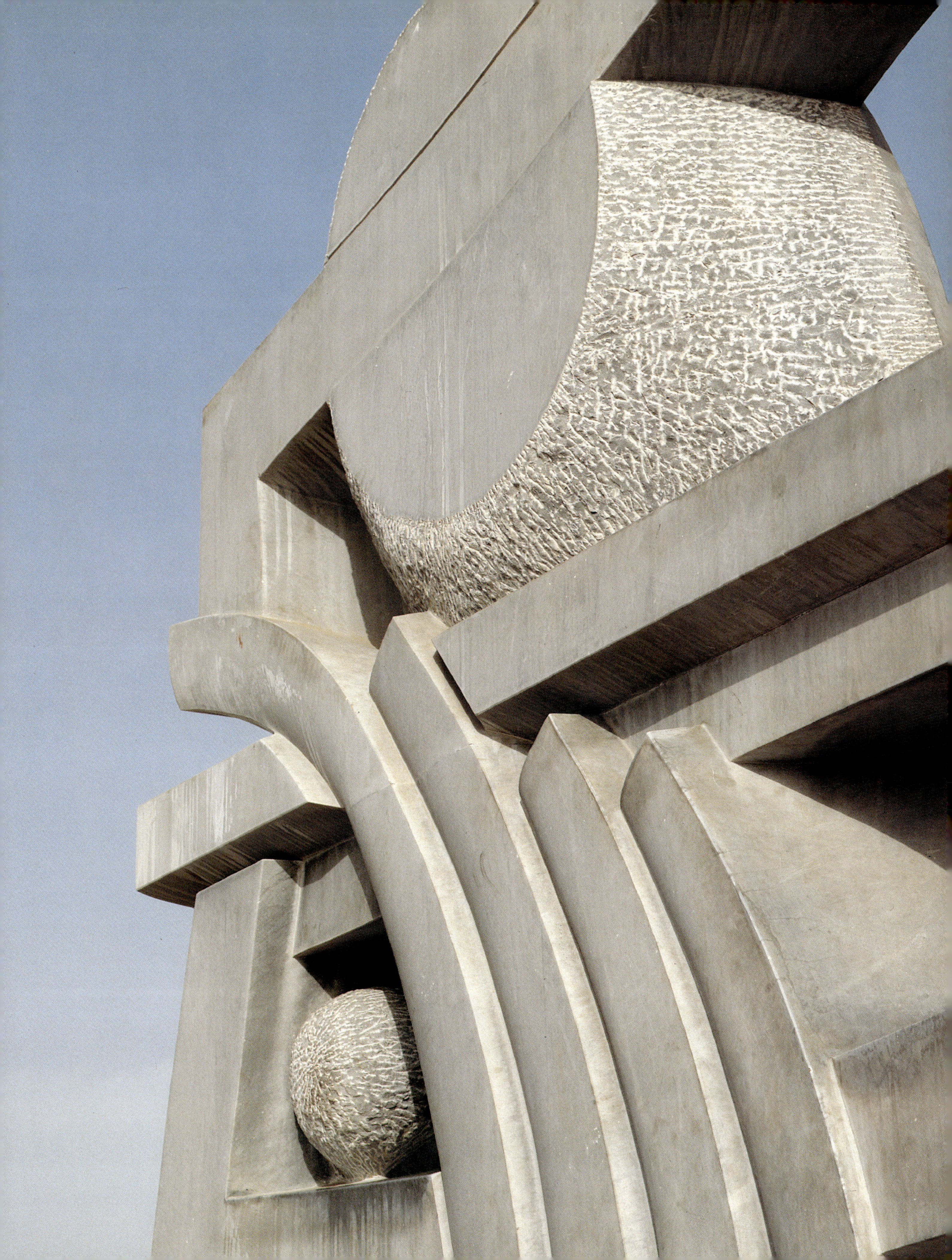

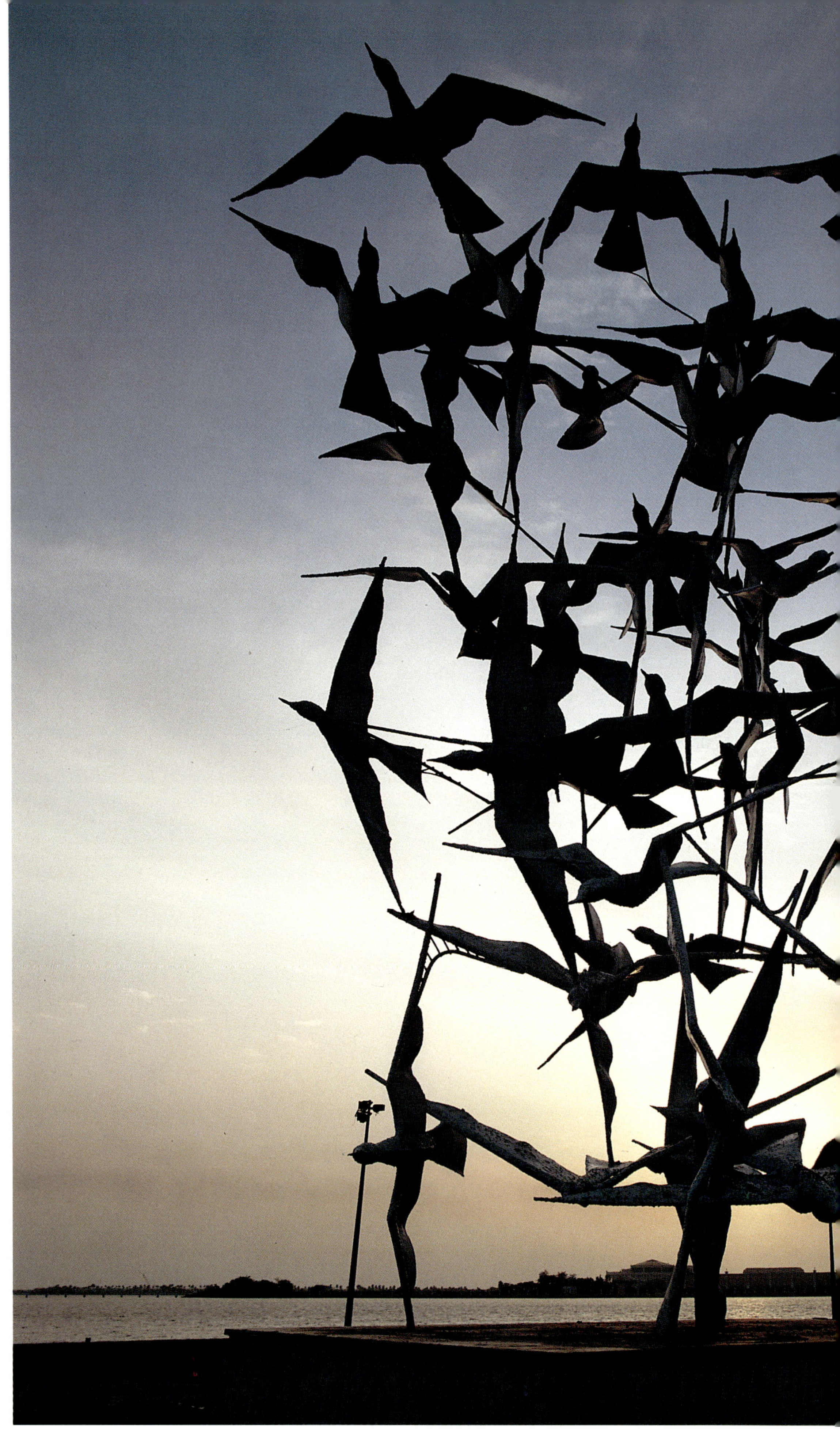

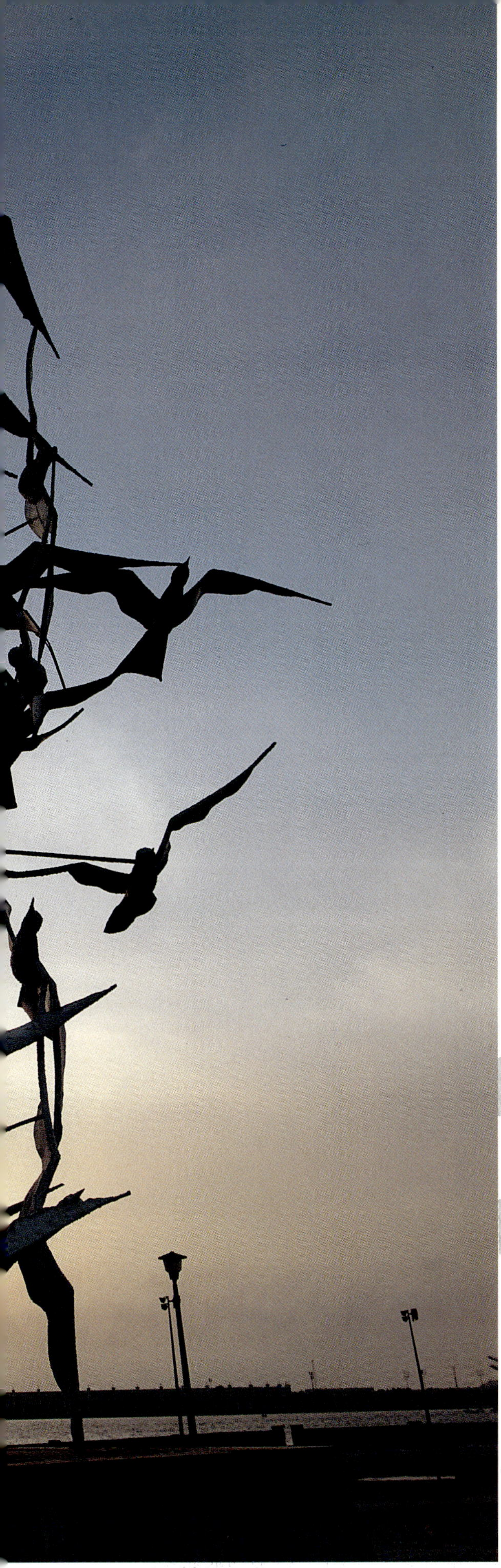

□ **MIGRANT BIRDS** (97)
Sylvestre Giovanni
Steel

This work, by an Italian artist who Mohamed Said Farsi met in Milan, represents one of the flocks of birds which migrate from Africa northwards via the Arabian Peninsula.

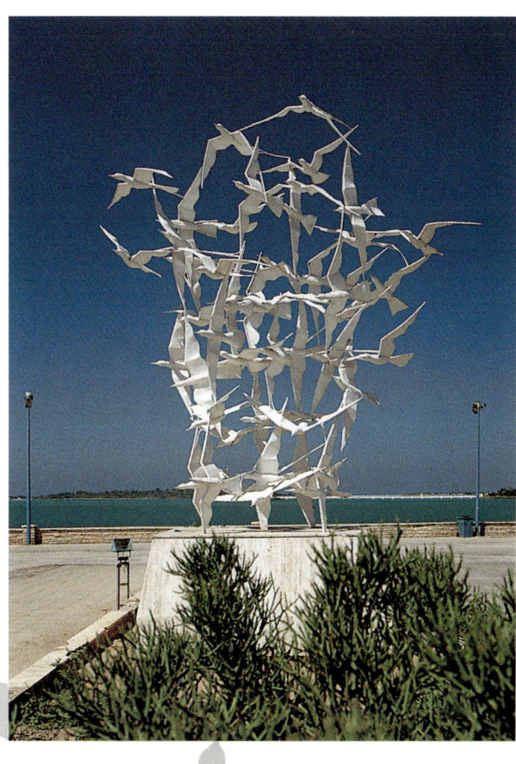

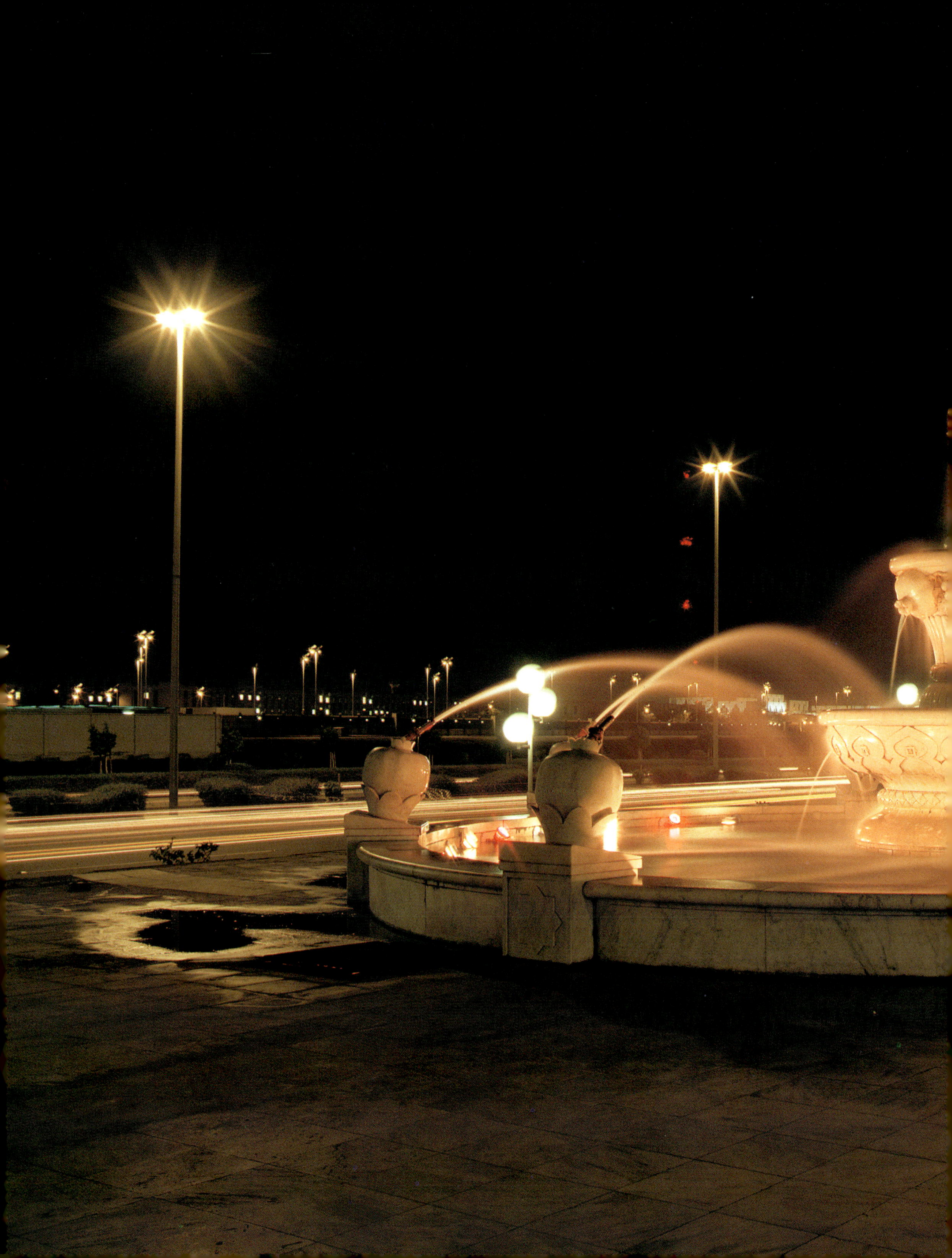

The INTERSECTIONS and PARKS

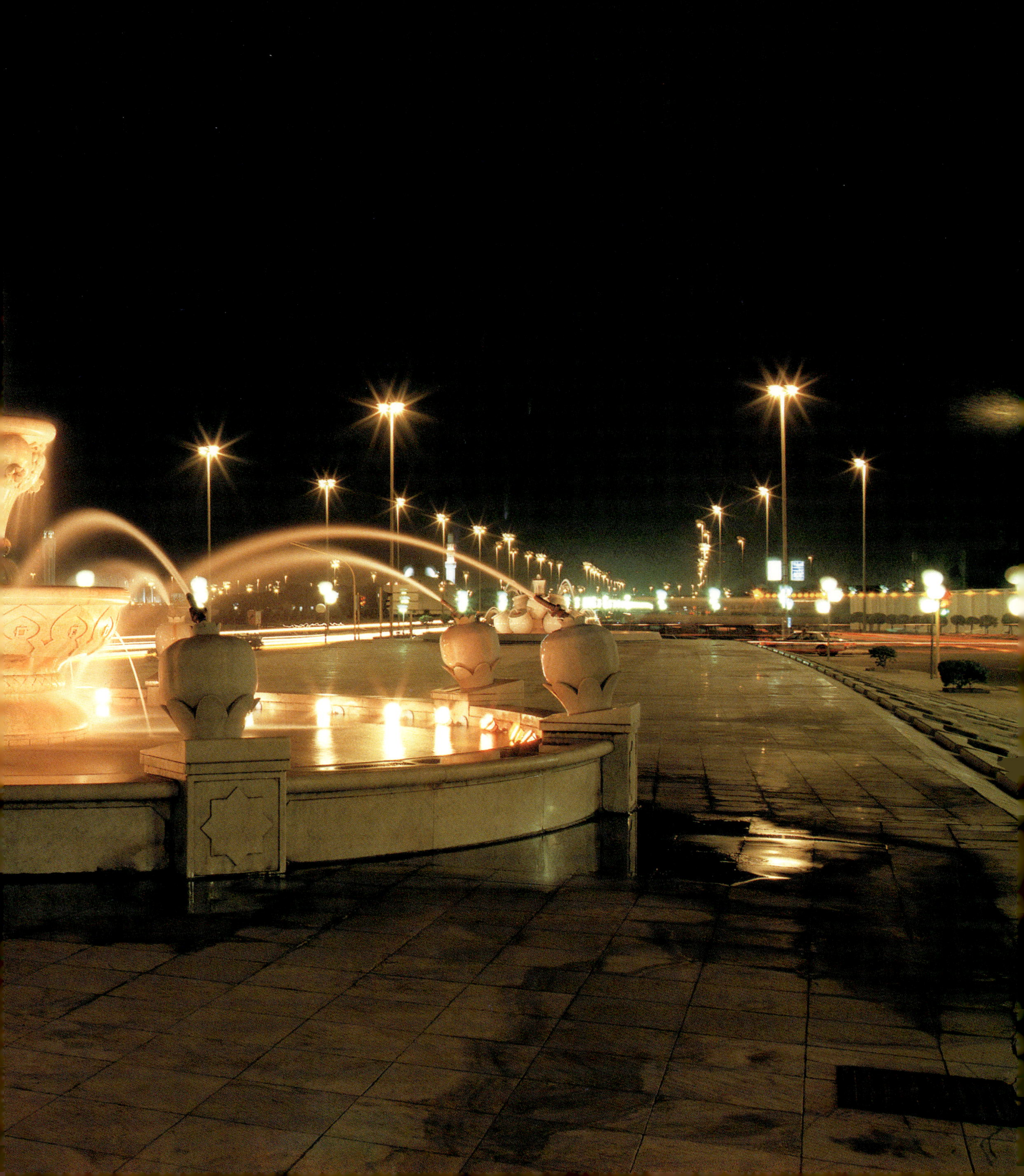

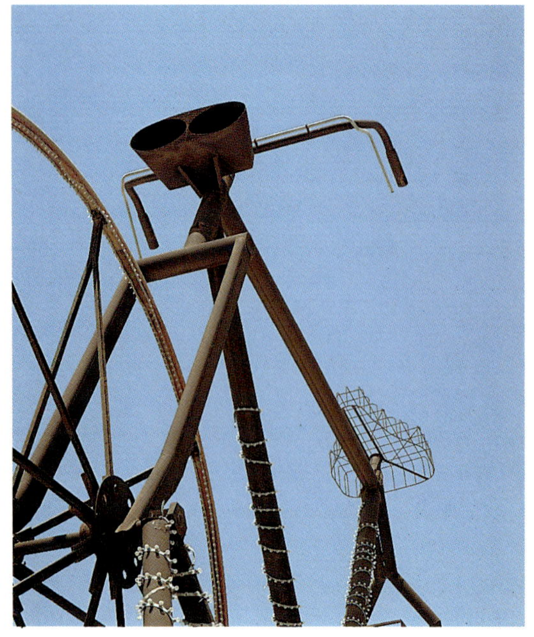

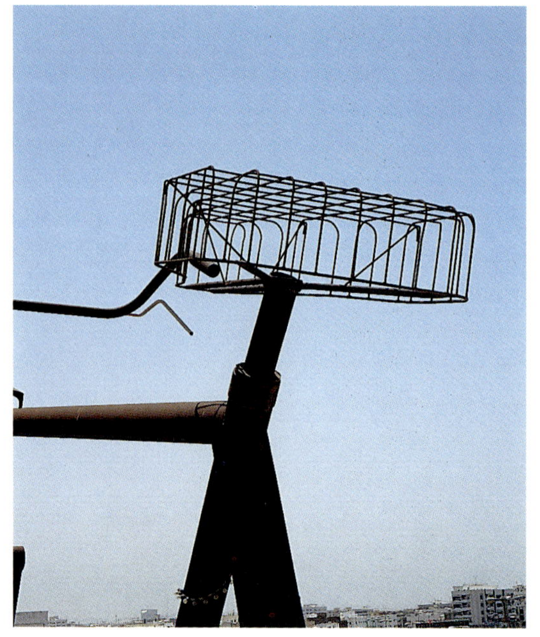

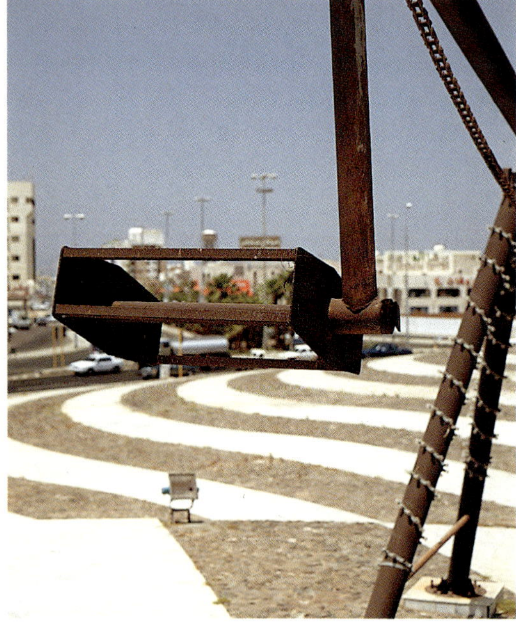

This *'Monument to the Unknown Cyclist'* by the ever-inventive Julio Lafuente is probably Jeddah's best-known sculpture. The Spanish architect-turned-sculptor used scrap materials from a derelict factory to create this 15 metre high boneshaker. Here, as in other monuments, Lafuente has also invested much time and effort in the design of the base, and the placing of the Spare Wheel (100) some 90 metres away helps to emphasise the scale of the work.

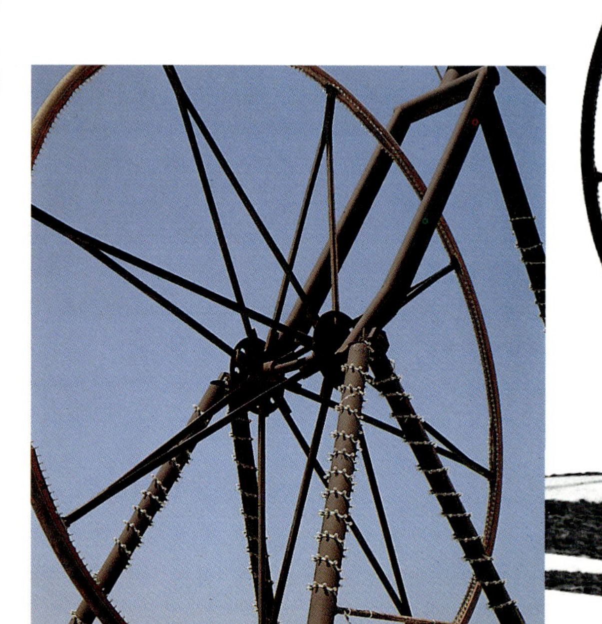

◄◄◄ POMEGRANATE FOUNTAIN (98)
Julio Lafuente
Marble

□ **THE BICYCLE** (Al-Darrajah) (99)
Julio Lafuente
Steel

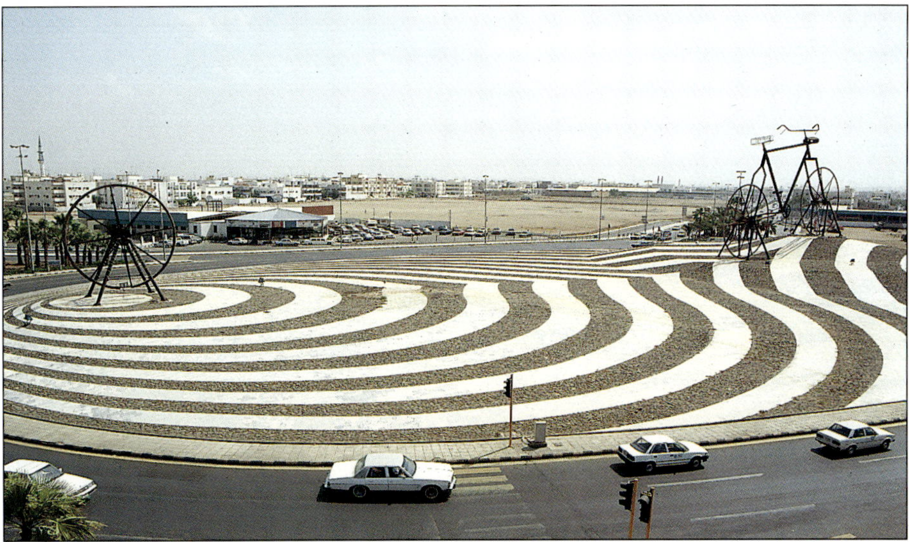

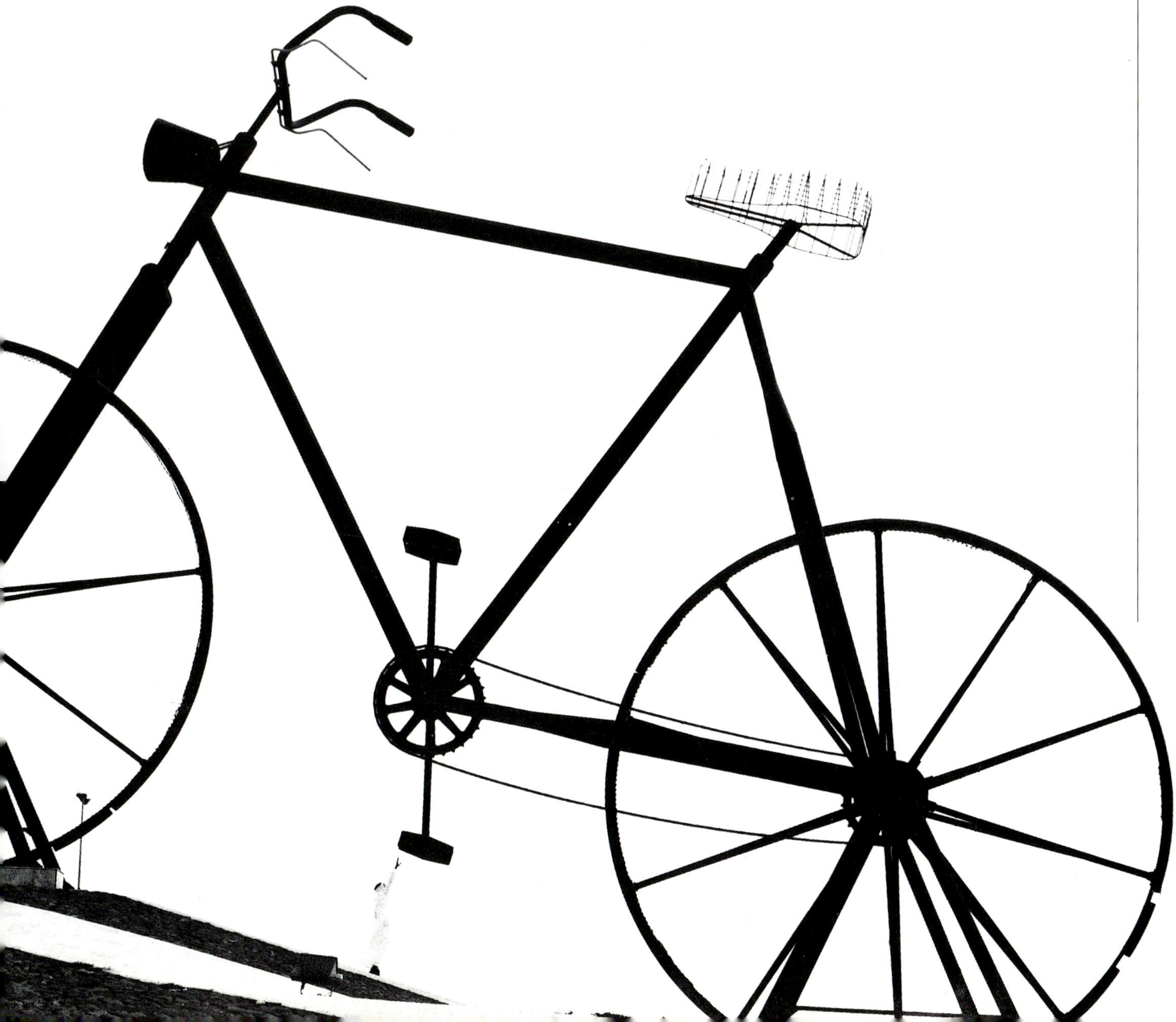

□ **VERSE BOAT** (Qareb Al-Doa'a) (101)
Julio Lafuente
Bronze

Computer Aided Design (CAD) techniques were used in the creation of this 20-tonne bronze calligraphic sculpture to ensure the accuracy of the proportions of its mould. The text reads: *"And say: 'My Lord, lead me in with a just ingoing, and lead me out with a just outgoing: Grant me authority from thee to help me.'"* (Holy Koran 17:80)

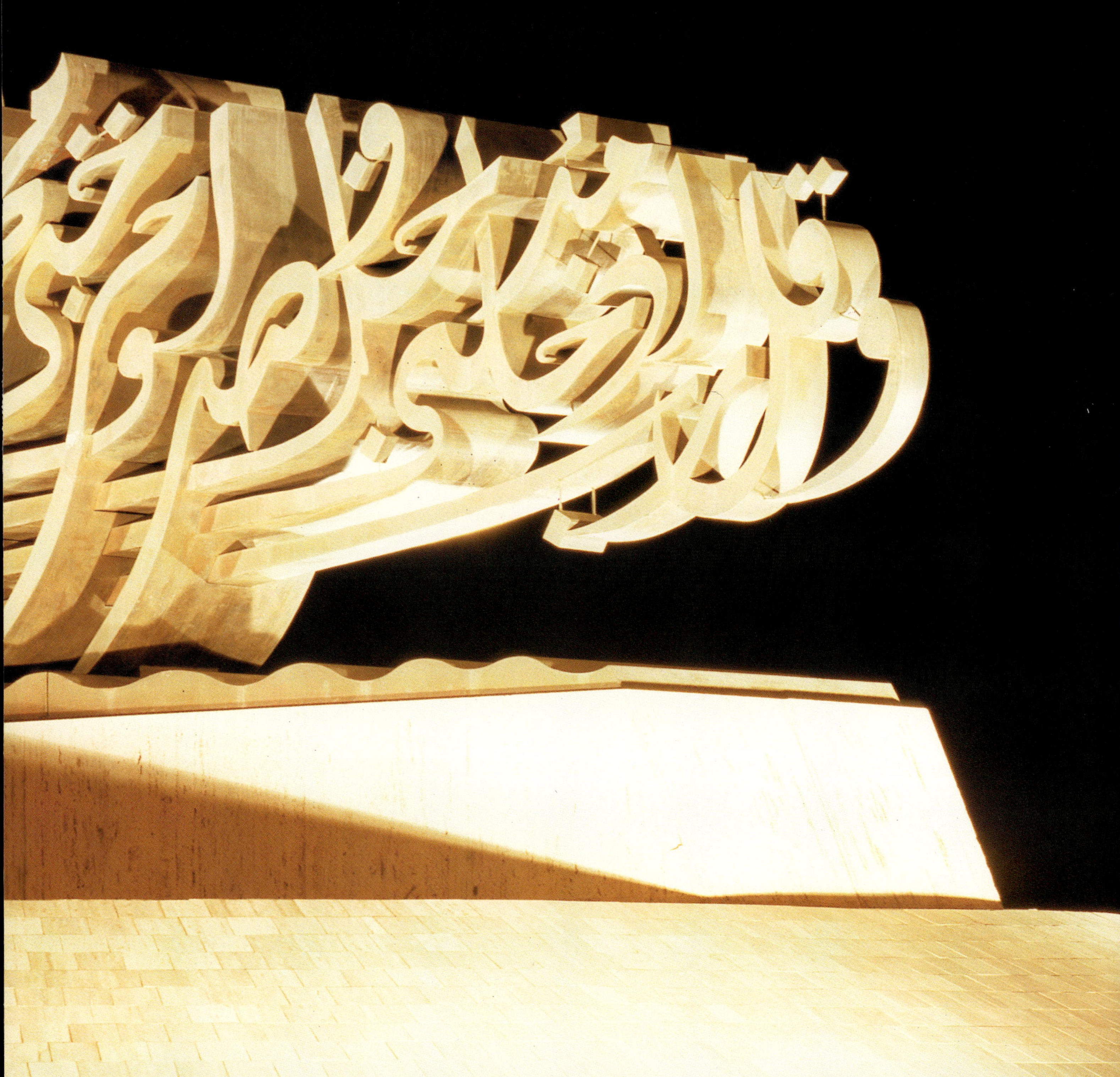

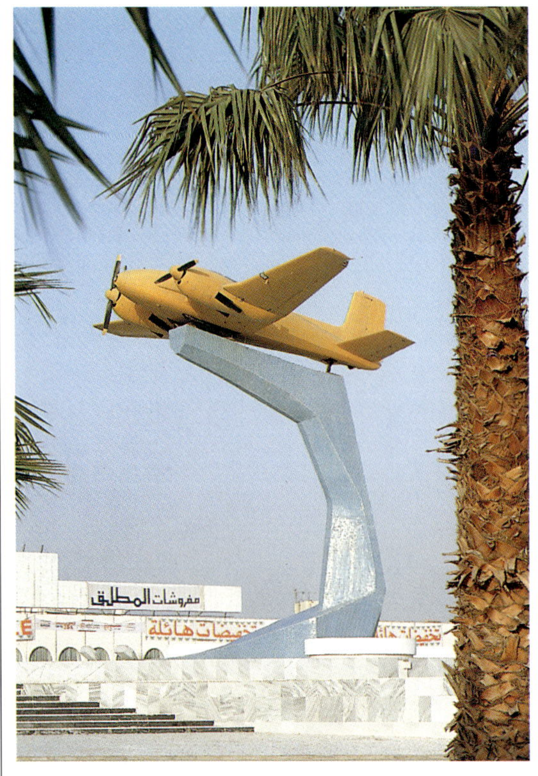

▲ TWIN-ENGINED AIRCRAFT (102)

□ Jeddah has enough aircraft monuments to fill a small aviation museum, ranging from a Vampire jet fighter to one of Saudia's veteran Dakotas. The Lockheed which stands in simulated take-off on a plinth at the end of the old airport's runway, was a gift to King Abdul Aziz from President Roosevelt.

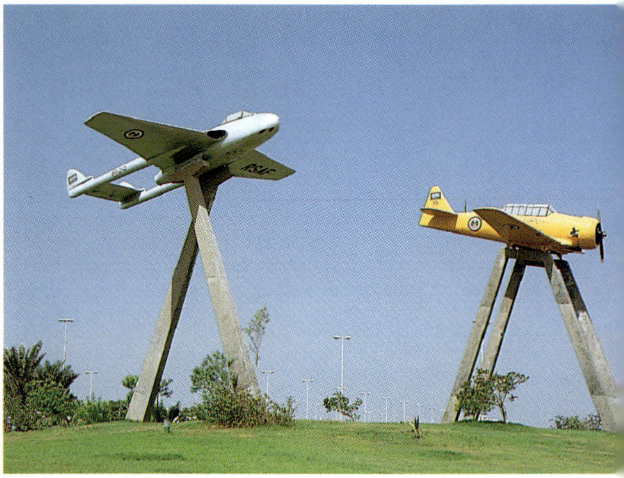

▲ FIGHTER AIRCRAFT AND TRAINER (104)

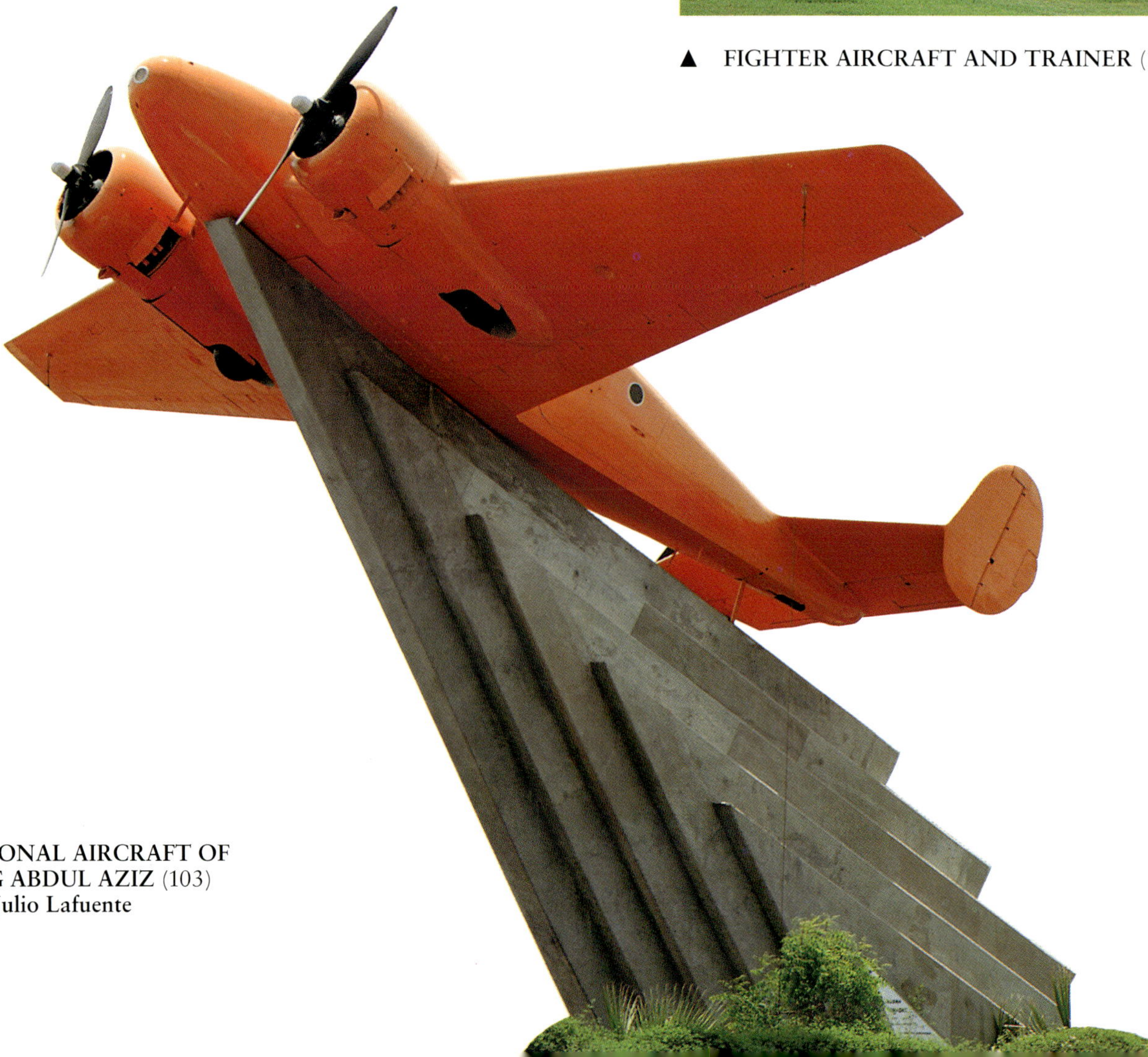

► PERSONAL AIRCRAFT OF KING ABDUL AZIZ (103)
Plinth by Julio Lafuente

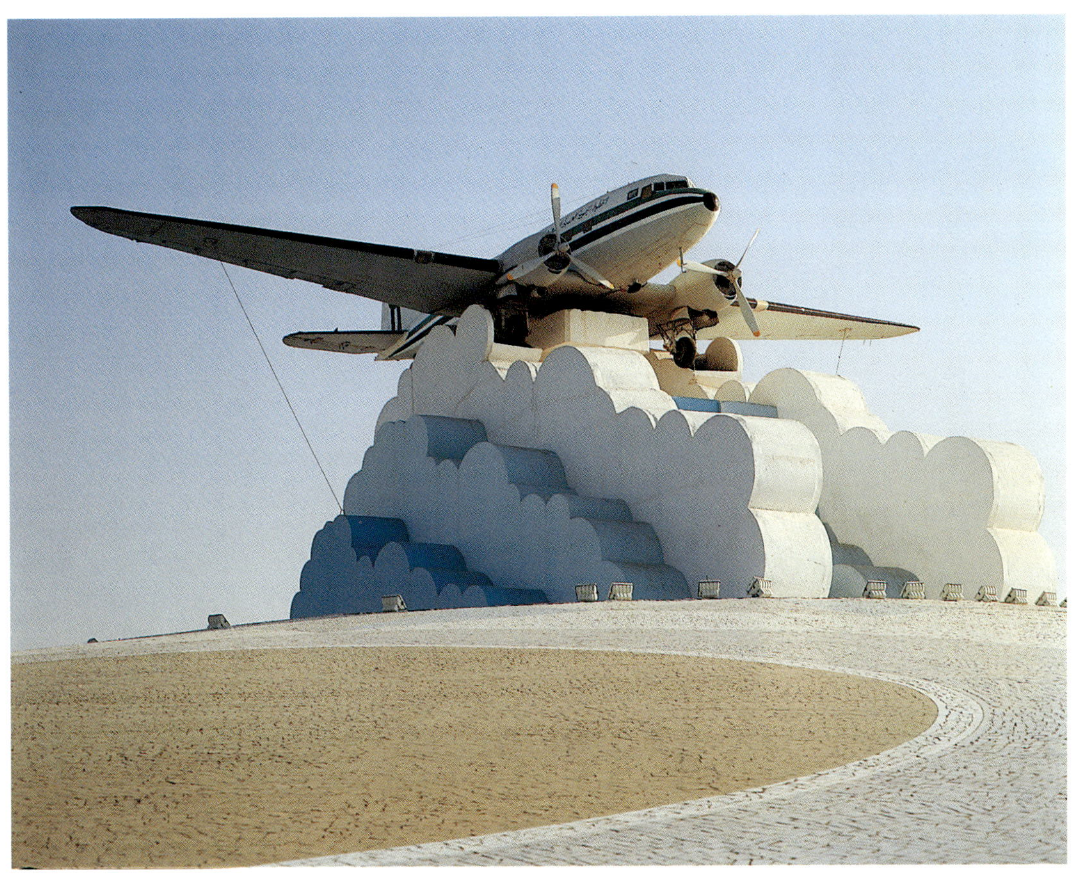

▲ **CLOUDS** (105)
Julio Lafuente
DC3 and reinforced concrete

This veteran Dakota in authentic period livery was a gift from Saudia and is a relic from the days when the airline's entire fleet consisted of this and two similar aircraft. Illuminated at night this spectacular monument is located on Prince Majed Street between the old airport and KAIA.

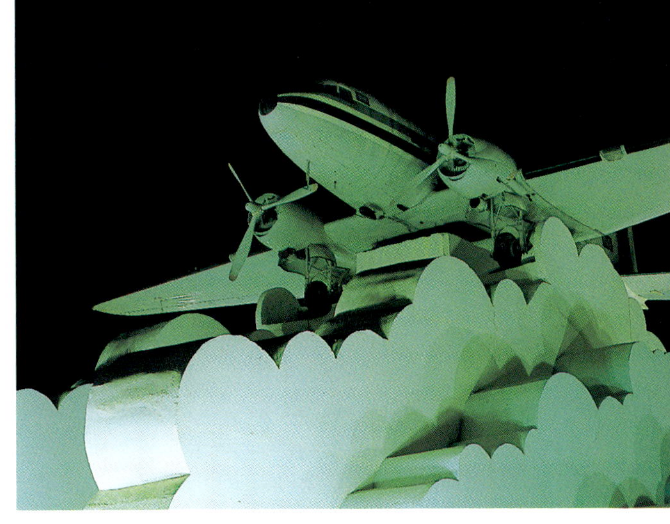

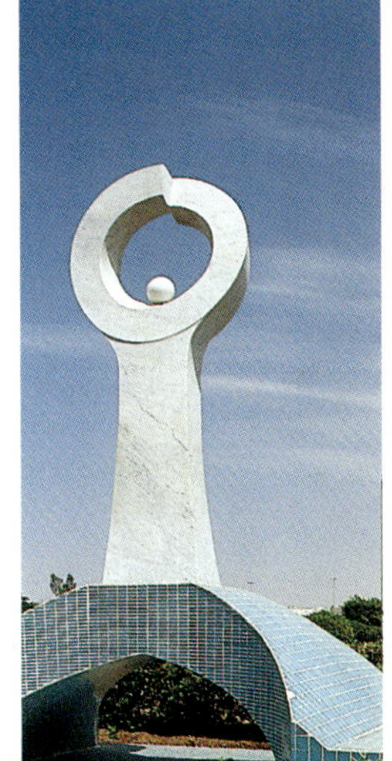

◄ **RATCHET SPANNER** (106)
Artist Unknown

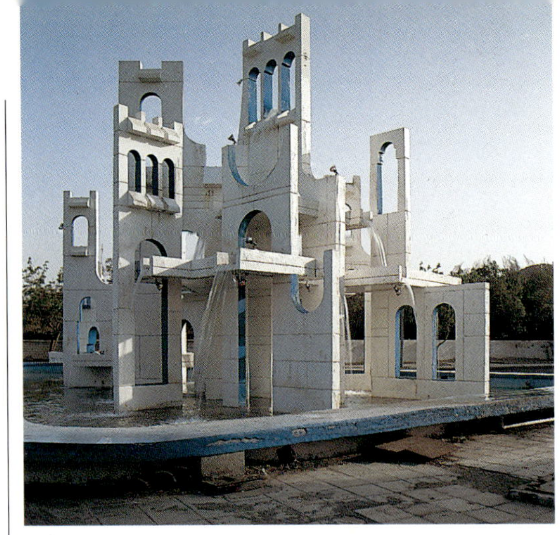

◀ ARCH AND WATERSPOUTS FOUNTAIN (107)
Shafiq Mazloum
Marble

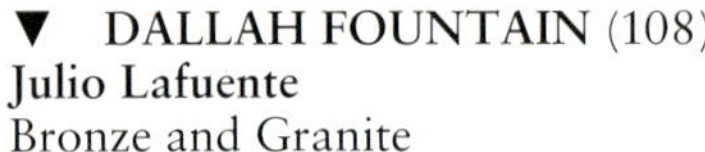

▼ DALLAH FOUNTAIN (108)
Julio Lafuente
Bronze and Granite

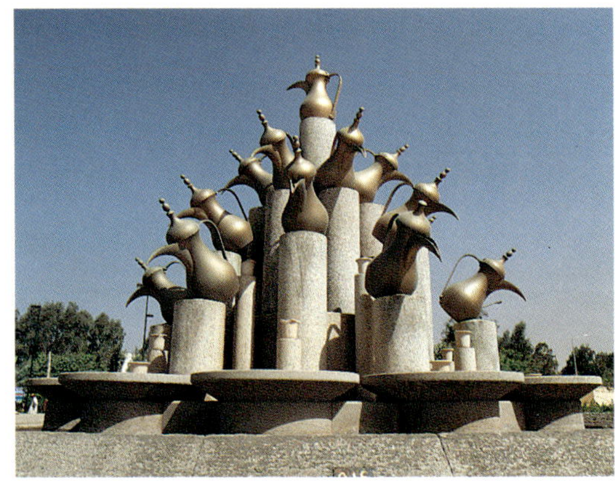

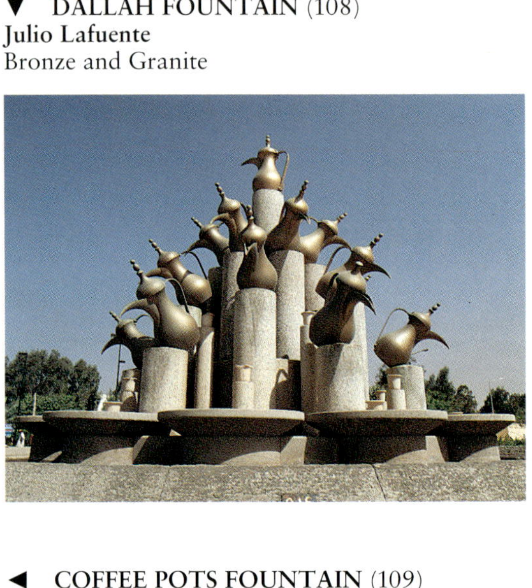

◀ COFFEE POTS FOUNTAIN (109)
Julio Lafuente
Bronze and Granite

◀ THE TREASURE TROVE (110)
Julio Lafuente
Wood, Bronze and Marble

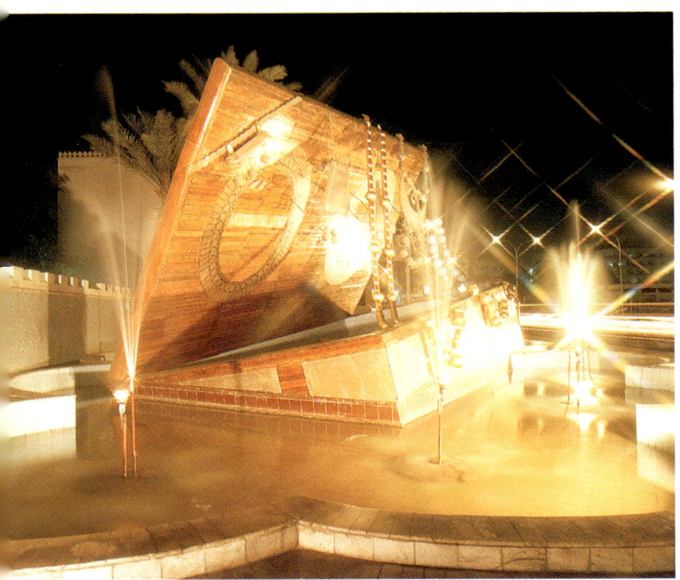

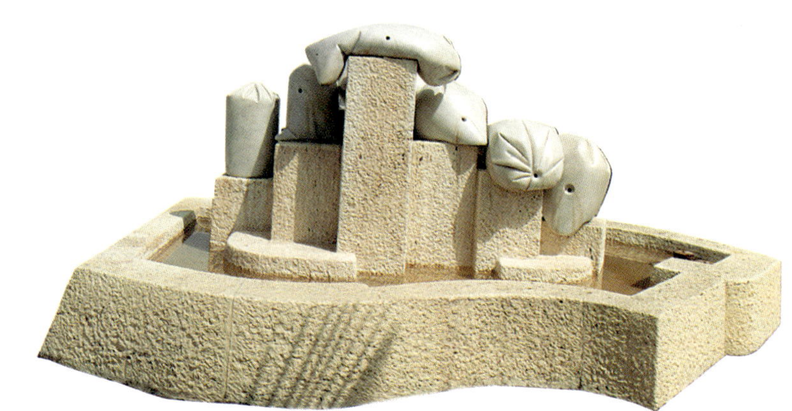

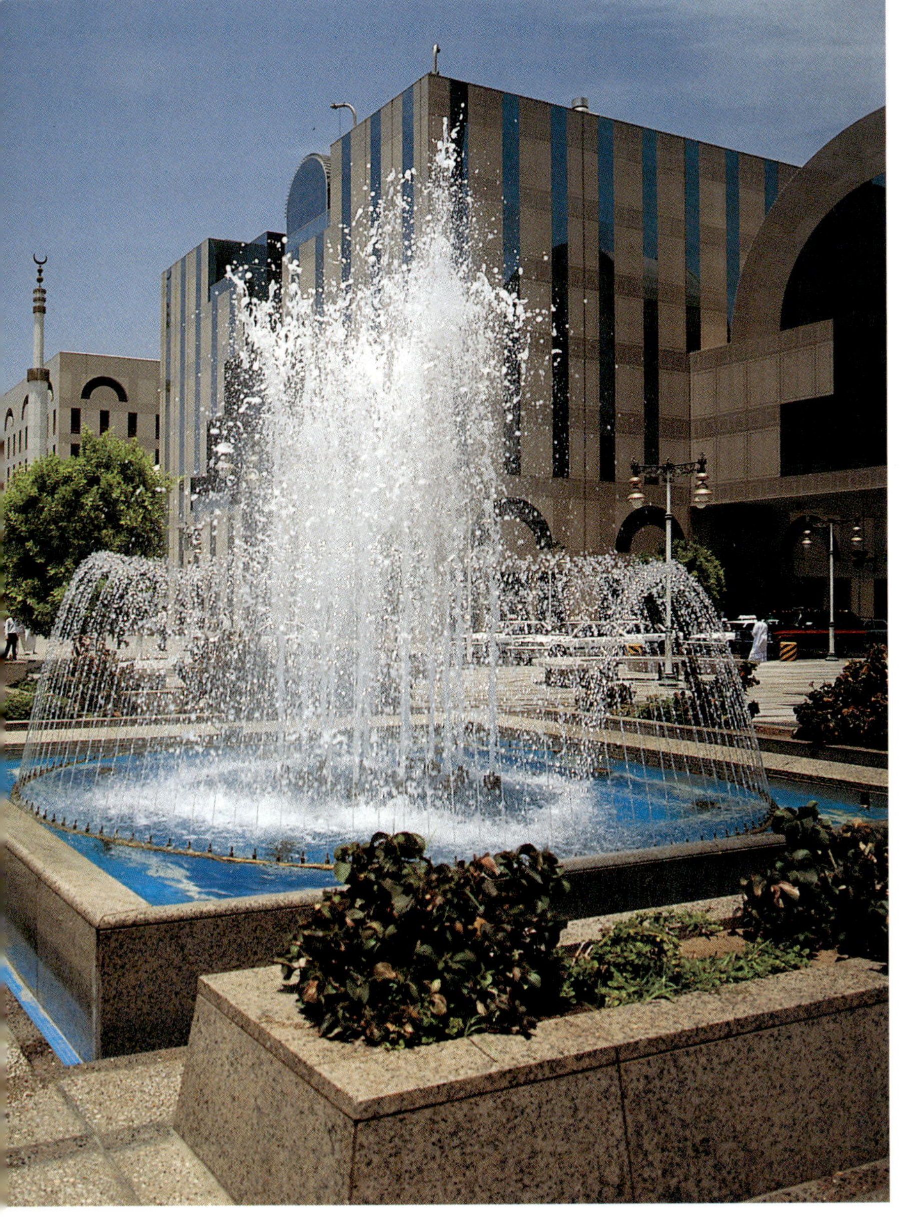

▼ **THE ROSE-WATER SPRINKLER** (112)
Julio Lafuente
Bronze

□ Traditional hospitality is acknowledged in this sculpture of the sprinkler used to greet guests. Also visible in this photograph is Mustafa Senbel's *Samovar* Fountain.

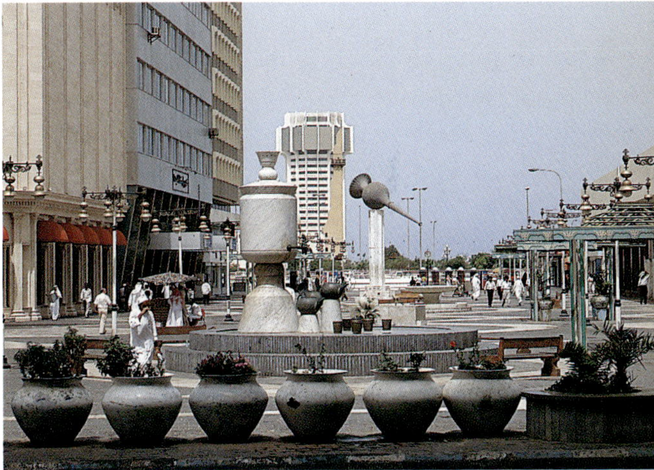

□ Throughout most of its long history Jeddah has had to make do with limited water supplies. Now, with the benefit of modern desalination technology, the city has fresh water in abundance – sufficient to use some in the many fountains which are to be found in its plazas and gardens. The main photograph shows one such fountain near the Mahmal Centre.

◀ **SACK FOUNTAIN** (111)
Aref el Rayess
Marble

▼ **WATER SKINS FOUNTAIN** (113)
Eila Hiltunen
Marble

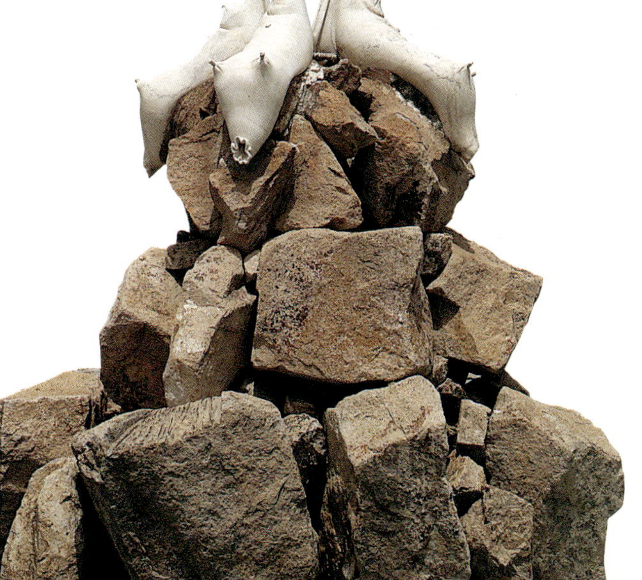

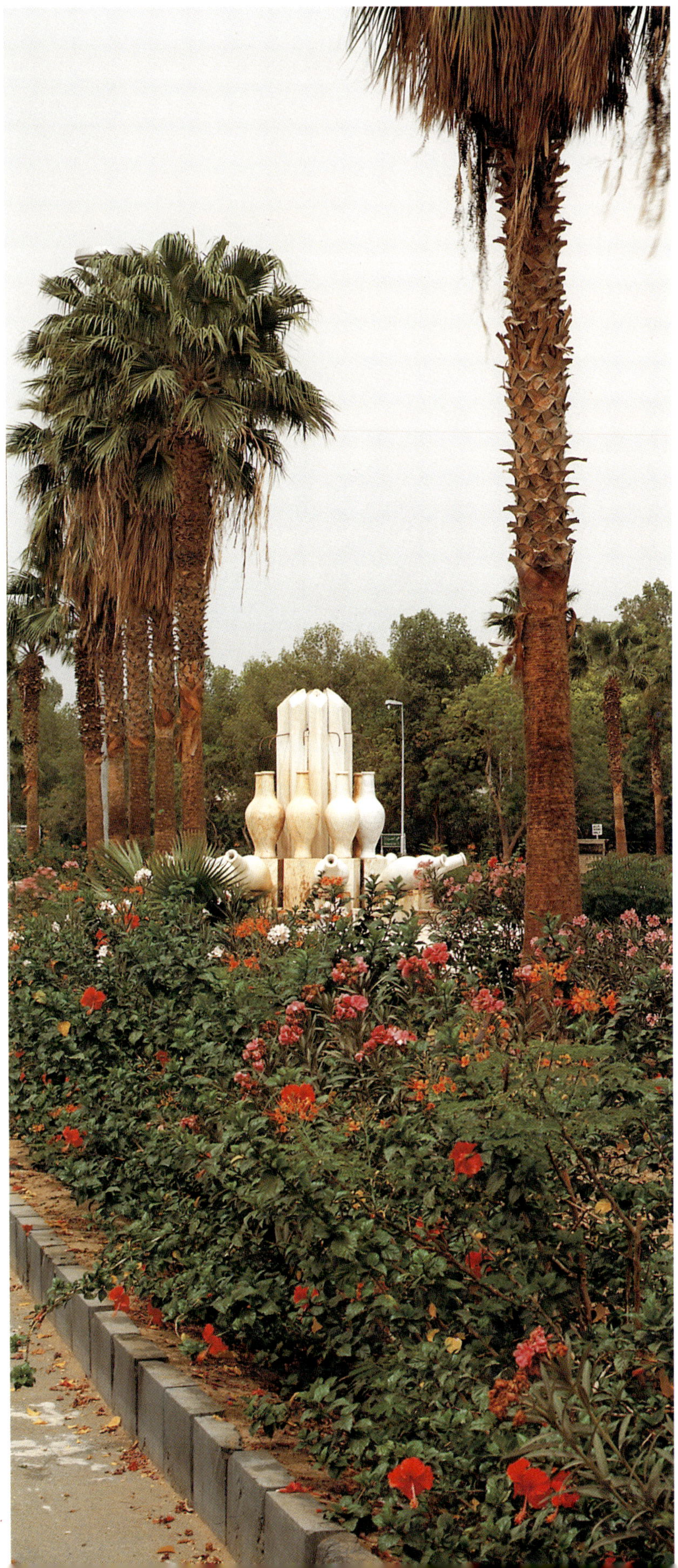

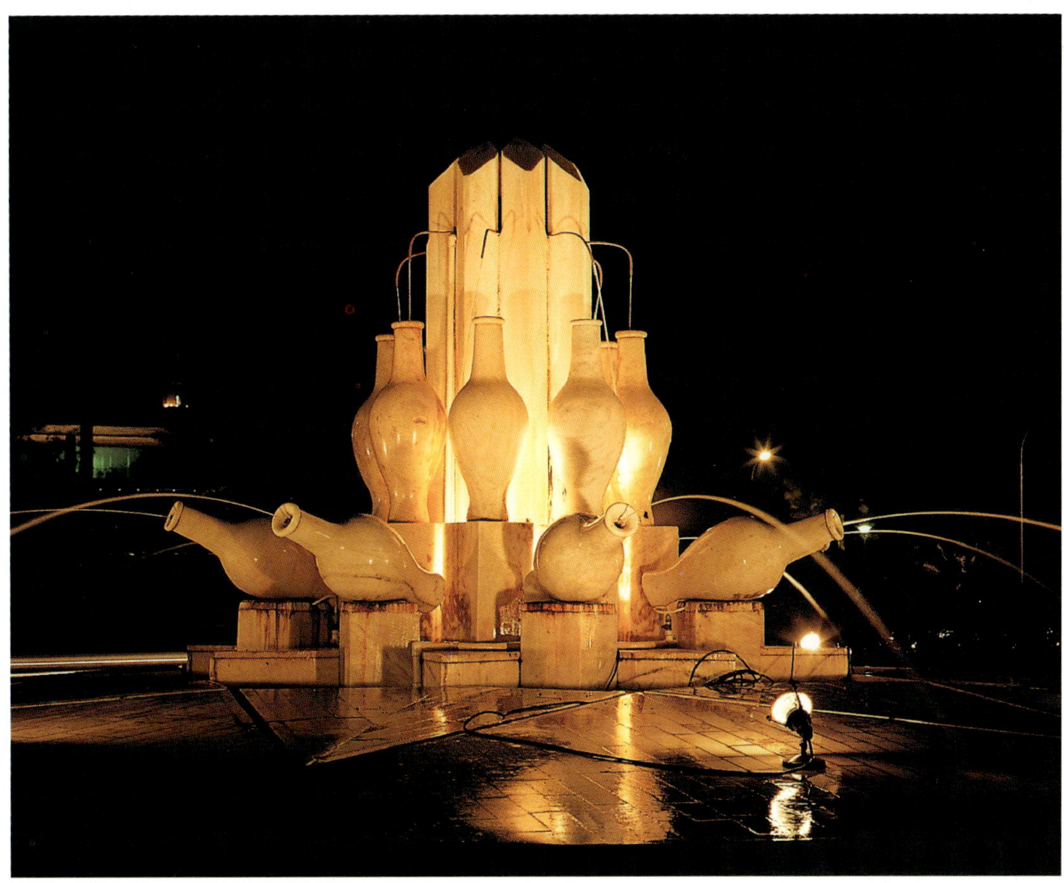

◄▲ **WATER JARS FOUNTAIN** (114)
Julio Lafuente
Marble

► **WATER JAR FOUNTAIN** (115)
Julio Lafuente
Marble

Although he is better known for his monumental pieces – *The Bicycle, the Mameluke Mosque Lanterns, the Condenser* etc. – Lafuente also created several fountains based upon traditional Arab water vessels and coffee pots.

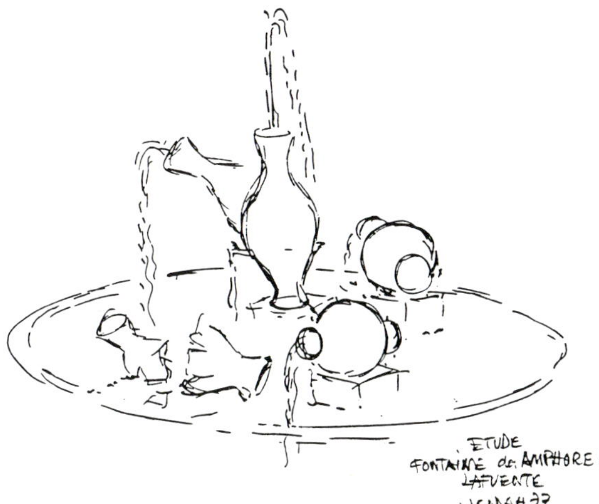

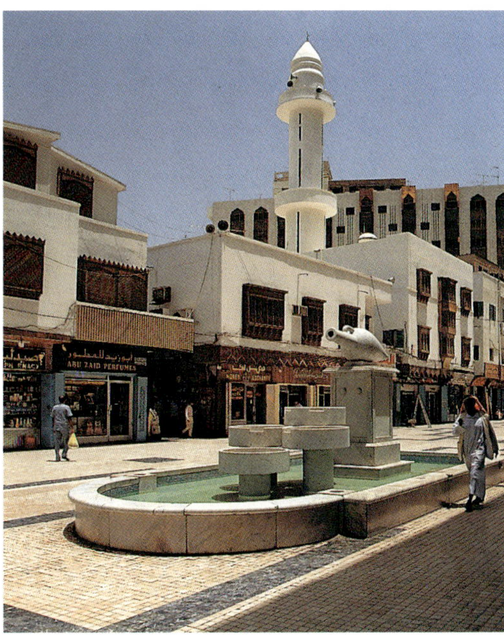

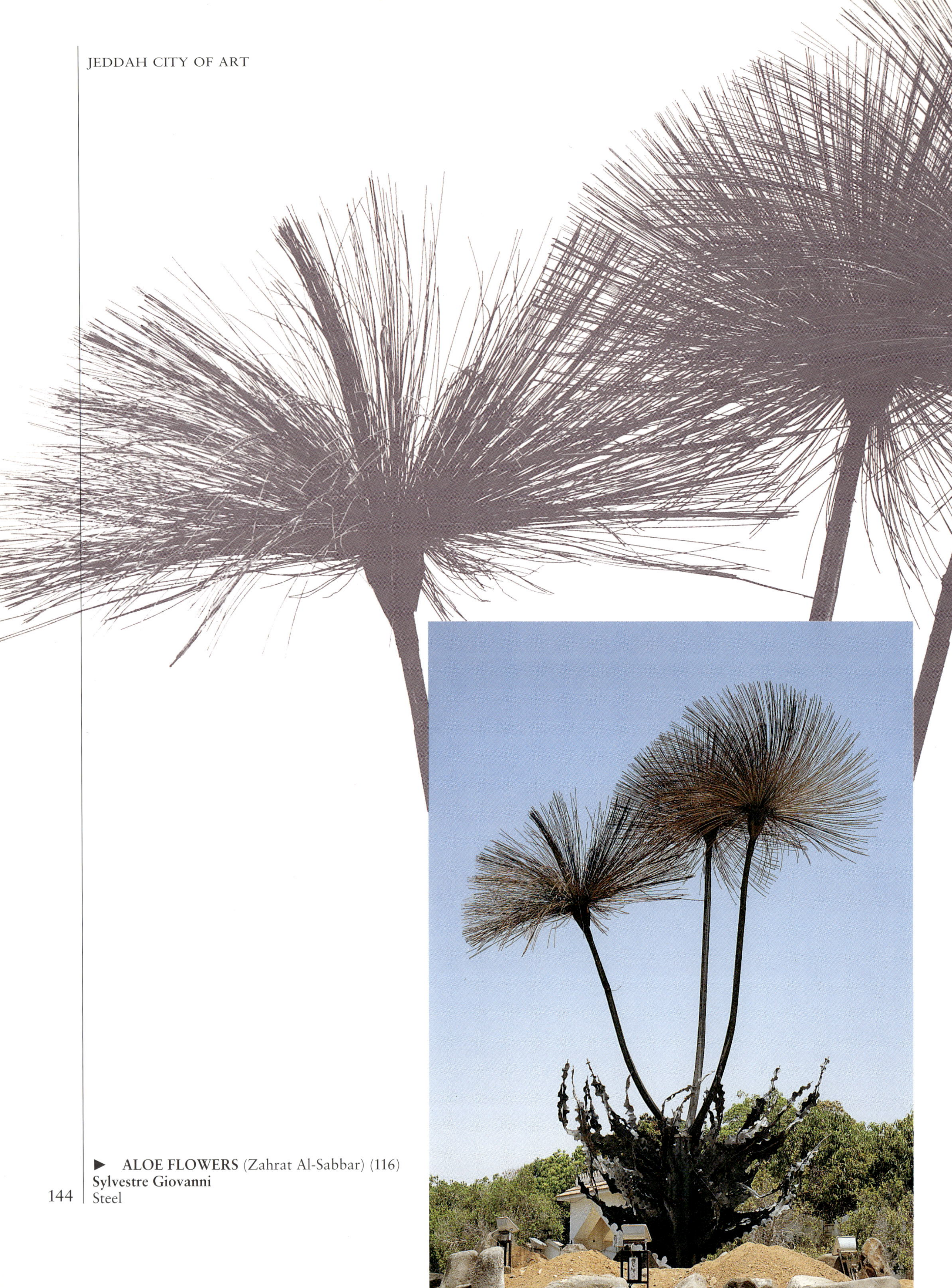

► **ALOE FLOWERS** (Zahrat Al-Sabbar) (116)
Sylvestre Giovanni
Steel

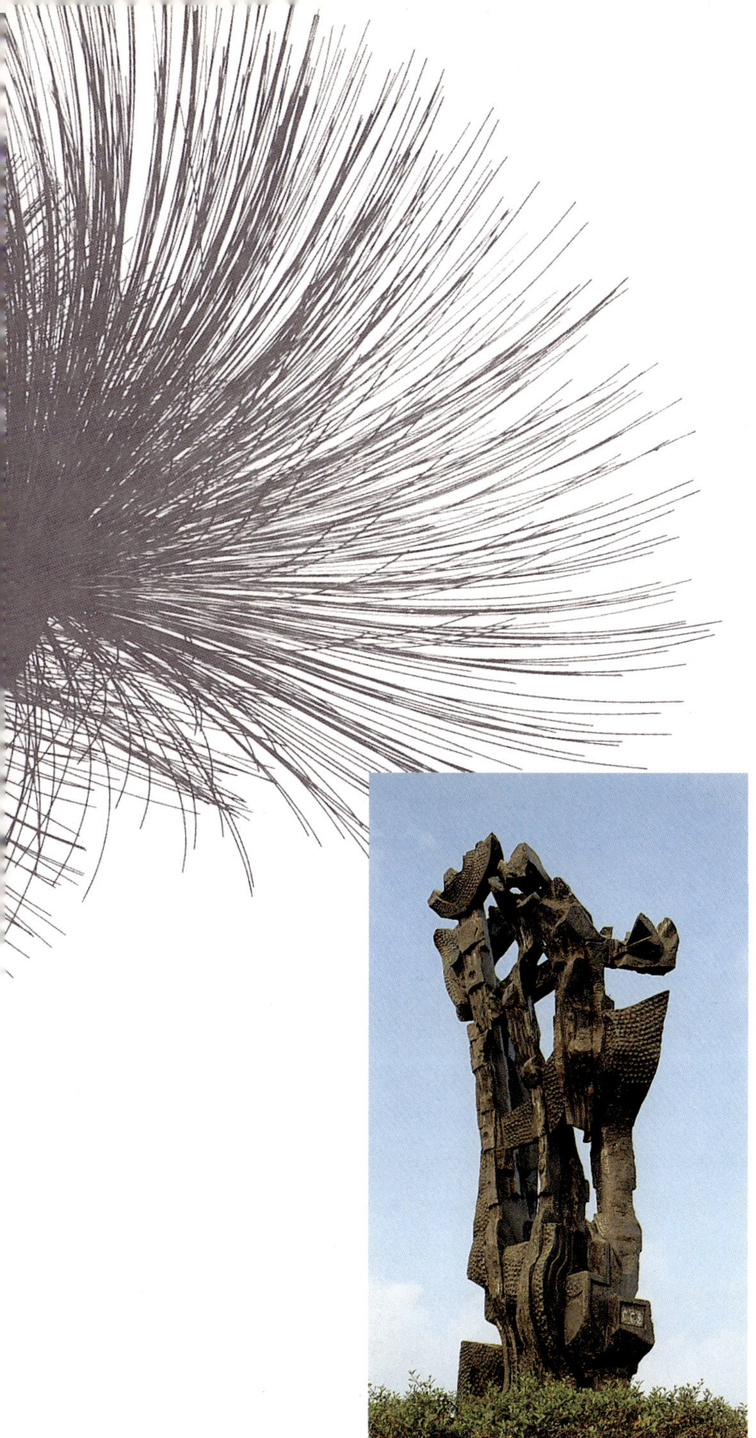

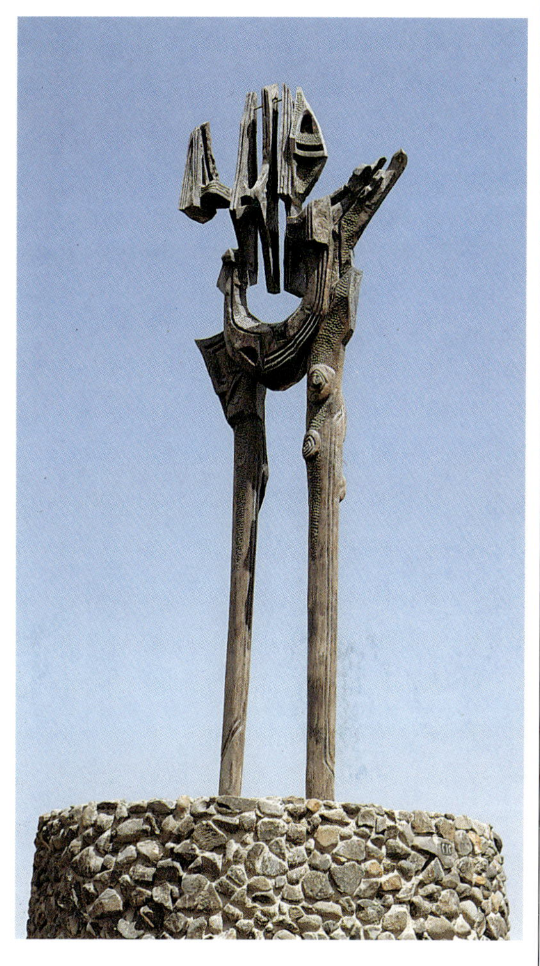

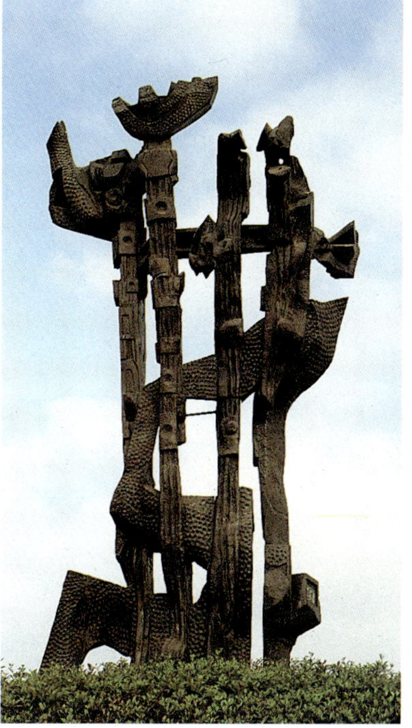

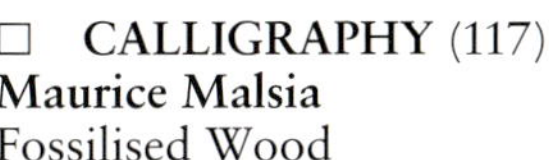

☐ **CALLIGRAPHY** (117)
Maurice Malsia
Fossilised Wood

Petrified wood found deep in the jungles of Indonesia was the preferred medium of Maurice Malsia. In the sculptures which Mohamed Said Farsi commissioned him to create for the Jeddah collection, the Indonesian artist crafted calligraphic forms which read: "There is no God but God".

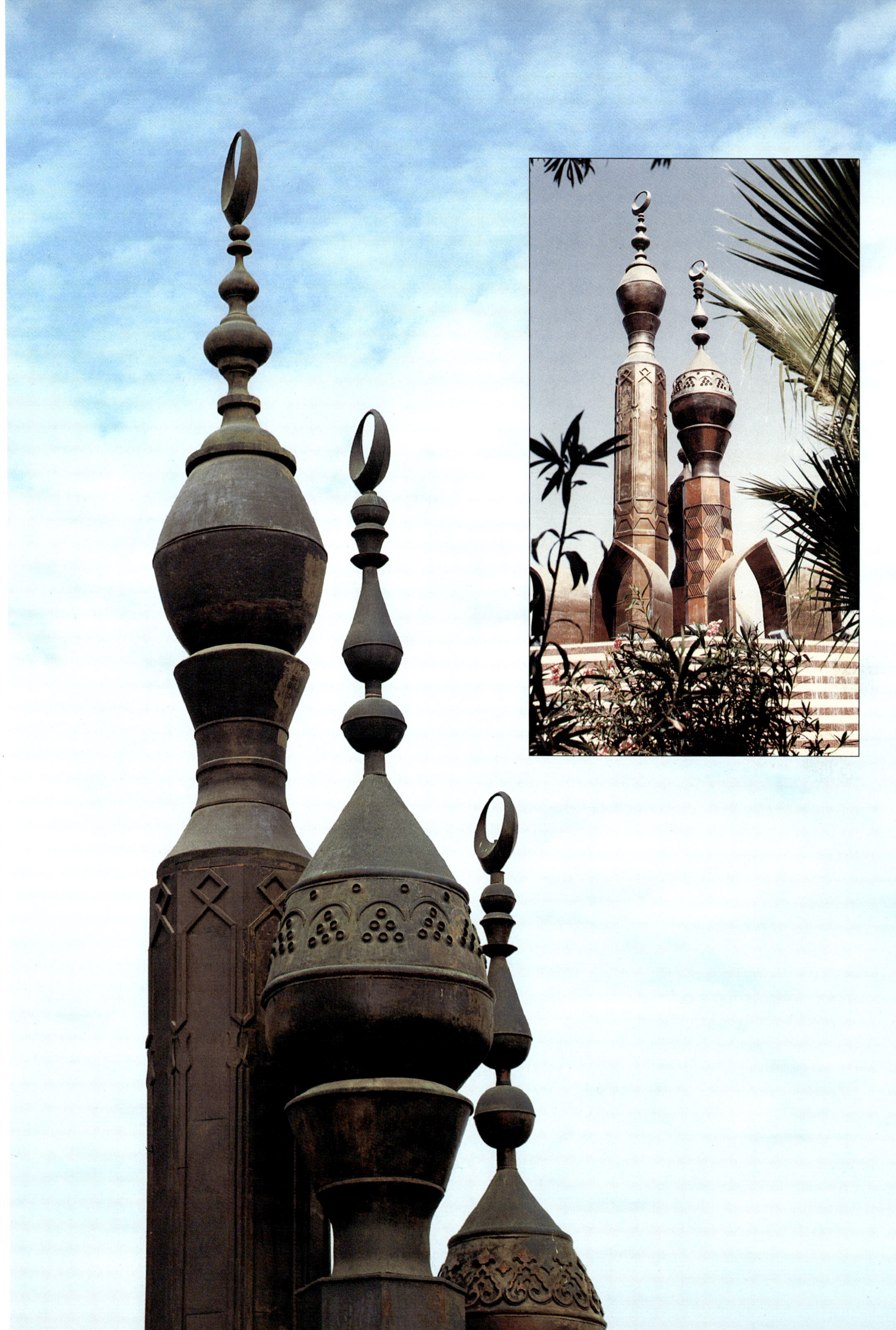

◄ **THE MAMELUKE MINARETS** (118)
Salah Abdulkarim
Copper on a steel frame

The monument was inspired by the mosque architecture of Egypt's Mameluke period, as typified by Cairo's Al-Azhar mosque. It was placed in a suitably dominant position in Al-Bayah Square by Mohamed Said Farsi, who couples the piece with the same artist's Pendentive in his description of them as "an outstanding achievement in the history of urban beautification and art in Islamic cities".

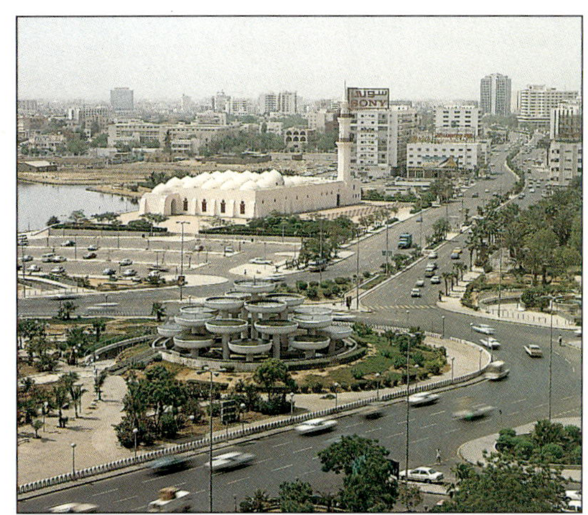

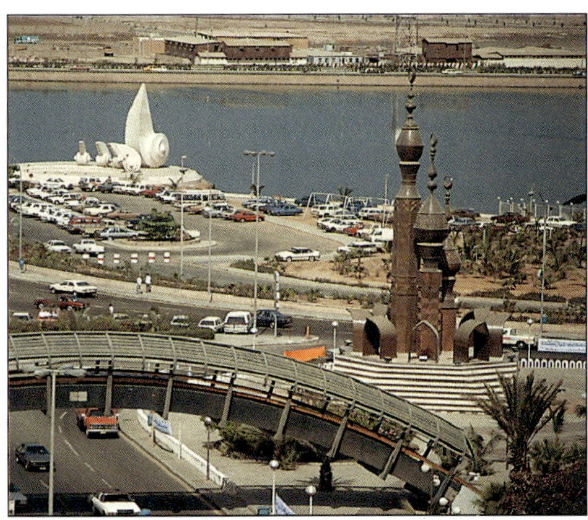

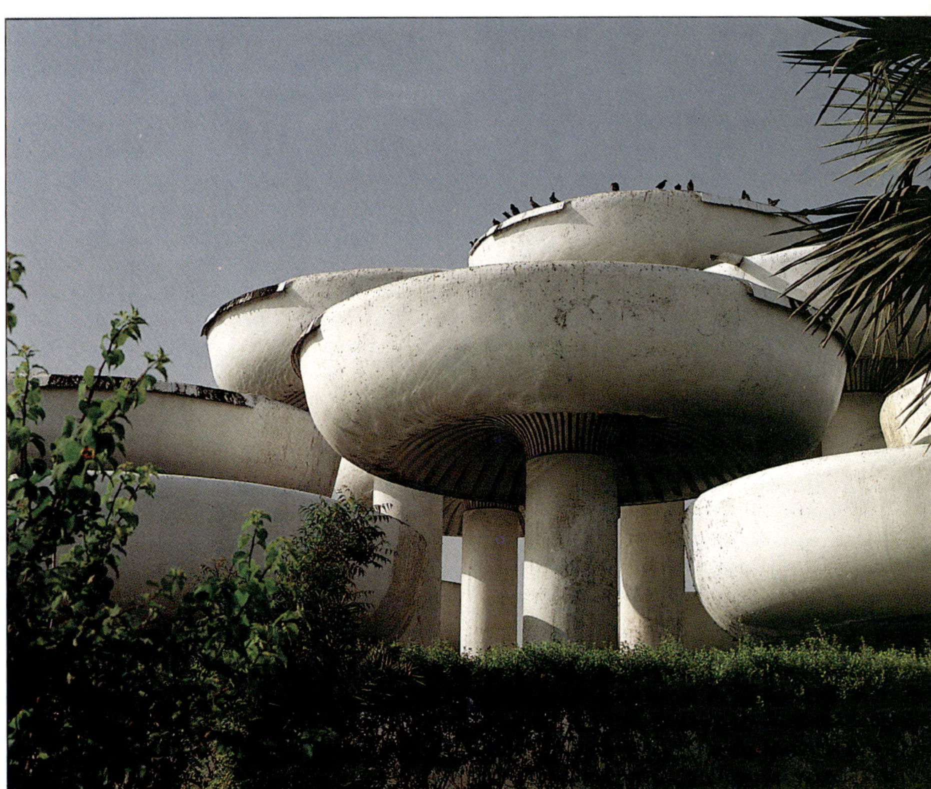

► **THE MARKET FOUNTAIN** (119)
Julio Lafuente
Reinforced Concrete

With the exception of the King Fahd Fountain, this 'mushroom' group is the city's largest fountain.

□ **COSMOS** (Al-Falak) (2)
Ottmar Hollmann
Steel and Aluminium

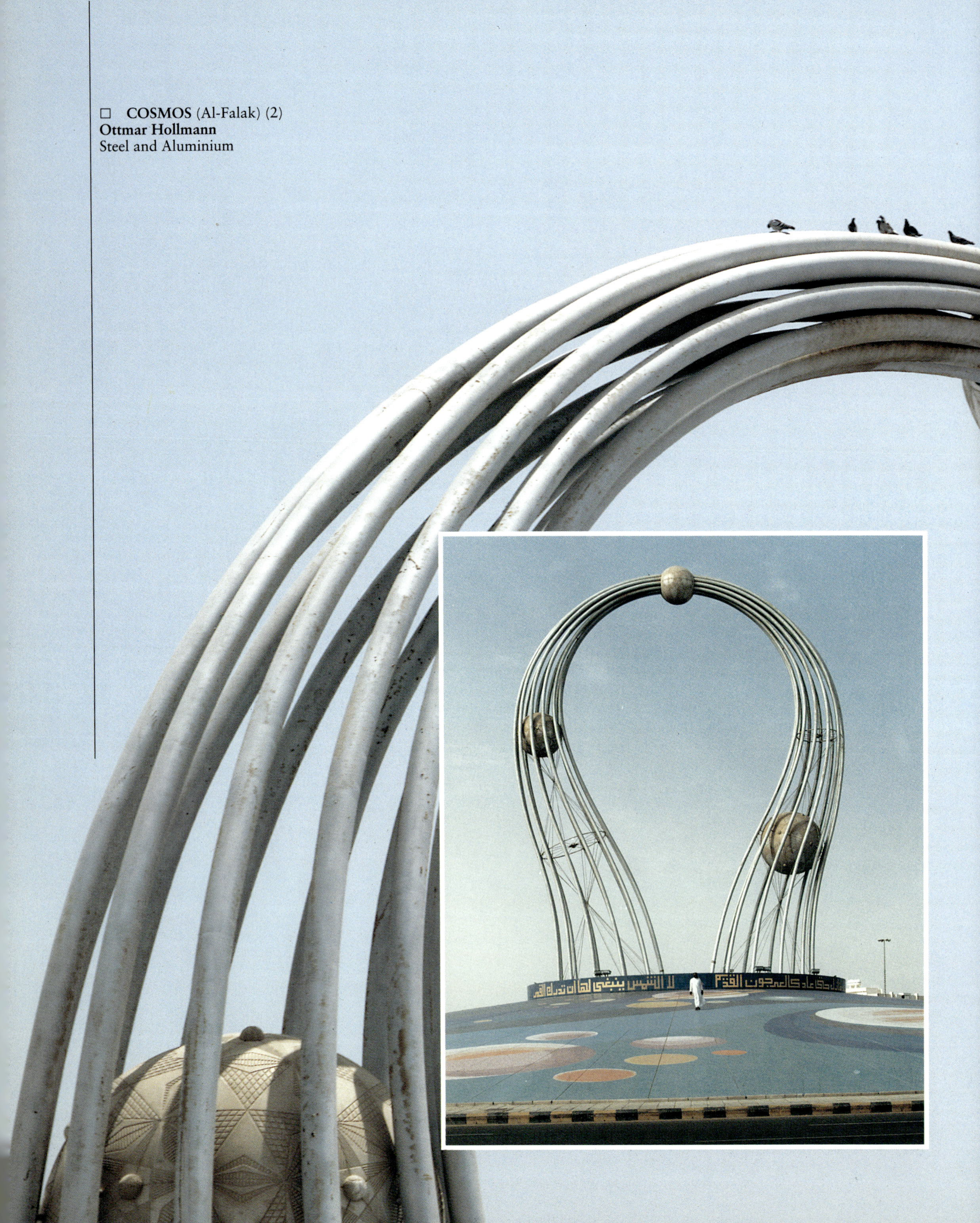

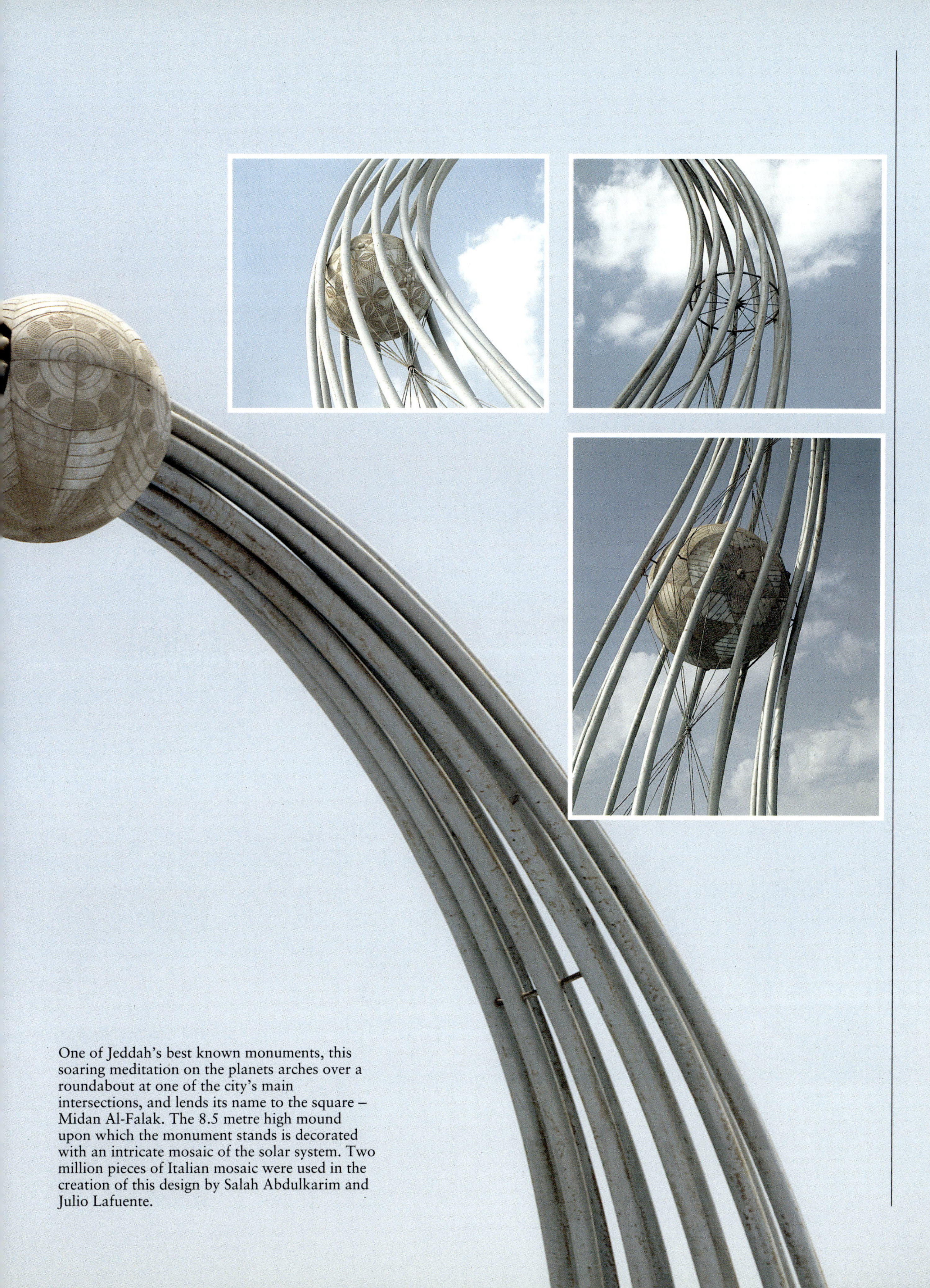

One of Jeddah's best known monuments, this soaring meditation on the planets arches over a roundabout at one of the city's main intersections, and lends its name to the square – Midan Al-Falak. The 8.5 metre high mound upon which the monument stands is decorated with an intricate mosaic of the solar system. Two million pieces of Italian mosaic were used in the creation of this design by Salah Abdulkarim and Julio Lafuente.

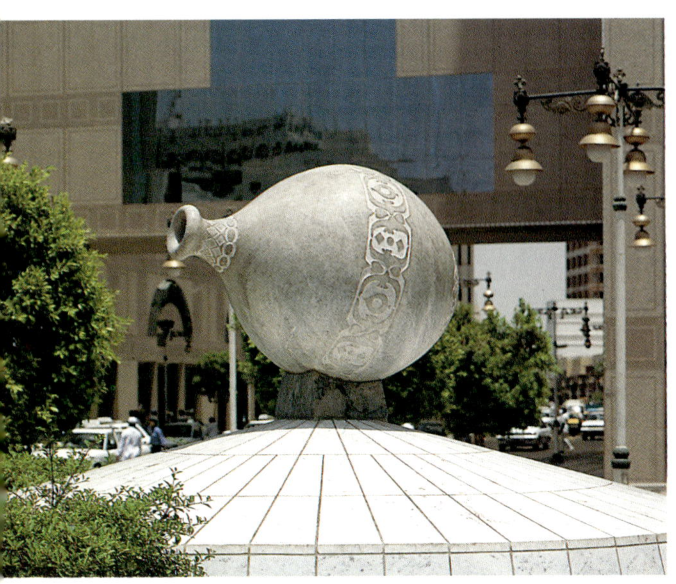

▲ THE BEAN POT (120)
Abdulhalim Radwi
Clay and Plaster

▲ INKWELL, PEN AND PAPER (121)
Abdulhalim Radwi
Clay and Plaster

The Koranic inscription on the scroll is: "*Read in the name of your Lord who teaches with the pen.*" (Holy Koran 96:1-4)

▼ BIRDS (122)
Abdulhalim Radwi

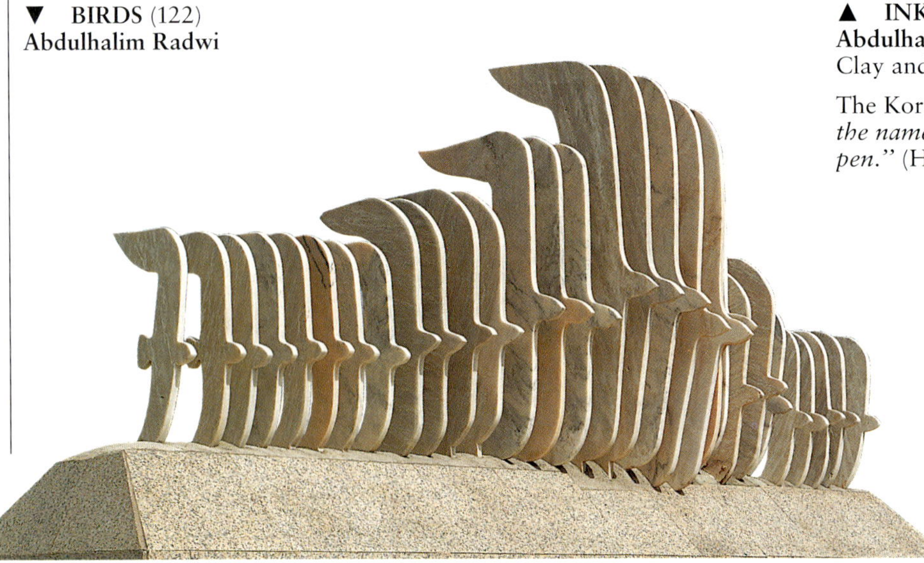

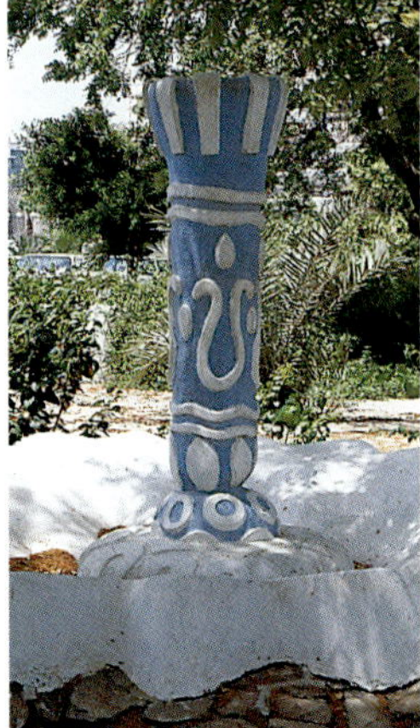

► TRADITIONAL JAR (123)
Abdulhalim Radwi
Clay and Plaster

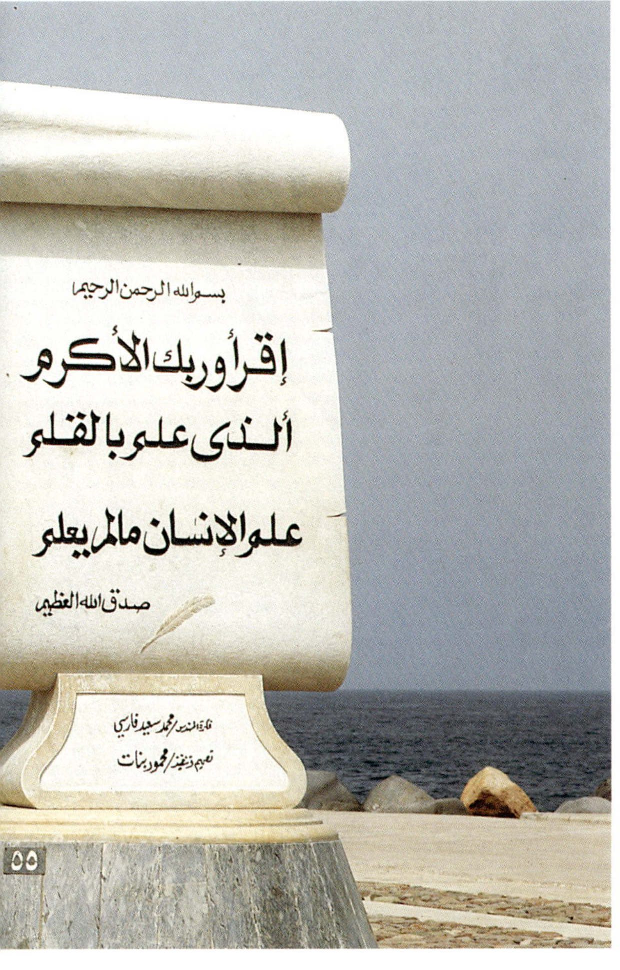

□ Makkah-born Abdulhalim Radwi was the first of many artists to contribute towards the beautification of Jeddah, his adopted home. Apart from his distinctive sculptures, he also contributed to the city's landscaping programme and designed decorative screens to enclose rooftop water tanks. His collection in the Poet's Garden may be seen as a precursor to the larger scale Open Air Museum.

► THE GLOBE OF KNOWLEDGE AND LIFE (124)
Abdulhalim Radwi
Clay and Plaster

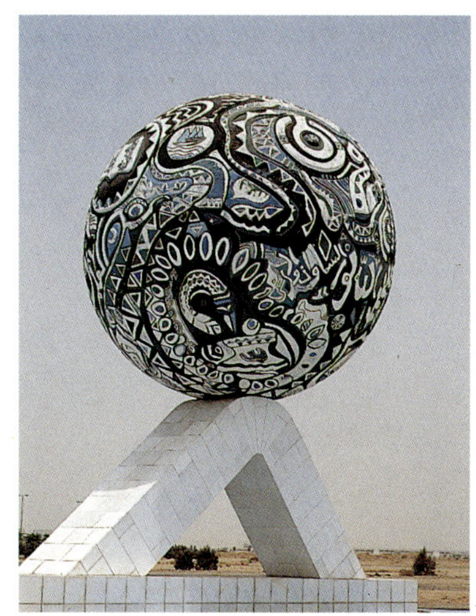

▼ SILENT FORMATION (125)
Abdulhalim Radwi
Clay and Plaster

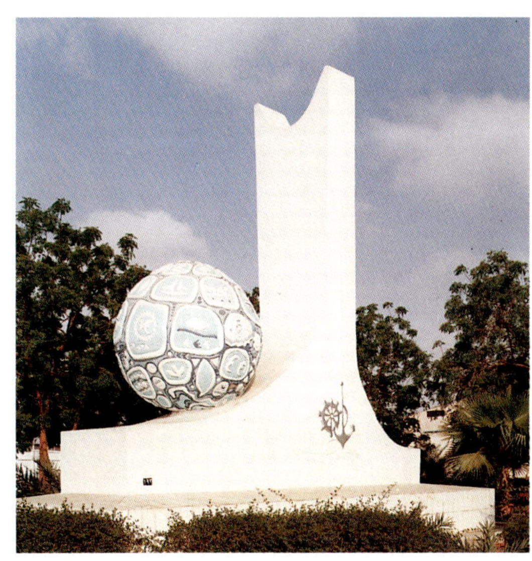

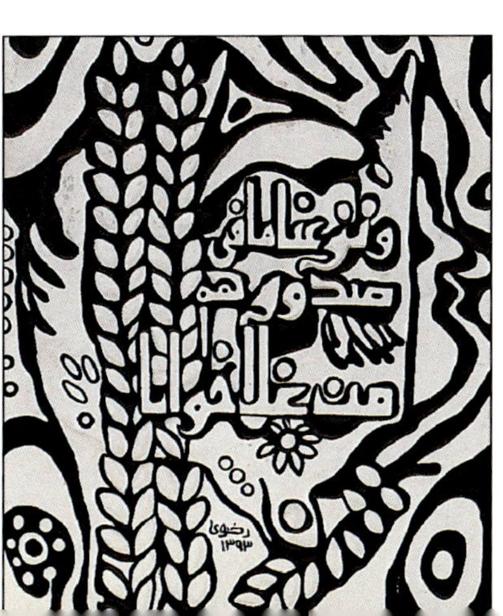

◄ AND WE BECAME FRIENDS (126)
Abdulhalim Radwi
Clay and Plaster

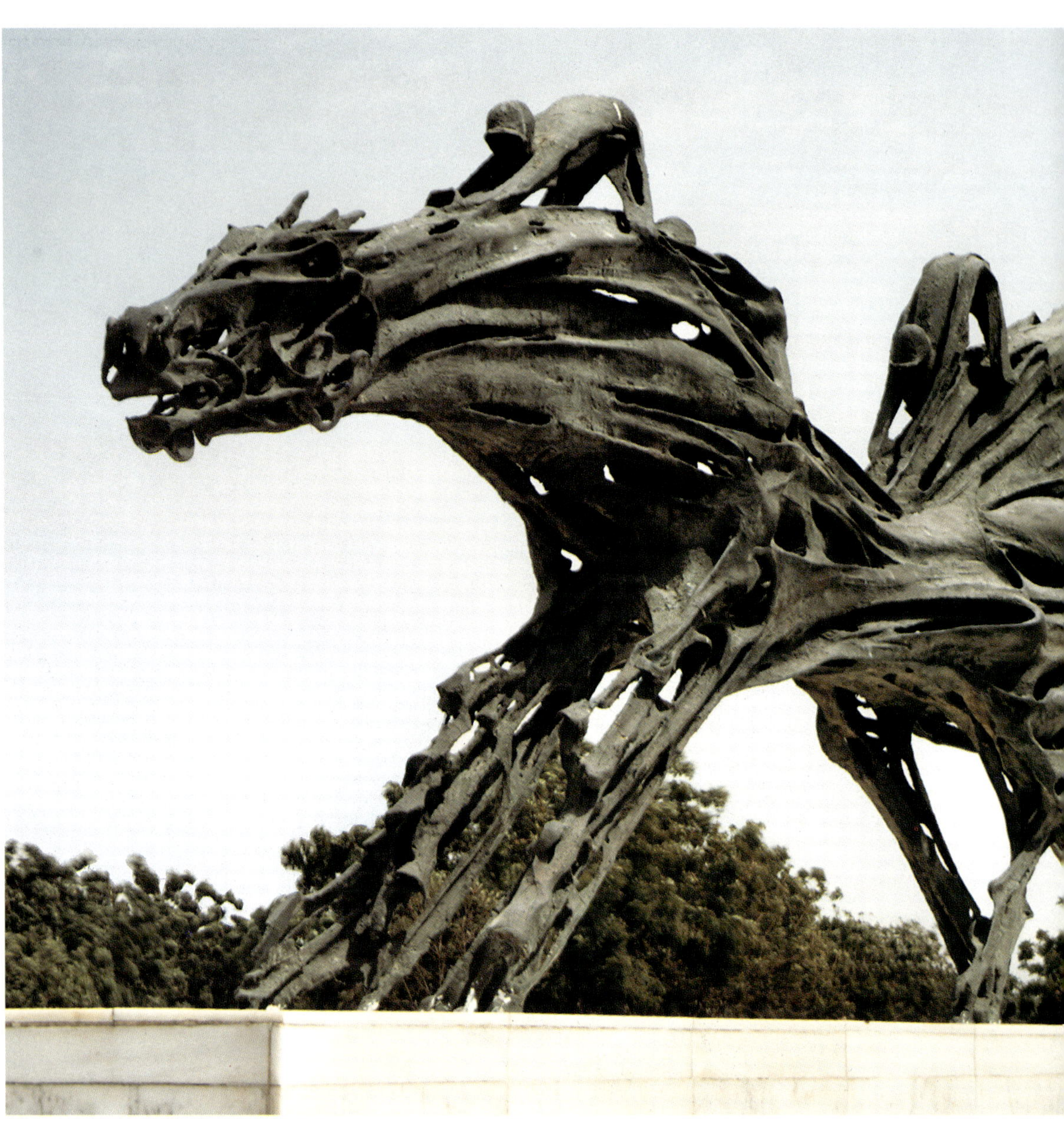

□ **HORSE AND JOCKEY** (127)
Artist unknown
Bronze

The Arab's love of the horse – as expressed in the poems of Al-Mutanabbi – is celebrated in this explosive representation of racing horses.

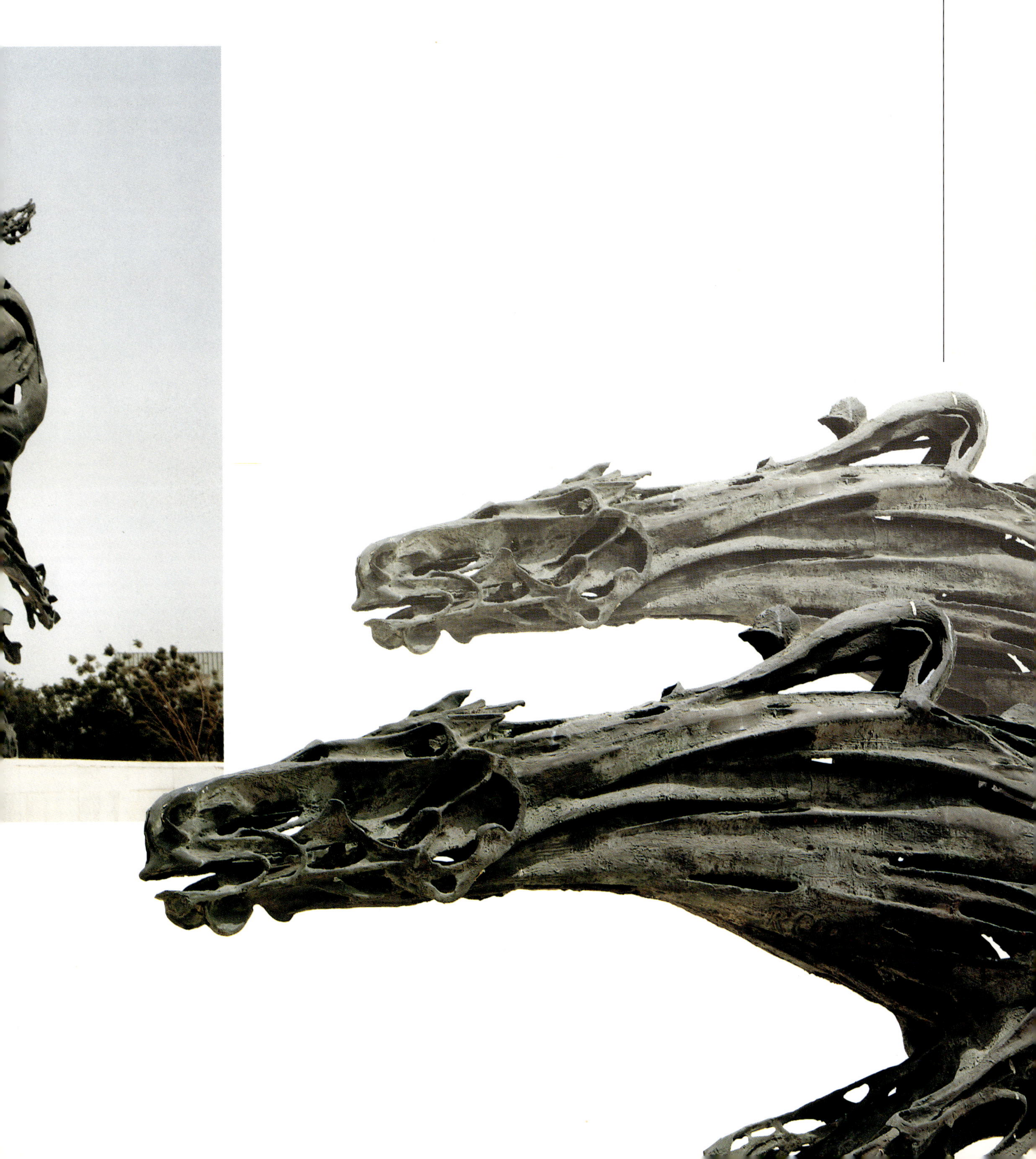

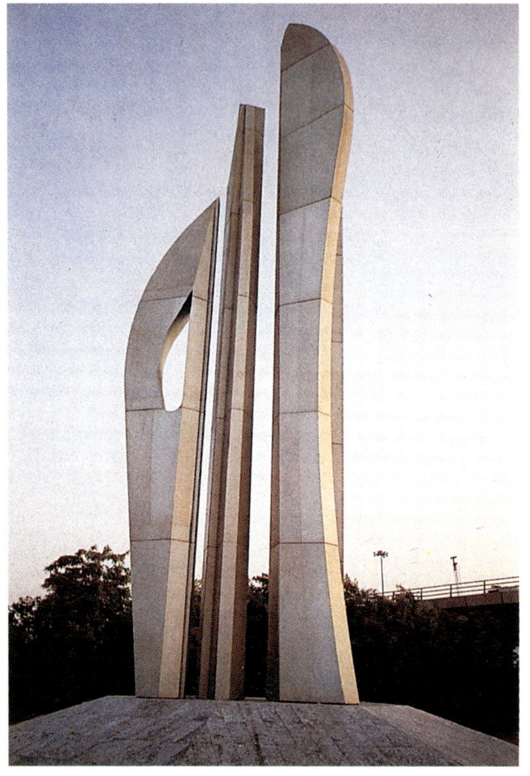

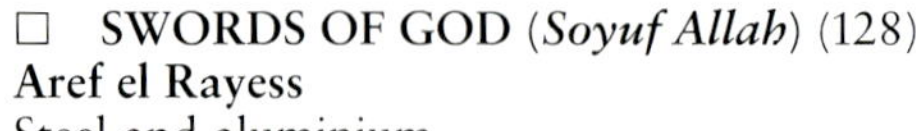

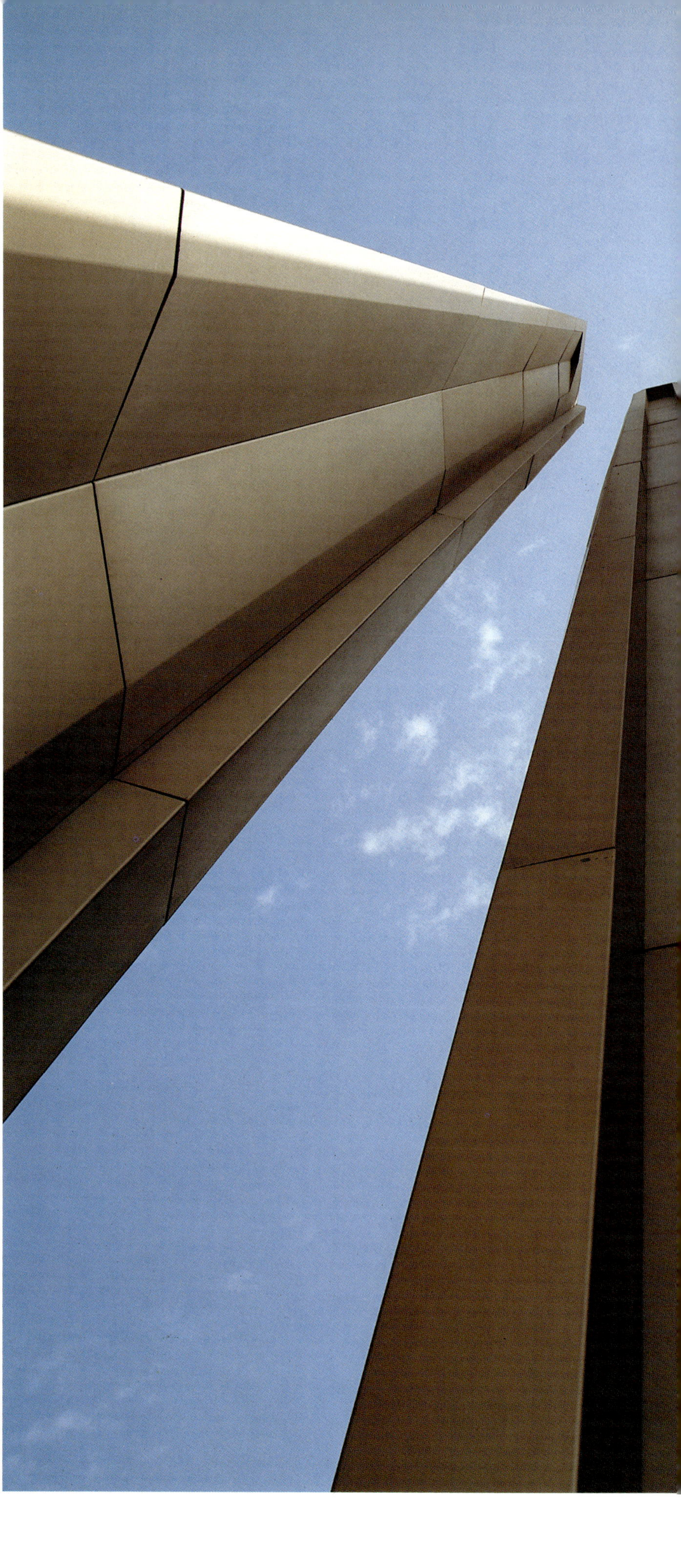

□ SWORDS OF GOD (*Soyuf Allah*) (128)
Aref el Rayess
Steel and aluminium

Despite the name by which it is most commonly known, the artist believes that this sculpture is open to a more peaceful, spiritual interpretation: the light streaming between the columns can be seen as a symbol of the universal love and respect preached by the Prophet Mohamed. El Rayess had planned to use marble as his medium, but it was decided that this was impractical for such a large monument (30 m) and the work was made from a steel frame clad with aluminium. Although it is not immediately apparent that this is a calligraphic work, the elements of the sculpture spell out the name of God.

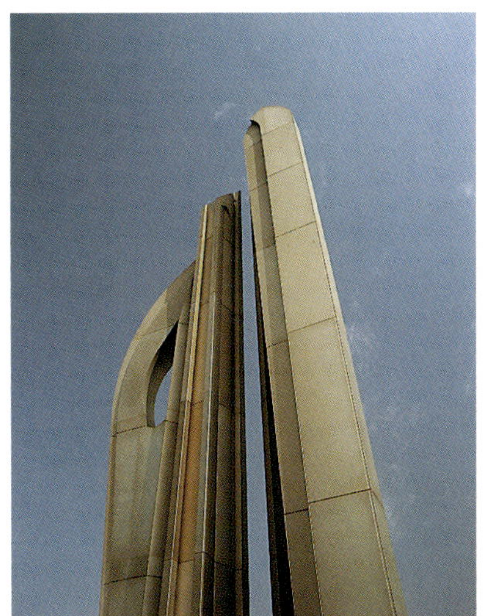

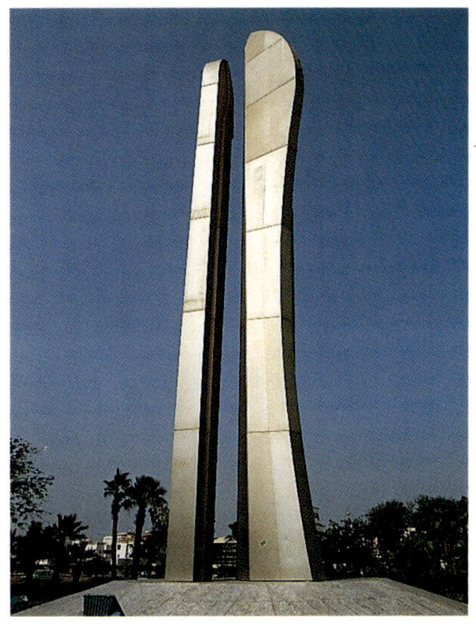

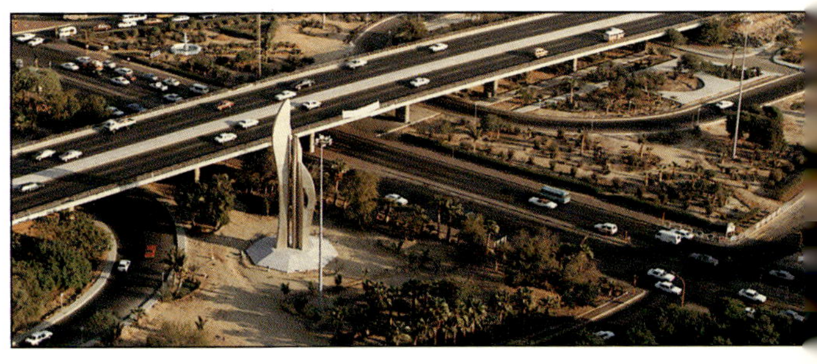

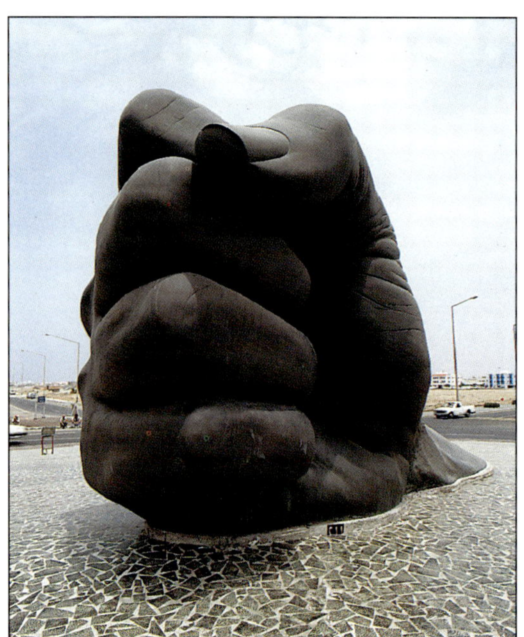

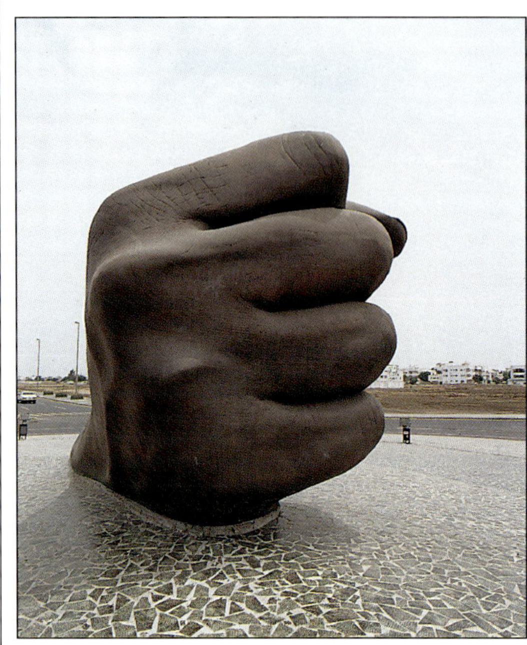

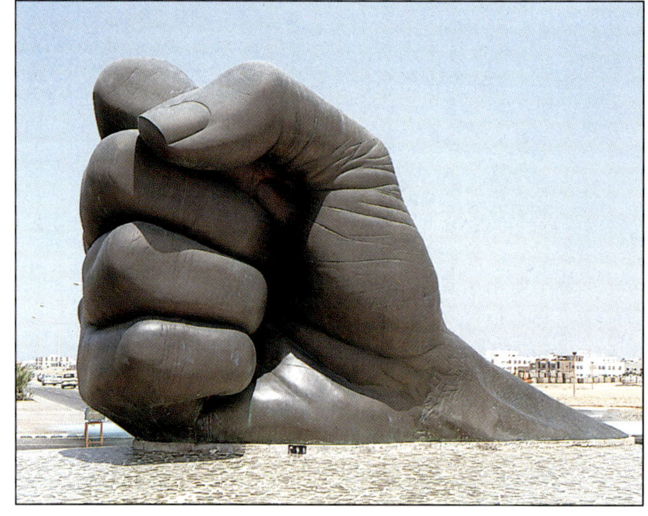

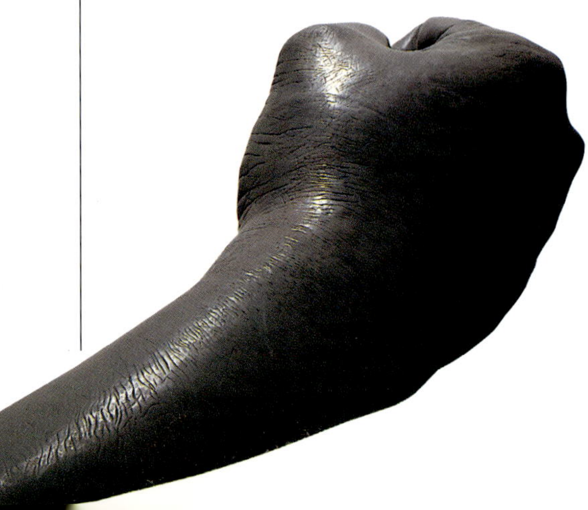

□ **THE FIST** (129)
César
Bronze

Menacing and potent, *The Fist* symbolises strength and, appropriately, was donated to the city by the Minister of Defence and Aviation H.R.H. Prince Sultan ibn Abdul Aziz.

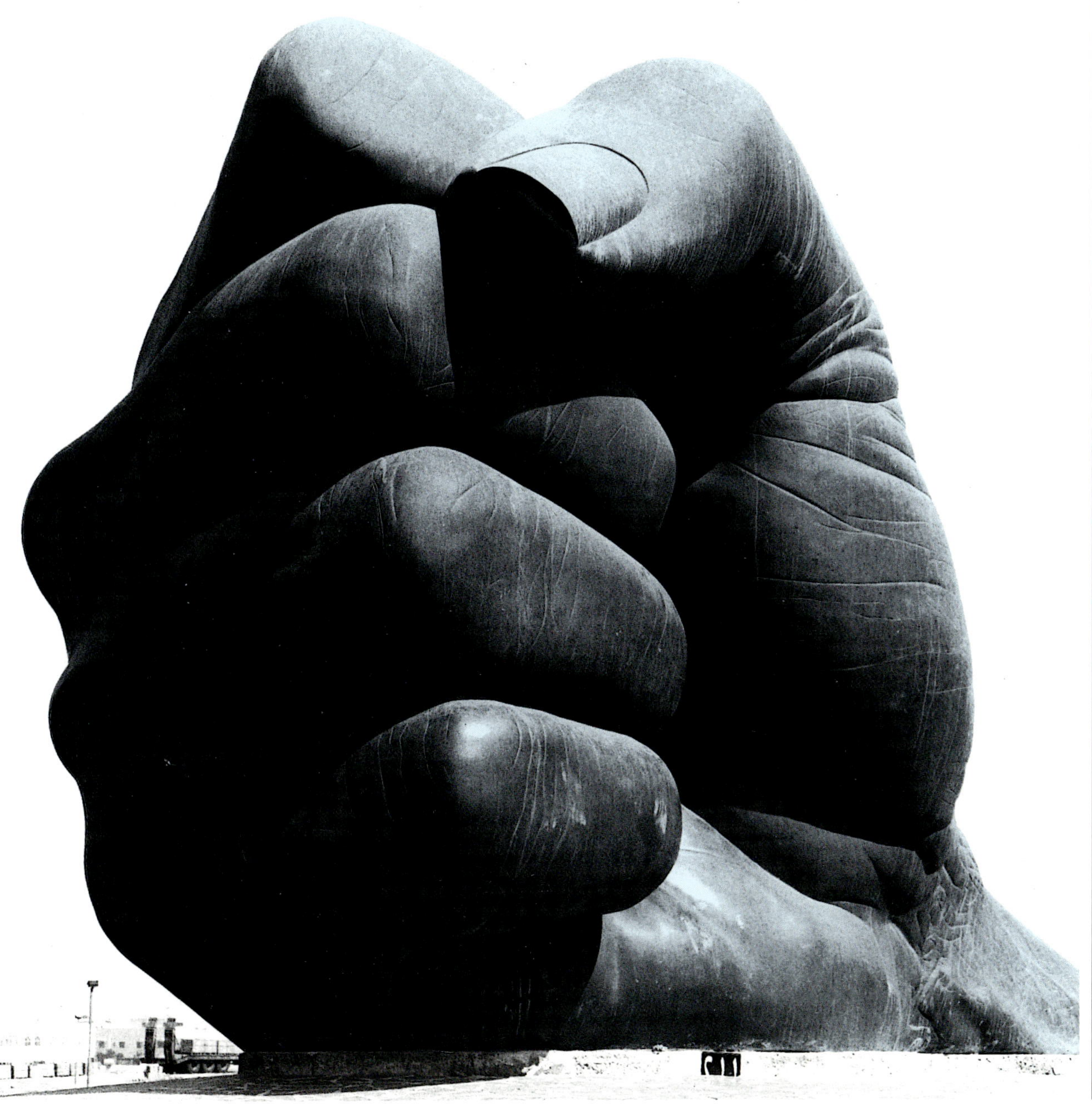

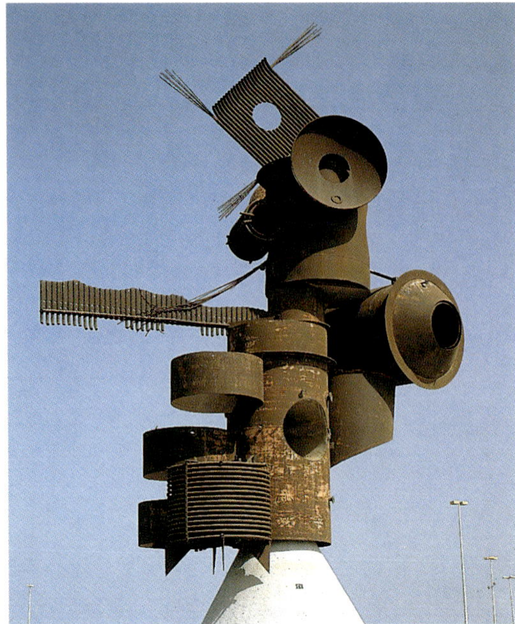

◀ **THE CONDENSER I** (130)
Julio Lafuente
Scrap metal

▼ **BANNERS IN THE WIND** (131)
Julio Lafuente
Scrap metal

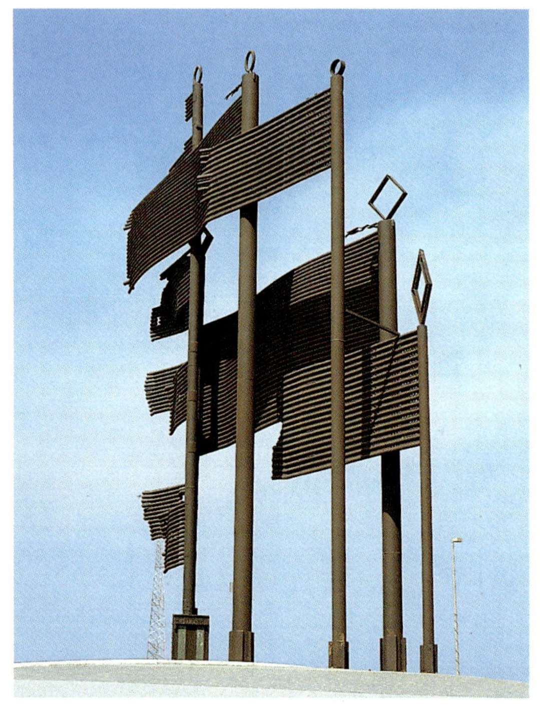

☐ During the first half of this century much of Jeddah's water was provided by two British-built condensers – primitive precursors to today's sophisticated desalination plants. The roar of the 'Lancashire boilers' – audible throughout the city – prompted one local poet to write: 'Save us from the clamour of the *kindasah*' – a prayer which was answered when, in 1947, completion of a pipeline from the wells of Wadi Fatimah made the condensers redundant. The equipment stood rusting for decades until Lafuente used the scrap metal in these three sculptures.

The flagstaffs of these banners – made from scrap iron from the old condensers – are topped by symbols used by some of the conquering armies of Arab history.

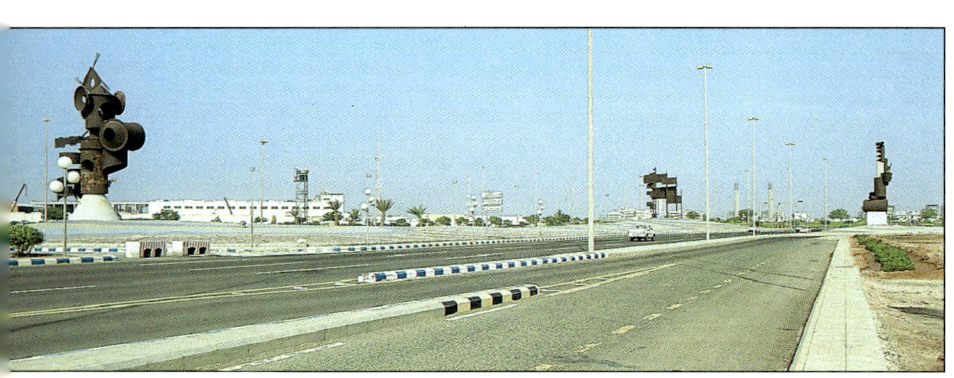

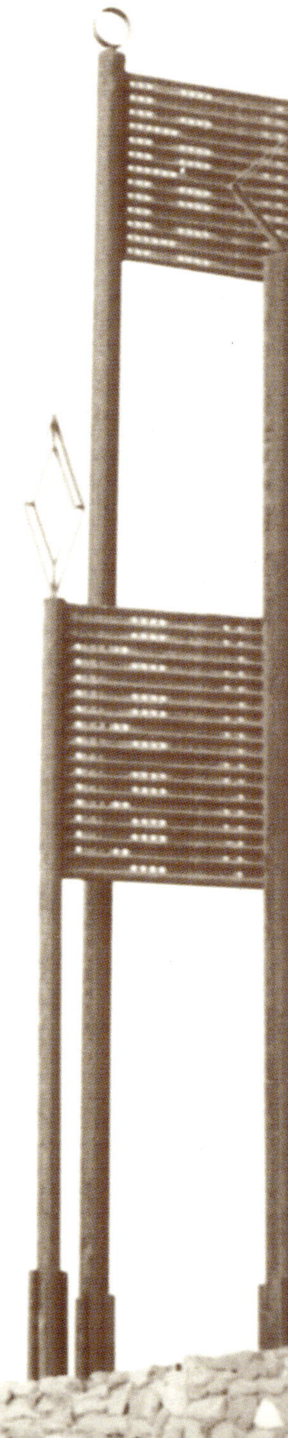

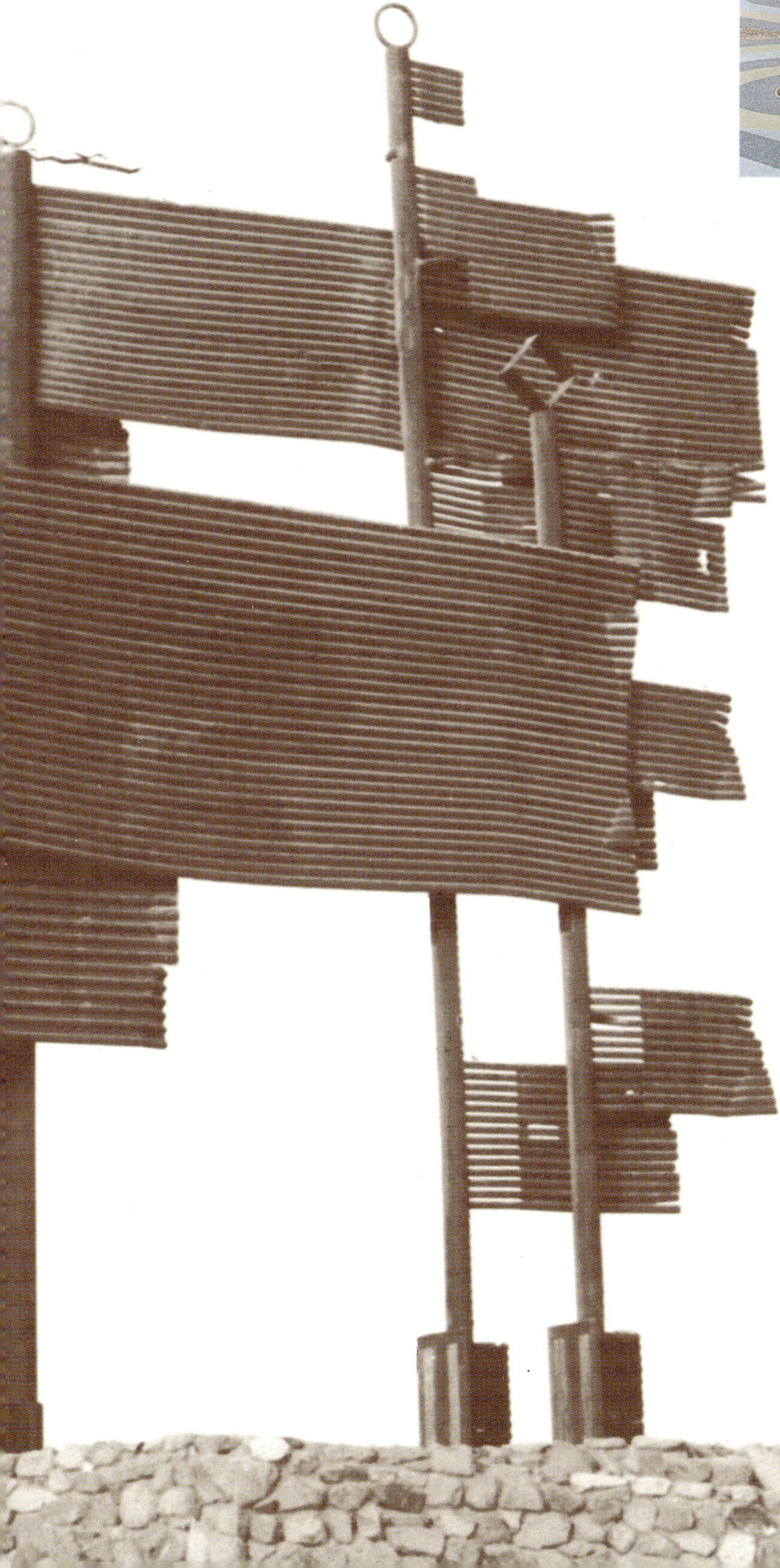

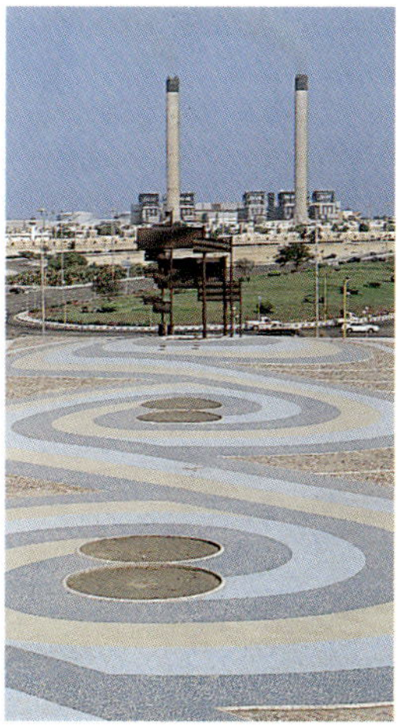

▼ **THE CONDENSER II** (132)
Julio Lafuente
Scrap metal

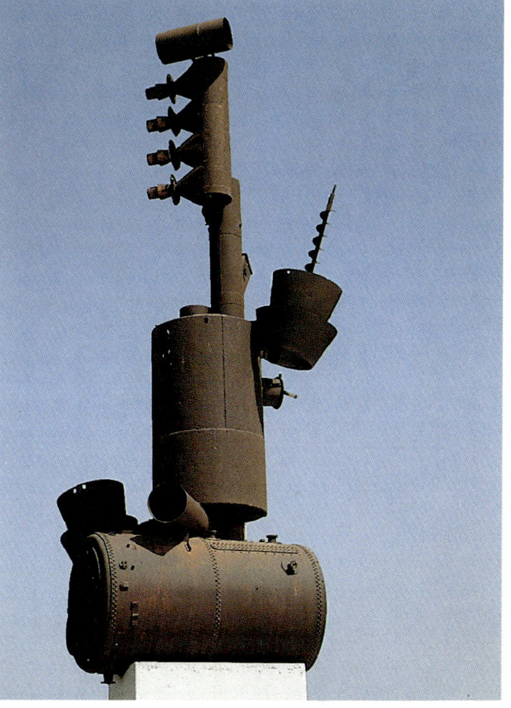

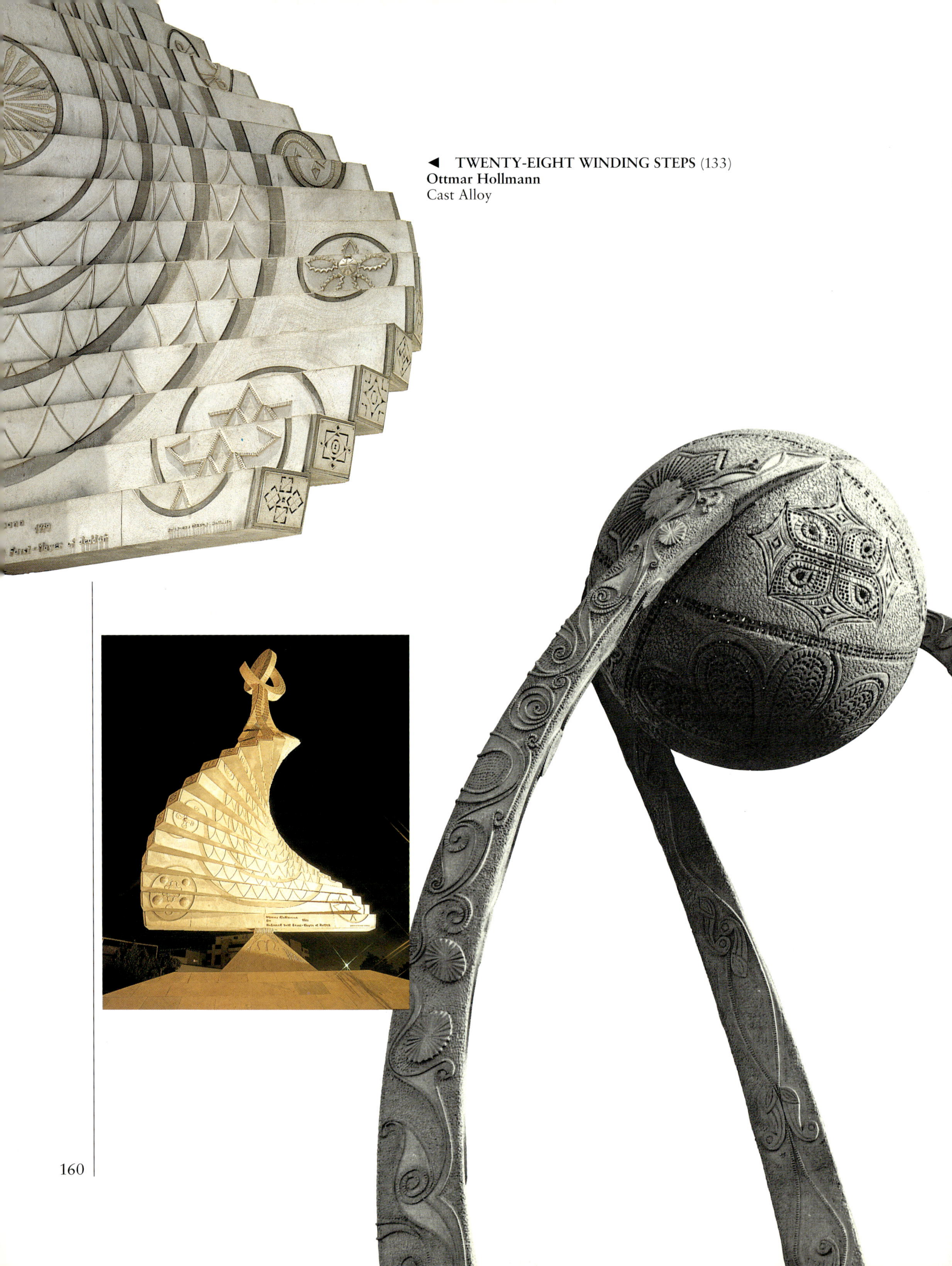

◄ TWENTY-EIGHT WINDING STEPS (133)
Ottmar Hollmann
Cast Alloy

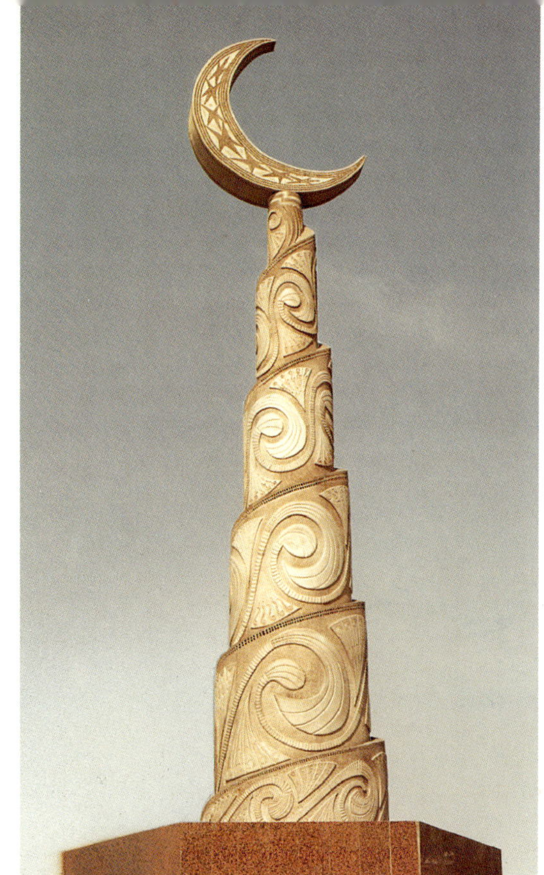

▲ SPIRAL WITH MOON (135)
Ottmar Hollmann
Cast Alloy

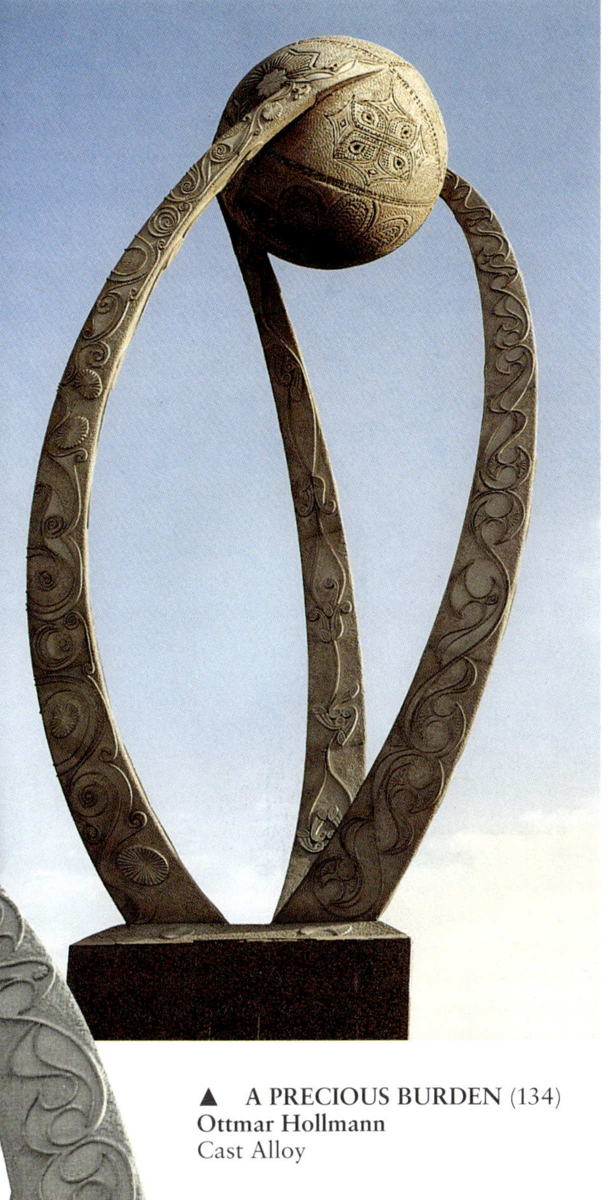

▲ A PRECIOUS BURDEN (134)
Ottmar Hollmann
Cast Alloy

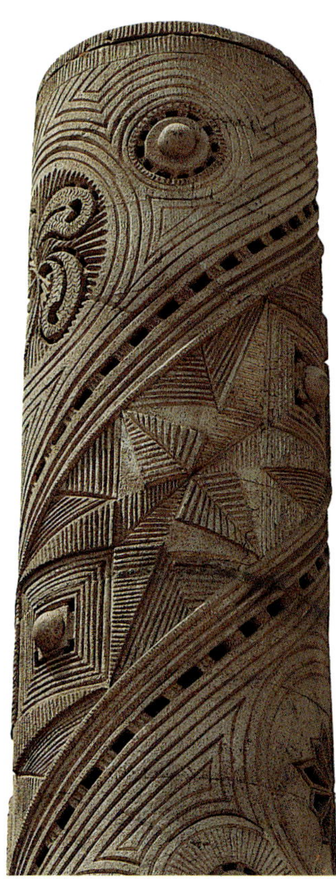

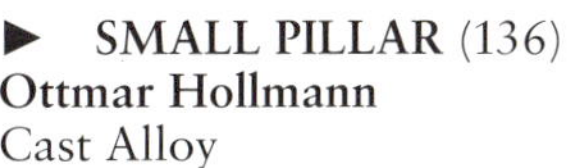

► SMALL PILLAR (136)
Ottmar Hollmann
Cast Alloy

Hollmann's richly textured work explores a variety of themes including ideas of balance and movement which are often contained in sculptures that combine strength with delicacy.

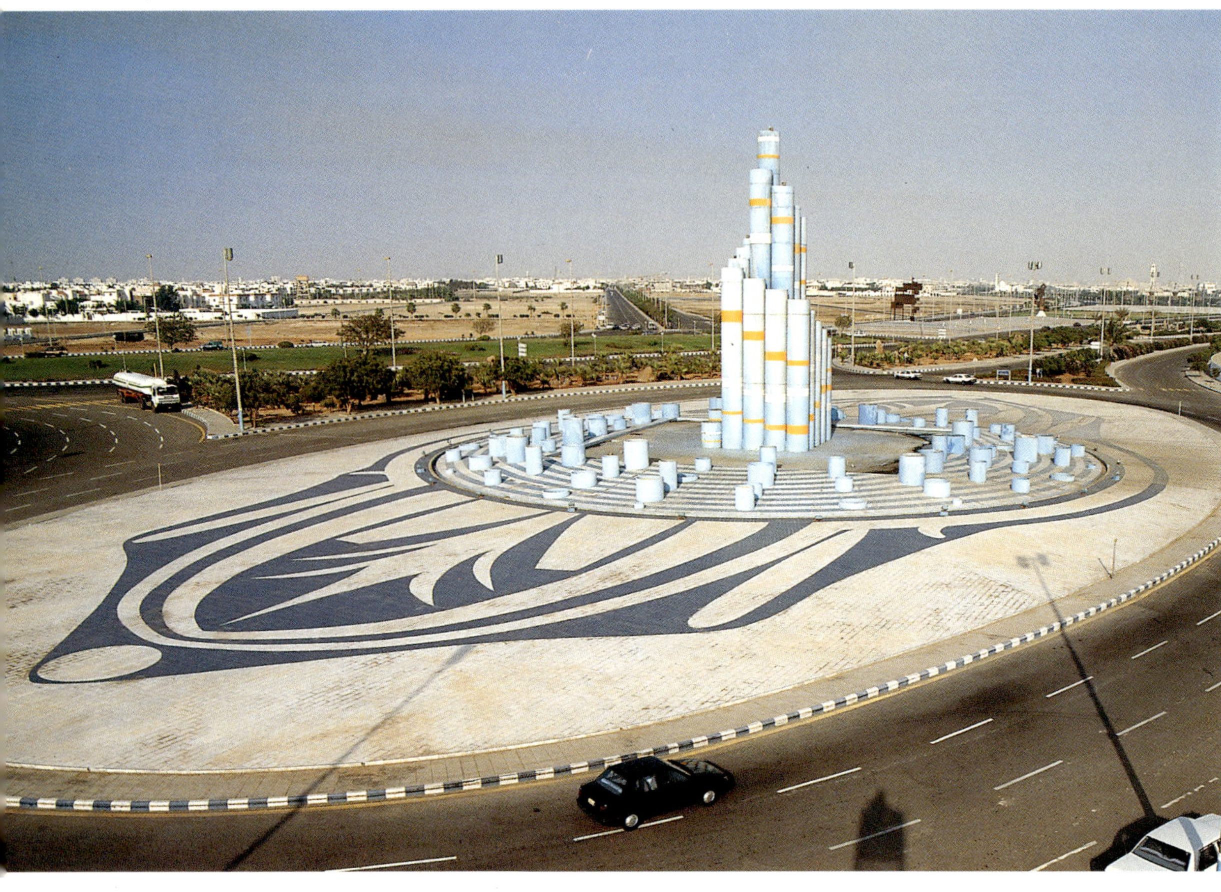

◄ **DESALINATION PIPES I** (Mawasi Al-Tahlia) (137)

□ The materials for these three works by Mustafa Senbel were donated by Amiantit Corporation, the manufacturer of the cement and glass reinforced plastic pipes used in the city's new water mains. The form of *Desalination Pipes I* derives its inspiration from the minarets of the great mosque of Samarra in Iraq. The sculptures are located at both ends of Al-Tahlia Street, marking the route to the desalination plant.

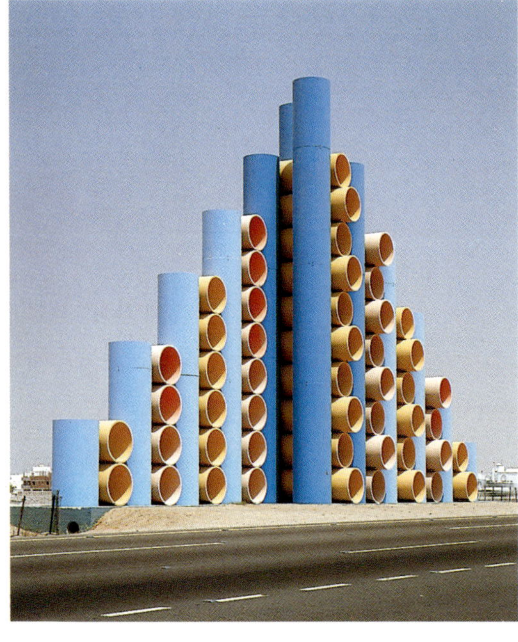

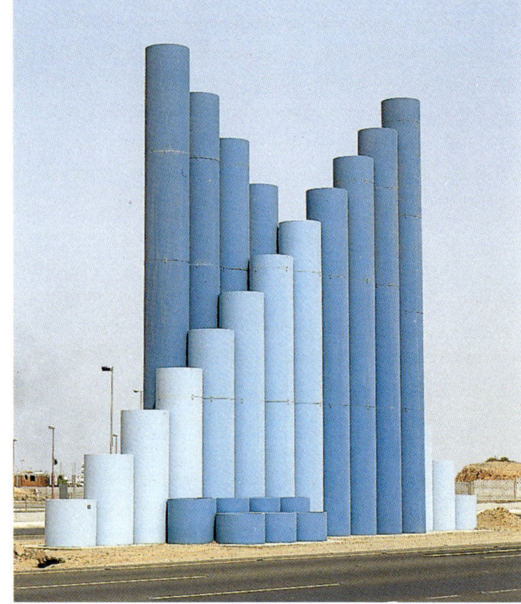

► **DESALINATION PIPES II** (138)

►► **DESALINATION PIPES III** (139)

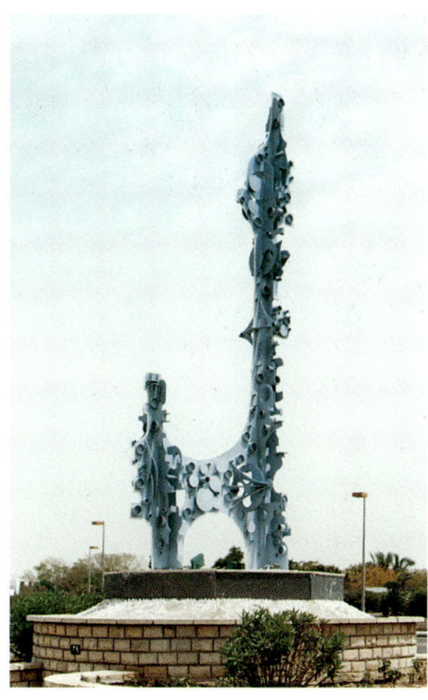

▲ **THE LETTER J** (140)
Shafiq Mazloum
Steel

In the last work before his premature death in a car crash Mazloum incorporated the letter J – standing for Jeddah – in a form which represents a gazelle. The base of the work is studded with sea shells in a further allusion to the maritime city.

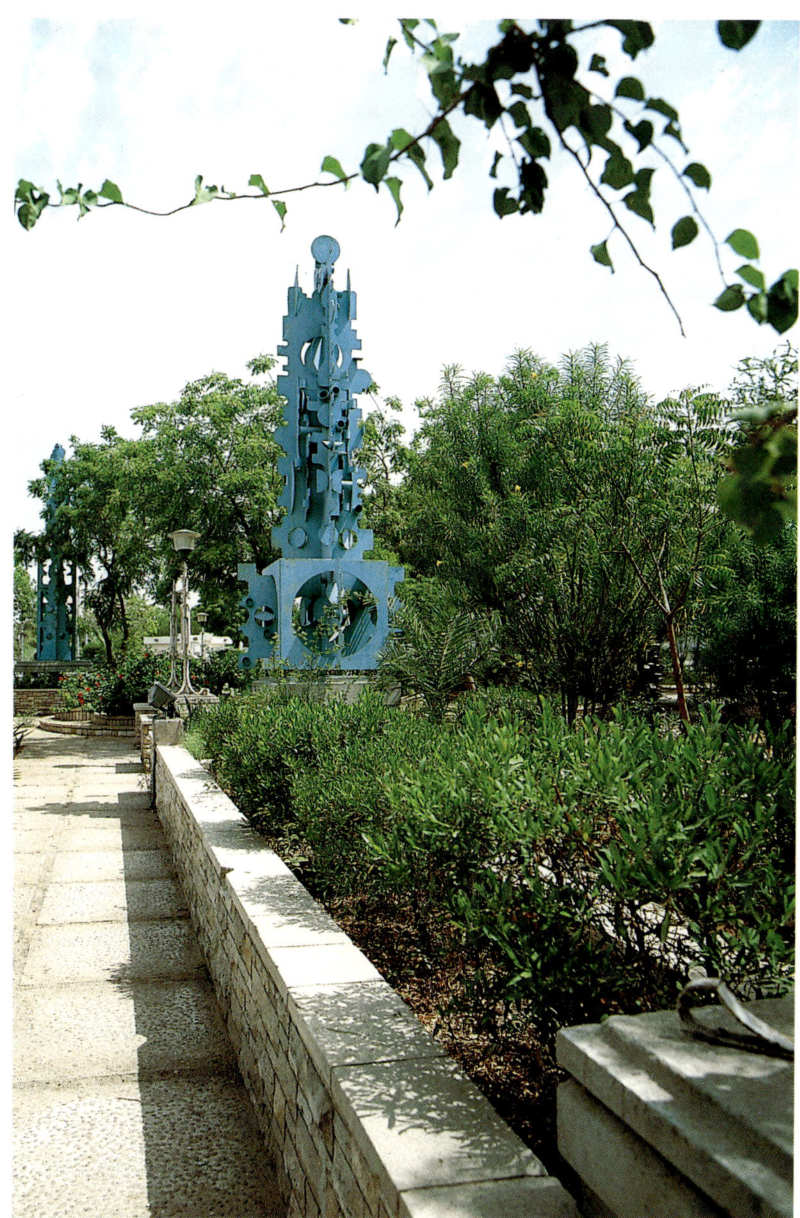

▲ **RECYCLED IRON I** (141)
Shafiq Mazloum

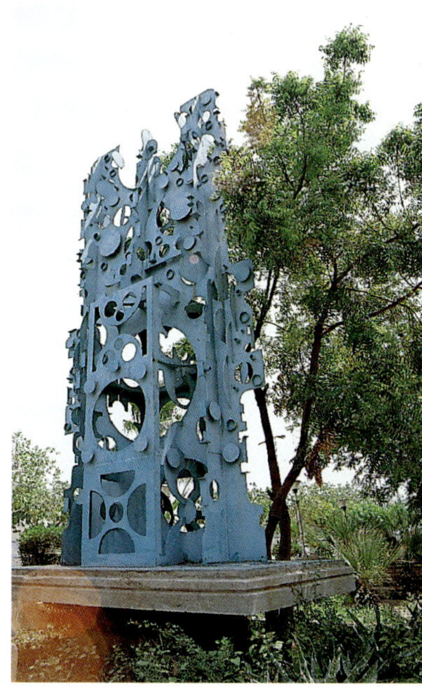

► **RECYCLED IRON II** (142)
Shafiq Mazloum

◄ **RECYCLED IRON III** (143)
Shafiq Mazloum

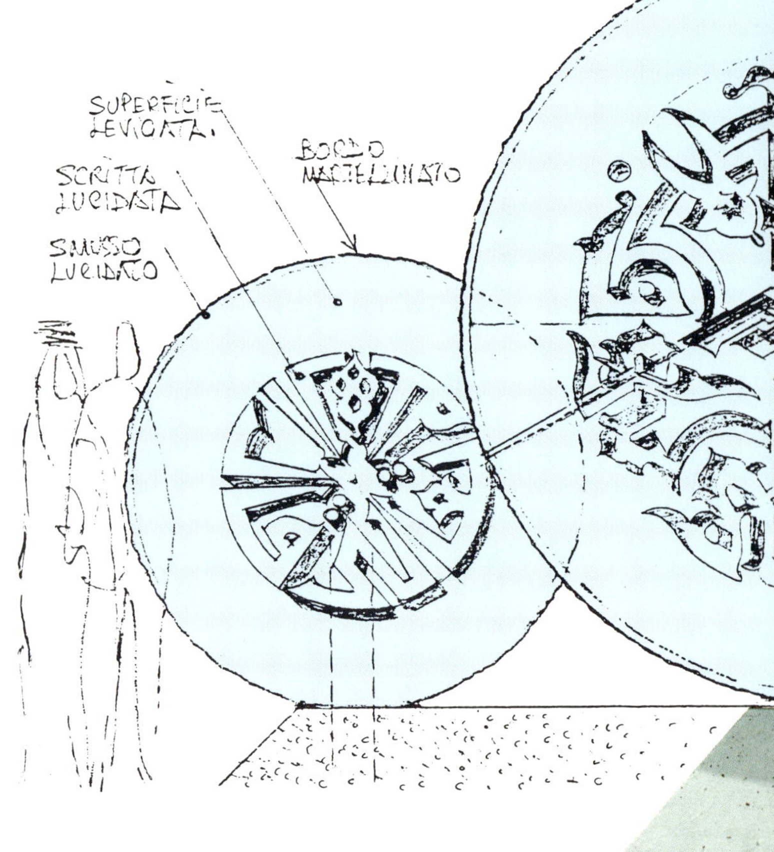

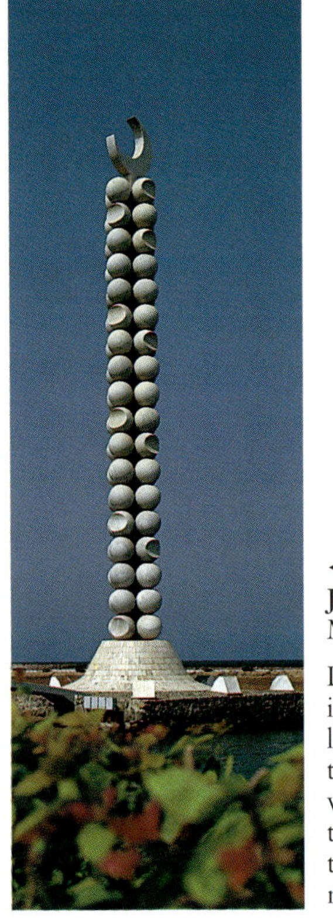

◄ **SCIENCE AND RELIGION** (144)
Julio Lafuente
Marble

Lafuente's towering obelisk, which stands on an island in one of the Corniche's ornamental lagoons, is one of many sculptures which explore the symbolism in Islam of the waxing and waning moon. Each of the 72 marble 'moons' in this column weighs 1.8 tonnes and such care had to be taken in positioning them that the monument took six weeks to erect.

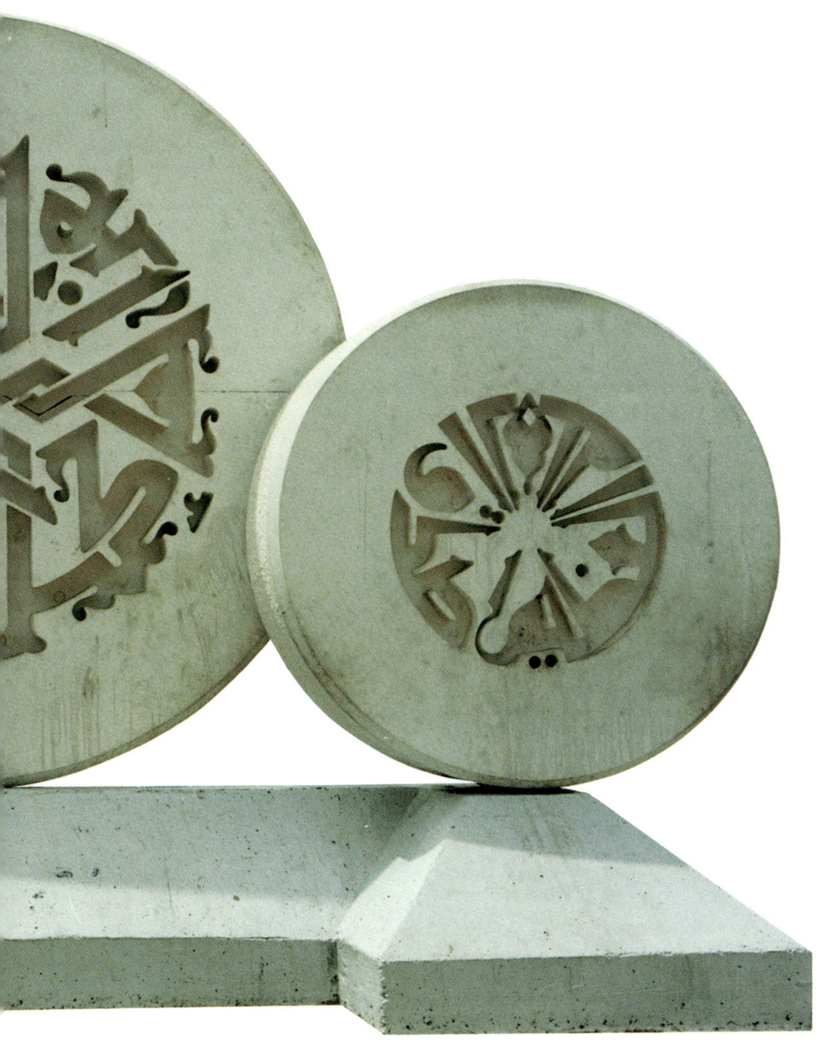

◀ **CALLIGRAPHIC DISCS** (145)
Julio Lafuente
Marble

The discs were inspired by an example of late Abbasid calligraphy which was presented by Mayor Farsi.
"Have not the unbelievers then beheld that the heavens and the earth were a mass all sewn up, and then we unstitched them and of water fashioned every living thing?" (Holy Koran 21:30)

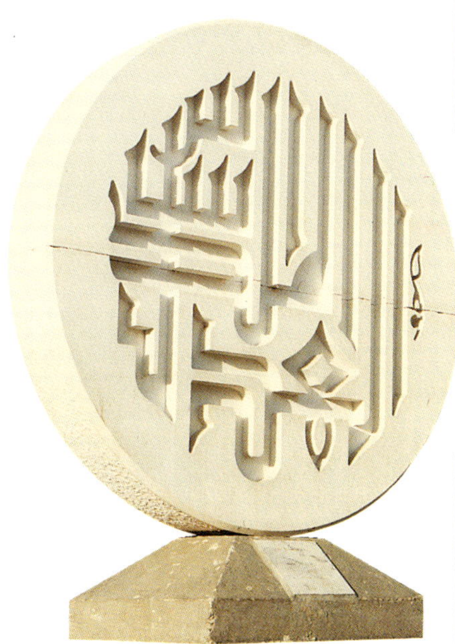

▲ **CALLIGRAPHIC DISC** (146)
Julio Lafuente
Marble

'Justice is the basis of authority'.

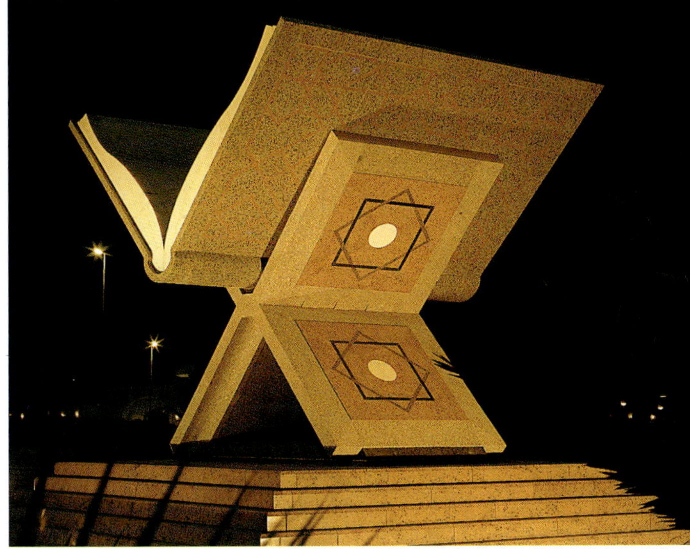

◀ **HOLY KORAN** (146)
Julio Lafuente
Granite

In this sculpture the Holy Koran rests on a stand such as is used throughout the Kingdom and beyond, by worshippers reading as they sit on the floor.

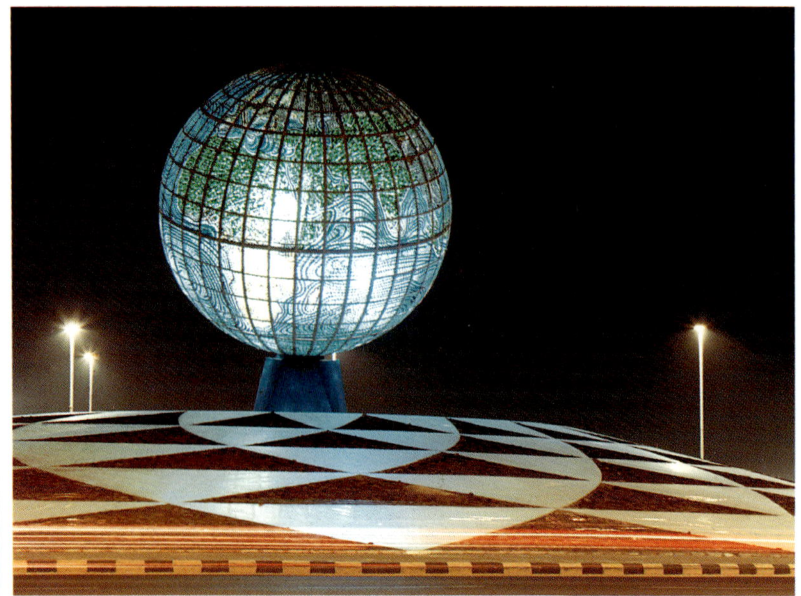

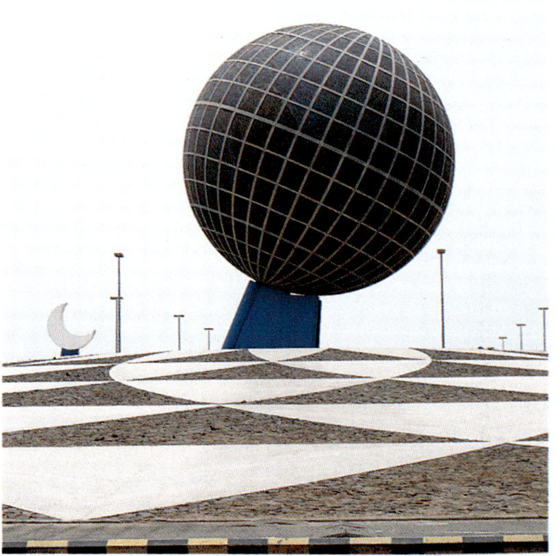

▲ **THE ILLUMINATED GLOBE** (Al-Korah Al-Ardiah) (148)
Julio Lafuente
Steel and Glass

The Illuminated Globe is designed to show Makkah as the centre of the Islamic world. It has a surface area of some 600 square metres and had to be put together to allow it to expand in the high temperatures of Jeddah's summer. The sculpture was fabricated in Italy and cost more than $1 million, excluding the base.

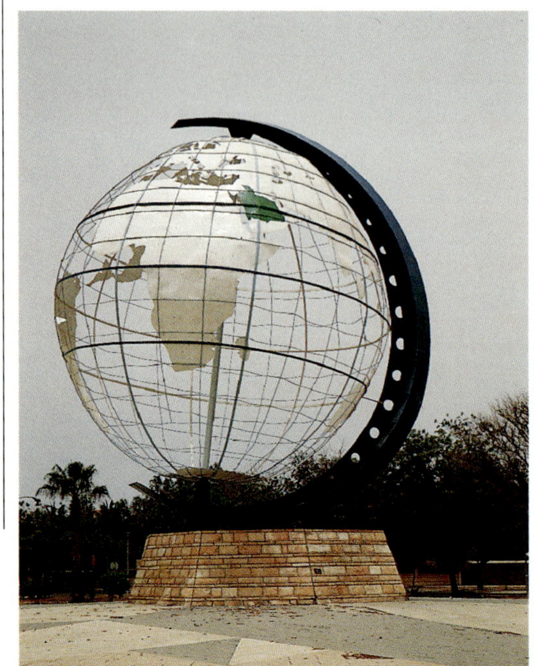

◄ **GLOBE IN SCRAP IRON** (149)
Julio Lafuente
Scrap Metal

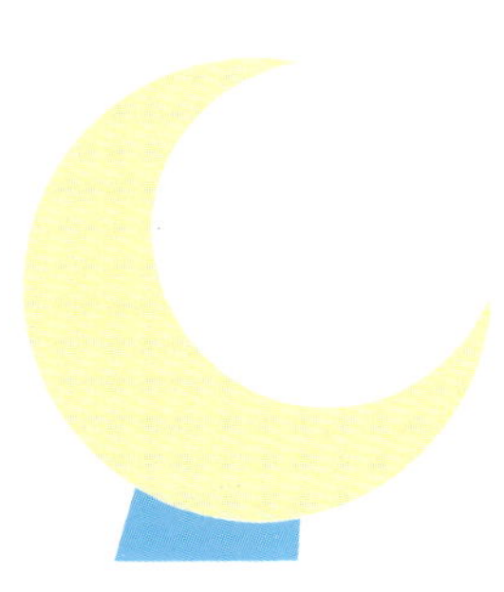

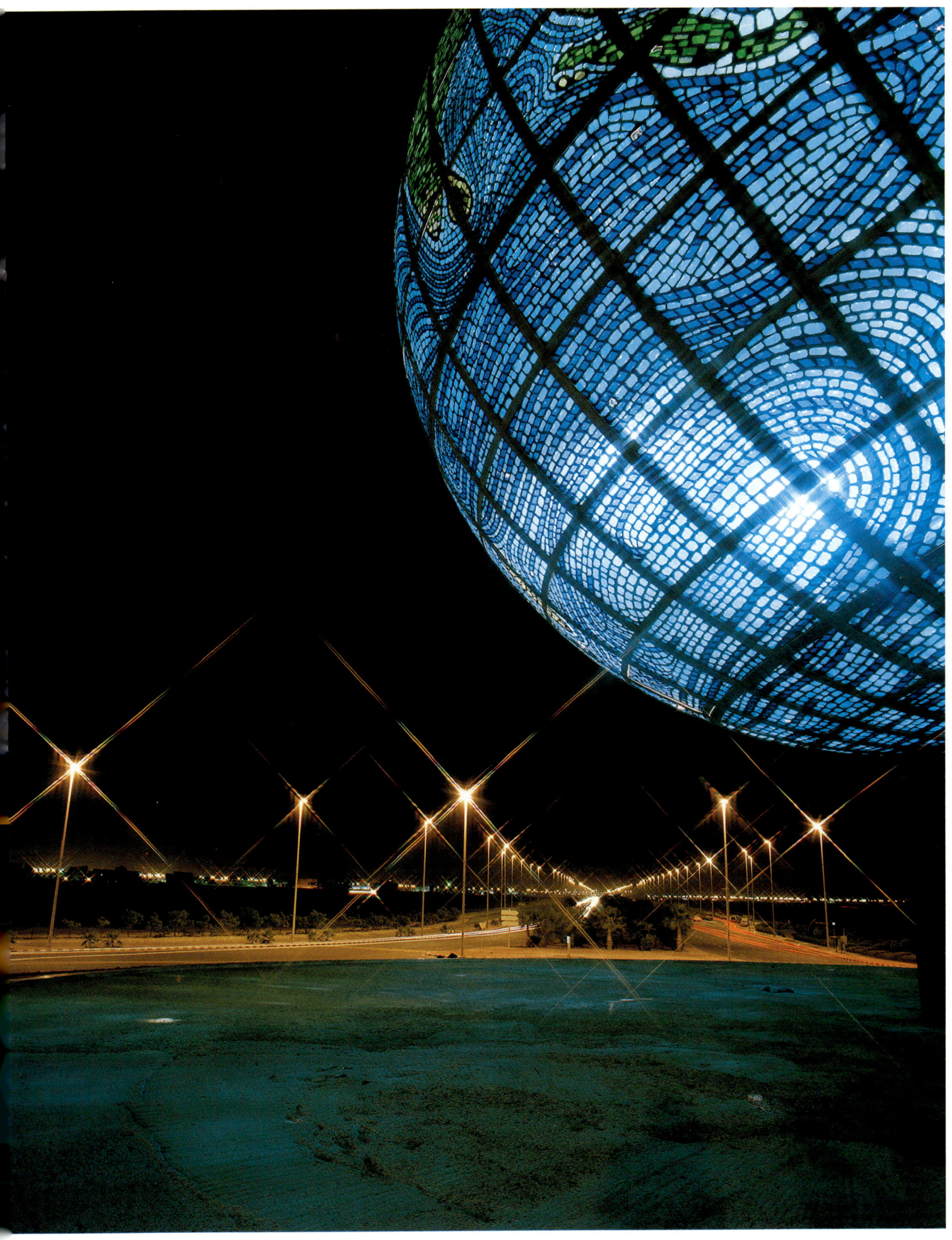

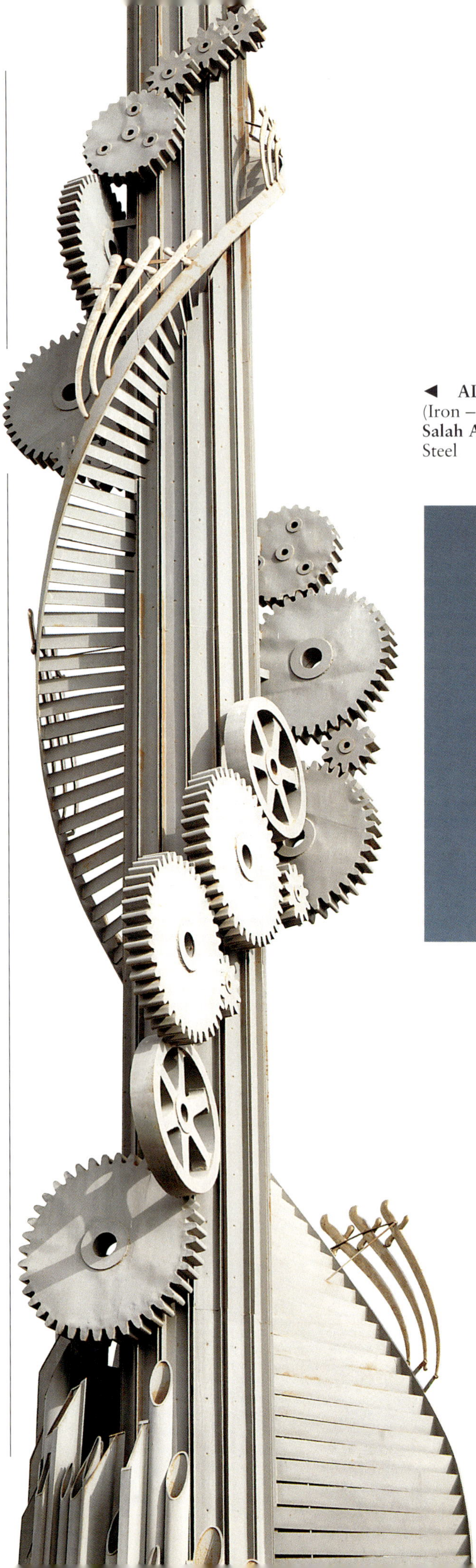

◄ **AL-SAROUKH I** (150)
(Iron – Its benefits and strengths)
Salah Abdulkarim
Steel

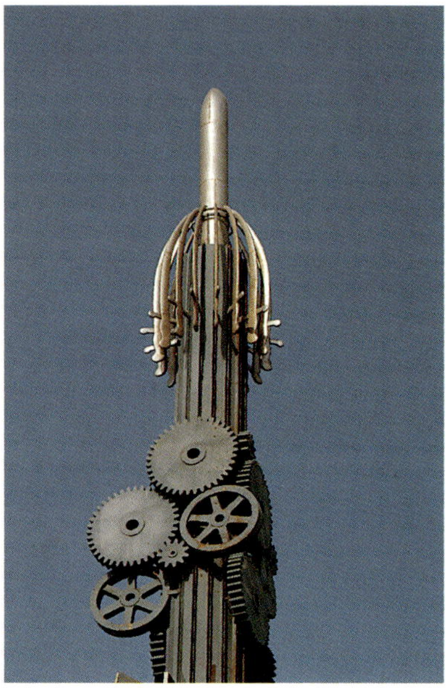

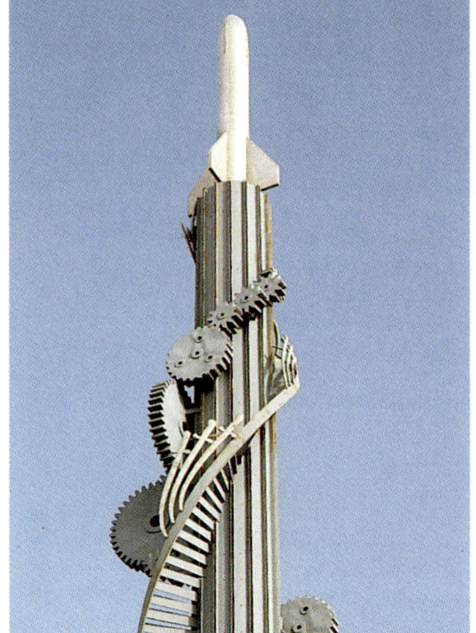

▲ **AL-SAROUKH II** (151)
Salah Abdulkarim
Steel

□ The artist produced two designs for this piece and asked Mohamed Said Farsi to choose one of them. However, the Mayor liked both versions and decided to go ahead with both. The monuments trace the different uses to which man has put steel, from swords, to machinery to spacecraft.

► **BALANCING CUBE** (Moka'ab Lafz Al-Jalalah) (152)
Abdulhalim Radwi
Steel

This sculpture is a large scale copy of the desk-top ornament given to winners of the Aga Khan Award for Islamic Architecture. Mohamed Said Farsi conceived the idea for the sculpture after seeing one of the 'trophies' in the office of Said Amin who, as Saudi Arabia's Director of International Airport Projects, was closely involved in the award-winning Haj Terminal project.

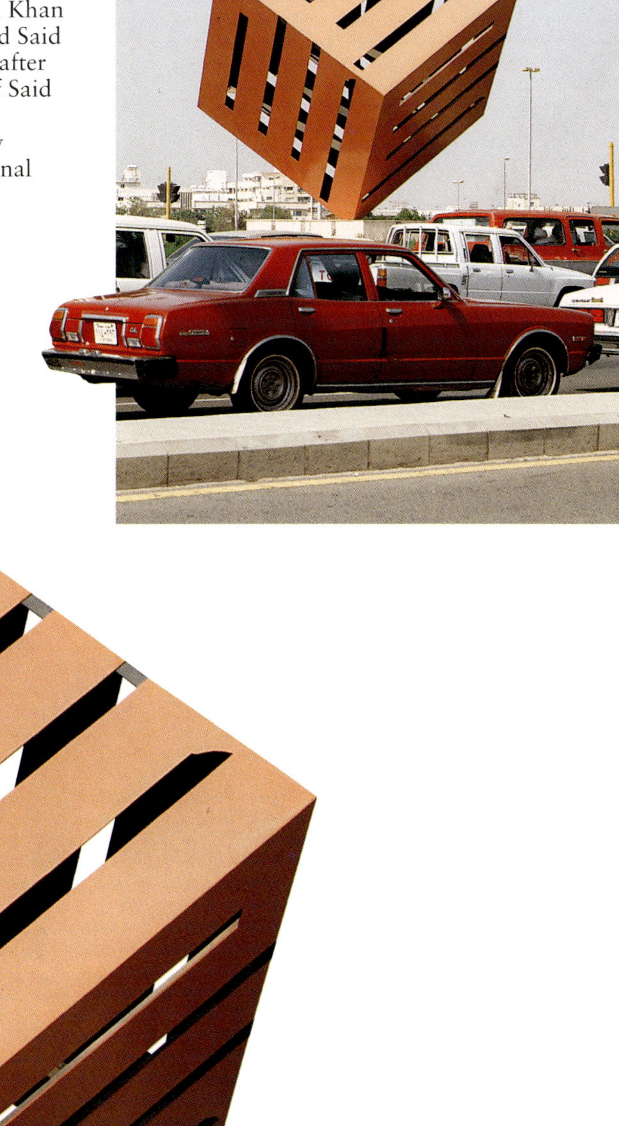

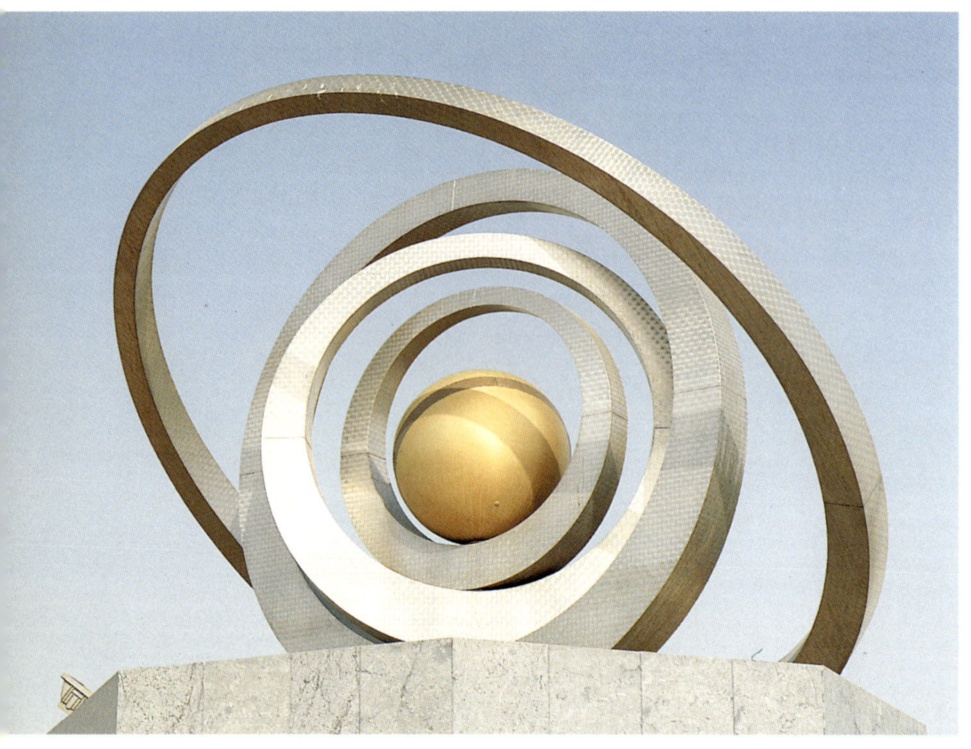

► **GRAVITY** (155)
Mustafa Senbel
Reinforced concrete and steel

Science undergraduates at Jeddah's King Abdul Aziz University may find inspiration in this dynamic work which stands at the entrance to the campus.

▲ **STRUCTURE OF THE ATOM** (153)
Artist Unknown
Aluminium

In this sculpture – a gift from the Italian car manufacturers FIAT – the rings denoting the orbits of the atomic particles rotate, driven by an electric motor.

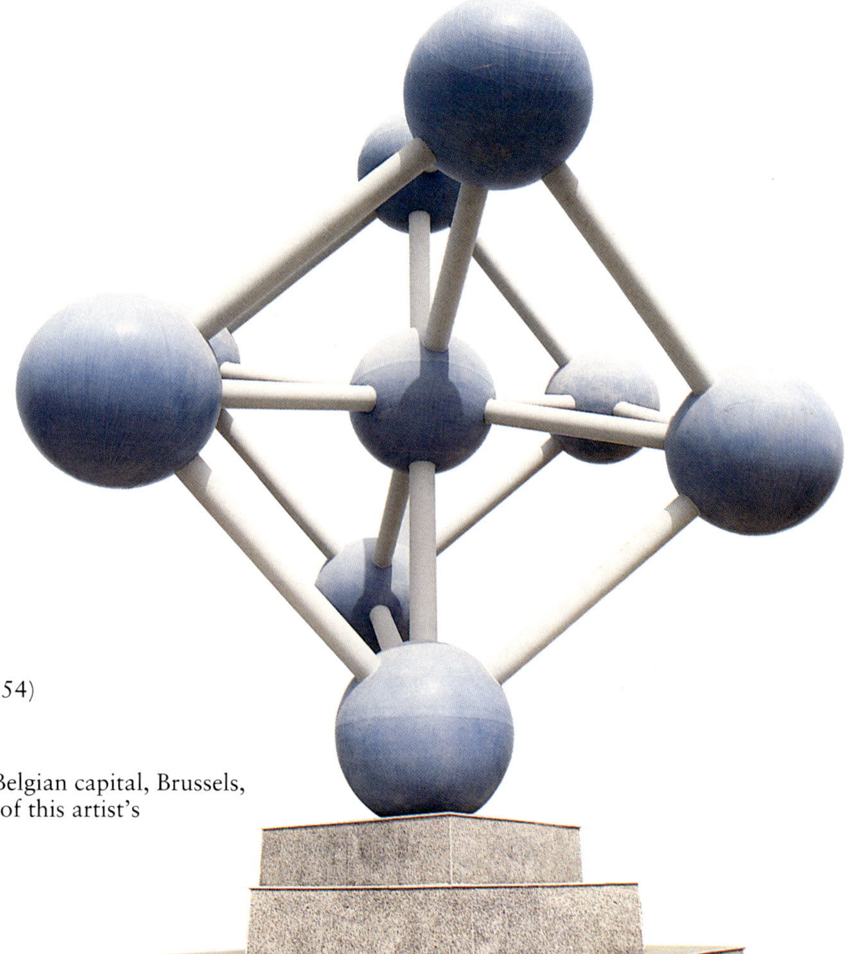

► **THE ATOMIUM** (154)
Ali Amin
Steel

Anyone who knows the Belgian capital, Brussels, will recognise the source of this artist's inspiration.

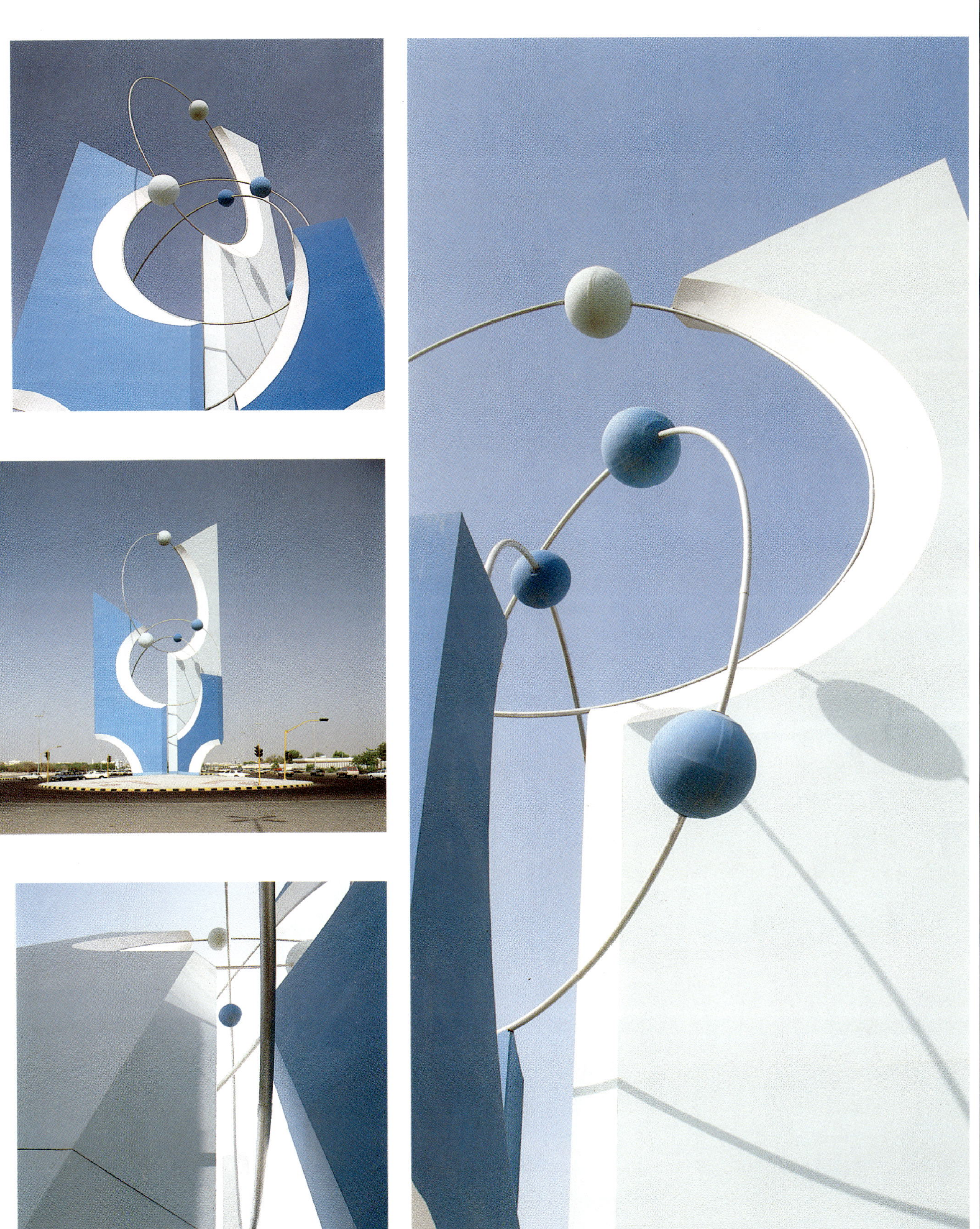

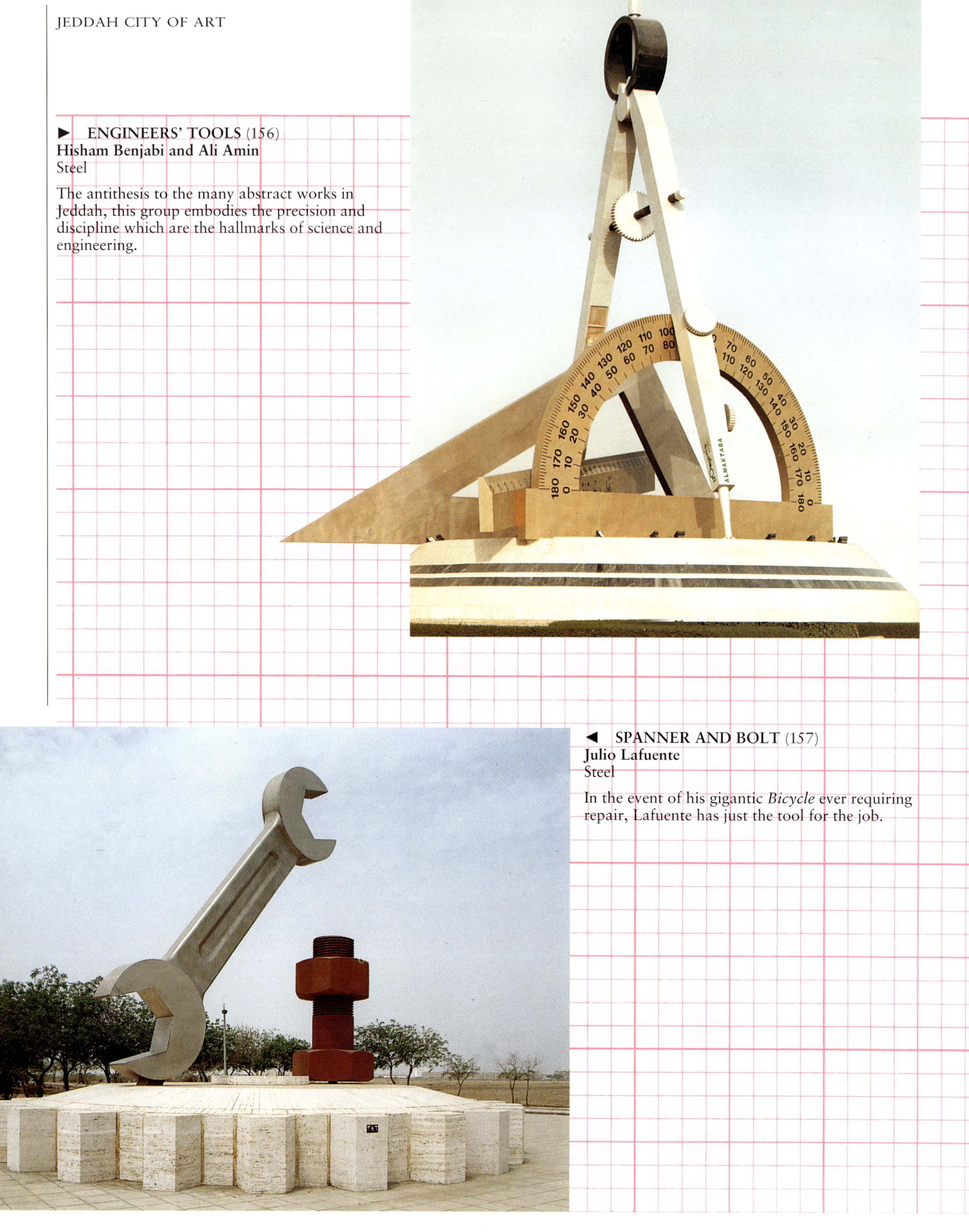

► **ENGINEERS' TOOLS** (156)
Hisham Benjabi and Ali Amin
Steel

The antithesis to the many abstract works in Jeddah, this group embodies the precision and discipline which are the hallmarks of science and engineering.

◄ **SPANNER AND BOLT** (157)
Julio Lafuente
Steel

In the event of his gigantic *Bicycle* ever requiring repair, Lafuente has just the tool for the job.

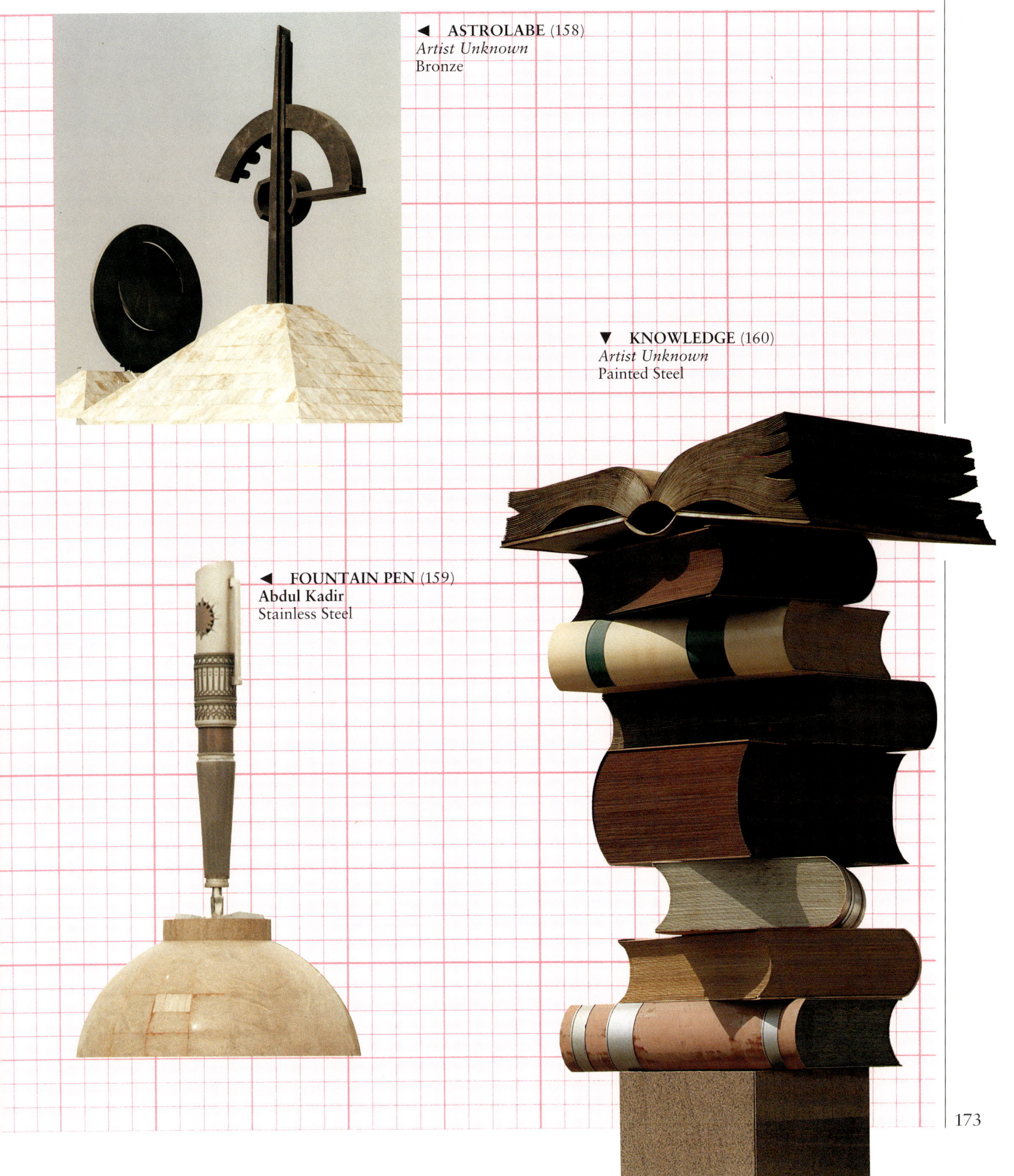

◀ **ASTROLABE** (158)
Artist Unknown
Bronze

▼ **KNOWLEDGE** (160)
Artist Unknown
Painted Steel

◀ **FOUNTAIN PEN** (159)
Abdul Kadir
Stainless Steel

INDEX

Page Numbers in **bold** *refer to photographs*

A Abbasid 19
Abdul Aziz ibn Abd Ar-Rahman ibn Saud, King 28, 31
Abdulkarim, Salah 27, 33, 44, 46
Abstract I **78**
Abstract II **78**
Abu Hayyan Al-Tawhidi 20, 30
Accident! 39, **80**
Aga Khan Award for Islamic Architecture 15, 32
Al-Anani Mosque **96**
Al-Nada 17
Al-Akhras, Rabi 123
Al-Farabi 19, 21
Al-Idrisi 31
Al-Jazirah Mosque **70-71**
Al-Khasikiyah 17
Al-Kindi 19
Al-Makdisi 12
Al-Waseti 19
Allah - In Arabic 45
Aloe Flowers 44-45, **144-145**
Alterations in Space **119**
Amin, Ali 90
Arab Knight **123**
Arch and Waterspouts Fountain 35, **140**
Arp, Jean 23, 125
Arrangements **119**
Astrolabe 30-31, **173**
At Sea 76
Atomium, The **171**
Avicenna (Ibn Sina) 30-31, 44

B *Baghdadi Fountain* 35
Balance 35, **118**
Balance in the Air 41, **116**
Balancing Cube 34, **169**
Baldaccini, see César
Banat, Mahmoud 72
Banners in the Wind 39, **158-159**
Beach Themes, 45, **69**
Bean Pot, The 34, **150**
Benjabi, Hisham 172
Bicycle, The 28, 32, 39, **134-135**
Bird's Wing 34
Birds 34, **150**
Bracelet, The 34
Builder's Plumbline 45, **84**

C César 23, 42
Calder, Alexander 118
Calligraphic Discs **164-165**
Calligraphy 19, 23, 39, 40, 42-44, 47
Calligraphy, Fossilised Wood **144-145**
Candles, The 32
Cannons, The 29
Cascella, Pietro 123
Censer, The 32, 39
Changing Positions 41, **116**
Chimney Form 32, 45, **84**
Circle and Square **122**
Clouds 31, 39, **139**
Coffee Pot, The 32
Coffee Pots Fountain, The 39-40, **140**
Condenser, The 15, 23, 39, **158-159**
Cook, A. 119
Cosmos **2-3**, 26, 28, 31, 43-44, 46, **148-149**
Crescent and Moon **123**
Cross-section of the Heart **79**
Cube **114**

D Dali, Salvador 23, 41
Dallah Fountain **140**
Desalination Pipe Fountain 46, **162**
Desalination Pipes 45, **162**
Dest, E. 110
Dialogue 45, **76**

E *Early Cubism* **125**
Egypt 12, 18-19, 21, 35, 45-46
El Rayess, Aref 120
El-Wakil Mosque **75**
Engineers' Tools **172**
Estranoma, Oscar 124
Eye, The 42-43, **100-101**

F Faisal ibn Abdul Aziz, King 13
Family **122**
Fighter Aircraft and Trainer **138**
Fisherman's Net (Large) **117**
Fisherman's Net 45, **76**
Fist, The 42-43, **156-157**
Five Fan Palms 43, **88-89**
Flame of Life **115**
Flexibility of Balance **118**
Flower basins, The **44-45**
Formation of Ships 46
Fossilised Nautilus Shell **91**
Fountain of Shells, The 45, **90-91**
Fountain Pen, The 32, **173**
Frustration **128**

G Gabel 17
Gathering of the Ships at Night 39, **64-65**
Giovanni, Sylvestre 32, 44-45
Globe in Scrap Iron, The 39, **166**
Globe of Knowledge and Life, The 34, **151**
Gravity 45, **170-171**
Guitar of Love, The **120**

H Haj 14
Haj terminal 15, 32
Harvest of the Sea 34
Heart, The 29, 33, **46-47**
Hejaz 11-12, 5, 19
Helmi, Dr Raouf 31
Hiltunen, Eila 5, 115, 141
Hollmann, Ottmar 26, 28, 30-31, 43-44, 4
Holy Cities 7, 15, 18, 40, 45
Horse and Jockey **152-153**

I Ibrahim, Dr Abdulbaki 46-47
Illuminated Globe, The 39, **166-167**
Illusion of a Second Cube, The 41, **116**
Inkwell Pen and Paper 34, **150-151**
Invocation **78**
Islam *7, 12, 14, 16, 19-20, 25, 30-31, 33-34, 38, 40, 42-43, 44-47*

J *Jeddah Bride of the Sea* **69**
Jeddah Past and Present 34
Jeddah Yesterday and Today 32

K Kadir, Abdul 173
Kibla, Al 28, 39, **60-61**
Kindil 43
King Abdul Aziz International Airport 15, 31-32, 39
King Abdul Aziz University 32
King Fahd Fountain **1**
Knowledge **173**
Kofax 119
Koran, The **165**
Koranic Verse: "And we became friends." 34, **151**
Koranic Verse: "Man can only achieve what he has worked for." 34
Koranic Verse: "Surely thou art upon a mighty morality" 72
Kufic Inscriptions 39

L Lafuente, Julio 23, 27, 31, 38-40, 44
Large Ball Bearing Symbols 43, **111-113**
Large Pillar 43, **86**
Large Spindle Piece 37, **104-105**
Lawrence, T. E. 12
Light and Shade 44

Lipchitz, Jacques 125

M *Mafrookah, Al* 41-42, **116**
Makkah 7, 11-15, 17-18, 33, 36, 39-40, 45
Malsia, Maurice 27, 40
Mamelukes 47
Mameluke Minarets, The 46-47, **146-147**
Mameluke Mosque Lanterns, The 28, 39, **92-94**
Market Fountain, The 39, **147**
Mazloum, Shafiq 35
Medinah 7, 47
Migrant Birds 44-45, **130-131**
Mina 19
Miró, Joan 23, 28, 38
Moon and Bow, The 30, 43, **84-85**
Moore, Sir Henry 23, 28-29, 37-38
Mukarnasat, Al (see Pendentive)
Music **22**

N *Name of Allah, The* **72**
Name of Allah (Kufic) 73
National Commercial Bank 16, 47, **54**
New Wave of Cars, The **81**
Newman 9
Non-Parallel Cubes and Rectangles 41

O *Obsolete Coastguard Vessels* 45
Obsolete Motor Launches 45, **68**
Oil Lamp, The 45, **63**
Open Air Museum 37-38, 40, 42-43, 47
Oval with Points 37, **106-107**

P *Peace (Al-Salam)* **59**
Pendentive, The 46-47, **52-55**
Personage I **126**
Personage II **127**
Personal Aircraft of King Abdul Aziz **138**
Pilgrims 11, 14, 32
Plaza of Missiles, The 45
Poets' Garden 34
Pomegranate Fountain, The 39, **132**
Pomodoro, Arnaldo 23, 35, **114**
Precious Burden, A 43, **160-161**
Pure Abstraction **121**

Q Qummusani, Kamal 81

R Radwi, Abdulhalim 33, 35
Ramadan Lantern, The 45, **62-63**
Ratchet Spanner **139**
Recycled Iron 35, **163**
Rose-water Sprinkler, The 39, 46, **141**
Rotation and Balance **122**
Rotation of the Crescent and Moon 31, 39, **96-97**

S *Sack Fountain* **140**
Sail, The 45
Sail Formation 32, 35, 45, **69**
Sails 44-47, **68**
Sails Formation 32, 35
Salamah, Darwish 36
Samarra 4
Samovar, The 45-46, **141**
Saroukh, Al 32, 46-47, **168**
Sassanian 19
School of Dolphins **76**
Science and Religion 39, **164**
Scrap Materials 23, 31-32, 42, 45
Scrap Iron 46-47, **115**
Sea Fountain 44-45
Sea Harvest Trellis 44, **76-77**
Seagull, The 28, 31, 45-46, **56-58**
Semsemiah, The **124**
Senbel, Mustafa 28, 45
Shahadat Al-Tawheed 39, 70
Shell, The **90-91**
Sign for the Fish Market 45
Signs of the Zodiac, The 43-44, **86-88**
Silent Formation 34, **151**
Skidmore Owings and Merrill 32, 47
Small Pillar 43, **161**
Solar Clock **113**
Solidarity (Al-Tadamun) 46
Spanner and Bolt 39, **172**
Speld, Paul 123
Spiral with Moon 43-44, **161**
Step Forward, A **125**
Stalks of Wheat 46-47, **74**
Structure of the Atom 31-32, **170**
Sublimity **78**
Sunflower Fountain, The **5**
Sunrise 45
Supplication, The **72**
Sweet Box, The 32
Swirl **120**
Swords of God **154-155**
Symbols of Victory **123**
Symmetry **122**

T *Telephone* **122**
The Balance between Science, Art and Life 34
The Essence is Gold **110**
The Letter "J" 35, **163**
Three Flowers 35, 43-44, **87**
Three-piece Reclining Figure 37, **102-103**
Thumb, The 42
Traditional Arabian Architecture **82-83**
Traditional Jar **150**
Traveller's Post, The **114**
Treasure Trove, The 32, 39, **140**
Twenty-eight Winding Steps 31, 43-44, **160**
Twin-engined Aircraft **138**
Two Poles 43-44, **89**
Two Vases 45, **95**

U Umayyad 19
Umra 14
United Nations 13, 37, 4
Unity is Strength **123**
Upright Motive 37, **108-109**

V Vasarely, Victor 23, 41-42
Verse Boat 39, **136-137**
Verse in White 39, 73

W Wadi Fatimah 12, 1
Wadi Khulays 15
Waiting **120**
Warships Square 27, 39, **66-67**
Water Jars Fountains 32, 39, **60**, **142-143**
Water Skins Fountain **141**
Wave, The 45-46
Waxing and Waning Moons 39
White Horse, The 32, **123**
White Minaret, The 34
Worked Iron Formations 45, **69**

Y Yacoub, Halem 46
Yemen 12, 14

Z Zamzam, Well of 17

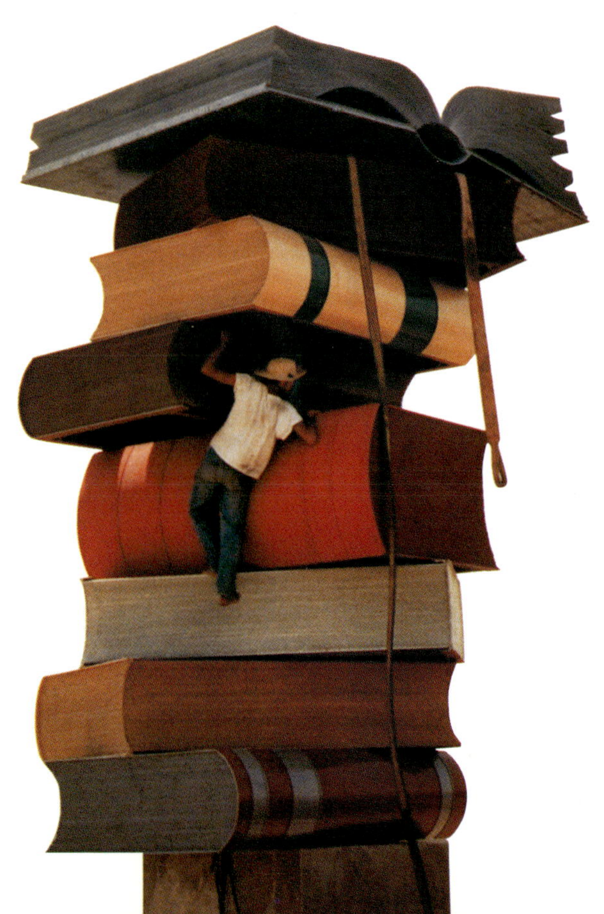

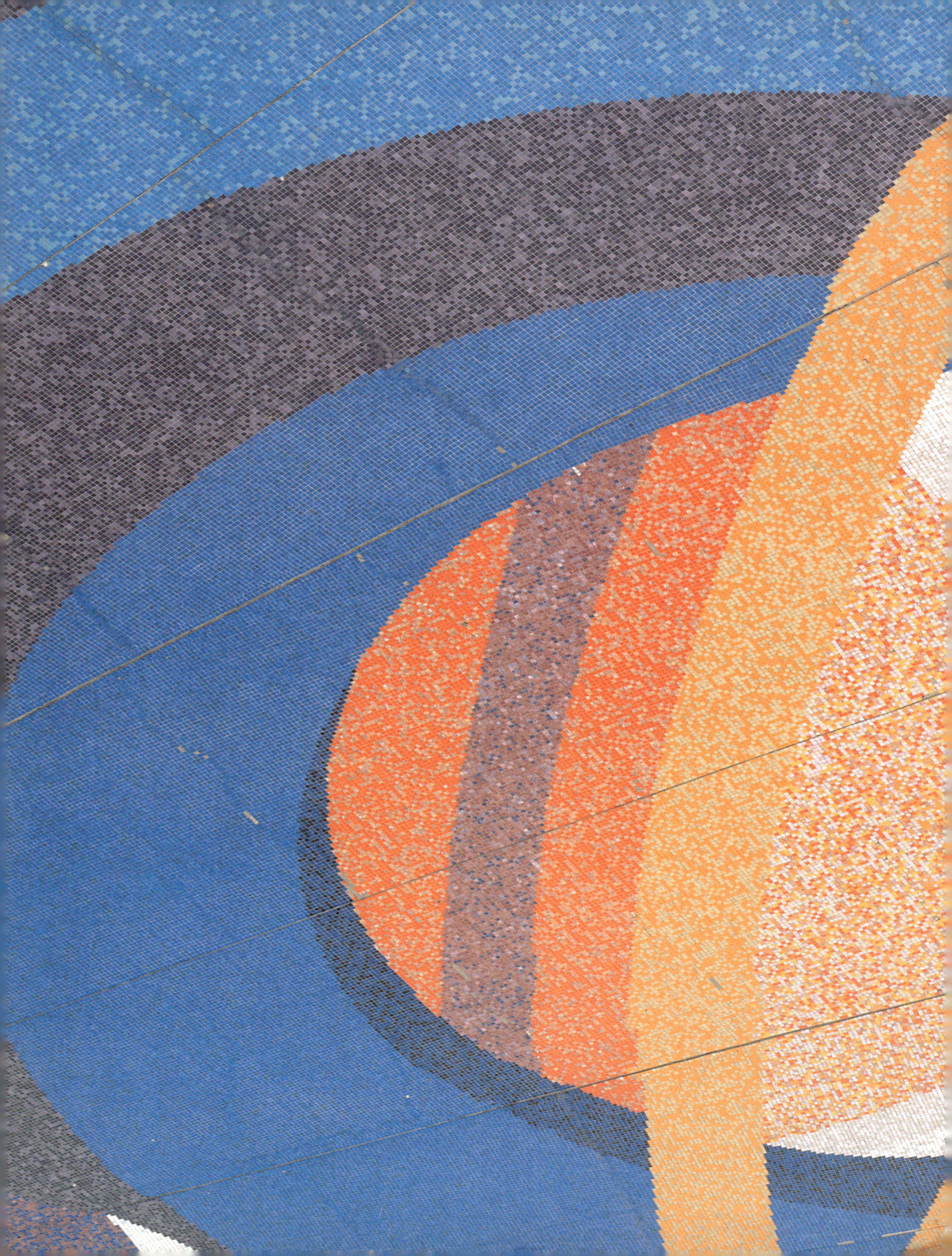